BEYOND TWO WORLDS

SUNY series, Tribal Worlds: Critical Studies in American Indian Nation Building

---

Brian Hosmer and Larry Nesper, editors

BEYOND TWO WORLDS

Critical Conversations on Language and Power in Native North America

Edited by

James Joseph Buss

and

C. Joseph Genetin-Pilawa

SUNY PRESS

“Wabansi Lakeside Chicago-Beyond Swag,” Jodi Webster. Graphite and Colored Pencil on Paper, Courtesy of Artist.

Published by State University of New York Press, Albany

Printed in the United States of America

For information, contact State University of New York Press, Albany, NY
www.sunypress.edu

Production by Ryan Morris
Marketing by Anne M. Valentine

Library of Congress Cataloging-in-Publication Data

Beyond two worlds : critical conversations on language and power in native North America / edited by James Joseph Buss and C. Joseph Genetin-Pilawa.
pages cm. — (SUNY series, tribal worlds : critical studies in American Indian nation building)
Includes bibliographical references and index.
ISBN 978-1-4384-5341-5 (hardcover : alk. paper)
1. Indians of North America—Ethinic identity. 2. Indians of North America—Cultural assimilation. I. Buss, James Joseph, author, editor of compilation. II. Genetin-Pilawa, C. Joseph, author, editor of compilation.

E98.E85B49 2014
970.004'97—dc23 2013047048

10 9 8 7 6 5 4 3 2 1

Contents

List of Illustrations ix

Preface xi
MALINDA MAYNOR LOWERY

Acknowledgments xv

Introduction: The World Is Not Enough 1
JAMES JOSEPH BUSS AND C. JOSEPH GENETIN-PILAWA

Part I: Historical Antecedents

1. "To Live and Die with Them": Wendat Reactions to "Wordly" Rhetoric in the Land of the Dead 15
KATHRYN MAGEE LABELLE

2. "Willingly Complied and Removed to the Fort": The Secret History of Competing Anglo-Visions for Virginia's Southwest 39
KRISTALYN MARIE SHEFVELAND

3. The Development of Two Worlds: British and Cherokee Spatial Understandings in the Eighteenth-Century Southeast 65
IAN D. CHAMBERS

Interlude: Diagramming Worlds 87
NANCY SHOEMAKER

Part II: The Real and the Imagined

4. Imagined Worlds and Archival Realities: The Patchwork World of Early Nineteenth-Century Indiana 97
James Joseph Buss

5. The Indians' Capital City: Diplomatic Visits, Place, and Two-Worlds Discourse in Nineteenth-Century Washington, DC 117
C. Joseph Genetin-Pilawa

6. Under One Big Tent: Race, Resistance, and Community Building in Two Nineteenth-Century Circus Towns 137
Sakina M. Hughes

Interlude: Of Two Worlds and Intimate Domains 161
Susan E. Gray

Part III: Consequences and Implications

7. nahi meehtohseeniwinki: iilinweeyankwi neehi iši meehtohseeniwiyankwi aatotamankwi: To Live Well: Our Language and Our Lives 181
George Ironstrack

8. Moving in Multiple Worlds: Native Indian Service Employees 209
Cathleen D. Cahill

Interlude: Working and *Between-ness* 237
Brian Hosmer

Part IV: Beyond Two Worlds

9. "born in the opposition": D'Arcy McNickle, Ethnobiographically 253
Daniel M. Cobb, Kyle D. Fields, and Joseph Cheatle

10. To Come to a Better Understanding: Complicating the "Two-Worlds" Trope 269
SANDE GARNER

Afterword: How Many Worlds?: Place, Power, and Incommensurability 295
COLL THRUSH

Contributor Biographies 319

Index 323

Illustrations

Figure 1	Euler Diagram of Eastern North America as Suggested by the Three Preceding Essays.	88
Figure 2	Euler Diagram of Richard White's *The Middle Ground.*	89
Figure 3	Euler Diagram of Nancy Shoemaker's *A Strange Likeness.*	90
Figure 4	Euler Diagram Comparing European Visions of Colonization.	91
Figure 5	Euler Diagram of Wendat Worlds.	92
Figure 6	Euler Diagram of Indian-European Relations in the Eighteenth-Century Southeast.	93
Figure 7	Antonio Capellano, *Preservation of Captain Smith by Pocahontas.*	120
Figure 8	Enrico Causici, *Landing of the Pilgrims.*	121
Figure 9	Nicholas Gevelot, *William Penn's Treaty with the Indians.*	122
Figure 10	Enrico Causici, *Conflict of Daniel Boone and the Indians.*	122
Figure 11	Kitsilano Point.	298
Figure 12	University of British Columbia, Museum of Anthropology.	304
Figure 13	Neely Mansion.	311

Preface

The Lumber River, the home of the Lumbee Indians to whom I belong, hosts our stories and our graves. The river is a generous host; it knew our flaws before we knew them ourselves; it keeps our secrets and our bodies. Then, in the time before the present time, our land as we now know it began to form. At that time there was the Upper World and the Lower World, two perfect opposites held in ideal tension. Lest we mistake it for John the Revelator's more recent visions of heaven and hell, the Upper World and Lower World are not rewards or punishments for human behavior in This World. No, these worlds are ancient systems of creation in their own right, generating powerful forces of harmony and disharmony, both of which are essential for all to be right within the nation, in This World. When one world is out of balance, the others are affected.[1] Humans who travel between Worlds have extraordinary spiritual power, and great need. The farmer who puts a dead snake in a tree attempts to bring the Lower World of the snake together with the Upper World of nourishment, to generate rain, prosperity, and harmony in This World.

Some of our ancestors said that in the beginning, the Creator took the form of a Great Hare, a rabbit. With the hare were four invisible forces, each taking shape as a wind from the North, South, East, and West. The hare made humans first, and then protected them from spirits who wanted to consume them. In the meantime, the Hare created the land, water, plants, and other animals. When he had created the deer, he placed his people on the land and instructed them in how to hunt.[2]

Other storytellers among our ancestors put the woman, not the animals, at the center of Creation. But as the eternal feminine sustains the nation, creation was a communal affair. It took a congregation of animals, men, women, elders, and particularly unruly children, to make the world. In the time before the present time, all of This World was water, and the

Elder Spirits of This World wanted land as well. So they consulted the Sky People, whose world was held together by a great tree, one of our tall pines. The Sky People created a baby girl and nurtured her into womanhood; she became known as Sky Woman. Accidentally or by force, the tree toppled. Sky Woman fell through the firmament, grabbing at the roots of the tree to save herself. The roots gave her seeds: in her right hand, corn, beans, and squash; in her left hand, tobacco. In her womb she also carried her own seed, a lynx whose name is sometimes translated as "Hanging Flowers." When she fell, the animals of the water decided to build a place for her, and a turtle volunteered to serve as her home. The water beings mounded mud on top of the turtle's back, and Sky Woman and her daughter Hanging Flowers proceeded to plant their seeds.[3]

The turtle can hinder as well as help; sometimes he needs a rabbit to remind him to share. Some of our ancestors may have told a tale about how the People obtained water. A big-headed, arrogant, snapping turtle sat over a spring—what we call a "branch" off of a swamp—and wanted all the water for himself. Sweet and cunning as a child, Rabbit went to Snapping Turtle and said cheerfully, "if you give me a drink I'll say thank you!" Snapping Turtle refused but Rabbit had a plan. He scratched a ditch in the soft, wet dirt beneath the turtle, and the water escaped: "Run much so the earth all over was a water branch," said a Catawba storyteller. And so the water flows easily.[4]

These stories of our creation come from three "different" peoples, the Algonquian, Siouan, and the Iroquoian, but in our history they are shared. That is what it means to be Lumbee: like the rabbit, we defy the powerful and share the water, sometimes at great risk to ourselves, but always with the blessing of the ancestors. Those ancestors are also non-Indians—newcomers from other continents who we adopted if we loved them, killed them if they insisted.

"Land" is hardly the right term for the Lumbees' homeplace—it is water and soil, two perfect opposites flowing together since ancient times. There are dense swamps where the water runs southwest, finger-like, toward the river. But the river is not the wide Shenandoah or roaring Colorado; the Lumber meanders slowly, twisting and turning an intricate design that changes periodically as her waters forge new paths.

In the Indian section of the county, seen from above, the Lumber River looks like a great snake, twisting and turning, swelling and breathing with the spring and summer rains. Snakes, in fact, have found a comfortable home there; the river hosts brown water snakes and cottonmouths (or water moccasins), which are often confused with each other. The difference is important; Cottonmouths are deadly and brown snakes are not. Varieties of turtles—what we and lots of other Southerners call "cooters"—continue to bear up the river mud that makes the planting possible for Sky Woman and her descendants. "Cooter" is, of course, also a slang term for the wet passage to the wellspring of birth. Perhaps that is no coincidence, that women not only produce babies but crops, and that turtles are their allies. Perhaps the big-headed turtle learned his lesson from the rabbit.

Between the swamps there are wide, shallow basins that never dry out, called pocosins. European newcomers retained the word from our Algonquian ancestors; it translates to "swamp-on-a-hill." Pocosins are home to the Venus flytrap, the carnivorous threat to unwitting insects and a precious specimen to mystified humans. Charmed by its murderous manner, Charles Darwin called it "the most wonderful plant in the world." Our land has been a safe place for some, but not for everyone.[5]

Pocosin soil is peat, the vegetative material that becomes coal under proper conditions. Peat began forming 360 million years ago, and in the peat the eternal feminine took root. Like Lumbee women who will cry as they laugh, peat itself can burn when it's dry—burning peat is probably why one of our swamp is called "Burnt Swamp." Our ancestors gazed at that peat fire which burned indefinitely, beneath flowing water. Water would never put out that fire, so long as the peat was there to fuel it.

What spirits inhabit land where fire and water coexist, neither extinguishing the other? No wonder they named one of these places a burning swamp; the name is a contradiction, and our contradictions hold great power. They remind us of the powerful spirits whose names we have since forgotten, but whose presence we still revere. We used to place our cemeteries at the edge of pocosins, perhaps because of the spiritual power we recognized there. We also planted a cedar tree, as cedar is the herb that heals—death, and its partner, eternal life, ultimately healed the body's frailties.

Darwin's world was different from our Worlds, but no less contested; it requires no less strength to navigate. Our relationships to our land and water, fueled by pocosins, changes, forms, and re-forms again and again, challenging our received wisdom. This is the World in which the Lumbee, and other indigenous peoples, live.

Since the Ancient Days, the time before the present time, newer people—settlers brought here by will or by force—have come to live with us and share this challenge. Some have responded by trying to be controlling and owning, others have responded by embracing and surviving. Our ancestors took both approaches and created a safe space, one where our children are encouraged to achieve, loyal to the relationships that created that safety, the places where they can return to be comforted, challenged, and renewed again. We strive, every day, to maintain that place of renewal because we recognize that it cannot be found anywhere. An elder told me once, "the blood of your ancestors is buried here"; indeed, there is only one World in which to find their resting places.

Malinda Maynor Lowery

Notes

1. This paraphrasing on the Upper World, Lower World, and This World are borrowed from Charles Hudson, *Conversations with the High Priest of Coosa* (Chapel Hill: University of North Carolina Press, 2003), 39ff

2. Michael Leroy Oberg, *The Head in Edward Nugent's Hand* (Philadelphia: University of Pennsylvania Press, 2007), 10–11.

3. Barbara Alice Mann, *Iroquois Women: The Gantowisas* (New York: Peter Lang, 2004), 32–34.

4. See Frank G. Speck, "Catawba Texts" (New York: Columbia University Press, 1934), 10–11.

5. Craig M. Stinson, "Venus Flytrap," in William S. Powell, ed., *The Encyclopedia of North Carolina* (Chapel Hill: University of North Carolina Press, 2006), 1158.

Acknowledgments

Friends and colleagues warned us that editing a volume with so many contributors could be like "herding cats" or "orchestrating a circus." We are pleased to report that such dire warnings proved as ill metaphors for our own experience. Instead, the type of collaborative work that accompanied this volume provided opportunities for us to engage in long, rich conversations with some really smart people. This particular volume changed a lot over the past five years, as compiling these chapters and working with the wonderful people who wrote them brought both jubilation and frustration. Some contributors withdrew in the early stages of drafting for personal and/or professional reasons. Other courageous authors agreed to write for the volume in the months before final submission. Regardless of whether they weathered the proverbial storm and saw this volume through, or took part in the conference panels that made this book possible, we thank you. This book is better because you were involved.

Some specific people deserve mention for influencing the pages herein by offering their sage advice. They include John Larson, Susan Sleeper-Smith, Cailin Murray, Tracy Floreani, Dennis Jowaisas, Steven Gooch, Alyssa Mt. Pleasant, David Martinez, Marc DiPaolo, Rachel Buff, Jean O'Brien, Larry Nesper, Brendan Gallagher, Scott Stevens, Boyd Cothran, Christina Snyder, Tsianina Lomawaima, students in Oklahoma City University's Native American History and Methodologies course, Paul Chaat Smith, Dan Dalrymple, Kent Blansett, Philip J. Deloria, Jenny Tone-Pah-Hote, Justin Carroll, Lucy Murphy, and Kellie Jean Hogue.

We also learned that life changes quite a bit in the time that it takes to complete an edited volume; one of our families doubled in size (thanks to the birth of twins) and the other moved halfway across the country. We both owe a deep and genuine gratitude to our family and friends who supported us over the half decade that it took to complete this collection. Joe would like to thank Sara Genetin-Pilawa and Onnalea and Parker Genetin. Jim would like to thank Kenneth, Sandra, Kevin, Charles, Tonya, Jonah, Annabelle, and Magdalynn Buss, as well as, Robert and Joann Brinkman.

Introduction

The World Is Not Enough

James Joseph Buss and C. Joseph Genetin-Pilawa

Malinda Maynor Lowery's powerful Preface reminds us that any conversation about the concept of worldedness links the past with the present, the spiritual with the terrestrial, the mind with the body. It is at once rich with cohesion as well as contradiction. It is mutually constructed and bound to place. In the words of the late anthropologist Keith Basso, "[w]e *are*, in a sense, the place-worlds we imagine."[1]

More than four decades ago Vine Deloria, Jr. complained that scholars of all types had created a crisis by theorizing Native people as individuals and communities trapped "BETWEEN TWO WORLDS."[2] This volume began with a seemingly simple set of inquiries. From where did the two-worlds framework come? How has it changed over time? And, how and why does it still persist? The trope itself has birthed a bifurcated lexicon—Savage and Civilized, East and West, Primitive and Modern—that serves as a grammar for settler colonialism. And, while many scholars have chastised this terminology in recent years, it is clear that the ideas behind these words still persist in American culture and society. As scholars of Native histories in North America, the editors of this volume are acutely aware of how this language of two worldedness has influenced earlier research—perhaps best exemplified by the enduring legacy of Frederick Jackson Turner's frontier thesis. While most modern scholars have come to critique or utterly reject Turner's ethnocentric claims, the concept of differing worlds, existing on opposite sides of clearly defined boundaries, still influences more recent works—especially those that have sought to explain how individuals struggle to exist in what they frame as diametrically opposed Native and non-Native worlds.

In scholarship and popular culture, Native people often are viewed as "trapped between worlds," forced to "walk between worlds," or simply must exist "in two worlds." Our own initial query into the origins of the two-worlds trope yielded a growing list of examples—some of which better illustrate our initial contempt for the use of two worldeness as an academic framework.[3]

Perhaps the most striking example is that of Ishi. More than a century ago an approximately fifty-year-old man wandered into the corral of a slaughterhouse near Oroville, California. Dressed in rags, starving, and disoriented, he became known as "Ishi" and was dubbed the "last of the Yahi." Ishi's story resonated with the public and local scholars—a man who seemingly stepped out of a bygone era and into the twentieth century—precisely because it represented the two-worlds framework in its most visible and corporal form. For the remainder of his life, Ishi lived as a human relic—studied by anthropologists, linguists, and historians. In 1960, Theodora Kroeber (wife of anthropologist Albert Kroeber) used her husband's notes to compile a biography of the "last of the Yahi."[4] Ishi's story is instructive here, because it points to the public's and academia's shared fixation with worldness and indigeneity. It also points to the ability of this obsession to obscure. As Cherokee author Thomas King reminds us, "His name wasn't Ishi. He never told anyone his name. Kroeber, under pressure from reporters who got tired of calling the Indian the Wild Man of Oroville, named him Ishi, a Yahi word that means simply 'man.' "[5]

For one of the editors of this volume, the language of two worldedness invaded the very sources he was using to conduct an individual manuscript project. The title of William Armstrong's 1978 book about the Tonawanda Seneca leader and government official, Ely Parker, illustrates the problems of flippantly employing the two-worlds framework to describe historical actors. Armstrong's *Warrior in Two Camps: Ely S. Parker, Union General and Seneca Chief* stressed the internal dilemma Parker faced by "walking between two worlds"—a dilemma seemingly lost on the real Parker who never used such language to describe his own life. More disturbing, Armstrong's book helped solidify this imagined internal dilemma for subsequent historians and storytellers. In 2004, PBS invited viewers to watch, *Ely S. Parker: A Warrior in Two Worlds*. Without attempting to critique the same framework embedded in the documentary's title, prominent scholars and Native American leaders spoke about Parker's life and made clear the damage wrought by a lifetime of straddling Native and non-Native worlds. An historian and archivist at the Rochester Museum and Science Center, for example, warned that Parker's life reminds students "to be careful when going out to be a bridge between two worlds, because if you don't step carefully, you lose who you are, you lose who you can become." In other words, she suggested that Parker's case provided an example of how attempting to meet a multitude of conflicting expectations could erode one's sense of self. Perhaps more startling, a historian and Tuscarora Beaver clan member, stated that Parker "was a traitor, because there was a betrayal to his people." When shown a picture of Parker just before his death, he lamented that what he saw was "a guy with a broken heart." In both the book and documentary, scholars viewed Parker's life as a series of conflicts that resulted from a man straddling two very different existences.

Historians and filmmakers have long populated the minds of historical actors with the internalized dilemma brought about by the two-worlds framework. HBO's 2007 adaptation of Dee Brown's *Bury My Heart at Wounded Knee* provides a solid case study and illustrates an American fascination with psychoanalyzing the internal crises among people, especially Native people, who are forced to choose between identities. In it, filmmakers focused on the lives of three Native leaders—Sitting Bull, Red Cloud, and Charles Eastman—from the Battle of Little Big Horn to the massacre at Wounded Knee. In the HBO adaptation, the three men choose very different routes in navigating between Native and non-Native worlds. Sitting Bull resists the non-Native world by leading his Lakota followers first in armed resistance against the U.S. Army, then by escaping north to Canada, and finally by facilitating a religious resistance in the Ghost Dance. He is murdered as a result. In comparison, Red Cloud attempts to forge a middle path through compromise, but in so doing, loses the respect of his own people. In one dramatic—but entirely fictionalized—scene, Sitting Bull (August Schellenberg) argues with Colonel Nelson Miles (Shaun Johnston). When Miles states that Red Cloud signed a treaty with the United States, Sitting Bull fires back "Red Cloud is no longer a chief. He is a woman you have mounted and had your way with. Do not speak to me of Red Cloud!" Charles Eastman (Adam Beach), however, is portrayed as a Native man who abandoned his people, seeking fame and recognition in a "white world." Near the end of the film, Eastman bears witness to the atrocities of the Wounded Knee massacre and, in a telling moment, realizes his error in abandoning "his people" and has a falling out with Senator Henry Dawes (Aiden Quinn), a man who the screenwriters imagined as a father-like figure to the younger Eastman. Later, down on his luck, Eastman begs Dawes for a job and is soon employed in the "naming project," randomly assigning Euro-American names to Native men and women on the Dawes Rolls. Eastman experiences an intense psychological breakdown as he is reminded of the moment when he was forced to give up his own Dakota name, Ohiyesa.

One of the final scenes in the film depicts Eastman, unable to sleep, crying and talking to himself in his den.

It is easy to critique the makers of the HBO film for over-simplifying the complex and brutal history of American Indian affairs, but doing so belittles the actual consequences of a bifurcated language of settler colonialism. As a settler population has attempted to mollify the threat of indigeneity through discursive practices, it has created paradoxes and paradigms that are not easily dismantled on the pages of scholarly volumes. The "nonsensical scholarly dribble," as Vine Deloria called it, also influences the lived experiences of Native and non-Native people alike who inhabit the North American continent.

Paul Chaat Smith, writing forty years after Deloria, referred to the two worlds dichotomy as a "rusting, broken contraption held together with stubbornness, colonized thinking, and baling wire."[6] Smith, associate curator at the Smithsonian Institution's National Museum of the American Indian, argued that the two-worlds trope was and is not simply something non-Native people impose upon Native persons; it is something American Indian people have internalized. In a humorous, yet insightful passage, he refers to the concept of "walking between two worlds" as Native peoples' own "ideological Vicodin."[7] In other words, worlding exists beyond the lexicon of settler language. It has created a real world fraught with expectations that Native people are forced to navigate. For literary theorist Scott Lyons, "That is precisely the 'problematic' part of the peoplehood paradigm. If you do not conform to the model—land, religion, language, sacred history, ceremonial cycle, and so on—if you happen to live away from your homeland, speak English, practice Christianity, or know more songs by the Dave Matthews Band than by the ancestor, you effectively 'cease to exist' as one of the People."[8] This is precisely the reason we asked the scholars of this volume to engage in a larger conversation about the concept of worldedness—our own initial disdain soon led to larger questions about how the maintenance, consequences, and lived experiences of Native people are shaped by four-plus centuries of two-world language.

For American Indian Studies scholar Joanne Barker (Lenni-Lenape), two worldedness and expectations are not abstract notions. In her study of the confluence of popular notions of indigeneity, identity, and American jurisprudence, Barker reveals her own struggles with racialized perceptions and the bifurcated language of difference. In writing about her own personal experiences with American preconceptions of Indianness that are largely based on phenotype and cultural performance, she writes:

> In these exchanges, people are looking to resolve preconceptions about Native peoples that my physical appearance and presumed blood degree contradicts. Often these efforts just make me tired, particularly of the disrespect to me and my family that I experience in these kids of interactions. So much so that on occasions when I have gone out after work for drinks with colleagues, when I just want to relax and unwind, I have disguised the work that I do so that I do not have to deal with the questions about my identity that its disclosure too often solicits.[9]

All this is to say that the binaries underlying the two-worlds trope manifest themselves in real ways for Native people day in and day out. Moreover, these discursive practices of settler colonialism also breed legal, economic, and political boundaries that extend well beyond a critique of words. It leads young children, as you will read in George Ironstrack's chapter on Myaamia language reclamation and history, to ask "George, if you come from a couple of tribes, do you have to choose one?" And, perhaps more importantly, it requires a response couched in both the determination of courts and communities. "In one way, yes, you do have to choose," Ironstrack replied, "Our politics requires that you can only be a voting member of one tribe. But outside of that, no you don't have to choose. If you can learn the language, kinship networks, and the responsibilities of each group, then it is possible to belong to all of the communities that your family connects you to."

In *Indians in Unexpected Places* historian Phil Deloria called for a broader examination of how Native people's defiance of external expectations help us better understand the limits of language and identity in the twentieth and twenty-first centuries.

> Taken together, it seems to me, the cumulative experiences of such anomalous Indians point to new questions concerning the turn of the twentieth century—perhaps toward a reimagining of the contours of modernity itself. They suggest a secret history of the unexpected, of the complex lineaments of personal and cultural identity that can never be captured by dichotomies built around crude notions of difference and assimilation, white and Indian, primitive and advanced. Those secret histories of unexpectedness are, I believe, worth further pursuit, for they can change our sense of the past and lead us quietly, but directly, to the present moment.[10]

We hope that the examinations of the "crude" dichotomies involved with the identity, politics, and history of worlded expectations will help move forward the conversation that Deloria implored nearly a decade ago. While the work of the aforementioned scholars and activists, along with the horrible examples that we encountered in the archive and on the television screen, provoked us to question the two-worlds framework, we ultimately concluded that answering, or even attempting to answer those questions was the work of more than two scholars. In order to address these issues we assembled a group of really smart people to address its use in history, society, contemporary scholarship, and popular culture.

The genesis of this book began in 2009, when we asked scholars to question the role of the two-worlds framework in a historical context by presenting papers at the annual meeting of the American Society for Ethnohistory in New Orleans. Through a series of three linked panels that comprised more than a dozen scholars, we discovered many others had critical questions about the two-worlds trope and wanted to speak about it. Our conversation could have ended there, and this volume would have been little more than a collection of essays challenging the use of the two-worlds framework in a historical context. What we've discovered in conversations with scholars, activists, Native peoples, and non-Native allies is that the idea of walking between two worlds, a framework birthed from a colonial past and adapted over time to produce an institutionalized ethnocentrism, maintains a significant legacy in a settler present.[11] These essays promise to engage more deeply the foundations of this framework by exploring the historical, imagined, and real forms of the two-worlds framework both in the historical record and within contemporary society.

We hope that a quick perusal of this volume indicates a different kind of academic conversation than the traditional edited volume. Instead, we sought to provide a forum where a series of linked conversations might take place between individual scholars. The book is divided into four parts, each addressing a separate aspect of the two-worlds trope. An "interlude" follows each part. In these interludes, we asked prominent scholars to reflect generally upon the issues raised by the chapters within the preceding section. They could reference their own work, reference the chapters themselves, or simply raise additional suggestions for the questions asked of the original contributors. Ultimately, we felt that this latitude would produce some provocative thoughts for our readers. In the end, we believe they have done just that.

As editors, we encouraged individual contributors in each section to explore the two-worlds framework by asking broad questions that were structured around general themes. In that way, each author was permitted to reflect upon the questions specific to their section, yet use their own research and personal experiences to address some or all of our queries. The authors in Part I were given the unenviable task of tracing the historical antecedents of the two-worlds framework in a North American context. We asked: Where did it come from? And, where do you see the language of worldedness in the historical literature? Our contributors responded by providing examples of how eighteenth-century Europeans and Native Americans employed the language of two worlds in three different geographical regions of North America. Katie Magee Labelle, examining French and Wendat experiences of the Upper Great Lakes, demonstrates intersections between corporal and spiritual worlds in the context of the colonial experience. As French missionaries attempted to describe the difference between Wendat and French worlds, their Indigenous counterparts reflected upon the division between the land of the living and the land of the dead. In Kristalyn Shefveland's essay we are exposed to the lexicon employed by early English settlers in colonial Virginia. Shefveland discovers that not all Englishman thought alike. While some described their surroundings as a stark contrast between Native and non-Native worlds, other Englishmen chronicled a far more complex story in their private journals. Ian Chambers examines the two-worlds trope through both English and Cherokee eyes. By assessing the perspective of each, Chambers is able to illustrate how single events, like council meetings between English and Cherokee leaders, could be "read" so differently. Nancy Shoemaker offers our first interlude and reflects on the previous essays. She also offers a way to map and visualize the spaces occupied by the varying worlds described by our first three authors.

In Part II, we asked authors to discuss how the two-worlds discourse has functioned in a historical context. How has it been used to categorize individuals or communities? How has it historically functioned in literature, art, or other forms of cultural expression? James Joseph Buss demonstrates how the two-worlds framework has led historians and others to place judgment on historical actors of the past. In this way, the language employed by nineteenth-century Americans in the Great Lakes has continued to influence our understanding of those individuals today. C. Joseph Genetin-Pilawa focuses on the commemorative and lived Indigenous landscapes of nineteenth-century Washington, DC and suggests that the public discourse of the capital fixed spatially and therefore legitimated the two-worlds trope. More importantly perhaps, he suggests that in studying the ways Native people engaged with the built environment of conquest, we can see a much more complex and challenging local history in the capital city. Sakina Hughes returns this section to the Great Lakes by examining the small Indiana community of Peru. Her study demonstrates that descriptors like Native and non-Native obscure a complicated regional history that includes Native Americans, African Americans, and other ethnic groups. Susan Gray's intriguing interlude suggests that postcolonial scholars and their recent emphasis on intimate encounters might provide a new, or renewed, lens through which to (re)envision the two-world framework.

Next, we asked how the two-worlds discourse functions in contemporary society? In Part III, authors discussed where they witnessed the manifestations of the two-worlds framework in political, artistic, and literary expressions. George Ironstrack retraces his own work in reconstructing the Miami language. By exploring the history of the Miami people of Indiana and Ohio in both historical and contemporary contexts, Ironstrack demonstrates the importance of looking beyond those restrictions to the importance of community and language. In her essay, Cathleen Cahill uses the micro-history of federal Indian Service employees to demonstrate how obfuscating the two-worlds trope can be, especially when considering multitribal experiences. Brian Hosmer's interlude explores the role of capitalism, wage-labor, and commercialism in influencing our understanding of "modern *tribal* nations as active participants in local and global marketplaces."

Finally, we asked authors: Where do we go from here? What new questions or frameworks might guide a new and meaningful discussion of the issues raised by scholars, artists, writers, activists, and others in this volume? Daniel Cobb, Kyle Fields, and Joseph Cheatle employ "ethnobiography" to provide an alternate retelling of D'Arcy McNickle's life, one that challenges the two-worlds trope and the way that biographies have traditionally been written in Indigenous studies. Ethnobiography, these authors submit, reject the occlusion of "two worlds" by allowing space for the unexpected, the improbable, even the impossible. Sandra Garner argues that to imagine Native futures, we have to attend to the layered and complex interactions so common in settler-colonialism as well as to the "complex personhood" of Native historical actors. To disrupt the two-worlds dichotomy, she asserts that scholars and others must take up multiple positionalities. Coll Thrush provides the final words of this collection, but hopefully not the last words on this issue. In his powerful Afterword, Thrush reminds us that these issues, and our suggestions for rethinking them, require a delicate dissection of the past and present.

Overall, the authors in this volume offer a range of views about how we might move forward—some outright reject the two-worlds framework, others attempt to explain how it has functioned in the past, still others attempt to problematize our very understanding of how it functions in historical and contemporary settings. Nancy Shoemaker, perhaps picking up a cue from Gayatri Spivak—who argued, "it is not possible, within discourse to escape essentializing somewhere"—suggests that binaries might still have their place in the academy.[12] "I do not believe that a two-worlds perspective is in itself a problem," she writes in this volume, "Instead, it seems a natural offshoot of a human predilection for binary thought, as in self and other, us and them. Moreover, for people in the past as well as for scholars, conceiving of two worlds in relationship could serve as a useful analytical tool for making sense of chaos. The problem with two worlds seems to rest mainly with our dependence on the construct of an Indian world juxtaposed against a European world." Coll Thrush pushes us further as he suggests that perhaps thinking in terms of one or two worlds is not enough. As he writes in the Afterword, "All of this is to say that Indigenous history (like so many other kinds of history, when done well and honestly) is full of paradoxes. There is only one world, except for the occasions when two worlds are necessary, and two worlds are insufficient. Each of these things is true, just as so many other seeming paradoxes are also true of Indigenous-settler relations."

Attempting to eliminate the two-worlds framework altogether is problematic, worldedness is, after all, more than just an abstract idea. For many Native people, it is a lived experience. For people of settler ancestry, it is the very language of settler colonialism. It is pervasive and imposes the conceptual map for understanding the terrestrial world upon which Native people and others are forced to engage. N. Scott Momaday's Pulitzer Prize-winning novel *House Made of Dawn*—long credited with launching a Native American literary renaissance—exemplifies the ubiquitous nature of the idea. The tagline on a recent edition of the work explains that the main character, Abel, is "a young Native American" who finds himself "caught between two worlds." Abel is a World War Two veteran, who after returning home to New Mexico, discovers that he no longer feels like he belongs—a stranger in his own house. When life's circumstances take him to urban Los Angeles after serving time in prison, he again finds himself an outsider—an Indian in the city. But the quip on the dust jacket, and the author who penned it, miss the larger point of Momaday's work. *House Made of Dawn* pushes its reader to reconceptualize the most entrenched binary of all: that of good and evil. In doing so, the book and its author provoke us to rethink the terms of worldedness. "How we love our binaries," Thomas King explains, "But what Momaday and other Native writers suggest is that there are other ways of imagining the world, ways that do not depend so much on oppositions as they do on co-operations."[13]

So, *where do we go from here*? Rethinking the two-worlds trope requires imagination and a critical evaluation of how language, politics, economics, and cultural all influence the expectations that we place on one another. This book does not seek to leave you with a concrete answer; rather, we hope that it inspires additional conversations and discussions about what it means to classify ourselves in terms of worlds. For Paul Chaat Smith a project of this type requires careful attention and great imagination. "The great project that awaits," he explains, "is to acknowledge the awesome complexity and find new avenues of investigation. Simply reversing bogus binaries doesn't get us anywhere. The project isn't about the good guys being bad, and the bad guys being good, but about finding new ways of seeing and thinking about the history that is all around us . . . That isn't only subversive, it's really difficult. Few can do it at all; hardly anyone knows how to do it well." In the end, we have tried to leave you with new ways of addressing the issue of worlding and, perhaps, a new understanding of the legacies of settler colonialism. In terms of this introduction, we leave you with a final example of how we might reimagine the confluence of the past and present.

Wabansi Lakeside Chicago-Beyond Swag

After looking through pictures of a family trip to Chicago, artist Jodi Webster (Ho-Chunk Nation/Prairie Band of Potawatomi) found herself wondering, "What if the Potawatomi or Indians in general, were never forcibly removed from their homelands or forced to assimilate?"[14] Her response, "Wabansi Lakeside Chicago-Beyond Swag," (the cover image of this book) defies expectations. Webster places her son in front of a familiar Chicago skyline wearing both a Chicago Bulls jersey and an intricately beaded bandolier bag (the only aspect of the drawing rendered in color). "He feels pride for the distinct nation he is representing," Webster explains, "and is willing to defend his style of dress to onlookers." Ultimately, Webster's reinterpretation of the urban landscape and decision to place of her son at the center of the painting helps us reach beyond the limitations of worldedness, while simultaneously using that same language to mark significance. "My goal was to inspire my children and encourage them to be proud of their lineage."[15] Perhaps, trying to render This World, as Malinda Maynor Lowery suggests in the Preface and Webster does so beautifully in her artwork, requires us to think beyond a mathematical language of worlds. Perhaps, in the end, thinking in terms one or two or even three worlds is not enough.

Notes

1. Keith Basso, *Wisdom Sits in Places: Landscape and Language among the Western Apache* (Albuquerque: University of New Mexico Press, 1996), 7.

2. Vine Deloria, Jr., *Custer Died for Your Sins: An Indian Manifesto* (New York: Macmillian, 1969), 86.

3. Cataloguing examples of the two-worlds trope is a herculean task. We thought about providing a broad list of examples here, but even we were surprised to find how many times the two-worlds notion ends up in scholarly works. Go to your computer and open a search engine. Then type in the words "two worlds" and "Native American." The number of results is mind-boggling. If you want to limit those examples to scholarly works, use Google scholar or (as we did) insert them into the academic database "America: History and Life." The hundreds of results suggest that historians are particularly fond of binary thinking. If you limit the search with the subject terms "INDIANS" and "WHITES—Relations with Indians" you will still likely find dozens of results and these are only articles or book reviews that reference two worlds in their titles and abstracts. On March 9, 2012, our initial search on "America: History and Life" returned 309 results using the basic search terms "two worlds." When we limited the results using the subject terms "INDIANS" and "WHITES—Relations with Indians," we still found 69 references. A similar search using the "Worldcat" database revealed thousands of results.

4. Theodora Kroeber, *Ishi in Two Worlds: A Biography of the Last Wild Indian in North America* (Berkeley: University of California Press, 2011, 50th anniversary edition).

5. Thomas King, *The Truth About Stories: A Native Narrative* (Minneapolis: University of Minnesota Press, 2003), 64.

6. Paul Chaat Smith, *Everything You Know About Indians is Wrong* (Minneapolis: University of Minnesota Press, 2009), 34–35.

7. Ibid., 36.

8. Scott Richard Lyons, *X-Marks: Native Signatures of Assent* (Minneapolis: University of Minnesota Press, 2010), 139.

9. Joanne Barker, *Native Acts: Law, Recognition, and Cultural Authenticity* (Durham, NC: Duke University Press, 2011), 3.

10. Philip Deloria, *Indians in Unexpected Places* (Lawrence: University Press of Kansas, 2004), 14.

11. Or what Edward Said labeled "positional superiority" and Michel Foucault called a society's "regime of truth." Edward Said, *Orientalism* (New York: Vintage Books, 1979), 7; and Michel Foucault, *Power/Knowledge: Selected Interviews and Other Writings, 1972–1977* (New York: Pantheon, 1980), 131.

12. Gayatri Chakravorty Spivak in *The Post-Colonial Critic: Interviews, Strategies, Dialogues,* ed. Sarah Harasym (New York: Routledge, 1990), 51.

13. King, 110.

14. Jodi Webster, artist statement for "Wabansi Lakeside Chicago-Beyond Swag," 2012.

15. Facebook conversation between James Joseph Buss and Jodi Webster, June 26, 2013.

I

Historical Antecedents

1

"To Live and Die with Them"

Wendat Reactions to "Worldly" Rhetoric in the Land of the Dead

Kathryn Magee Labelle

In 1637 an unnamed Native man, faced with the possibility of death, explained his plans for the afterlife. "I remembered having heard . . . that the French go after death to a place full of joy," he asserted. "Hence I said to myself, 'It is well that I die with them; for I will not leave them, I shall be very careful to take the same route that they do, after my death.' "[1] The "route" to which this man referred was a European-Christian path, one most likely explained to him through conversations with missionaries. Cross-cultural encounters, such as interactions between Natives and European missionaries, inevitably were complicated by the obstacles of communication faced by these groups. Yet, this man seems to have grasped not only the differences between French and Native worldviews, through his understanding of Christian concepts of the afterlife, but also chose to adopt this new doctrine into his own cosmology. These types of cultural transformations shaped the nature of encounters between the two groups in ways that would have long-lasting effects for all parties and future generations.

Take the case of the seventeenth-century Wendats and the French Jesuit missionaries. In planning their venture to visit the Wendats, whom the French would call "les Hurons," the Jesuits included objects that they hoped would enable them to better communicate with their North American hosts. Packed among Father Jean de Brébeuf's belongings was a small model of a globe.[2] This item, spherical in shape, depicted the world according to the French in the 1630s. It most likely included outlines of labeled continental land masses, large bodies of oceanic and sea water, as well as the lines of longitude and latitude measurements.[3] The globe acted as a visual aid to Brébeuf, as both Jesuits and Wendats attempted to understand each other's belief systems. Later, as communication became easier through linguistic fluency, the globe still remained a vital instrument in order to clarify misunderstandings about Jesuit concepts of Heaven and Hell, the earth and God. In fact, Brébeuf reflected on the success of this strategy in winning over Wendats who rejected the missionary's teachings, explaining ". . . when we preach to them of one God, Creator of Heaven and earth, and of all things, and even when we talk to them of Hell and Paradise and of our mysteries, the headstrong [Wendats] reply that this is good for our Country and not for theirs . . . But having pointed out to them, by means of a little globe that we had brought . . . they remain without reply."[4]

This was neither the first, nor the last time that European notions of worldly rhetoric and concrete objects would re-shape North American perceptions of the world, both in the physical and metaphysical sense. Although, in Brébeuf's example, the silence expressed by the Wendats is not a clear indication of their acceptance of Jesuit teachings, there are many other instances that signify a reorientation toward Europeanized cosmologies. Items, such as the globe, were tools implemented by Europeans to aid them in this process.

Undoubtedly one of the foremost factors influencing the change in North American belief systems was the introduction of Christianity. There is a wealth of scholarship dedicated to the subject, which emphasizes both the detrimental and positive repercussions of conversion within Native communities.[5] Within this field there is a considerable amount of work focused on the Wendat experience.[6] For the most part, these historical investigations serve to clarify our understanding of the impact that the introduction of Christianity had on Native women, politics, economies, and social systems. Furthermore, they have clarified the process of religious conversion and cultural encounters within the North American context.

This chapter is an attempt to contribute to this important field of research through an exploration of Wendat perceptions of a two-world rhetoric introduced by French missionaries in the seventeenth century. Prior to encounters with Europeans, the Wendats supported and maintained the notion that there was one collective world shaped by the alliances and kinship connections of various groups, whether they were Wendat, Algonquian, or French. This was apparent in both their understanding of the living world as well as what they called the "Land of the Dead." The introduction of Christianity by the French, however, led Wendat society to reconsider its "one-world" vision and eventually shift to a two-world discourse. Consequently, through the lens of Wendat afterlife, this chapter examines the process in which the missionaries introduced and shaped Wendat notions of separate worlds, highlighting Wendat articulations of resistance and acceptance to such a concept.

Wendat Perceptions of the Afterlife

The Wendat Confederacy was a coalition of four or five separate nations. These included: The Bear Nation (*Attignawantan*), Nation of the Rock (*Arendarhonon*), The People of the Cord (*Attigneenongnahac*), The People of the Deer (*Tahontaenrat*) and perhaps a fifth group, The People of the Marsh (*Ataronchronon*). The Confederacy occupied territory around the Great Lakes region along the shores of Georgian Bay, Ontario, Canada. This area was known as "Wendake." They were culturally an Iroquoian people, speaking an Iroquoian dialect, living a predominantly sedentary and agricultural lifestyle, and organizing their social structures around a matricentric and matrilocal body-politique.

Spiritual beliefs infused every aspect of Wendat life. At the center of this belief system was the "soul." In reality, the Wendats perceived there to be two immortal souls, one that remained with the body after death and the other that traveled to the Land of the Dead. The former was referred to as atisken, while the latter was called by a different name, esken.[7]

The Land of the Dead, or ahahabreti onaskenonteta (the place where the souls of the dead went), was to the west of Wendake.[8] Roger Carpenter has summarized both the spiritual and physical sense of the Wendat afterlife as a "single, shared, yet segregated community."[9] It was comprised of several villages, each representing one of the Wendat nations. The villagers took part in similar activities to the living, maintaining fields, sowing corn, as well as hunting and fishing throughout the year.[10] Not all Wendats settled in this western hamlet, however. Those who were killed in battle or who committed suicide, for instance, were relegated to a separate village in and of itself and were feared by the other villages. In addition, those Wendats who died in old age or very young remained in another village closer to Wendake because they were too weak to make the voyage out west. This group planted corn in the abandoned fields of the living Wendats and many believed that you could hear the voices of children's souls chasing birds in the fields.[11] There was no equivalent to the Christian concepts of Heaven and Hell in relation to the Land of the Dead, and no mention of reward or punishment in the afterlife.[12]

The journey to the Land of the Dead was not an easy one. Although there is some discrepancy as to the exact path (there are accounts of both a path in the sky along the Milky Way and a path on earth) most Wendat descriptions of the journey seem to favor the earthbound route.[13] This is corroborated by the Wendat spiritual leader Tonneraouanont's explanation to the Jesuits that "We have . . . a certain road that our souls take after death."[14] It was a well-beaten, broad trail that was about four leagues or thirty-two kilometers from Wendake proper. Along the way travelers passed by a sacred rock called Ecaregniondi, which was often marked by a paint that the Wendats used to color their faces.[15] Further down the path was the house of Oscotarach, which translates into "Pierced-Head." It was this individual's job to draw the brains of the deceased out of their head, keeping them for himself. Next, the traveling soul was faced with a river. The only way to cross it was by crossing an unstable fallen tree trunk. Additionally, this natural bridge was guarded by a dog that continuously jumped at travelers, often throwing them off balance and into the cold current of the river.[16] In the end, the Land of the Dead was not an easily accessible route. It required determination and perseverance to arrive at the final destination.

Information about the afterlife was attained in large part by living individuals who had managed to visit the Land of the Dead and then subsequently returned to the living. These accounts gave insight into the journey, and verified the existence of such a place. Travelers became witnesses, giving testimony that supported Wendat concepts of the afterlife that served as a source of information to perpetuate the belief system. Take the account of a Wendat man who accomplished this feat in the hopes that he might find his recently deceased sister and bring her back to life. It took him twelve days to make the journey throughout which time he did not eat or drink anything. On the first night of his arrival to the Land of the Dead, his sister appeared to him, giving him a dish of cornmeal cooked in water. At this time, she disappeared too quickly for him to tell her his purpose and bring her back with him. The man, therefore, remained in the Land of the Dead for the next three months. It was during this time that he came across the home of Oscotarach. Oscotarach told the man where he could find his sister and gave him a pumpkin to hold her soul for the return journey. Eventually he was able to capture his sister and he returned to Oscotarach who gave him his sister's brains and instructed him on how to make the return journey back, as well as the process of how to revive the woman. The man followed the directions and although he was able to bring his sister back to Wendake, her soul ended up escaping due to an accident during the resuscitation ceremony.[17] On the whole, it was accounts such as this that enticed Wendats to continue their belief in the Land of the Dead by verifying a number of aspects of Wendat afterlife. It gave details about the journey west, the existence of villages occupied by the dead, and insight into the role of Oscotarach.

New Ideas: Missionaries in Wendake

By the time Brébeuf presented his "little globe" to the Wendats, missionaries had been visiting Wendake for over a decade. In 1615 the Récollet friar Joseph le Caron ventured to live with the Wendats for a year before returning to Quebec. In 1620, William Poulin took up the task, and was later joined in 1623 by Le Caron, as well as missionaries Father Nicholas Viel and Brother Gabriel Sagard. Historians have viewed the Récollet mission in Wendake as a venture with little influence, arguing that this was the result of language barriers and a lack of evangelical zeal.[18]

The Récollet period, abandoned for the most part by 1625, was followed by a new wave of missionaries that began with the arrival of Jesuits Jean de Brébeuf and Anne de Nouë in 1626. The Jesuits remained for several years, in order to Christianize the Wendats. This venture was cut short, however, when Brébeuf was recalled to Quebec in 1629 and New France fell to the English. Within a few years, however, New France was restored to France through the treaty of St. Germaine and the Jesuits were given sole authority over the Native missions within the territory. Consequently, Jesuit missionaries took up residence within Wendake as of 1634 and would continue to have a close relationship with the Confederacy and its descendants for many generations.[19]

Language training was an important component to the success of the missions in Wendake. Converts had to understand the concepts of Christianity before attaining baptism and without a comprehension of the language this goal would be almost impossible. From the very beginning of French missionary activity in Wendake, attempts were made to learn the Wendat language. Le Caron spent most of his first year trying to become fluent, while Sagard documented the language into a dictionary as an additional aid for future missionaries. This knowledge was later passed on to Brébeuf and de Nouë as they made their own preparations to visit the Wendats.[20] By 1636, Brébeuf reported that most Jesuits were able to understand the

Wendats and vice versa. In addition, he boasted that the Jesuits were also compiling a new dictionary as a demonstration of the progress they had made.[21] This was the first step in a series of calculated tactics used by the missionaries to convince the Wendats of the benefits of conversion and sway them to adopt Christianity as their own religious system.

Once the linguistic boundaries were overcome, the Jesuits were able to convey a series of teachable concepts most pertinent to the conversion process. For the most part, the emphasis was on the afterlife and the differences between Heaven and Hell. Brébeuf, for instance, told the Wendat *Martin Tsicok* that "souls after death all go to Hell or to Paradise, that Paradise is a place full of delights and contentment, and on the contrary that Hell is a place of fires, of pains, and eternal torments."[22] Moreover, the teachings emphasized that the actions of the living would decide which of these two places the soul would go to after death. Brébeuf tried to clarify the important repercussions of such an afterlife by enticing *Tsicok* to "think, while he was yet still in life, to which of these places he desired to go and dwell forever."[23] *Tsicok* acknowledged the Jesuit's message and replied he was fearful of the fires of Hell, subsequently asking for more lessons on the topic.[24]

Despite the attempts of missionaries to present a relatively simplified description of the Christian afterlife, many Wendats found the details confusing in comparison to their own beliefs. For example, when the Jesuits taught that Heaven was a place of peace, the Wendat Elder Tendoutsahoronc questioned "How? . . . we people think that the dead make war among themselves as well as the living."[25] Similar questions surfaced when the Jesuits tried to clarify what they meant by "Paradise" in stating: "[T]here are no fields and no grain there; that people do not go trading, nor fishing there, and that they do not marry."[26] Thus, "Paradise" represented a place lacking all forms of familiar and cherished Wendat activities. Wendats also questioned the height of Heaven, and the logistics of how they would get there—a detail deemed ridiculous by the Jesuits who rendered Wendat beliefs in a tangible trail or path to the Land of the Dead as pagan mythology.[27] Jesuit reactions were the same when they were asked about the fires and burning that took place in Hell. Wendats challenged the idea on the basis that "there could be no fire where there was no wood . . . [and] what forests could sustain so many fires through such a long space of time?"[28] On other occasions the missionary's own communication skills were questioned, rather than the content contained in the message. A sick Wendat man, for instance, became insulted by Father Pijart's attempt to discuss conversion. The Father asked this man where he would like to go after death, Heaven or Hell? "[This] is not right," the man replied, "we people do not ask such questions, for we always hope that they will not die, and that they will recover their health."[29] In this case, Pijart's lack of cultural awareness cost him a potential convert.

Taken as a whole, the Jesuit's afterlife departed drastically from the Wendat's Land of the Dead. This made discussion and linguistic fluency all the more critical, so that the French could respond to questions and clarify their interpretation in regards to Heaven and Hell. In particular the Jesuits relied heavily on their theological training to help respond to these inquiries. In one instance, Brébeuf was questioned about the nature of God and more specifically "where God was before the creation of the world."[30] The Jesuit responded without hesitation, drawing from the works of St. Augustine. He then followed this answer with a series of questions to the Wendats including "who created Heaven and earth?" According to Brébeuf, the Wendats had no immediate answer and thus conceded to accept his own explanations as the truth.[31]

European scientific knowledge also helped the Jesuits resolve Wendat questions about their teachings. In regard to Hell's fires and the lack of wood, for instance, a Jesuit responded "the lower world possessed no wood, and that it burned by itself." [32] He then produced a lump of sulfur and passed it around to his Wendat spectators. The group was then led to a nearby kettle placed on several coals. The missionary sprinkled a few pieces of the sulfur on the coals and within seconds the kettle was engulfed in flames. After three more similar demonstrations the Wendats were convinced of the possibility of the "lower world" and its ability to make fire without wood.[33]

Beyond the concepts of Heaven and Hell, missionaries needed to communicate the exclusivity of Christian afterlife. Heaven was reserved for Christians alone, dividing the afterlife into converts and infidels. The Jesuits contextualized this idea in terms of Wendat kinship practices, describing the "Sky-dwellers" as Christian souls in Heaven. They were also called, the "heavenly family" or a "lineage of believers."[34] Through this rhetoric, Jesuits hoped to illustrate how baptized Wendats could become adopted members of this Christian celestial family. Adoption and familial ties were paramount to Wendat social order and thus provided a familiar framework for explaining an appealing Christian afterlife.

One of the ways the Jesuits demonstrated the important role exclusivity played in Christian religion was by imposing strict rules about the burials of Wendat converts. Traditionally, Wendats buried their dead in a communal ossuary pit every eight to ten years during their Feast of Souls ceremony. The burial itself required that all bones that had been temporarily buried since the last Feast be dug up and placed within the ossuary pit. There were five or six people in the pit in charge of mixing the bones. Gifts, furniture, ornaments, kettles, corn, as well as other goods were also placed in the pit. Once everything had been deposited, mats and bark were placed on top of the bones, along with sand, poles, and wooden stakes. The rest of the day was taken up by gift giving, songs, and feasts. Combined, these activities marked a symbolic confirmation of kinship ties and alliances. Just as the bones were physically united within the same ossuary pit, the living relatives of the deceased were united in a similar synchronic state.[35]

Missionaries rejected this practice from the very beginning. Jesuits noted it as a "useless" and "foolish" custom, reporting explicitly "if divine goodness does not stop the course of its blessings upon these [Wendats], the feast will cease. . . ."[36] On some level the Jesuits' prayers were answered. As they slowly gained favor within the Wendat community and members began to adopt Christian customs, burials became just as segregated and exclusive as their lessons on Christian afterlife. Christians were not allowed to be buried with Traditionalists—a practice that was both in tune with Christian doctrine, and also acted as a symbolic reminder to the Wendats that there was a metaphysical and tangible division between converts and non-converts.

As early as 1635, Jesuits enforced the rule that baptized Wendats be buried outside the ossuary pit in a Christian manner. This engendered a ripple effect, in which friends and relatives of interred Christians desired to be buried in a similar way. Joseph Sondaarouhane, a Wendat man of roughly fifty, was buried "solemnly in a separate place," for instance. As a result, when his friend, Joachim Tsindacaiendoua, a Christian elder of eighty years, also died, his family requested a similar burial so that they could be sure the two would meet in Heaven.[37]

In 1636, Wendats asked the Jesuits if they would consent to bury a number of Frenchmen within the Feast of Souls burial pit. This was meant as a symbolic gesture signifying the close relationship between the two groups of people. The Jesuits rejected the idea immediately, but suggested an alternative that included reburying the Frenchmen in a private grave along with the bones of Wendat Christians.[38] Father Brébeuf gave four reasons for this decision. First, he explained that that "we were already granting to them on this point what they wished, and were making it appear thereby that we desired to love them as our brothers, and *to live and die with them*."[39] The justification continues:

> 2. We hoped that God would be glorified thereby,—mainly in this, that, in thus separating, with the consent of the whole Country, the bodies of Christians from those of Unbelievers, it

> would not have been difficult afterwards to obtain from private persons that their Christians should be interred in a Cemetery apart, which we would consecrate for that purpose. 3. We were intending to inter them with all the ceremonies of the Church. 4. The Elders, of their own accord, wished us to erect a beautiful and magnificent Cross, as they stated afterwards more particularly. Thus the Cross would have been authorized by the whole Country, and honored in the midst of this Barbarism, and they would not have taken pains thereafter to impute to it, as they have done in the past, the misfortunes that might overtake them.[40]

Ultimately, through Jesuit lessons, quizzical debates, emphasis on the "heavenly family" and burial ceremonies, the missionaries were able to effectively communicate an alternatively new perspective on the afterlife. Their evangelical drive pushed them to spread their knowledge of Christianity and persuade Wendats to join them in "Paradise." In order for them to accomplish this task Wendats had to reconfigure their understanding of the afterlife from a unified, inclusive, yet carefully segregated world of villages reflecting the same lifestyle of the living, to a divided world—exclusive to Christians and hostile to non-believers.

Wendat Resistance

Not all Wendats were ready to endorse Christian perceptions of the afterlife and frequently voiced their reasons for opposition to the Jesuits. Initial arguments against Heaven and Hell were rooted in a desire to continue the traditional beliefs in the Land of the Dead, and to retain connections with Wendat ancestors. One line of argument was simply that the Wendats were not a people who desired change. They respected the French notions of Heaven and Hell, but were satisfied with their own beliefs. Brébeuf found this argument frustrating, as he was repeatedly faced with Wendats who explained "[our] Country is not like [the French], that [the French] have another God, another Paradise, in a word, other customs."[41] Some went further in saying "that [the Jesuit teachings] were good for [the French] Country and not for theirs, that every Country has its own fashions."[42] The Wendats were not denying the French their version of the afterlife, but maintained that each people had their own ideas and customs that were unique to them. They contended that each "Country" had its own unique practices, acknowledging that difference in tradition was a universal human trait, differentiating people from one another, but not privileging one custom above the rest. This was difficult, if not impossible for the Jesuits to accept, as they believed Christianity to be the ultimate "truth."[43] Further, the use of the term "Country" signifies a much more complex discussion than strictly one based on religious difference. It is unclear what the Wendats meant by "Country" at this time and within this context. Was it employed in a customary sense in order to differentiate between different people and territory—synonymous with "Neutral Country" or "Iroquois Country?" Or had the meaning changed as a result of European contact, indicating a more abstract notion of different "worlds?" In the case of the latter, the implication is that Wendats ironically used Jesuit concepts and rhetoric in order to combat the missionaries. If this was the situation, it was not necessarily a shift in cosmology, but a strategic linguistic turn in order to better communicate Wendat ideas to the Jesuits. Without more evidence, however, we are left with only speculation.

Another popular Wendat argument was that there was no need for baptism because the Wendats did not concede to committing sins, nor did they seek to understand what "sins" were. A dying woman explained "she could not do it [be baptized],—that she had not offended God, and that she did not know what sin was."[44] Her relatives supported her claim in saying that she had always "lived correctly."[45] The Jesuits tried to counter her argument with the explanation that everyone was subject to sin and that she was no exception. Still, the woman maintained her stance for over an hour of debate with the priests until her weakened state drained her ability to argue any further.[46]

Other Wendats argued that they were disillusioned with the final destinations for their departed soul, rejecting Heaven as it was seen as a location of perpetual dissatisfaction. Arguments were made that Heaven was a place of idleness, for instance. Without fields, fishing, hunting, and trading, people would become bored and lazy—how would they be able to endure an eternity subjected to that type of lifestyle?[47] Furthermore, there were rumors that there was no tobacco in Heaven.[48] This would have deterred the Wendats as tobacco was essential to many of their cultural practices.

Much like the details of the Land of the Dead, Wendats gained further insight into Heaven from individuals who had made the trip there and returned to share their experiences. Wendats used the information acquired by these accounts as material to justify further resistance to baptism. In 1638, a man described his journey to Heaven where he encountered two English women. These women, he said, warned him that he should not go to Heaven and that the Jesuits were evil. This report was delivered at a general council and was circulated widely throughout Wendake.[49]

A similar account took place in 1646. In this case, a Christian Wendat woman had ventured to Heaven. Upon arrival she was tormented by the French in the same manner as the Iroquois welcomed war captives into their villages. She received repeated beatings with sticks and fire-branding, as well as other forms of torture. She then divulged that Heaven was full of fire and that the French take pleasure in burning Wendat souls. She concluded that those individuals who had managed to evade the French in the living world and who rejected their foreign rules and regulations went to a place of "delights," where everything good abounds, and whence all evil is banished.[50] This report spread more widely than the one in 1638. According to the Jesuits, and much to their dismay, "This news was soon spread everywhere: it was believed in the country without gainsaying."[51] Traditionalists used this report as a means to convince others of the evils of Heaven, while fractions of already converted Wendats became skeptical of their predestined afterlife. In short, these negative firsthand accounts of Heaven confirmed Wendat resistors' desires to maintain their Wendat customs, and general contempt toward a Christian vision of the afterlife.

By far, the most popular reason for resistance articulated by Wendats was their desire to reconnect with deceased relatives.[52] In the early years of French/Wendat encounters, there were very few Wendats who had been baptized; consequently they believed that very few Wendats had made their way to Heaven. Conversely, there were generations of Wendat kinsmen who had settled in the Land of the Dead. The husband of a dying woman, for instance, presented his case against his wife's decision to be baptized by reminding her, "What then? Do you wish to leave your relatives, your fathers, mothers, and children who are dead, in order to go with strangers?"[53] Certainly, at least in the early decades of missionary work, many Wendats expressed similar fears. The chance that they would never see their dead relatives again would have served as sufficient reason to reject a journey to Heaven entirely.

The "Sky-dwellers"

Eventually Wendat justifications for resistance gave way to equally influential arguments to reconsider the Christian option. Jesuit skillful communication tactics notwithstanding, epidemics and warfare were the major factors that began to loosen Wendat attachments to the Land of the Dead. Throughout the 1630s Wendake lost up to 60 percent of its population.[54] The exact number of people affected by disease is uncertain, but Bruce Trigger argued, "there can be no doubt that many [Wendat] were stricken by this epidemic."[55] Commenting on the loss of Wendat life throughout this period, Brébeuf stated that "he personally did not know anyone who had escaped [the epidemic] and that a large number had died."[56] This unprecedented death rate forced Wendats to make decisions about burials and the afterlife on a daily basis. Furthermore, the dying were often baptized by the Jesuits, sending a good portion of the deceased to Heaven rather than to the Land of the Dead. These circumstances combined to create the ideal situation for a Jesuit "Harvest of Souls."[57] Essentially, Wendats were weak, vulnerable, and in search of solutions. The Jesuits argued that baptism would save their souls, and for many, this was worth considering.

Wendat arguments in support of Christian conversion were based along similar lines as those who presented resistance. Wendat public articulations indicate that these decisions were focused primarily on first-hand accounts of Heaven, and above all else, the desire to reconnect with loved ones. For example, a woman who was ill for some time was said to have traveled to Heaven and it was because of this trip that she resolved to attain baptism. She reported her experience to her father, who then passed it on to the missionaries and the rest of the village. According to this woman, she did not find fires as previously reported, nor was there any indication of Iroquoian captive torture. Instead, she reported that there were large numbers of handsome looking Frenchmen and women. In addition, she saw several Christian Wendats who had recently deceased. Among these kinsmen were her uncle and a sister who had died only a few days before. The woman approached them and to her surprise they began to speak to her. Her uncle began the conversation, "Well, my niece, so you have come here," which was followed by her sister's request to see the wampum bracelet the Jesuits had given her.[58] The sick woman was confused because she had not yet received a bracelet. The sister then explained that it was a gift reserved for Christians upon entering Heaven and that if she was baptized, she too could have a similar bracelet of her own—at which point the sister presented the woman with the bracelet she had received from Father Brébeuf upon her departure for Heaven. Shortly after her return to life, the woman was baptized and died soon after.[59]

Trips to the Land of the Dead could also serve as an indication that Heaven may be a better alternative than the traditional Wendat afterlife. For example, a man returned from the Land of the Dead to report with great enthusiasm, "Rejoice . . . for I have returned from the country of the souls, and I have found none there any longer; they have all gone to Heaven."[60] Before this journey he had been reluctant to accept baptism because he was determined to follow his ancestors. After his observations of the Country of the Souls (Land of the Dead), however, he went immediately to the missionaries to explain that he had changed his mind.

Other Wendats did not need this type of first-hand account to accept a Christian version of the afterlife. For them, the desire to connect with loved-ones and join the "Sky-dwellers" was reason enough.[61] This was the most frequently articulated argument by Wendats. Many parents, for instance, asked for baptism so that they could join their children in Heaven.[62] This was directly correlated with the fact that the Jesuits had taken it upon themselves to baptize many infants who had succumbed to the epidemics and were too young to resist and/or understand the missionaries' actions. Thus, the parents were forced to decide which was more important, seeing their young children in Heaven, or going to the Land of the Dead.

Another group who began to convert more frequently in the wake of disease and warfare were Wendat warriors. Specifically, missionaries remarked on the increased baptisms of war leaders, linking the "marked degree" of Wendat Christian converts to the number of Christian war chiefs.[63] Reflecting upon this apparent shift in conversions, Father Le Jeune noted that during the 1630s "hardly could one find, hitherto, among our Christians two or three warriors . . ." but almost a decade later "we have counted in a single band as many as twenty-two Believers,—all men of courage, and mostly Captains or people of importance."[64]

One of the reasons behind this shift was the need to be reunited with fallen comrades. When the popular Wendat war chief, Eustace Ahasistari was killed in a battle in 1642, many of his fellow warriors decided to convert.[65] Ahasistari was a Christian, baptized just before he ventured out on his last expedition.[66] With the news of his death, many of his comrades converted to the Christian faith out of respect and a desire to see the fallen warrior in the afterlife.[67] These men justified their decision in relation to a speech delivered by Ahasistari to other Wendat Christians just before he left. The surviving war chiefs used this message as a guide to their actions. "Let us inform our Relatives," Ahasistari said, "who are not of the same Faith as we, even if they may be our fathers and our children, that we do not wish our bones to be mingled together after our death since our Souls will be eternally separated, and our affection will not continue beyond this life."[68] As a result, we find a close friend of Ahasistari, Martin Tehoachiakwan, making a public declaration of his support for baptism in the aftermath of Ahasistari's death. Tehoachiakwan's speech was as follows:

> The enemies are at our doors . . . I withdraw from misfortune, let who will, follow me; our affairs are in a desperate state . . . I

> do not fear the Iroquois; I dread the more inhuman cruelties of the devils in hell, in a fire that is never extinguished. I abandon you, without abandoning you, or rather I abandon your follies; I abandon our evil customs; from this moment, I renounce all kinds of sin, and know ye that tomorrow I shall be a Christian.[69]

Overall, factors such as disease and warfare heightened the need for Wendats to make decisions concerning the fate of their souls. Jesuits conducted a skillful campaign to try to entice them towards Heaven, while the number of Christian Wendats was growing and to some extent this increase in conversions diffused the arguments in favor of the Land of the Dead. Indeed, by the 1640s we find Wendats who endorsed the Christian afterlife wholeheartedly, stating, as one Wendat man did: "I no longer fear death at all, and I would thank God if I saw myself at the end of my life, in the firm hope that I have, that I should go to Heaven: in like manner, I no longer apprehend the death of any of my relatives, provided that they die in the grace of God."[70] He later elaborated on the kinship connection made possible by joining the "Heavenly family," explaining his vision as follows:

> When a young woman who lives in her father-in-law's house is invited by her own father to come and spend some months in his house; if he is a rich and liberal man, the father-in-law rejoices in the thought that his daughter-in-law will be much at her ease, Likewise, if some one of our family died, I should have the thought that God, her father, had drawn her to his house: I should rejoice in the same, since she would be better off there than with me.[71]

This man's view of Heaven reiterates the messages communicated by the missionaries. He accepted that Heaven was a place of refuge and a place exclusive to Christian Wendats and their Christian relatives. Ultimately, the "Sky-dwellers" would reconnect in Heaven with their "father" (God), who would serve as an eternal protector and provider of good things.

Notions of exclusivity among the "Sky-dwellers" soon flowed into exceptionality and division within the Wendat living community as well. Christians were no longer buried with their unbaptized Wendat brethren, ultimately leading to calls from Christians to form a unified faction within Wendat society. Joseph Taondechoren, for instance, addressed the Christians of his village before departing on a trade venture to Quebec City:

> My brothers . . . here I am, about to depart; and perhaps we shall never have the consolation of seeing one another again here on earth. This makes me feel a desire to speak to you, as if I saw myself about to die, with the truest sentiments of my heart. Whatever misfortune may befall us, let us remember that we are Christians; that the object of our hopes is Heaven; that the earth contains nothing worthy of us . . . My brothers, let us kneel and all offer ourselves to God both for life and for death; let all of you follow my words, so that, having but one heart, we may also have but one tongue, and the same prayer in our mouths.[72]

Taondechoren's message clearly depicts a call to create and maintain a unity exclusive to Wendat converts. His metaphorical desire for them to have "one heart," and "one tongue" is similar to Wendat rhetoric in regards to alliance making and political policy. For Taondechoren, Christian Wendats should represent a cohesive group in both thought and action. Their desires and exploits should reflect a consistent dedication to the Christian faith, a belief system that distinguished them from other Wendats. Thus, through rhetoric such as Taondechoren's address, the differentiation between "Sky-dwellers" and Traditionalists began to replicate itself among the living. Discussions of different cosmologies were infused with worldly discourse, a useful way of depicting the shifting divide between Christians and non-Christians. Eventually we find Wendats using this language to describe these changing circumstances. Simply put, the situation, as one Wendat expressed to the Jesuits, was that "your world is different from ours; the God who created yours . . . did not create ours."[73]

Comparable Circumstances

The Wendat shift towards a two-world discourse was not an isolated incident. Jesuits expanded their missions among other Native Nations throughout New France. The Innu (Montagnais-Neskapi), for instance, were exposed to analogous rhetoric and conversion tactics as the Wendats. A review of the Innu experience underscores a potential pattern throughout Native communities who engaged with the Jesuits, highlighting similar discussions and results as the Wendat case study.

The seventeenth-century Innu were some of the most populous Algonquian-speaking Native people in the region encompassing the present-day

Canadian provinces of Quebec, Newfoundland, and Labrador. Theirs' was a society based predominantly on hunting and fishing and they led a less sedentary lifestyle then the Wendats.[74] Much like the Wendats, Innu customary perceptions of the afterlife differed greatly from those of the Christian French missionaries. They believed the earth to be flat and that once a person died their soul traveled west, toward the setting sun, until they reached the end of the earth. Houses were built upon the ledge, overlooking the watery basin that formed beneath the earth. If a soul fell off the ledge then it was turned into a fish. The routine of the Innu soul was the same as the living. It was thought that the majority of the time was spent eating, drinking, and dancing, while the departed soul continued to form relationships, and marry, just as the living did.[75] On the whole, the Innu maintained a comparable vision of the afterlife to the Wendats. Both believed that the Land of the Dead was a tangible place, located out west where souls participated in similar activities as the living.

The missionaries viewed the Innu version of the afterlife as pure "nonsense" and devoted many years to persuading the Innu to accept a Christian notion of Heaven.[76] This type of missionary work may have predated the Wendake missions, as both Innu and French missionaries came in contact with one another as early as 1603, when French explorer Samuel de Champlain traveled up the St. Lawrence with a number of Récollet missionaries. More official missions were established in the following decades. In 1637, for instance, the Jesuits established the Sillery mission (originally named St. Joseph). This was a semi-permanent community, located approximately three miles from Quebec City and had roughly twenty Innu and Algonkin residents to begin with. On 2 August, 1646, the Governor of New France, Charles Huault Montmangy reinstated the Jesuit's authority over Sillery by signing over the land around it (which the French considered their own) to the Jesuits in order to "better convert" the Natives.[77] Later in 1647, the Jesuits received 5,000 livres to aid them in this task.[78] This type of community organization fostered similar interactions between the French missionaries and Native residents as those in Wendake, and the Jesuits' ability to engage in frequent meetings, lessons and discussions with Innu created similar results.

Communication between the Jesuits and Innu was difficult at first, but by the 1630s there were at least several Innu and French who could converse with relative success.[79] The content delivered by the Jesuits was consistent with the information they shared with the Wendats. The main focus was on discounting Innu traditional beliefs of the afterworld and most importantly communicating the metaphysical certainty of Heaven and Hell. According to a very satisfied Jesuit observer, the Christian Innu Makeabichtichiou was able to summarize these teachings with clarity for his Innu village members. In brief, Makeabichtichiou explained, "the creation of man, the inundation of the world caused by men's sins, how the universe was re-peopled by Noah and his children, [and] how all men would die and be again brought to life."[80] He then elaborated on the afterlife stating, "Heaven kept very great blessings for the good and that there were horrible punishments prepared for the wicked . . . that those who believed in God were protected against sorcerers."[81] The Jesuit's support for this interpretation indicates the extent to which it was a true testament to the Jesuit's original teachings. Makeabichtichiou was not only taught by the missionaries, but understood the lessons to such a degree that he was able to explain and reiterate the Christian message to others.

Just as they did in Wendake, the Jesuits promoted separate burials among the Innu Christian converts in order to demonstrate further the exclusivity of the Christian afterlife. In one case, we find an Innu man pleading with the Jesuits to be baptized so that he might be buried beside his daughter and wife. Apparently both these women had received a Christian burial and the Jesuits had interred them in the French cemetery, a location set apart from the graves of the non-Christians. In order to convince the Jesuits, the man declared,

> Hast thou not heard . . . of my daughter, whom thy brothers baptized in the Winter, who died in your faith, and was buried in the place where they bury the French? Hast thou not been told how my wife also believed in God before her death, and how the same favor was granted to her as to my daughter? It is I who induced them to embrace what you teach. I wish to take for myself the advice I have them; I wish to die a Christian, and to be buried with your people.[82]

The Jesuits, therefore, enforced systematic separation of Christian Innus from Traditionalists through both discussions of the afterlife, and the gravesite and funerary practices. It was through these forums of cultural communication that Innus eventually came to view their world, once thought to be characteristically flat and inclusive, as a domain based on the principles of division and selectivity in accordance with Jesuit teachings.

The reasoning behind Innu conversions, as articulated by converts, were made along the same lines as the Wendats, with the most popular argument rooted to kinship ties and familial reunions. Makeabichtichiou's desire for baptism, for example, was primarily because he wanted to follow the path of his daughter and wife. Likewise, the Christian Innu François Xavier had converted because his dead wife and two deceased children had been baptized.[83] This also led *Xavier* to persuade his remaining family members, and especially his living children, to convert. Upon his deathbed he called to them, asserting "My children, believe in God; imitate your Father in this respect. I believe in him with as much certainty as if I saw him with my eyes; do not offend him, and he will help you. I am already dead; when my body is in the earth, remain near the Fathers, and obey them."[84] This was both a request for his children to attain baptism, but also an appeal to make sure that *Xavier* would be reunited with his children in Heaven. In his eyes, because his wife and children had died as Christians, his own baptism, as well as that of his surviving children, was the only way to ensure an eventual family reunion in Heaven.

The process in which the Innus and the Wendats became aware of Christian concepts of the afterlife were strikingly similar; so too were the means by which these new ideas were communicated to them by the Jesuit missionaries. Discussions surrounding Heaven and Hell, in addition to the fundamentally divisive and exclusionary nature of these metaphysical locations, were crucial in shifting Innu Traditional beliefs to a Christian worldview. Taking this into consideration, it would seem that the Wendat case was not an isolated experience and that other Native groups also adopted a language and conceptual cosmology based on notions of separate worlds put forth by missionaries.

Conclusion

In a website publication, the late Chief Bearskin of the Oklahoma Wyandotte, a confederated member of four modern Wendat nations,[85] concluded his presentation of a traditional legend by stating: "Other stories will follow from time to time covering all aspects of our Indian world."[86] The use of the term "Indian world" by Bearskin, nearly 400 years after the Jesuit missions to Wendake, demonstrates the ways in which two-world rhetoric has been incorporated and internalized by the Wendats and their ancestors after European contact. Missionaries worked hard to communicate an afterlife that promoted a two-world dichotomy. Through discussions of Heaven and Hell, burial practices, as well as significant waves of baptisms in the wake of disease and warfare, Wendats began the process of re-shaping their worldview. Although at first orchestrated along religious lines, ethnic and cultural differences could not be ignored, furthering this development and deepening the divide. By means of discussions on the afterlife, Christian and Traditionalist worlds transformed into similar subsequent articulations about French and Wendat worlds, as well as non-Native and Native ones. As a result, we find generations of modern Wendats expressing a European constructed two-world rhetoric, rather than a precontact one-world philosophy.

The concept of Native and non-Native worlds has been adopted widely within the North American context by both Indigenous peoples and settler society. Bearkskin's "Indian world," much like the popular term "Indian Country," has become a common label that enable contemporary peoples, both Native and non-Natives to differentiate between each other. The process by which this type of multiworld discourse developed may have several origins. Indeed, the Wendat/Jesuit case study, along with similar circumstances of the Innu, does not negate alternative factors leading to comparable results. Put another way, this examination into Wendat concepts of the afterlife signifies but one version of this process. Other Native Nations may have had preconceived traditions of separate worlds before European contact, or in some circumstances it may have been Native people themselves that instigated frameworks of cultural exclusivity. Therefore, the Wendat model provides a unique, but not isolated, prism for studying power negotiations within a new emerging North American order. There is no doubt that Native contact with Europeans sparked significant cultural repercussions for both parties. This re-orientation required a shift in both continental and metaphysical geography. As for the Wendats, Father Brébeuf's use of one globe may have been more efficient and representative of the Jesuit mission and its ultimate outcome if he had packed two.

Notes

1. Reuben G. Thwaites, ed., *The Jesuit Relations and Allied Documents, 1600–1791.* (Cleveland: Burrows, 1896–1901), vol. 12, 175. (Hereafter cited as *JR* 12:175).

2. *JR* 8: 119.

3. Allain Manesson Mallet, *Description de l'univers* (Paris, 1683), 209.

4. *JR* 8: 119.

5. For representative examples see: Susan Sleeper-Smith, "Women, Kin, and Catholicism: New Perspectives on the Fur Trade" *Ethnohistory* 47, No. 2, (Spring 2000), 423–52; Kenneth M. Morrison, "Discourse and the Accommodation of Values: Toward a Revision of Mission History," *Journal of the American Academy of Religion* 53, no. 3 (September1985): 365–82; Robert S. Michaelsen, "Red Man's

Religion /White Man's Religious History," *Journal of the American Academy of Religion* 51 (December 1983): 667–84; Neil Salisbury, "Religious Encounters in a Colonial Context: New England and New France in the Seventeenth Century," *American Indian Quarterly* 16, no. 4 (Autumn 1992): 501–09; James P. Ronda, "'We Are Well As We Are': An Indian Critique of Seventeenth-Century Christian Missions" *The William and Mary Quarterly*, Third Series, Vol. 34, No. 1 (Jan., 1977), 66–82.

6. For representative examples that include specific discussions on Wendats and Christianity see: Bruce G. Trigger, Ch. 10 "The Storm Within" in *The Children of Aataentsic: A History of the Huron People to 1660* (Montreal and Kingston: McGill-Queen's University Press, 1976), 665–724; Roger M. Carpenter, Ch. 4 "The Jesuit Assault of the Huron Thought World" in *The Renewed, The Destroyed, and The Remade: The Three Thought Worlds of the Iroquois and the Huron, 1609–1650* (East Lansing: Michigan State University Press, 2004), 46–63; Denys Delâge, *Bitter Feast: Amerindians and Europeans in Northeastern North America, 1600–64* transl. Jane Brierley (Vancouver: University of British Columbia Press, 1993), 178–224; Michael Pomedli, "The Concept of 'Soul' in the Jesuit Relations: Were there any Philosophers among the North American Indians?" *Laval théologique et philosophique*, vol. 41, no. 1, (1985), 57–64; Lee Irwin, "Contesting world views: Dreams among the Huron and Jesuits" *Religion*, Vol. 22, Is. 3 (July 1992), 259–69; Bruce G. Trigger, "The Jesuits and the Fur Trade" *Ethnohistory*, Vol. 12, No. 1 (Winter, 1965), 30–53; Karen Anderson, "Commodity Exchange and Subordination: Montagnais-Naskapi and Huron Women, 1600–1650" *Signs*, Vol. 11, No. 1 (Autumn, 1985), 48–62; John Steckley, "The Warrior and the Lineage: Jesuit Use of Iroquoian Images to Communicate Christianity" *Ethnohistory*, Vol. 39, No. 4 (Autumn, 1992), 478–509; Daniel K. Richter, "Iroquois versus Iroquois: Jesuit Missions and Christianity in Village Politics, 1642–1686" *Ethnohistory*, Vol. 32, No. 1 (Winter, 1985), 1–16.

7. Michael M Pomedli, *Ethnophilosophical and Ethnolinguistic Perspectives on the Huron Indian Soul* (Lewiston/Queenston/Lampeter: The Edwin Mellen Press, 1991); *JR* 10: 141, 287.

8. *JR* 13: 251.

9. Roger M. Carpenter, *The Renewed, The Destroyed, and The Remade,* 50.

10. *JR* 10:143–47.

11. *JR* 10:145.

12. *JR* 8: 119; 121.

13. The Récollet missionary Gabriel Sagard wrote about the Wendat belief in "the path of souls," or *atiskein andahatey.* Alternatively, the Jesuits transcribed numerous accounts of an earthly route. Gabriel Sagard, *The Long Journey to the Country of the Hurons.* (Toronto: Champlain Society, 1939), 172; *JR* 10: 145; 10: 153–55; 13: 251.

14. *JR* 13: 251.

15. *JR* 10: 145.

16. *JR* 10: 147.

17. *JR* 10: 149–53.

18. *JR* 1: 23; Georges E. Sioui, *Huron-Wendat: The Heritage of the Circle* (Vancouver: University of British Columbia Press, 1999), 135–136; W. J. Eccles, *France in America*, Rev. ed. (East Lansing: Michigan State University Press, 1990), 25.

19. *JR* 1: 23–25; Roger M. Carpenter, *The Renewed, The Destroyed, and The Remade,* 50; Denys Delâge, *Bitter Feast*, 191; W. J. Eccles, *France in America*, 41–42.

20. *JR* 1 23–25.

21. *JR* 10:55.

22. *JR* 8:137.

23. *JR* 8: 137.

24. *JR* 8: 137.

25. *JR* 13: 179

26. *JR* 13: 179.

27. *JR* 17:127.

28. *JR* 1: 289.

29. *JR* 13: 127.

30. *JR* 8: 145.

31. *JR* 8: 147.

32. *JR* 1:289.

33. *JR* 1: 289–91.

34. Michael M. Pomedli, *Ethnophilosophical and Ethnolinguistic Perspectives on the Huron Indian Soul,* 55.

35. Gabriel Sagard, *The Long Journey to the Country of the Hurons*, 211–12; *JR* 10: 279–303.

36. *JR* 10: 301.

37. *JR* 8: 137.

38. *JR* 10:305.

39. Emphasis is my own. *JR* 10: 305.

40. *JR* 10: 305–07.

41. *JR* 8: 147.

42. *JR* 8:119.

43. *JR* 8: 147.

44. *JR* 13: 199.

45. *JR* 13: 201.

46. *JR* 13: 201.

47. *JR* 13: 179.

48. *JR* 17: 127.

49. *JR* 15:51.

50. *JR* 30: 29–31.

51. *JR* 30: 31.

52. The *Jesuit Relations* are replete with accounts of Wendats who use this line of argument in order to resist baptism. For examples see: *JR* 13:251; 15: 71; 13: 127; 19: 189–91.

53. *JR* 19: 189.

54. Gary Warrick, "A Population History of the Huron-Petun, A.D. 900–1650," PhD diss. (McGill University, 1990), 399.

55. Bruce G. Trigger, *The Children of Aataentsic*, 500.

56. Bruce G. Trigger, *The Children of Aataentsic*, 500–01.

57. "Harvest of souls" was originally used by Father Paul Le Jeune in his 1942 missionary report. More recently Carol Blackburn uses it as the title of her manuscript: Carol Blackburn, *Harvest of Souls: The Jesuit Missions and Colonialism in North America, 1632–1650* (Montreal: McGill University Press, 2000).

58. *JR* 13:151. Wampum is sacred shell beads used for a number of different purposes.

59. *JR* 13: 151.

60. *JR* 8: 145–47.

61. Historians are in agreement with this argument, but none have dedicated a full examination into its implications, dedicating one or two sentences to the topic. Bruce Trigger, *Children of Aataentsic*, 516; Roger Carpenter, *The Renewed, The Destroyed, and The Remade*, 50; Denys Delâge, *Bitter Feast*, 185.

62. *JR* 11: 9.

63. *JR* 26: 273.

64. *JR* 25:27.

65. Of particular note were the influential war chiefs *Thomas Sondakwa*, *Mathurin Astiskw*, and *Martin Tehoachiakwan*; *JR* 26: 273. See also, Kathryn Magee Labelle, "They Spoke Only In Sighs": The Loss of Leaders and Life In Wendake, 1632–1640" *The Journal of Historical Biography*, Vol. (Spring, 2010), 1–33.

66. *JR* 23: 31.

67. *JR* 26: 273.

68. *JR* 23: 31.

69. *JR* 23: 31

70. *JR* 19: 147.

71. *JR* 19:147.

72. *JR* 26: 233–35.

73. *JR* 11:9.

74. Peter Armitage, *The Innu* (*The Montagnais-Naskapi*) (New York: Chelsea House Publishers, 1991).

75. *JR* 12: 29.

76. *JR* 12: 29.

77. Léo-Paul Hébert, *Le Registre de Sillery (1638–1690) Introduction, Présentation et notes de* (Quebec: Presses de L'Université du Quebec, 1994), 38; Governor Charles Hualt Montmagny, Wendake Archives [WA] Fonds Marguerite Vincent [FMV], "Concession des Terres pour les Sauvages Chrétiens à Sillery en a août 1646," Box 8552, Folder 8552-03, Cote E-1-18.

78. Letter from Du Tillet (July 1650, Paris), "Ratification par le roi de la concession de Sillery, par la compagnie de la nouvelle France, en faveur des sauvages,

sous la direction des Peres Jesuits" WA, Collection Francois Vincent [CFV], Folder 1-b.

79. *JR* 12: 151.

80. *JR* 12: 151.

81. *JR* 12: 151.

82. *JR* 12: 223–25.

83. *JR* 14:135.

84. *JR* 14: 137–39.

85. The modern Wendat (Wyandotte/Wyandot/Hurons) nations are represented presently within four branches located in Quebec, Ontario/Michigan, Kansas, and Oklahoma.

86. Emphasis is my own. Chief Leaford Bearskin Wyandotte website. Accessed online at_<http://www.wyandotte-nation.org/community/tribal-profiles/bearskin/yellow-eyes/> (11 August, 2010).

2

"Willingly Complied and Removed to the Fort"

The Secret History of Competing Anglo-Visions of Virginia's Southwest

Kristalyn Marie Shefveland

In their descriptive letters and petitions, colonial leaders shaped the landscape of Virginia in their attempts to persuade investors, merchants, the English clergy, and the members of the Lords of Trade and Plantations of the value of trading with and educating the Indian populace. Through careful consideration of their audiences and by portraying their own interactions with Native inhabitants and their Indigenous world, these colonists drafted persuasive letters and petitions to produce a representation of progress—of civilization emerging from the wilderness. The colonists intentionally constructed a representation of a separate Indigenous world that found fertile ground in European minds. At the center of their plans, the English hoped that Native children would be the bridge between two worlds. The record, however, highlights a more nuanced reflection of multiple worlds—both real and imagined—that were far more diverse than the static representation of Native and English, worlds that included the enslavement of Native children and the trade worlds of Indians aligned with the English.

This essay outlines early attempts at education, particularly with captured Native tributary children, and culminates with an examination of Virginia Lieutenant Governor Alexander Spotswood's persuasive letters in favor of his plans for the Virginia Natives juxtaposed against the journal of John Fontaine's encounters at the Virginia Indian Company's Fort Christanna as well as the diary and letters of Indian trader and colonist William Byrd II. Spotswood sought a Virginia that was poised between two worlds but Fontaine's journal and Byrd's writings expose Virginia as a much more complex place. This essay argues that by visiting Fort Christanna, the Indian trade and education site, through Fontaine's and Byrd's eyes one sees the vision of a hybrid landscape emerging at the fort rather than the starkly contrasted one advertised by Spotswood. All three of these English colonials provide examples of a diverging landscape, one rooted in the arbitrary lines within Spotswood's mind, and the other in the reality of the Virginia trade world.

Unlike the Spanish and French in their areas of colonization, the English colonists of Virginia did little in their first years of contact with Virginia Natives to proselytize and convert the population en masse. Although the official promoters of the colony in England often urged that the Indians be educated, the three Anglo-Powhatan wars prevented any serious attempts. There is little evidence that the majority of colonists had any desire to fully assimilate the Indians, and the Indians most likely felt the same way as one scholar opines that the Powhatan saw little need to "emulate the institutions, customs, and beliefs," of the English.[1] That being stated, although not a "civilizing" mission from its outset, the Virginia colony grappled with the concept of conversion in between the Anglo-Powhatan wars.

Early Official Attempts at Conversion via Tributary Trade Relationships

Although some effort to convert Indians began with the settlement of Jamestown, the colonists focused on "civilizing" their Powhatan neighbors by setting boundaries to settlements and by teaching captive Indian children the English language, converting them to Christianity, and teaching them useful English trades such as carpentry or cobbling. Children became more readily available for English households after the last Anglo-Powhatan war. The 1646 Peace with Necotowance created the tributary system that yielded all legal authority over the former Powhatan Chiefdom to the English colonists. English expansion after the war led to interaction with tributary Natives and foreign Indians of the piedmont as the English sought trade allies in skins and slaves.[2] The practice of taking Indian children hostage, although present from the beginning of the colony, quickly became the avenue to convert Indian children as the legalized practice allowed for the taking of hostage children to ensure their parents' compliance with the treaty. The English believed that only children would be open to conversion and instruction. The former Powhatan agreed to a stipulation "that such Indian children as shall or will freely and voluntarily come in and live with the English may remain without breach of the articles of peace, provided they be not above twelve years old."3 Still, there is no evidence that they made any formal attempts to educate or convert them. While agreements dictated that children were not to be kidnapped, treated as slaves, or transferred to other families, in fact, Virginians tended to ignore the law.4 In effect, the period after 1646 highlights an attempt by the English to codify an English and Indian world, however, in their haphazard attempts to create and/or maintain two separate worlds, some English colonists raised concerns over the need to convert their Native neighbors to English modes of religion and habits of work.

Ten years passed before the colonial Assembly further codified children-taking and what should happen to those children brought into English homes: cautioning English settlers to "do their best to bring them up in Christianity, civility and the knowledge of necessary trades."[5] In September 1656, as part of tributary agreements and as a sign of faith between the two parties, colonists and local Natives in Rappahannock County agreed to have Indian orphans sent to the English to be trained in Christianity.[6] By 1660, in order to encourage families to take in Indian orphans, the legislature allotted a one-thousand two-hundred pound allowance for each English family for the maintenance and education of Indian children.[7] Despite laws preventing the abuse of hostage children and regulations for their treatment, genuine efforts at educating the Indian youth were sporadic.[8] The tributaries were coerced into giving up their children and when given the opportunity to speak they told of their pain in realizing that many of these children were sold into slavery. The tributary Pamunkey later complained on October 26, 1708, of a long history of the colonists taking away "diverse of their nation," including children.[9]

A renewed interest in conversion began with shifting concerns about the tributaries' fidelity to the colony and fear of Indians following a series of wars and skirmishes throughout the Southeastern colonies. One proposed solution, intended to remove the threat of Indians, was to assimilate and convert the existing Indigenous population, beginning with tributaries but extending to foreign Indians as well. This changing perspective was coupled with a general rise in religious activity in the colony due to the arrival of a charismatic missionary and educator aligned with the Bishop of London who sought to bring spiritual vitality to the American colonies. The arrival of Reverend James Blair in 1685 marked a change in Virginia toward revitalizing the colonial Anglican Church and led to Virginia's first successful formal efforts at educating and converting hostage Indian children whom colonists hoped would become missionaries to their home communities.

At this juncture in the Virginia colony, one might describe it as deeply rooted in a two-worlds mindset, especially as glimpsed through the lens of religious conversion. After failing early at converting Native people to Christianity, English Virginians viewed the Indians as living in a separate world, one that could not be bridged. However, as English settlers increasingly moved closer to Indian territories in the post-1646 era and as tributaries moved into English towns as servants and slaves, a new perspective emerged. Leaders such as Spotswood began to argue that Indians could be proselytized and that education of children would lead to ministries in not only the tributary populations but hopefully in every Indian town in Virginia, blurring the distinctions between Native and English worlds. It is important here to recognize that many English leaders did not adequately grasp the hybrid worlds already present in Virginia that emerged through the trade. Those unable to see the blurred lines of their two-world dichotomy might find that their allies and foes would be one and the same in the ensuing debates over proselytization and conversion of the Native populace.

William and Mary College

Earlier formal efforts at Indian conversion and education were unsuccessful in part because of the strife within the colony and a lack of support from the majority of English colonists. The 1622 Anglo-Powhatan War, along with financial mismanagement on the part of Virginia Company proprietor, Sir Edwin Sandys, ended English plans for the first school intended for Indian education at Henrico. Later, the demise of the Virginia Company led to the end of the proposed East India School in Charles City for Indians. Thus ended all formal efforts toward Indian education and began the informal housing of Indian children, a plan that did little to further conversion of Native tributaries. Efforts to revitalize conversion attempts began in earnest with the arrival of Reverend James Blair in 1685, a Scottish missionary and educator. Blair acted as the catalyst for the founding of the College of William and Mary in 1693, which eventually enrolled somewhere between two and twenty-four tributary Indians a year in its first fifteen years of existence.[10] At the college, the English instructors intended to teach the Indians not only the rudiments of reading and writing English but also sought to train these students as missionaries to convert the Native populace.[11] Blair later wrote a proposition for the "encouragement of the

Christian Education of our Negro and Indian Children" which stipulated that the training of Indians should include the Creed, Ten Commandments, and the Lord's Prayer.[12] The philanthropist Robert Boyle, a director of the East India Company, who contributed funds to missionaries throughout the British colonies, created a relatively large fund for Indian education at William and Mary. Yet, despite his generous bequest, the colony anticipated that they would need to find supplementary ways to finance the college. In October 1693, legislators sought to bring levies against the Indian trade in order to finance the school.[13] In addition, the colonists had to reapportion tributary lands in order to make room for the college by allotting twenty-thousand acres of land from Pamunkey Neck and Blackwater Swamp from the Chickahominy.[14]

Despite efforts by the colonists to create a school where Indian children could be educated, tributaries were not eager to send their children to the college. Additionally, little evidence exists that supports the claim that a majority of colonists supported the plan. At least one historian has argued that the college never seemed to have "a workable plan" for the education of the Indians.[15] According to Reverend Hugh Jones, many of the young Natives, procured by the colonists with "much Difficulty," died "often for want of Proper Necessaries and due Care taken with them."[16] The Brafferton estate records tell a story of hope for the college, indicating a desire to keep "soe many Indian children in Sicknesse and health in meat Drink Washing Lodgeing Cloathes Medicines Bookes and Educacon from the first beginning of Letters til they are ready to receive Orders and be thought Sufficient to be sent abroad to preach and Convert the Indians."[17] Thus was the English desire for children who could become missionaries. But what of the tributaries' desires? Peripheral tributary settlements gained some English skills, as is evident in the case of Robin, a Pamunkey shoemaker who requested to stay with the English. Additionally, there are many examples of adult tributaries who adopted some English habits as hunters and trackers, but who remained outside English settlements in a hybrid society based off the needs of the trade.[18] Of great concern, however, was the issue of the Indian slave trade, particularly of children, and the tributary fears were not without warrant. Although Boyle endowed the college with a fund of two-hundred pounds for the education of Indian children, most scholars agree that, while there are clear attempts by some Virginians toward education, many children were sold into labor or died, never returning to their communities to proselytize. Thus, Virginians had to coerce Indians into turning their children over or bought them outright; as noted by Robert Beverley in his *History and Present State of Virginia*, the Boyle fund was used to purchase "half a Dozen captive Indian Children Slaves and put them to the College."[19] Little is known about these first pupils of the college and whether they successfully became missionaries.

With the arrival of Lieutenant Governor Alexander Spotswood, however, the English Virginians began to change their tactics with the tributaries and hoped that finally Indian children would be educated in English ways and then begin to serve as missionaries to their communities and lessen the gap between the two worlds: English and Native. According to one scholar, Spotswood was appalled and "shocked by the government's deplorable disinterest in Indian welfare—namely, conversion and education."[20] In 1711, Spotswood decided to employ a different tactic. He remitted tribute of skins and furs to encourage attendance; if the tributaries sent their children, he would consider their tribute paid in full for the year. This persuaded a few Powhatan, including the Queen of the Pamunkey's son, to attend.[21]

Spotswood's plan to educate and convert the Virginia Indians was ambitious, and he intended it to reach beyond the current tributary groups. In a letter to the Bishop of London on November 11, 1711, he expressed hope that educating and converting the tributaries close to the colony would give the English a good start toward "a greater progress among those more remote, when they see the advantages these reap by it." He then described the negotiations with the upper Tuscarora towns and his plans for expanding Virginia's sphere of influence through tributary peace agreements that would bring more children into his school. Spotswood desired a plan of conversion and wanted to bring all Indians interacting and moving through Virginia into peace agreements with the Virginia government, peace agreements that were contingent upon captive exchange. First, he had to convince the tributaries to bring their children to the school, and he did so by focusing on halting the illicit Indian slave trade.[22]

Spotswood's plans to curb the abuses of the Indian slave trade inspired trust from the tributaries and the Pamunkey sent twice the number of required children. The Nansemond, Nottoway, and Meherrin began to send children and Spotswood anticipated that the Chickahominy would send their sons soon.[23] So successful were Spotswood's "recruitment" techniques that the school had twenty-four Indian students in 1712, and soon depleted the Boyle endowment and Indian trade taxation funds. Spotswood hoped to eventually pay for the school by public levy: forty pounds of tobacco levied against every titheable person.[24] In the interim, Spotswood tried to solve the problem of funding by appealing to the General Assembly and then to financiers in England, including making a plea to the Society for the Propagation of the Gospel, who by this time were bolstered by a decree by King William III to send priests and schoolteachers to America.

In the spring of 1712, Spotswood was in need of funds in large part because of political wrangling between himself and the Virginia Executive Council and House of Burgesses, so Spotswood sought outside resources, writing to the Bishop of London, Henry Compton, about instruction of Indian children. He also wrote to the Archbishop of Canterbury. Spotswood indicated that his efforts to secure funding through a public levy had failed but insisted that he had not "for that reason slackened my endeavors for the conversion of that people."[25] He informed the Bishop of the current enrollment of fourteen students and told him that he expected six more. He continued that he hoped this news would generate "encouragement both from the Society for Propagating the Gospel [SPG] and from Nobility and Gentry of England, who cannot in my opinion imploy their Charity to better purpose than by laying such a Foundation for bringing a great many Souls to the Christian faith."[26]

While the Bishop supported Spotswood's plans and attempted to influence the SPG on his behalf, Spotswood did not receive immediate funds and support, so he tried again, anxious and enthusiastic about prospects for the world he intended to create. He wrote that he wanted each tributary town to send two sons of their "Chief men" to William and Mary and that once there they would be "instructed in Literature and the principles of Christianity, at the expence of the College." Spotswood also said that he "offered to quitt all the Tribute which they [the Indians] used formerly to pay yearly to the Governor so long as their Children continued with us."[27] He explained that by discontinuing tribute he obtained additional children and that the children and their parents and other observers seemed "pleased" and expressed "much satisfaction with the care that is taken of them, and frequently lament their own misfortune in not having like advantages in their Youth."[28] Finally, Spotswood warned that the funds would run out soon. He also discussed lofty plans for the future, describing his ultimate goal of converting the entire Indian populace. Thus, monetary assistance was essential. He confided, "I hope the Society will the more easily agree to this since 'tis the expence that has ever been demanded of them [the SPG] of this Colony, tho' every other plantation has been in a manner supplied [with monetary assistance for Indian conversion] at their charge."[29]

Spotswood's letter to the Archbishop of Canterbury was no less impassioned in requesting assistance. In order to convert the entire Indian populace, Spotswood asserted that he would need one or two missionaries, of "good lifes and zealous in their Offices" to place at the largest of the Indian towns where there "would be no hard matter to bring them all over in a generation or two from their own Pagan Superstitions to the true faith." Once settled there, missionaries could build churches and schoolhouses where they would teach not only the inhabitants of the town but also assist in teaching the Indians throughout the interior. Spotswood intended for all the legal trappings of English settlements to exist at these towns, allowing the missionaries to have the "power of Justices of the peace for deciding differences between the Indians and their Neighbours." This was an essential provision because the remoteness of the Indian towns from the English often caused their "frequent injurys [to go] unredressed, w'ch, in a great measure, irreconcile the Indians both to our Religion and Government."[30] Spotswood argued in favor of his idea in part by rationalizing that it would prevent further injuries to the Indians and help in settling their disagreements with English settlers.[31]

Despite these elaborate plans, Spotswood had to put everything on hold when the colony became embroiled in the peripheral events of the Tuscarora War in 1711. However, the war also presented an opportunity for Spotswood, and, after the failure of his fundraising efforts and in part because of the concerns over the war with the Tuscarora, Spotswood decided to cut costs and raise funds himself by consolidating the military rangers and creating a buffer policy between the colony and North Carolina. He hoped this buffer policy would involve resettling tributary and foreign Indians that would then leave excess funds to pay for education efforts. Conditions in the region favored Spotswood's policy because many smaller Indian groups desired to move closer to colonial settlements for protection from raiding Indians in the piedmont.[32] Enrollment at William and Mary declined during the Tuscarora War, but Spotswood had a new vision for his world and thus he continued in his efforts to regulate the Indian trade and develop a new frontier policy that would further his plans for Indian education, a plan that would push the limits of his administration. Instead of focusing on bringing Native children to William and Mary College, Spotswood intended to create a trade site in the piedmont that would work toward proselytizing not only children, but the entire Native community of new tributaries Spotswood hoped to bring in.

Fort Christanna and the Virginia Indian Company

After the outbreak of war with the Tuscarora, Spotswood hatched a plan to resettle various existing and new tributaries on the southwest periphery of the colony. There, according to Spotswood's plans, these tributaries would act as a buffer between hostile Indian raiders with themselves benefiting from the protection of the English militia. Spotswood also intended to use the settlement as a trading outpost and a place to further his education goals. Even though the Tuscarora threat was subdued with their migration after the Tuscarora War, in late 1713, the House of Burgesses approved Spotswood's plan. The Tuscarora War inspired fear within the colony and Spotswood hoped a tributary settlement, called Fort Christanna, would provide a remedy for these concerns. Spotswood insisted that his buffer plan would work to reorganize trade, protect the south side of the James River residents and Indians, and create a better working relationship with Indians in Virginia.[33] To Spotswood, who was desperate to rein in the traders and develop his ideal, the education of Indian children would prepare the way for the conversion of the whole Native populace which would, in turn, ensure the fidelity and compliance of Native elders. The colony successfully built Fort Christanna by October 14, 1714.[34] To encourage the Indians providing children for education Spotswood suggested to the Bishop of London that he intended to combine trade with education, allowing Indians moving to Christanna or sending their children to William and Mary privileges to trade within the Virginia Indian Company, "which, by former Laws of the Colony, they were prohibited to do."[35]

In 1714, Spotswood himself visited the fort and successfully persuaded the Saponi, Tutelo, Occaneechee, and Nahyssan to occupy a tract on the south side of the Meherrin River. Despite these successes, the Nottoway and Meherrin refused to move to Christanna. At one point, Spotswood went so far as to abduct the Great Men of the Nottoway and Meherrin. The Great Men of local Indians, according to colonist John Fontaine, were a council of twelve men who had the "power to act for the whole nation, and they will stand to every thing that thos twelve men agree to, as their own act."[36] In August 1715, when the Nottoway refused to hand over twelve of the Nottoway children for Christanna, the Council held the Nottoway Great Men hostage until they sent the boys to Christanna.[37] Despite such difficulties, Spotswood persevered with his plans to expand his influence to foreign Indians into his tributary designs adding Carolinian Indians, the Sara, and the Esaws (later known as the Catawba), to the list of Indians he intended to settle at Christanna.[38] Spotswood eventually turned his attention onto his education plans and vigorously championed his efforts in a series of letters back to London that detailed his conversion plans under the direction of Reverend Charles Griffin.

The College of William and Mary sponsored the school at Christanna, and so desirous was Spotswood to succeed with his education schemes that he initially paid Griffin fifty pounds a year out of his own pocket.[39] Once at Fort Christanna, Griffin, a Quaker settler from North Carolina, took over the education of the Native Americans. By all European accounts, Griffin had great initial success. Writing after the fact, the Reverend Hugh Jones stated that the "Indians so loved and adored him, that I have seen them hug him and lift him up in their Arms, and sain would have chosen him for a King of the Sapony Nation."[40] Spotswood wrote a glowing report to the Bishop of London. Indian children, he said, could now read and write "tolerably well," repeat the catechism and knew "how to make their responses in ye Church," and showed "a great desire" to be baptized. Spotswood departed from previous policies of baptism by not requiring individual godparents for each child but instead allowing the schoolmaster to act as the godparent for the Indian children. Spotswood acted as though the approval of the clergy on this matter would be forthcoming and was surprised by the refusal of the clergy to grant permission, on the grounds that they were not born to Christian parents. According to Jack Morpurgo, "the Church's logic defies understanding," and was one "incredible convolution and absurdity."[41] On the issue of baptism, the Reverend Hugh Jones wrote that objections to baptizing Indians could easily be "refuted, if the Persons be sensible, good, and understand English, and have been taught (or are willing to learn) the *Principles of Christianity* . . . [for] *Christianity* encourages and orders them to become more humble and better Servants." Jones was likely speaking of tributaries with the previous statement for he follows with the question whether baptizing "wild Indians" was a "prostitution of a Thing so *sacred.*"[42] To the Lords Commissioners of the Trade he related on June 4, 1715, that the Saponi are of "good disposition" to have their children educated at the fort and, "there is all human probability of the Success of this undertaking, whereby a Foundation will be laid for a more lasting Friendship w'th those Indians than can be expected while they retain their Savage principles and Heathenish Superstitions."[43]

By October 26, 1715, Spotswood told the Bishop that many of these children could already say the Lord's Prayer and Apostle's Creed. He mentioned, in particular, a young girl aged ten who died before she could be baptized. Her death appeared to bother Spotswood on a personal note as he had promised to be her godfather, noting, "at her death she seem'd to express her self with much concern that she could not see us." He opined, "I look upon the education of these Indians to be so feasible that I should be very sorry if it miscarry for want of a suitable support."[44] In 1716, he was happy to report to the Lords Commissioners of the Trade that there were one hundred students at Fort Christanna.[45]

Spotswood's reports were naturally glowing since they were in part public relations advertisements designed to garner support from the Bishop of London and others. Yet there are two other accounts to consider. The journals of John Fontaine and William Byrd II allow for a more nuanced understanding of the educational undertaking at Christanna. John Fontaine traveled with Spotswood to the Fort in April 1716. William Byrd II was a member of Spotswood's Executive Council and an Indian trader who made numerous trips to the fort. Of the two, Fontaine's account is the more detailed in regard to activities at Fort Christanna. Spotswood sought a Virginia that was poised between two worlds, a converted Indian world and a "civilized" European world. Spotswood hoped to converge these worlds, but Fontaine's journal reveals that Virginia was a much more complex place. By viewing Christanna through Fontaine's eyes, one can see a vision of the hybrid landscape that was emerging at the fort.

Christanna was at the peak of its success upon Fontaine's arrival. Fontaine toured the peripheral region of the Virginia colony on three separate trips covering nearly two-hundred miles over the course of ten days. He first journeyed through the southwest toward the settlement at Christanna on November 12, 1715. Passing by Indian settlements along the way, he described in detail a cabin, "built four square," covered with the bark of trees in lieu of an English style roof. Fontaine skeptically reported, "they say it keeps out the rain very well." He also noted that the women were naked from the waist up with "only a girdle they had tied about their waist, and they had about a yard of blanketing which they passed one end under the fore part of the girdle, and other end under the girdle behind." The only sign of English trade, according to Fontaine, were blankets and one pot.[46] In his journal, he repeatedly seemed surprised that despite their proximity to the English fort the Indians had few outward trappings of English life. Ultimately, this assessment reveals more about Fontaine's relative inexperience with the trade than it does about the lack of English influence in the region. Repeatedly, Fontaine commented on the lack of English civility, simultaneously highlighting the presence of English trade and the influence of English traders, such as the presence of trade blankets and pots as well as the simple, yet telling, fact that nearly all the Natives he encountered spoke English.

Fontaine's next trip to the Virginia interior began on April 14, 1716. Setting out in the morning and noting the distance from the interior of the colony, Fontaine stated, "we have no roads here to conduct us, nor inhabitants to direct the traveller." They arrived near noon at the Meherrin River opposite the fort and there met "several Indians," and saw "several fine tracts of land and plains."[47] After breakfast he and Spotswood met with Charles Griffin the schoolmaster. Fontaine writes that Griffin lived with the Indians and taught them to read "the Bible and Common Prayers, as also to write, and the English tongue." He further related that Griffin had "good success amongst them," after being there for over a year.[48] At their meeting, Griffin told the Lt. Governor that the Saponi Great Men intended to come to the Fort to meet with them. The arriving Indians, the Saponi, consisted of approximately two hundred men, women, and children, all of whom lived within a musket shot of the fort, and "are always at peace with the English."[49]

The Saponi arrived at the fort around noon bringing with them several skins that they laid at the feet of Spotswood, and then, after bowing to the Governor they asked for an interpreter, "saying they had something to represent to him." Fontaine mused that some of them could speak good English but noted, that when it came down to matters of diplomacy or trade they would not discuss it in English, desiring instead an interpreter by whom they "will not answer to any question made to them without it be in their own tongue."[50] Fontaine may have exaggerated the Great Men's ability to speak English, but at the very least, they surely felt more comfortable conducting such business in their own language. Once an interpreter had been found, they spoke to Spotswood regarding both their satisfaction with him and their grievances against some English with whom they had problems.[51] Spotswood assured them he would examine their concerns. Another grievance the Great Men raised involved other Indians Fontaine called the "Genitos," a group who the Saponi alleged had murdered fifteen members of a hunting party. Spotswood refused to retaliate against the Genitos, but instead promised them powder and shot so they could seek their own revenge. The Saponi also claimed that English traders had defrauded them. The Governor paid for the damages, which according to Fontaine, "satisfied them."[52]

Later in the day, younger men of the Saponi arrived. Much to the surprise of Fontaine, they had feathers in their shorn hair, pierced ears, and faces painted blue and vermillion. Fontaine describes their hair, "some left one side of their hair on, and others had their hair cut on both sides and on the upper part of the head, made it stand like a cock's comb."[53] Again, Fontaine shows relative inexperience with the nature of exchange between the Virginian English and Indians. He commented that they dressed in blue and red trade blankets, a clear example of trade exchanges. Fontaine ascertained that their outfits were "war dress, which really is very terrible and makes them look like so many furies." Although they did not speak they made quite an impression upon Fontaine.[54] Following the young men were young women who wore trade blankets around their waists but were naked from the waist up except for some who wore deerskins across their shoulders. Fontaine thought their skin ugly because of the bear's oil they used to grease their bodies. Despite his dislike for this habit, he noted that they were "straight, well limbed, good shape and extraordinarily good features as well the men as the women."[55] He also noted, however, that "they look wild and are mighty shy of an Englishman and will not let you touch them." Intriguingly, William Byrd had already been in the area for quite some time, his noted exploit with Jenny at Saponi Town during the Tuscarora War might lend some understanding to the Saponi women's reaction to Fontaine. Byrd was a known philanderer and when previously at Saponi Town he and some other Englishmen had taken advantage of Jenny by getting her drunk, they said it made her "good sport."[56]

On April 17, Fontaine journeyed to Saponi Town outside Fort Christanna where he described his impressions of the households along the Meherrin River that were arranged in a circle facing one another in a circle around a tree stump. Fontaine asked the reason for the stump, and the Saponi informed him that it was for when one of their head men made an announcement, that "he may the better be heard."[57] The houses were large, and he also described several huts with small doors near the riverside. These were sweathouses for sick people to enter, with a trade blanket as their only clothing, to sweat out the disease.[58] Similar to the previous Indian town through which he had traveled, Fontaine found at Saponi Town evidence of trade, including pots, blankets, dishes, and trays.

On the sixth day, Fontaine and Spotswood witnessed a sporting event performed by the young boys of the fort. Spotswood placed an axe at about twenty-yards distance from where they stood and the boys competed for prizes as they all took turns shooting at the axe. Fontaine complimented the Saponi boys for their dexterity at the task as the boys frequently shot arrows through the eye of the axe.[59] The contest lasted around an hour, and afterward, Spotswood asked the boys to prepare a "war dance" in a ring. A musician sat in the middle of the ring and played a board with two sticks that he struck while singing a "doleful tune," sometimes "shrieking hideously, which was answered by the boys," as the Saponi danced in a circle to the rhythm of the music.[60] Fontaine surmised that the dance represented how they attacked enemy combatants and how many Indians they killed. Fontaine's opinion of the event, similar to his earlier perceptions of the Great Men, towns, and dwellings, was rather low. He believed that it showcased the inhuman and barbarous nature of war, by which the Indians might surprise their enemies and their "inhuman way of murdering all their prisoners, and what terrible cries they have when they are conquerors."[61] After the dance finished, Spotswood provided food for the boys, who, Spotswood commented, ate with gusto. On the seventh day, April 19, 1716, after breakfasting, Spotswood and Fontaine read the Common Prayer with eight young Indian boys who "answered very well to the prayers and understood," finally impressing Fontaine very much.[62]

Of interest to Fontaine was the arrival on April 20 of ten Meherrin who came to trade at the fort. They arrived with beaver, dear, and bear skins, delivering them to the fort but refusing to stay; opting instead for the woods to stay overnight.[63] Given episodes such as this, Fontaine's journal suggests that Spotswood's overt Christian conversion project barely went beneath the surface. However, Fontaine's repeated denial of any trappings of English life does not highlight a lack of interaction or influence in the peripheral Native settlements. Rather it does the exact opposite: it shows that the English and the Natives were not just trading goods but also likely trading ideas. While there is little evidence of complete Christian assimilation, Fontaine's journal shows Native and Virginian immersion in a frontier exchange economy in a world that was not Native, not English, but a hybrid world based not on the needs or desires of the Lords of Trade and Plantations or the Bishop of London but on those of the local Virginia traders and their Native counterparts.

Included in Fontaine's detailed description of the Indians at Christanna is a glossary of words, possibly the trade language alluded to by Robert Beverley in his 1705 history, that he called "a sort of general Language."[64] Many of these words and phrases were necessary for the simplest of dialogue in a trade relationship such as greetings, "Jog de log" (How d'ye do?) "Kihoe" (Come here); numbers, "Nacout, Tock, Nos," (one, two three); and trade items, "Mahinkt" (shot bag), "Tabike" (powder horse), and "Mosnukhe" (otter). However, the nature of this list is telling in and of itself. It is a trade list at first glance, but it also reflects upon the nature of social interaction especially concerning sexual relations within a multi-ethnic trade town. Such phrases as "Ke ly pomerin" (will you kiss me) coupled with "Conopana" (come to bed) and "Mihu mima mikito" (my dear wife) speak to exchanges other than trade goods.[65]

Spotswood and Fontaine left the fort on April 21, to the sound of cannons firing, and several Indians from Saponi Town assured Spotswood that they were sorry to see him go, "but that they would guard him safe to the Inhabitants."[66] Spotswood's official letters to the Bishop and to the Lords of Trade make no mention of this journey with Fontaine, yet by May he was relating to the Bishop of London his successes at Christanna and expanding settlement to the region and its positive effects on his proselytizing efforts, writing that he could not fathom an endeavor more worthy of funds and support than the conversion of the Natives in Virginia.[67]

The Virginia Indian Company and Its Detractors

Despite his proclamations of great successes at Christanna, ultimately the fate of the fort and its Indian inhabitants became mired in the discourse on the Virginia Indian Company. In a letter to a Mr. Popple of the Council on Trade on April 16, 1717, Spotswood related the precarious nature of southside settlements and again related the need for conversion and ordered Indian settlement at the fort. This time, however, Spotswood emphasized the threat of individual English traders inflaming the South Carolina Indians and the Seneca. Spotswood again became passionate regarding his beloved project as he described the death of a number of Catawba and others who brought eleven children to Christanna. A party of Seneca attacked the Catawba at night, killing five of them, and while wounding two, carried off an additional five prisoners. The Catawba were "highly enraged at this insult," feeling that the English had some part in it, and it was "with abundance of difficulty, and not without running some hazard in my person," that Spotswood was able to persuade them to leave their children at the fort.[68] The Catawba were part of Spotswood's trading and diplomatic strategies to further lure Southern Indians into the tributary system. Describing his efforts with the Catawba, he wrote that he convinced them to send children for education as part of a promise to live in peace with the Virginians. He blamed the English traders for this attack, "some loose fellows" who while carrying on an illegal trade with the Tuscarora informed the Seneca of the Catawba arrival at Christanna, which then "thereby encouraged the one to fall upon the other." He included this information to show that he was not at fault for this failure and to persuade the Lords of Trade of the necessity to back him on the Virginia Indian Company and Fort Christanna and to take aim at his foes, the English traders, to show "how little regard [they] have to the Peace of this Country."[69]

William Byrd II, the trader with whom Spotswood most frequently came to verbal blows and fought most viciously over the Virginia Indian Company, also commented on the Christanna experiment. While Spotswood envisioned an orderly Indian settlement at Fort Christanna and a regulated Indian trade company, Byrd (likely angry that he was repeatedly denied trade monopolies) sought to destroy Spotswood's visions which were directly contrary to Byrd's desires in his world of the Virginia Indian trade. Reflecting on the Boyle Trust at William and Mary, the efforts of Spotswood, Griffin, and the failure of the education plans, William Byrd II related that the Indians knew how to read and write, and knew the principles of Christianity. But he felt the conversion was only skin deep as the Indians did not react as missionaries to their own people as Spotswood had hoped.[70] Instead, after they returned home Byrd relates that he felt they almost immediately relapsed into what he referred to as "infidelity and barbarism."[71] Reflecting on these types of ideas, Byrd feared that educating Indians allowed some to use knowledge they acquired against their benefactors, as the Indians likely learned to dislike the English in their time spent amongst them and remembering any refraction would likely become "more vicious and disorderly than the rest of their countrymen." Still Byrd contradicted himself as he wrote of Spotswood's "great prudence," opining that it was necessary to keep a close eye on the Native tributaries in order to prevent an uprising.[72] Referring to Griffin, he called him a "man of a good family," who was by "the innocence of his life and the sweetness of his temper was perfectly well qualified for that pious undertaking."[73] Byrd felt that Griffin enthusiastically took to instructing his pupils and was met with affection from his pupils. Yet Byrd also lamented that in the end, "all the pains he had taken among the infidels had not other effect but to make them something cleanlier than other Indians are."[74] Byrd related an epigram, "not published during his [Spotswood's] administration for fear it might then have looked like flatter,"

> Long has the furious priest assayed in vain. With sword and faggot, infidels to gain, But now the milder soldier wisely tries By gentler methods to unveil their eyes. Wonders apart, he knew 'twere vain t'engage The fixed preventions of misguided age. With fairer hopes he forms the Indian youth To early manners, probity, and truth. The lion's whelp thus, on the Libyan shore, Is tamed and gentled by the artful Moor, Not the grim sire, inured to blood before.[75]

Byrd, for his part, felt that Spotswood's efforts were too little too late and that the only way to really succeed at converting the Indians was through intermarriage, and he apologized that he could not provide a better account of the "poor Indians." Spotswood and Byrd II had very different ideas about the role of Indians in the colony and conversion. Byrd believed that the only way to convert Indians was through intermarriage. He continued that he felt all men had the "same natural dignity" and that Indian wives "would have made altogether as honest wives for the first planters as the damsels they used to purchase from aboard the ships." Byrd completed his thought by disparaging the English women sent to the colonists and wives and wrote, " 'Tis strange, therefore, that any good Christian should have refused a wholesome, straight bedfellow when he might have had so fair a portion with her as the merit of saving her soul."[76] This is not the final comment Byrd had on the Natives of Virginia and his thoughts on their religion and the inability of the English to convert them.[77] Byrd's private writings hold some insight into his interaction with Native peoples. In In his commonplace book and diary he recorded his frequent dreams and oracles. In the spring of 1709, Byrd had a dream regarding an Indian woman he owned that foretold her death from illness. In 1710, he had similar dreams regarding African and Indian slaves including an Indian boy named Harry who was sick from the early summer into the late fall when he passed away.[78]

In an interaction that took place well after the demise of Fort Christanna, a Saponi tracker, hired by Byrd and named Bearskin, spoke to his employer about the deities of the Saponi, that there was one god with several, "subaltern deities under him." That in the beginning, "he told the sun, the moon, and stars," what their role was, and they "with good looking-after, have faithfully performed ever since." Bearskin told Byrd, although "God had formed many worlds before he formed this," those worlds had become either "ruinous" or were obliterated for the "dishonesty of the inhabitants." God, to Bearskin, was "very just and very good, ever well pleased with those men who possess those godlike qualities." Therefore, he protects the good by making them "very rich," providing bountiful amounts of food and preventing illness and "from being surprised or overcome by their enemies." But he also punishes "all such as tell lies and cheat," never failing to punish this wicked men with "sickness, poverty, and hunger and, after all that, suffers them to be knocked on the head and scalped by those that fight against them." Byrd's impression of the tale told by Bearskin was that the Saponi religion was a "natural" religion that contained three traditional articles, that is, "a belief in god, a moral distinction between good and evil, and the expectation of reward or punishment in the next world.[79] In his A Journey in the Land of Eden, where he also spoke of his dialogue with Bearskin, Byrd asserts that the Indians have "no notion of the Sabbath," and will hunt for dinner for the English on this day, and on occasion brought a young doe back for dinner. According to Byrd, "They laughed at the English for losing one day in seven," but he placed his judgment upon the Natives when he said "the joke may be turned upon them for losing the whole seven, if idleness and doing nothing to the purpose may be called loss of time." This again, says more about Byrd than it does about the Native population. Byrd was obsessed with his daily schedule and routine and felt that he must never be idle, yet he, too, had his personal quirks regarding relaxation and enjoyment, never missing an opportunity to relish a rich meal or the company of women.[80] While these exchanges might have been part of everyday conversations between English traders and their Native counterparts, they do not show any real effort on the part of the English to convert the Natives to Christianity and in part bolster Byrd's argument that any conversion taking place at Christanna was not genuine. What Byrd did not discuss, however, was his role in the Native dissatisfaction with the English, the role he played in the demise of Spotswood's efforts at Christanna, or the Indian's motivations for being there.

So confident was he in his plans at the fort that Spotswood contemplated building a house of his own at Christanna and bringing his family to live there as well. Instead, the monopoly of the Virginia Indian Company came under fire from William Byrd II and other traders within the colonies of Virginia and South Carolina resulting in the dismantling of the company and the fort.[81] The Lords of Trade proclaimed that trade companies never contributed much to the conversion of Natives, as evidenced by the Royal African Company, the Dutch East India Company, and others. Instead, the Lords of Trade wrote these companies had a history of instigating wars in the name of private gain that in the end proved to be a great dishonor to the name of Christianity. Spotswood hoped to stave off the closing and dismantling of the fort, writing to the Lords of Trade that the fort at Christanna had been "so usefull to the Security," of the tributaries and the English settlers in the region that "the slighting therof would have proved of ill consequence."[82] He argued that it would be dangerous to disperse the Indians in part because of threats by the Five Nations to the safety of the peripheral settlements. Spotswood related that he planned to maintain the fort until at least April 23, 1718, when the Assembly could meet to decide a course of action.[83] Even so, in May of that year, the House of Burgesses determined that the fort was no longer necessary for the maintenance of the colony's borders and resolved that the government should send home the Natives of Christanna with trade goods in order to preserve their friendly relationship to the Virginia colony.[84]

The demise of the Virginia Indian Company and the closing of the fort left Spotswood to secure the safety of Virginia colonists and Natives by seeking diplomatic relations with the Five Nations. A treaty whereby the Five Nations agreed not to travel west of the mountains further made Fort Christanna obsolete, and the Virginians made plans to return Catawba children to their homes and to disperse the other Indian settlers. Local histories of the area allege that the Saponi and Tutelo remained there until 1740, when they moved to Pennsylvania and joined the Iroquois.[85]

The attempts to convert the Indians of Virginia can be described as haphazard at best. However, one could easily argue that the colonists themselves were in need of civilizing, at least from the vantage point of the Anglican Church and the Lords of Trade and Plantation. English colonists used captive Indian children as a means to culturally coerce conversion, yet they often sold these children into slavery and servitude thus hobbling any genuine attempt to assimilate the Native tributaries.

Naturally, the official record is quite scant on the subject of Indian children in English homes, aside from the evidence that the colonists traded children and the Assembly attempted to ban the practice. Only with the arrival of Reverend Blair is there a documentary trail of the curriculum and expectations for conversion and assimilation. Building upon Blair's enlightened thinking toward Natives was Spotswood, whose plans, although lofty and intended to be far-reaching, can also be described as disorganized and disjointed. In the world Spotswood was trying to create, he desired a plan of conversion, to expand upon Governor Berkeley's 1646 and 1677 tributary agreements and to bring any and all Indians interacting and moving through Virginia into a treaty with the Virginia government. Spotswood sought to create two zones of settlement, one Indian and one English. Yet Spotswood clearly ignored the standing arrangements between the traders and the Indians, and he, himself, was a paradox, boasting proudly about his abilities to convert the Indians and yet when he went to Nottoway Town in October 1711, and asked his hosts for "war" dances and "love" dances from the Tuscarora delegates, he clearly encouraged Indigenous lifeways.

Providing commentary alongside Spotswood are William Byrd II and John Fontaine. What is particularly intriguing about each of their accounts are the ways in which they contradict themselves. At one point or another, all three are inconsistent in their descriptions of the English impact on Native people. This can only be reconciled by considering that they are mired in the differences between ideas and reality. Spotswood, for his part, seemed convinced that he was going to save the Native population from the abuses of the English traders by creating a separate world for them to inhabit, a world controlled by English regulation and wholly separate from the English settlements. Byrd, on the other hand, utilized Indian trackers, owned Indian slaves and servants, had Indians living on his plantation, and likely experienced more direct day-to-day contact with Indians than Spotswood ever imagined possible. At times it appears as though Byrd might have had some respect for his Native traders, but at other times he is wholly dismissive and more usually brutal. More work remains to be done on the role of the Native in Byrd's world and his families trading empire. Fontaine, as the other outsider alongside Spotswood, clearly illustrated his lack of understanding of the nature of exchange in the peripheral southwest of Virginia.

The Virginia Indians were in a strained position regarding their interaction with the English. Clearly, they were ambivalent at best about receiving an education from the English and moving to places such as the College of William and Mary and Fort Christanna. The colonists forced the tributaries to provide Indian children as hostages as part of the negotiating process to being a tributary. Certainly, there was an economic incentive motivating Indians to sign tributary agreements that lead to access to trade goods and protection from their enemies. Learning the English language and Christianity provided Natives with abilities to navigate the English world, a skill that would help them secure employment as traders and interpreters—increasingly valuable professions. Another factor that needs to be considered is why piedmont Indians who were autonomous from Virginia agreed to move to Christanna in the first place. The answer to this is the slave trade. With the arrival of the English Carolinians, piedmont Virginia and North Carolina Indians were surrounded by slavers and were very vulnerable to attacks by armed raiders and disease. It is very likely that Christanna provided a place of refuge from these attacks. The Indians relied on the promise of Spotswood that their children would be educated and not enslaved. This must have been seen as a way to avoid enslavement.

Conclusion

Spotswood arrived in the colony with a plan to "civilize" Virginia, to organize its trade, to assemble its Native inhabitants into orderly tributaries, and to shape the Virginian landscape into an English society. Spotswood's stated intentions for education were to convert the Natives in the hopes that they would then proselytize on behalf of Virginia to the entire Native populace of the colony and surrounding regions. He hoped to do so by starting at William and Mary and then Fort Christanna, eventually expanding further as necessary. Indeed, while construction was completed in 1723 on the Brafferton building at the College of William and Mary, there were no Indians at the school in 1722; by 1732 "not a single youth had passed through the institution to ordination" and Jack Morpurgo alleges the funds intended for Native education benefitted English boys instead.[86] Clearly, however, Spotswood was not in step with the general intentions of the English populace throughout Virginia, who had little need for a converted Indian population and who, instead, desired trading partners and a labor force, a fact reinforced by the musing of Hugh Jones who stated that the Natives should be converted and sent to work. Responding to criticisms of attempts to convert the native populace, the Reverend Hugh Jones opined in his 1724 State of Virginia, that while some may have "returned to their own Ways, chiefly because they can live with less Labour . . ." this problem might be easily remedied by "sending some to Sea, and putting out others to Trades, and not letting them idle away their Time, nor return to their Towns so soon." After being fully accustomed to English ways, Jones felt that if they then returned, "they might do Good to themselves and others."[87] Those genuinely interested in the education and conversion of the Native populace met obstructions at every turn from the Virginia populace. Thomas Dell wrote of his concerns to the Bishop of London, citing that the Natives "still grope in darkness at noon day, & how Xtians (Christians) prejudice the Heathens against the Gospel & hinder the Propagation of it, by their unchristian lives."[88]

Fontaine and Spotswood offer very different insights of the shaping of the Virginia landscape. They also highlight the ways English observers crafted a perspective of the interplay between Indians and colonists in Virginia. In the casc of Spotswood, he highlights his hopes and intentions for the colony. Through Fontaine's journal, an observer gains insight into the viewpoint of an Englishman not invested in Spotswood's experiment—a glance at the activities on the ground and at the reality of Spotswood's actions versus his stated intentions. Byrd's source highlights the investment of a trader in the process and, as an enemy of Spotswood, it also brings to bear a new avenue of discussion, the role of English rivalry regarding leadership in the colony and the conversion of the Natives. All of these sources illustrate how different the views could be, depending on the vantage point of the observer and how privileging one source over the other can dramatically change the landscape of Virginia to the historian. Spotswood and Fontaine were the outsiders to the Virginia world, while Byrd was an insider to the Virginia trade world.

Notes

1. Margaret Connell Szasz, *Indian Education in the American Colonies, 1607–1783* (Albuquerque: University of New Mexico Press, 1988), 55.

2. David K. Hazzard, and Martha W. McCartney, *Fort Christanna: Archaeological Reconnaissance Survey* (Williamsburg, Virginia: Virginia Research Center for Archaeology, 1979), 1. See W. Stitt Robinson, ed., *Early American Indian Documents: Treaties and Laws, 1607–1789: Volume IV Virginia Treaties 1607–1722* (Frederick, MD: University Publications of America, 1983), 67–69; Warren Billings, "Some

Acts Not in Hening's Statutes: The Acts of Assembly, April 1652, November 1652, and July 1653" *Virginia Magazine of History and Biography* (83: 22–26, 1975), 68; Frederic W. Gleach, *Powhatan's World and Colonial Virginia: A Conflict of Cultures* (Lincoln: The University of Nebraska Press, 1997), 185; Helen C. Rountree, *Powhatan Foreign Relations 1500–1722* (Charlottesville: University Press of Virginia, 1993), 173–205.

3. William Waller Hening, *The Statutes at Large: being a Collection of all the Laws of Virginia*, (Richmond, VA: Samuel Pleasants, 1810–1823), 1: 322–26.

4. Szasz, *Indian Education*, 64–65.

5. Hening, *Statutes at Large*, 1: 393–96.

6. Ruth Sparacio, ed., *Deed & Will Abstracts of (Old) Rappahannock County, Virginia 1656–1662; 1677–1682; 1683–1685; 1685–1687; 1687–1689; 1689–1692; 1688—1692* (McLean, VA: Antient Press, 1989) 1: 10–11.

7. Hening, *Statutes at Large*, 1: 193.

8. Certainly one can argue that the sale of Indian children as slaves and servants did much to hamper Indian interest in providing hostage children.

9. H. R. McIlwaine, ed., *Executive Journals of the Council of Colonial Virginia* (Richmond, VA: Virginia State Library, 1925), 3: 198.

10. Szasz, *Indian Education*, 68–69. Eventually the College established a separate building, the Brafferton School, for Indian education in 1723.

11. Ibid., 68.

12. Blair cited in W. Stitt Robinson, "Indian Education and Missions in Colonial Virginia," *Journal of Southern History* (Vol. 18, No. 2 (May, 1952), pp. 152–68), 161.

13. Hening, *Statutes at Large*, 3: 123,

14. McIlwaine, *Executive Journals*, 1: 311.

15. Jack Eric Morpurgo Papers, Special Collections Research Center, Earl Gregg Swem Library, College of William and Mary.

16. Rev. Hugh Jones, *The Present State of Virginia, 1724* (New York: Reprinted for Joseph Sabin, 1865), 92; Even the English presented some concerns over the corruptible nature of the schoolmasters charged with Indian pupils. In a letter from Henry Compton, Bishop of London, to Francis Nicholson dated January 5, 1698, Compton writes that "from ye example in Virginia" a school can be made "either unsafe or dangerous." Francis Nicholson Papers, Addition One, Manuscript # MS 86.10, John D. Rockefeller Library, Colonial Williamsburg Foundation.

17. Brafferton Estate Collection, Special Collections Research Center, Earl Gregg Swem Library, College of William and Mary.

18. Rountree, *Powhatan Foreign Relations 1500–1722*, 198.

19. Robert Beverley, ed. David Freeman Hawke, *Robert Beverley: The History & Present States of Virginia, 1705* (New York: The Bobbs-Merrill Company, Inc., 1971), 231–32.

20. Morpurgo Papers, College of William and Mary.

21. McIlwaine, *Executive Journals*, 3: 287–88, 290–91.

22. Alexander Spotswood, *The Official Letters of Alexander Spotswood, Lieutenant-Governor of the Colony of Virginia 1710–1722*, ed. R. A. Brock (Richmond,

Virginia: Virginia Historical Society, 1882), "To the Bishop of London, November 11, 1711," 2: 126–28.

23. Ibid.

24. Ibid.

25. Spotswood, *Letters*, "To the Bishop of London, November 11, 1711," 2: 126–28.

26. Spotswood, *Letters,* "To the Bishop of London, May 8, 1712," 1: 156–57.

27. Spotswood, *Letters*, "To the Bishop of London, July 26, 1712," 1: 174–75.

28. Ibid.

29. Ibid.

30. Spotswood, *Letters*, "To the Archbishop of Canterbury, July 26, 1712," 1: 176–77.

31. Ibid.

32. McIlwaine, *Executive Journals*, 3: 188, 296, 310.

33. According to Hazzard and McCartney, the two treaties concluded with the tributaries and the Tuscarora that spring dealt primarily with trade and then Christianizing the Indians. "Spotswood felt that conducting trade on a just and equal footing, with a fair administration of justice, would have created a respect for English laws and government and a dependency upon the English to supply all trade goods." Hazzard and McCartney, *Fort Christanna,* 7.

34. McIlwaine, *Executive Journals*, 3: 375–76; Winfree, *Laws of Virginia*, 104–13.

35. Spotswood, *Letters,* "To the Bishop of London, January 27, 1714," 2: 89.

36. John Fontaine, *The Journal of John Fontaine An Irish Huguenot Son in Spain and Virginia, 1710–1719,* ed. Edward Porter Alexander (Williamsburg, VA: The Colonial Williamsburg Foundation, 1972), 93.

37. McIlwaine, *Executive Journals*, 3: 405–08.

38. Ibid., 412, 440.

39. Leonidas Dodson, *Alexander Spotswood Governor of Colonial Virginia 1710–1722.* (Philadelphia: University of Pennsylvania Press, 1932), *Alexander Spotswood,* 84.

40. Jones, *Present State of Virginia,* 15.

41. Morpurgo Papers, College of William and Mary.

42. Spotswood, *Letters,* "To the Bishop of London, January 27, 1714," 2: 91; Jones, *State of Virginia,* 70–71.

43. Spotswood, *Letters,* "To Ye Lords Commiss'rs of Trade, June ye 4th, 1715," 2: 113.

44. Spotswood, *Letters,* "To the Bishop of London, October 26th, 1715," 2: 138.

45. Spotswood, *Letters,* "To the L'ds Comm'rs of Trade, Feb'y 16th, 1716," 2: 141.

46. Fontaine, *Journal,* 91.

47. Ibid.

48. Ibid.

49. Ibid., 92.

50. Ibid., 93.
51. Ibid.
52. Ibid., 94.
53. Ibid.
54. Ibid.
55. Ibid.
56. Ibid., 94; William Byrd, *The Secret Diary of William Byrd of Westover, 1709–1712*, eds. Louis B. Wright and Marion Tinling (Richmond: The Dietz Press, 1941), 424–25.
57. Fontaine, *Journal,* 97.
58. Ibid.
59. Ibid., 97.
60. Ibid., 98.
61. Ibid.
62. Ibid.
63. Ibid.
64. Ibid., 12. Robert Beverley quoted and Philip Alexander writes, "One may speculate as to how Fontaine secured the list. He may, of course, have talked with one or several Indians and spelled out the words phonetically as best he could." He likely learned them from Charles Griffin, the teacher.
65. Ibid., 95.
66. Ibid., 98.
67. Spotswood, *Letters,* "To the Bishop of London, May 23d, 1716," 2: 159.
68. Spotswood, *Letters*, "To Mr. Popple, April 16th 1717," 2: 236; James D. Rice, *Nature & History in the Potomac Country: From Hunter-Gatherers to the Age of Jefferson* (Baltimore: The Johns Hopkins University Press, 2009), 187. "The 1717 attack on Ft. Christanna was an important turning point. It set off a sustained burst of north-south warfare, which in turn set off a burst of diplomatic activity that would eventually open the backcountry to colonial farming . . . The attack on Ft. Christanna also inspired the first serious diplomatic initiative between Virginia and the Five Nations since the 1680s."
69. Spotswood, *Letters*, "To the Lords Commissioners for Trade and Plantations, Aug't 29th 1717," 2: 258.
70. It is relevant to consider Byrd's perspective not only as a contemporary of Spotswood and Fontaine but also because evidence clearly illustrates that Byrd considered himself to be a Christian man, for more on the religious beliefs of the emerging planter class in Virginia see Lauren F. Winner, *A Cheerful and Comfortable Faith: Anglican Religious Practice in the Elite Households of Eighteenth-Century Virginia* (New Haven, CT: Yale University Press, 2010), 103–09. Byrd clearly had a model of what "appropriately pious prayer looked like, and he measure himself against that model," it is clear that he did not feel Native students met the standard. Additionally, one must question Byrd's involvement in the opposition to Spotswood and Assembly's open hostility to Spotswood's proselytization plans. Their hostility is reflective of the colonial concept that indigenous peoples were not capable of

conversion through "hereditary heathenism," as described by Rebecca Anne Goetz with reference to Virginia as being endemic among the locally born colonists but not in English born men like Spotswood and Blair. See Rebecca Anne Goetz, *The Baptism of Early Virginia: How Christianity Created Race* (Baltimore: The Johns Hopkins Press, 2012), 140–48.

71. William Byrd, *The Prose Works of William Byrd of Westover: Narratives of a Colonial Virginian,* Edited by Louis B. Wright (Cambridge, MA: Harvard University Press, 1966), 220–21.

72. Byrd, *Prose Works,* 220–21.

73. Ibid.

74. Ibid.

75. Ibid.

76. Ibid., 115.

77. Byrd, *Prose Works*, 246–48, 284.

78. Byrd, *Secret Diary*, April 8, 1709, 19; July 21–November 10, 1710; 207–61.

79. Byrd, *Prose Works*, 246–48, 284. Byrd discussed at length the religion of his Saponi tracker, Bearskin, during his surveying of the Virginia and North Carolina boundary line in 1728, citing in two separate accounts his examination of his religion. Byrd's assessment of the Saponi religion, as we now know, was erroneous.

80. Byrd, *Prose Works*, 391, 397; Byrd, *Secret Diary*, 228. Byrd's diary provides recipes, religion commentary, and his sexual preferences.

81. Among the most damning of the allegations was that Spotswood was the biggest stockholder in the Virginia Indian Company, holding shares under the false name of Catherine Russell. Spotswood, *Letters*, 2: 207; Hazzard and McCartney, *Fort Christanna*, 26.

82. Spotswood, *Letters*, "Feb'ry ye 27th 1718 To the Lords of Trade," 2: 263.

83. Ibid.

84. McIlwaine, ed., *Executive Journals*, 3: 478; McIlwaine, ed., *Journals*, 207.

85. Ibid; Keith Egloff and Deborah Woodward, *First People: The Early Indians of Virginia* (Richmond, Virginia: The Virginia Department of Historic Resources, 1992), 50. Spotswood held council with the governors of New York, Pennsylvania, and Maryland where he suggested that the Iroquois might carry official passes and only travel west of the Blue Ridge Mountains while the Virginia Indians would stay in the east; For a history of Virginian/Iroquoian diplomacy and Spotswood's role see Matthew Lawson Rhoades, *Long Knives and the Longhouse: Anglo-Iroquois Politics and the Expansion of Colonial Virginia* (Lanham, MD: Fairleigh Dickinson University Press, 2011).

86. Morpurgo Papers, College of William and Mary.

87. Jones, *State of Virginia,* 19.

88. "Thomas Dell to the Bishop of London," June 1, 1724, quoted in Morpurgo Papers, College of William and Mary.

3

The Development of Two Worlds

British and Cherokee Spatial Understandings in the Eighteenth-Century Southeast

Ian D. Chambers

Native Americans have, as noted in the introduction to this book, been regularly represented as living in or being forced to live in two distinct worlds. My contribution to this discussion is to turn to the eighteenth century and examine a moment of colonial interaction, pursued with what one historian refers to as "tourist enterprise," that took place over a four-week period in 1730.[1] By examining this event I shall detail the manner in which English colonialism, in the guise of one the activities of one individual Sir Alexander Cumming, contributed to the creation of the concept of two worlds, in this case one English, one Cherokee. This tale of colonial contact, a positional imposition of the two-world paradigm by the British, is also read from a Cherokee perspective to detail how, even at the founding moments of this paradigm, Native peoples constructed understandings differently by recognizing a single world consisting of multiple, discrete, yet interlinked spaces within a single world. I thereby highlight that the two-world paradigm was not only created by but also needed by European colonists to make sense of their actions in America. This desire to control the Cherokee landscape, prompted by a fear of the unknown and therefore uncontrolled, drove Cumming and the British to attempt to incorporate the Cherokee within their intellectual and physical world. This development of a known and safe world had the effect of creating a separate and necessary second space which was outside British control and therefore available for condemnation and attack.

To give full meaning and explanation to the interaction I will be using two interrelated theoretical concepts; spatial habitus—the spatial understanding held within a community; and spatial persona—the understanding held by individuals within the community's broader spatial habitus.[2] As indicated by the term habitus this theoretical concept is drawn from and derives its impetus from the work of Pierre Bourdieu, for Bourdieu, who first used the term in 1967, defines habitus as:

> systems of durable, transposable dispositions, structured structures predisposed to function as structuring structures, that is, as principles of the generation and structuring of practices and representations which can be objectively "regulated" and "regular" without in anyway being in obedience to rules, objectively adapted to their goals without presupposing a conscious aiming at ends or an express mastery of the operations necessary to attain them and, being all this, collectively orchestrated without being the product of the orchestrating action of a conductor.[3]

Bourdieu therefore argues for a series of dispositions, or practices, which provide individuals with the knowledge necessary to act in any given circumstance, without this knowledge being driven by specific conscious rules of action. This is not a static objectivistic knowledge for, simultaneously, individuals' experiences inform their behavior and understanding allowing them to adapt and modify theses dispositions, which in turn adjusts the knowledge that helps to inform their decisions.

An individual's behavior, what I term their *persona*, is open to individual adaptation but is guided by, and informed by, the knowledge that they have been given through their existence within the community's habitus, that is, they have a pre-reflective level of awareness.[4] This construction of behavior, therefore, avoids both the concepts of mechanical determinism often found in structuralism, whilst simultaneously avoiding the idea that each individual has full rational agency for their actions.

Bourdieu's construction of habitus is not, however, without its critics and potential problems, as Bourdieu himself notes "it would be wrong to underestimate the pressure or oppression, continuous and often unnoticed or ordinary things."[5] Bourdieu himself utilizes spatial concepts in his discussion of the term, most notably in his descriptive analysis of Kabyle houses as representative, or instructive of, broader Kabyle society. However, it must also be noted that, in his discussion of distribution of cultural capital with the petite bourgeoisie of Paris and rural France, he delineates social space from geographic space, therefore separating two interlinked aspects, which I consider essential to consider simultaneously while detailing spatial habitus: the physical and the intellectual. The two inform and reflect upon each other to develop the groups spatial habitus; that is, location informs equally to conceptualization.[6]

Finally, as Bourdieu notes, "as habitus is not something natural, inborn: being a product of history, that is of social experience and education, it may be *changed by history*, that is by new experiences, education or training," although tending to perpetuate it is not eternal. This work will show the manner in which the collision of two differing spatial habitus, the "*dialectical confrontation* between habitus," affected the encounter between two nations and therefore advance understandings of the development of the two-world paradigm.[7]

The story begins not in the hills and mountains of the Cherokee but rather in the city of Edinburgh, Scotland, where on December 18, 1691, the protagonist of the story, Alexander Cumming, was born.[8] Thirty-eight years later, in 1729, Cumming "induced, by a dream of Lady Cummings [sic], undertook a voyage to America, for the purpose of visiting the Cherokee nation."[9] While the full manuscript of Cumming's Journal is now unfortunately lost, it was published in *The Daily Journal*, a London newspaper, upon his return to England.[10] The report was published in two different versions. The first version was published in September, 1730. It consisted of an overview, describing in broad strokes the daring deeds of Cumming, leading up to his arrival in London with seven Cherokees, when Cumming announced himself the appointed leader of the Cherokee nation. The second report, published the following month, gives a more detailed day-by-day description of his travels.[11]

Walking with Cumming as he took his journey into Cherokee space allows us to uncover the moments where both Europeans and Native Americans used their spatial personas to inform their understanding of the unfolding events. I do not wish to claim that spatial understanding alone prompted each action taken. Rather, the spatial aspect of the trip reveals significant insights into the development of a "two worlded" colonial process that might otherwise escape our knowledge.[12]

Since the eighteenth century, Cumming's position has been interpreted differently. During the nineteenth century, some historians ascribed Cumming the role of official ambassador from the British crown, something that Cumming himself had denied in his journal. Others also raised questions regarding Cumming's motives and even questioned his sanity.[13] In the twentieth century, he has been viewed as nothing more than an oddity, "a one-man firework display wildly emitting sparks and colored lights and blazing rockets," whose arrival coincided with the earliest steps of contemporary Cherokee state formation.[14] By returning to the journey and reintroducing Cumming as an important part of early eighteenth century Cherokee–British interaction, we see Cumming's actions emerge as an attempt to create two worlds, one British and one Native. This creation of separate worlds was an act both needed and claimed by Cumming, and in turn the British, in order to define space and claim the trip as a victory for British colonialism. However, for the Cherokee involved this assignment of a position within one of two distinct worlds was *not* accepted. Rather, they created a space within a single world accommodating the newcomer without the need for sites of inclusion and exclusion.

Arriving in Charles Town in early 1730 and using his title as collateral, Cumming convinced the colonists that he possessed great wealth and proposed to "settle in Carolina, and do wonderful Things for the Good of the Country."[15] To solidify his position, and signal his intent to assist the people of the colony, Cumming began to write promissory notes which "by his punctual Payment of them upon Sight, in a little Time they acquired a Credit and Currency equal with Money." With this secure footing, Cumming began to expand his financial dealings within the colony, buying "several large Plantations." In addition he opened a loan office, issuing more notes bearing a ten-percent interest payment. Using the money gained from these several ventures, he was able to buy an "abundance of Gold and Silver and a great Deal of Country Produce which he shipt [sic] away continually." With his financial and social position secured, Cumming was able to draw on the help of several leading traders and merchants to furnish his journey among the Cherokee.[16]

On the afternoon of March 13, 1730, at "about five," Cumming left the home of Mr. James Kinlock at New Gilmerton, South Carolina, in the company of Indian trader George Chicken and Surveyor George Hunter, and headed into Cherokee country. Three days later, Cumming and his companions, which now included William Cooper, "a bold Man, and skilled in the Cherrokee [sic] Language," traveled to an underground cave near the home of a Mr. Coxe.[17] Cumming, "Mr. Chicken, and Mr. Coxe, made several marks to show that they had been there." Not content to enter just his own name, Cumming branded the cave, and symbolically the land, for Britain, engraving "King George II of Great Britain, wrote by S.A.C."[18] By leaving this mark, Cumming attempted to ensure that the space in which he stood became known not only physically but was also conceived of as part of British jurisdictional and intellectual space. This desire to identify, fix, and record is seen throughout the journey. Whenever Cumming met an "Indian," he would "take his name down in his book saying that he had made a friend of him." By this act, Cumming, mirroring the act of cartographers who claim land by placing a country's name on a map, added each individual to the knowledge and control of the British, symbolically removing them from the "other" Cherokee world.

Over the next few days Cumming continued his journey along the Cherokee Path, the main trading trail into Cherokee Country.[19] Arriving at the Cherokee Town of Keowee on March 23, 1730, the true purpose of Cumming's journey was revealed to both the Cherokee and his traveling companions. Over dinner in the house of one of the Town's traders, Cumming was informed that there recently had been "Messengers from the lower Creeks, with the Cherokees, desiring them to come over to the French Interests."[20] Cumming suggested in his journal that this warning reinforced the danger that he was under and his bravery in undertaking such a journey. However, I argue that this warning provided the catalyst that forced Cumming's next action. As a self-conceived ambassador, acting, in his own mind, on behalf of Britain to visit, define, mark, and thereby incorporate the Cherokee nation into his known world, Cumming was forced to act by the threat of French incursion into the region. His response to the news is demonstrated in the events that unfurled in the Keowee Town House that evening.[21]

The Town House was full, with a reported 300 Cherokees in attendance as well as nine British traders. Cumming entered and waited patiently while the Town's leaders spoke before making his own speech.[22] Cumming began by informing the Cherokee who he was and that he had come as an individual citizen, not as an official ambassador on behalf of King George. He then proposed a toast to the King during which he hoped, if not demanded, that all others would pledge their loyalty and allegiance to King George. After encouraging the shocked traders to fall to their knees, he turned to the Cherokee and, revealing the four firearms and the cutlass he had under his cloak, demanded that the "head Warriors . . . acknowledge his Majesty King George's Sovereignty over them on their knee." Joseph Cooper, a trader who was the evening's interpreter also, declared:

> If he had known before hand what Sir Alexander would have order'd him to have said, he would not have ventured in the Town-House to have been Interpreter, nor would the Indian Traders have ventured to have been Spectators, believing none of them could have gone out of the Town-House without being

> murdered, considering how jealous that People had always been of their Liberties.[23]

Cumming and his contemporaries leave us no description of the Cherokee reaction to this alarming episode, although as all the British lived through the event, we must assume that some form of accommodation was met. For Cumming, situated within the British spatial persona, the meeting represented the conquest, or at least the first step in that process, of the Cherokee nation for the British crown and its incorporation into the known British world. Furthermore, for Cumming and the British readers of his journal the Town House no longer acted as a location for Cherokees to discuss and debate the affairs of their Town nor did it provide an avenue for encouraging clan affiliation throughout the broader Cherokee nation. Instead, the space functioned as a site where British authority and control had been established, thus leaving other towns in a separate, external, world. The Town House and the space it occupied personified Cumming's, and through him Britain's, control of this Cherokee village. Cumming viewed the population of the village as British subjects, informing them that if they failed to submit to the king "they would become no people," for any population beyond British space had no "fixidity" and therefore no existence.[24]

Cumming's intent to dominate the Cherokee is seen by his response to trader Ludovick Grant. When asked what he had planned to do if the Cherokees present had refused to submit:

> he [Cumming] answered with a Wild look, that . . . if any of the Indians had refused the King's health to have taken a brand out of the fuire (sic) that Burns in the middle of the room and to have set fire to the house. That he would have guarded the door himself and put to death every one that endeavored to make their Escape that they might have all been consumed to ashes.[25]

This statement, which worried the traders who heard it, indicated that Cumming believed there were only two positions available to the Cherokee—as subservient members in a British space or death.

To affirm his position and his claim of dominance and incorporation of the Cherokee, Cumming demanded a second meeting eleven days later, on April 3, 1730, at the Cherokee Town of Nequassee. Cumming informed the members of the Keowee community that he expected that "one of their head Men should bring full Power from the lower Settlements, another full Powers from the upper Settlements, and the third full Powers from the middle settlements" to this meeting.[26] In demanding individuals to represent the physical regions of the whole nation, Cumming planned to repeat his conquest of the single village on a national scale.

For those Cherokee in the Keowee Town House on March 23, 1730, operating in a different spatial persona, an alternative interpretation of the events would be realized. James Adair, a contemporary of Cumming, provides us with a clue as to the Cherokee understanding. Writing of Cherokee government Adair noted that:

> They can only persuade or dissuade the people, by their force of good-nature and clear reasoning, or colouring things, so as to suit their prevailing passions. It is reputed merit alone, that gives them any titles of distinction above the meanest of the people.[27]

What Adair saw as a lack of authority within the administration of the Cherokee was actually a recognition that each person's voice and opinion could, and would, be heard in debate. This belief in an egalitarian approach to politics did not mean, however, that every point contained equal value. As the quotation suggests, certain people could gain a greater degree of influence through their action or "merit." This opened up the possibility for someone with a proven history of success, in warfare or negotiation, to rise into a position of heightened influence, what Adair referred to as a "title of distinction."

Adair's quotation also suggests that strength of argument and oratorical skills played a large part in any debate. It is therefore possible that an individual could, through force of personality and argument, influence the policy of the Town. Accepting that all people could be heard and that a powerful debater could gain influence, is it possible that this was the route that allowed Cumming to, apparently, dominate the community of Keowee? Cumming's behavior in Charles Town prior to his journey into Cherokee space indicates that Cumming had self-confidence and skills of persuasion, and his willingness to make such a dramatic display of force in the Keeowe Town House suggests that he possessed tremendous bravery and assumed great authority. Both attributes may have allowed him to assert power within the space of the Town House.

If we view the episode at Keowee as an isolated and individual event, the apparent submission of the Cherokee appears puzzling, even allowing for Cumming's oratory skills and assertive behavior. However, if the events of the evening of March 23, 1730, are placed into a broader view, based within a Cherokee spatial persona, a different image begins to appear.

Although Europeans reported, and Cumming believed, that his actions had ensured control and domination over the Cherokees, the Cherokees viewed the events as acts which provided a means to be absorbed or adopted by Cumming into Cherokee space within a broader single world.

The first step in understanding this alternate view of Cumming's involvement with the Cherokee focuses on the role of negotiation with Cherokee political life. Cherokee individuals involved in negotiations had authority, in a loose sense, to represent the position of the larger group, but no authority to enter into additional negotiations or agreements without further consultation with the larger group. Cumming's actions might be reinterpreted through this understanding. Whereas Cumming saw his request at Keowee to summon other Cherokee leaders as an instruction to facilitate broader control, the Cherokee recognized it as an opportunity to adjourn the negotiations and return to the larger group to discuss the next step. For the Cherokee, the single Town of Keowee did not have the authority to commit the whole nation to a position of allegiance. The apparent Cherokee acquiescence in the Keowee Town House on March 23, 1730, was in actuality a necessary step in their political structure. That is, they deferred the negotiations until a larger Cherokee group was able to convene and discuss Cumming's proposal.[28]

Working in tandem with the need for larger group discussion was a second aspect of Cherokee political life: the need for harmony. The Cherokee spatial persona had at its core the recognition that separate and discrete places needed to be combined through ceremonial means into a single world for life to continue. Within political debate, this aspect of the spatial persona played out through the pursuit of harmony. When harmony was threatened, the deferral of decision making was a common method of maintaining harmony. When involved in negotiations, the Cherokee deflected requests for immediate resolutions and instead chose to withdraw, discuss, and return.

An example of the manner in which pursuit of harmony through deflection operated can be found by turning to another of Cummings's contemporaries. On this occasion Colonel George Chicken's 1725 mission to the Cherokee helps explain the Cherokee reaction to Cumming's demands. On Tuesday January 14, 1725, at the Town of Tugoloo, Chicken met with representatives from several Cherokee Towns. During the meeting Chicken put forward seven points for discussion, which ranged from details of recent activity among the Creek to the Cherokee relationships with the English. The fifth point raised by Chicken, detailed below, marked the beginning of the Cherokee process of decision deferral. Chicken raised the subject of a standing Cherokee army. He informed the Cherokee that,

> . . . if you would but Consider Yourselves how Numerous you are and how little you would Miss the drawing out of each Town in the Nation a small Number of Men, you would not talk of defending your Towns but would Raise an Army of Men and Defend your Enemies before they come Nigh your Towns.[29]

As the above quotation shows Chicken, operating from within the British spatial persona, assumed that the logic of a single unified national project, such as an army, would make sense and be acceptable to the Cherokee. For the Cherokee, however, the need for separate discrete spaces in the form of Towns—each responsible for its individual defense—was the logical answer to the challenges of external attacks. In order to preserve harmony within negotiations where British and Cherokee views were clearly divergent, and not likely to be easily resolved, the assembled Cherokee leaders attempted to defer a decision, assuming that Chicken would recognize and accept this tactic.

Initially the Cherokee promised to "all go and consult together abt [sic] what" Chicken proposed, promising to return later with an answer. Upon further discussion the Cherokee informed Chicken that they would take action upon his suggestion to send scouts to look for the enemy, but that with regard to his request for the formation of a national Cherokee army, they "had concluded to send to the other Towns in order to meet them to Concur abt [sic]" the suggestion. Chicken's response to this deferment was once more to push the concept of a unified army. He informed the Cherokee that "unless they had a body of men to go out against the enemy when they were discovered that their Scouts would be of little Service to them." The Cherokee attempted to defer a decision for a fourth time, and Chicken again pushed for the creation of an army.

The Cherokee then tried a different approach to defuse the situation. They informed Chicken that they accepted "if the enemy comes on them before they can gett a body it would not be the Englishes fault because they have given them Notice of it." Such an assurance that blame would not be apportioned to the English was an important concession in a clan-based society like the Cherokee where culpability was a key factor in decisions of retaliation. Despite this assurance, Chicken still refused to back off and once more pushed for a commitment to a standing army. In a final attempt to deflect the decision, driven, we must assume, by exasperation at Chicken's continued failure to recognize the correct form of negotiation, the Head Warrior of Toxsoah agreed to go out and "gett what men he could to goe along with him." This final act allowed for an acceptable solution to both parties. Chicken assumed that this was the beginning of a national army with the Head Warrior of Toxsoah as the commander, while the Cherokee saw it as the promise of one man, not of the whole group. Thus, after several hours of negotiation, harmony was restored.[30] The use of decision deferment was one intellectual tool available to the Cherokee during their interaction with Cumming. A second involved the Cherokee relationship to personal power.

Individual power for the Cherokee was not a fixed attribute possessed inherently. Rather, power was a potential strength that the correct behavior could reveal and incorrect actions could remove. Power was therefore flexible and, in the case of assessing an individual, unable to immediately gauge. Thus "overt deference and respect afforded the safest course to follow in interpersonal relations. Such behavior minimized the chance of giving offense and, perhaps, suffering hostile repercussions."[31] Cumming's actions of bringing weapons into the Town House and demanding subservience cast him outside the normal rules of behavior for Cherokee negotiations. It made eminent sense for the Cherokees to defer a decision and palliate someone behaving so boldly and aggressively. Yet, these same actions suggested to Cherokees that Cumming possibly possessed personal power. On March 27, as Cumming entered the Town of Tassetchee "there happen'd to be most terrible Thunder, Lightning, and Rain."[32] One European who had lived with the Cherokee for ten years in the early eighteenth century reported that Cherokees perceived thunder and lightning as messages from spiritual beings. They believed that individuals who assumed themselves to be superior to others and gave "themselves over to al sort of crulletie and abominations" would be struck down by lightning. In cases where lightning fell "hard by Them," but did not kill them, the Cherokees read it as a message for others to "ammend thire lives and To obay thire seperriors."[33] Cumming's decision to take guns into the Town House and demand the acquiescence of the Cherokees appeared to locate him as one claiming undue prestige and superiority. Yet a Cherokee reading of the meteorological events of the evening of March 27, when Cumming remained unscathed by the thunder and lightning, undoubtedly suggested to them that Cumming possessed strong spiritual power.

Cherokee caution regarding power combined with their preference to defer decisions when unanimity could not be reached suggests another way to understand the events involving Cumming between March 23 and April 3, 1730. Seen from a Cherokee perspective, Cumming neither controlled nor dominated the proceedings. Instead, Cherokees constructed a meaning and a place for Cumming that allowed him to be respected but not accepted. They recognized the potential Cumming held but did not ascribe him authority. Rather, the Cherokees found a way within their political and spatial understanding to defer any decision making to a later date.

After leaving Tassetchee, Cumming headed to Great Tellico where unwittingly he described an alternative set of political actions being played out. The actions taken by "Moytoy, the Head Warrior" shift Cumming's journey from a daring and aggressive act of British politics to capture the Cherokee within British space, to a move by the leader of one Cherokee Town to politically adopt Cumming, thereby creating a link between the Cherokee and the British.

Arriving at Great Tellico on March 29, 1730, Cumming commented that he saw "a great many Enemies Scalps, brought in and put upon Poles at the Warriors doors."[34] This is his first mention of the martial prowess of the Cherokee, within the telling of the trip. Two interpretations can be made of this display. The first would be to suggest that Cumming, influenced by the scalps, saw the Town and its leader as a dominant force in Cherokee society. That he would later position Moytoy as "Emperor of the Cherokee" reinforces this view. By asserting control over Moytoy, Cumming created a fixed hierarchical structure within Cherokee society, which as a member of the British aristocracy he would both understand and within which feel comfortable. The second interpretation inverts the first. That is the possibility that the scalps had been intentionally displayed by the Town not to assert Moytoy's primacy in Cherokee society but to suggest his strength as a warrior. As a warrior Moytoy was situated in the Cherokee space that dealt with diplomatic relations with outsiders, thereby, Moytoy may have been offering himself as a suitable person to be the focus of interaction between Cumming and the broader Cherokee polity. Cumming saw an opportunity to assert British domination and control over the Cherokee. The Head Warrior, Moytoy, by contrast saw an opportunity to create a link between the British and the Cherokee through Cumming. Thus, it appears that both parties viewed the meeting through the distinctive lens of their own spatial persona.

During an initial meeting in the Great Tellico Town House, Moytoy informed Cumming that there had been discussions the previous year "among the several Towns" of the Cherokee to make "Moytoy Emperor over the whole, but that now it must be whatever Sir Alexander pleased."[35] With this statement Cumming drops his first hint that he will personally assume a position of dominance among the Cherokee, for if the man whom the Cherokee have already considered for leadership is prepared to submit to Cumming, then what apart from total dominance are the British to expect?[36]

The events that unfolded are, however, given a different light when viewed through the Cherokee spatial persona. Moytoy did not claim power to position himself as Principal Chief among the Cherokee. Rather he sought to place himself as the man who could control the potential power that Cumming possessed and by that control form a link between the Cherokee and British.[37] The following day, March 30, while still in Great Tellico, Cumming was involved in another Cherokee ceremony, writing that he was "Particularly distinguished in the Town-house by Moytoy, where the Indians sung songs, danced, and stroked his Head and Body over with Eagles tails." This event was not included in Cumming's first published overview of his trip. In that document he included instead the later meeting at Nequassee on April 3, highlighting what he, and the British reading public, perceived as his coronation.

However, for the Cherokee the March 30 meeting had great importance, for it provided the first step in linking Cumming and the Cherokee. By ensuring that the ceremony took place in the Town House of Great Tellico, and by assuming a leading role in the ceremony, Moytoy placed himself in the center of this process and positioned himself to act as spatial ambassador of the Cherokee.

The next major incident, and for Cumming the culmination of his ascendancy to leadership of the Cherokee, was the bestowing of the crown of Tannassy during his alleged coronation. This occurred on April 3, 1730, at the Town of Nequassee, where the "Kings, Princes, Warriors, Conjurers, and Beloved Men were all met."[38] Cumming described the events in the Nequassee Town House in the following terms:

> Here with great Solemity Sir Alexander was placed in a Chair, by Moytoy's Orders, Moytoy and the Conjourers standing about him, while the warriors stroked him with 13 Eagles tails and their Singers sung from Morning to Night, and, as their Custom is on Solemn Occasions, they fasted the whole Day.[39]

Cumming informs us that he gave a speech during the coronation proceedings in which he detailed the power of the King and demanded the Cherokee's submission. Additionally he "ordered that the Head Warriors should answer for their Conduct of the People to Moytoy, whom he appointed their Head, by the unanimous Consent of the whole People."[40] For Cumming and his readers the image is clear. The Cherokee at this moment became subjects of Britain and, if not totally controlled, were at least no longer politically outside the British world. In order to give physical presence to the events, Cumming collected not only the signed affidavits of the British traders present but in addition "as Evidence of the Truth of what had happened," brought to London seven Cherokee.[41]

Cumming's actions on, and reaction and comments to, the events of April 3 indicate the manner in which a British spatial persona, based upon fixity and control, operated within a political act. Cumming reached out from British space, looking for an opportunity to act *upon* the Cherokee, not to interact *with* them. At the first opportunity Cumming used force in an attempt to dominate and control the Cherokee, and as he continued his journey, he attempted other forms of control, meeting Cherokees and recording names, fixing them in the record of his journey. Buoyed by early success he pushed his reach further, demanding a meeting with the leaders of the whole nation. At this later meeting at Nequassee, Cumming considers himself to have been crowned king of the Cherokee, thereby both securing his position and more importantly fixing the Cherokee nation within the knowledge and political orbit of the English. One of his first acts was to dictate the structure of society and outline the political relationship between the British and the Cherokee, ordering "the head Warriors should answer for the Conduct of their People to *Moytoy*, whom he appointed their head . . . and he to answer to Sir *Alexander*."[42]

Historian Verner W. Crane correctly argues that the Cherokee "had no real notion of acknowledging English 'sovereignty,' much less of parting with their lands to either Cumming himself or to the 'Great Man on the other side of the water.'" Nevertheless, it is clear that something of a political and ceremonial nature did occur on this date. The Cherokee did meet in national council and Cumming was involved in some form of ceremony in front of the assembled Cherokee. If the events do not portray Cherokee submission to British authority, then what do they represent? I suggested earlier that the events in Keowee, as described by Cumming, have a different meaning when viewed through the spatio-political behavior of the Cherokee. Therefore we can see in the events a clear step in the development of differing concepts of "worlding," for the British a second—Cherokee—world was being created whereas for the Cherokees an additional part was being added to their single world. I now want to expand this argument further and refocus our view of Cumming's whole journey through the spatial persona of the Cherokee.

Let us examine the importance and significance of the national council at Keowee which Cumming claims to have obtained sovereignty. The dramatic ceremony that Cumming viewed as a coronation may not be as dramatic or as singularly important as Cumming would have us believe.

In 1725, five years before Cumming's journey, Colonel George Chicken traveled throughout the Cherokee nation.[43] Chicken was not there to assert his control over the Cherokee, but rather to bring a message or "talk" from the South Carolina authorities. Like Cumming, Chicken spent only a short time in Cherokee space, traveling from Town to Town before speaking to a gathering of all Towns. Chicken's actions suggest that in contradiction to Cumming's claim that the meeting surrounding his coronation was such a gathering as "never was seen at any one time in that Country," in fact it was not unusual for the Cherokee to gather in large numbers to hear the "talks" of British visitors. Chicken's 1725 journey provides another inconsistency in Cumming's claims. Chicken describes his own arrival in Keewhohee (the Town Cumming referred to as Keowee), in the following manner:

> At my Arrival here King Crow and the head men were out of the Town at their Plantations and a Messanger being sent to inform them of my Arrival, they Imediatly [sic] Repaired to the Town and soon after, they after their Ceremonial way placed me in a Great Chair in the most Publick Place in the Town and set down by me themselv's faning me with Eagles Feathers.[44]

The similarity between this ceremony and that which Cumming experienced in Nequassee is obvious. Therefore, we can suggest that the ceremony Cumming experienced was not as he thought, a coronation, but rather an often-used method to incorporate an external individual. It represented a political adoption that allowed the Cherokees to form a link to an external discrete space. The act of political adoption allowed the voice of that outside space to be heard and such an act was in keeping with the Cherokee spatial persona. Additionally, Cumming's positioning of Moytoy as "Emperor" in order to verify British control over the Cherokee is also open to a Cherokee interpretation. Moytoy's efforts can be seen as an attempt to position himself as the gatekeeper for contact with the British. Moytoy did not declare himself sovereign over the Cherokee, although the British would increasingly view him as if he had, instead he offered himself as the person who would sponsor Cumming's interaction and linkage with the Cherokee nation.

The final point to be made with regard to the ceremony of April 3, 1730, concerns the artifact that gave Cumming's claim of coronation its greatest legitimacy, the crown of Tannassy.[45] Cumming, in the published details of his journey, mentions the crown and ceremony simultaneously, tying together the ceremony and the crown. However, a closer reading of the events reveals that Cumming did not receive the crown on the day of the ceremony, as his journal implied, but on the following day, suggesting a separation between event and artifact. There are other inconsistencies in the tale of the crown and how it came into Cumming's possession. The quotation below, from Cumming's initial overview report of the journey, details Moytoy's and the Cherokee's submission to him and positions the crown as a symbol of that capitulation.

> *April* 4. The Crown was brought from great *Tannassie*, which, with five Eagles tails and four Scalps of their Enemies, Moytoy presented to Sir *Alexander*, impowering him to lay the same at His Majesty's Feet.[46]

For the reading audience, this is a clear assertion that the Cherokee are within the British world as a people who are known and importantly controlled by the British. The next quotation, taken from Cumming's later day-by-day account, offers a subtle but important shift in the role of the crown.

> *April* 4. The Solemnity continued, Sir *Alexander* made some Presents, received their Crown, Eagles tails, and Scalps of their Enemies, to be laid at his Majesty King *George's* Feet.[47]

The crown shifted position; it no longer offered Cumming a symbol of obsequiousness but rather a gift, given after, and in return for, "Presents" given to the Cherokee by Cumming. This subtle movement in proceeding turned the object from a symbol of authority to a symbol of reciprocal contact and incorporations.

Examining the reports of other Europeans present at the presumed coronation ceremony further complicates the role of the crown. In his journal, Cumming suggested that as early as March 30 the possibility of his coronation was raised, writing that Moytoy "determined to present him [Cumming] with the crown of Tannassy."[48] This early introduction of the supposed coronation reinforces Cumming's later claim of authority. A different explanation comes from trader Ludovick Grant, who explains the crown's introduction in the following terms:

> From Telliguo we rode over to Tannassee and afterwards returned by Neguasse Where several Traders met us and a good many Indians. Sir Alexander had been informed of all the ceremonies

> that are used in making a head beloved man, of which there are a great many in the nation. They are called Ouka, and we translate that word king, so we call the Cap, he wears upon that occasion his Crown . . . Sir Alexander was very desirous to see one of them, and there being none at that Town One was sent for to some other Town. He Expressed Great Satisfaction at Seeing of it, and he told the Indians that he would carry it to England and give it to the great King George.[49]

Grant, who was with Cumming in both Great Tellico and Nequassee, indicates that, rather than being discussed prior to the ceremony of April 3, the crown was introduced at a later date. Additionally, it appears that the Cherokees had no intention of presenting the artifact to Cumming as a crown or any symbol of authority, but rather that it was an ethnographic artifact displayed only upon Cumming's insistence.

Finally we must consider the role that physical geography played in the events that occurred during Cumming's journey, exploring the role that different spaces played in the Cherokees interaction with Cumming. The claimed coronation took place in Nequassee and Cumming asserts that it is Moytoy, of Great Tellico, who performs the act. The crown itself comes from a third discrete Town location, Tannassee. This diversity of geographical location in the interaction between the Cherokee and Cumming is expanded following Cumming's supposed coronation. On April 6, 1730, during his return to Charles Town, Cumming informs us that they "proceeded to *Ookunny*, where Sir *Alexander* found a House built for him."[50] Cumming later claimed that the house came with "certain Territories there unto belonging as an acknowledgement" of his position "as their Governor & Lawgiver," stating that additional space was assigned to him "in every Town through which Sir Alexander had passed in his journey throughout the mountains."[51] This act, the linkage between landholding and political power, would appear logical in Cumming's spatial understanding, as it matched the associations seen within the system of hierarchical and political control that operated in the Britain at the time.

The act of constructing a house for Cumming adds a further aspect to the Cherokee understanding of Cumming's visit. By constructing a house for Cumming, in a Cherokee Town, Ookunny, and in a Cherokee style, the Cherokee have positioned and included Cumming in their physical and intellectual space. They have created a way for Cumming to have a stake in one of the two aspects of Cherokee national membership: Town affiliation.

The positioning of Cumming's residence in Ookunny, which appears to be a village with ties to the Township of Keowee, achieves two further objectives.[52] First, it places Cumming at the edge of Cherokee space in the region most closely related to Charles Town, thereby increasing the ease of communication between British and Cherokee space. Second, it offers the intriguing possibility that Cumming may have acquired some form of national Cherokee membership for he thereafter held links to the Upper Settlements through Great Tellico and Tannasse, to the Middle Settlements through Nequassee, and to the Lower Settlements through Ookunny and Keowee.

Taking all these points together, we find that an incident reported by an English traveler as representing a strong claim to English authority over the Cherokees is in fact a powerful display of Cherokee authority. Cummings journey graphically details the contrasting spatial personas of the Cherokee and the British, thereby allowing for a further understanding of the events from the point of view of both sets of participants. Each group's action and reaction were driven by differing spatial personas with each side comprehending the events in ways that made sense to themselves while simultaneously being unable to understand the other's reality. For Cumming, and the British readers of his adventures it was clear that two worlds had been created. The British world, containing members of the British colonial enterprise now including those natives who had submitted to British control, and a second world outside. Natives had the choice of existing within either of these two worlds, but to straddle them or exist in both was defined as impossible, something that would lead to danger and damage. However, for the Cherokee, what had been created was simply an addition to the single world in which all people existed.

Notes

1. The author would like to like to thank his colleague Adam Sowards for reading this chapter and providing comments and suggestions. Verner Winslow Crane, *The Southern Frontier, 1670–1732* (Ann Arbor, MI: University of Michigan Press, 1956), 277.

2. Taking a lead from Pierre Bourdieu's discussion of habitus in relation to class I suggest that there also exists a spatial habitus. We must also recognize that as Bourdieu notes habitus is not "a logical systematicity; it is a practical systematicity" to uncover the practice that informs this systematicity we need to examine acts of individuals living and operating within a habitus. For where group exists with

spatial habitus, individuals from that group, due to the multi-varied experience of possible permutations within the construction and use of group spatial habitus, possess a singular spatial persona. P. Bourdieu, *Outline of a Theory of Practice* (New York: Cambridge University Press, 1977), 53, 80–81; P. Bourdieu, "Habitus a sense of place" in *Habitus a Sense of Place*, Hillier and Rooksby, ed. (Burlington, UK: Ashgate Publishing, 2005), 44. Additional theoretical motivation in my construction of the analytical tool of the spatial persona is the work of theorists such as Edward Soja, Michel Foucault, and Henri Lefebvre. See Edward Soja, *Postmodern Geographies: The Reassertion of Space in Critical Social Theory* (New York: Verso, 1989); Henri Lefebvre (trans. Donald Nicholson-Smith), *The Production of Space* (New York: Blackwell, 1991, orig. 1974); Michel Foucault, (trans. Jay Miskowiec) "Of Other Spaces," *Diacritics*, Vol. 16, No. 1 (Spring, 1986); Michael Foucault, *The Order of Things: An Archaeology of the Human Sciences* (New York: Vintage Books, 1994); "Questions on Geography" (original "Questions á Michel Foucault sur la géographie"), *Hérodote*, 1, (1976)—interviewers: the editors of the Journal; Michel Foucault (ed. Colin Gordon), *Power/Knowledge Selected Interviews and other Writings 1972–1977* (Brighton, UK: Harvester Press, 1980).

3. Pierre Bourdieu (trans. Richard Nice), *Outline of a Theory of Practice*, (New York: Cambridge University Press, 2008), 72; The first use of the term by Bourdieu us found in the postface for his 1967 translation of Panofsky's *Gothic Architecture and Scholasticism.*

4. Instrumental in the construction of the analytical tool of the spatial persona is the work of theorists such as Edward Soja, Michel Foucault, and Henri Lefebvre. See Edward Soja, *Postmodern Geographies: The Reassertion of Space in Critical Social Theory* (New York: Verso, 1989); Henri Lefebvre (trans. Donald Nicholson-Smith), *The Production of Space*, (New York: Blackwell, 1991, orig. 1974); Michel Foucault (trans. Jay Miskowiec) "Of Other Spaces," *Diacritics*, Vol. 16, No. 1 (Spring, 1986); Michel Foucault, *The Order of Things: An Archaeology of the Human Sciences* (New York: Vintage Books, 1994); "Questions on Geography" (original "Questions á Michel Foucault sur la géographie") *Hérodote*, 1, (1976)—interviewers: the editors of the Journal; Michel Foucault (ed. Colin Gordon) *Power/Knowledge Selected Interviews and other Writings 1972–1977*, (Brighton UK: Harvester Press, 1980). See also Robert Thomas who writes that the Cherokee world is a "system" that "has parts and there are reciprocal obligations between the parts," Robert K. Thomas, *Cherokee Values and World View* MA thesis: University of North Carolina, 1958, 21. For a discussion on the importance of movement as part of identity for other Native American nations see Stephen Warren, "'The Greatest Travelers in America': Shawnee Survival in the Shatterzone," paper presented at American Society for Ethnohistory Conference Santa Fe, NM, November, 2005.

5. Pierre Bourdieu (trans. Richard Nice), *Pascalian Meditations*,(Stanford, CA: Stanford University Press, 2000), 141.

6. For Kabyle see Pierre Bourdieu (trans. Richard Nice), *The Logic of Practice*, (Stanford, CA: Stanford University Press, 1990), Appendix; for cultural capital in

France see Pierre Bourdieu (trans. Richard Nice), *Distinction: A Social Critique of the Judgement of Taste* (Cambridge, MA: Harvard University Press, 1987).

7. Pierre Bourdieu, "Introduction: Habitus" in *Habitus: A Sense of Place*, Hillier, Jean and Rooksby, Emma, (eds.), (Burlington, UK: Ashgate Publishing, 2005), 45–46 (emphasis in original).

8. In 1703 at the tender age of 12, Cumming was granted a Captain's commission in the Earl of Mar regiment by Queen Anne and ten years later gained a Doctorate of Law from the University of Aberdeen. Over the next few years Cumming was to lead a company against the Jacobites in the 1715 uprising, turn down the Governorship of Bermuda, and in 1725, after his father's death, became the second Baronet of Culter. As the decade drew to a close Cumming's eclectic career included a failed attempt to enter Scottish politics and admission to the Royal Society of London for Improving Natural Knowledge. Biographical details from The Scottish Tartans Museum website at http://www.scottishtartans.org/cumming.html. Accessed 22 February, 2006.

9. For details regarding the impetus for his trip see Daniel Lyons, *The Environs of London: Being an Historical Account of the Towns Villages and Hamlets, within Twelve Miles of that Capital: Interspersed with Biographical Anecdotes*, Vol. 4, (London, 1795–1796), 20.

10. *The Daily Journal*, Number 3037, (Wednesday, September 30, 1730) and Number 3044, (Thursday, October 8, 1730); The Journal was reprinted in *The Historical Register of 1731*. Note: Cumming refers to himself in the third person throughout the text.

11. There is considerable overlap between the two reports; however, the details left out of the first "claim to fame" piece that appear in the daily journal enable us to gain a better understanding of the events that unfolded.

12. In a period when the contest for control of what Herbert Eugene Bolton has termed the "Debatable land" of the southeast was intense any statement of spatial control was viewed by competing European powers not only as a geographical but also as a political success. The publication of Cumming's Journal, and the widely publicized presence of the Cherokee who accompanied him to London, reassured the British public of their country's position of strength in the region. It also allowed the British government to solidify its relationship with the Cherokee and score a political victory over the other competing European nations in the southeast, the French and Spanish. The combination of public and political recognition assured that in the eighteenth century the trip was seen by both the general public and the British government as a moment of great success for British colonial ambitions. See Herbert Eugene Bolton, *The Debatable Land, a Sketch of the Anglo-Spanish Contest for the Georgia County*, (Berkeley, CA: University of California Press, 1925).

13. For the claim of Cumming's official role see J. H. Stocqueler, *A Familiar History of the United States of America, From the Date of the Earliest Settlements Down to the Present Time*, (London: Darton and Hodge, 1865), 95. For his denial with regard to any official sanction of his trip see *The Daily Journal*, Thursday,

October 8, 1730. For details with regard to the question of Cummings sanity see J. H. Stocqueler, "Sir. Alexander Cumming," *Notes and Queries*, Series 1, Vol. V. No. 125, 278.

14. William O. Steele, *The Cherokee Crown of Tannassey*, (Charlotte, NC: J. F. Blair Publishers, 1977), xiii; and John Andrew Doyle, *English Colonies in America*, Vol. V (New York: Henry Holt and Company, 1882–1907).

15. "Extract of a Letter from South Carolina, June 12," *The ECCHO: or Edinburgh Weekly Journal*, Number LXXXIX (Wednesday, September 16, 1730); see also *The Grub Street Journal*, Number 36 (Thursday, September 10, 1730).

16. Cumming returned to England shortly before payment of his loans became due. After his departure, in an attempt to recoup their money, several members of the Charles Town community broke into his treasury. All they found inside were "some empty Boxes, old Iron and other Rubbish" and it was "computed" that he carried off "no less than £15000 sterling" a substantial amount for the period. "Extract of a Letter from South Carolina," Cumming's Manuscript, Ayer MS 204, Newberry Library, Chicago, 21.

17. *The Daily Journal*, Thursday, October 8, 1730.

18. *The Daily Journal*, Thursday, October 8, 1730. The cave is marked on George Hunter's map to the south side of the Santee River, slightly below the Township of Amelia.

19. The Cherokee Path, mapped in 1730 by George Hunter, the Surveyor-General of the Province of South Carolina, ran for 130 miles from Charles Town and passed though the Cherokee Lower and Middle Towns before terminating at Settico in the Overhill Towns.

20. *The Daily Journal*, Wednesday, September 30, 1730.

21. Veteran trader Ludovick Grant, who was in Keowee that evening, left a report corroborating the events that occurred in the Town House. See "Historical Relation of the Facts Delivered by Ludovick Grant, Indian Trader to His Excellency the Governor of South Carolina," *The South Carolina Historical and Genealogical Magazine*, Volume X (1909).

22. The named Europeans were Joseph Cooper, Ludovick Grant, Joseph Barker, Gregory Haines, Daniel Jenkinson, Thomas Goodale, William Cooper, William Hatton, and John Biles.

23. *The Daily Journal*, Thursday, October 8, 1730.

24. Although the word "fixity" is more frequently used today I have elected to use the eighteenth-century term "fixidity." See for example its use in Anton Friedrich Büsching, *A new system of geography: in which is given a general account of the situations and limits, the manners, history, and constitution of the several kingdoms and states in the known world: and a very particular description of their subdivisions and dependencies, their cities and towns, forts, sea-ports, produce, manufactures and commerce* (1762) I, 45.

25. *Historical Relation*, Grant, 56.

26. *The Daily Journal*, Thursday, October 8, 1730.

27. Adair, *History of the American Indian*, 460.

28. Long-term English traders also recognized this need for full national endorsement. While discussing a failed transfer of land from the Cherokee, Grant was to suggest that, the reason for failure was "because the head men were not present," Grant, 64. For a discussion of the "pragmatic" attitude by the Cherokee to external threats, see Robert K. Thomas, *Cherokee Values and World View*, MA thesis: University of North Carolina, 1958, esp. p. 14.

29. Randolph Boehm, ed., "Journal of the Commissioner for Indian Affairs on his Journey to the Cherokees and his Proceedings there," in *Records of the British Colonial Office, Class 5 Part 1: Westward Expansion 1700–1783*, Vol. 12, (Frederick, MD: University Publications of America, 1972).

30. This harmony ethic has continued to be an important part of Cherokee life. When John Gulick conducted research among the Eastern Cherokee in the mid-twentieth century, he observed a similar need writing that "When social decisions must be made, involving the resolution of differing points of view, the aim is circumspectly to work out a unanimous decision. An outvoted minority is regarded as a source of conflict and disharmony. Anyone whose views absolutely cannot be accommodated to the otherwise unanimous decision simply withdraws from the proceedings." John J. Gulick, "The self-corrective service and persistence in Conservation Eastern Cherokee culture," *Research Previews*, (1959), 6.

31. Raymond D. Fogelson, "Cherokee Notions of Power," in Raymond D. Fogelson, and Richard N. Adams (eds.,), *The Anthropology of Power: Ethnographic Studies from Asia, Oceania, and the New World*, (New York: Academic Press Inc., 1977), 189–90.

32. Cumming, "Account of the Cherokee Indians," 3.

33. Longe, "Small Postcript on the ways and manners of the Indians called Cherokees," *Southern Indian Studies,* Vol. XXI, (October, 1969), 39.

34. *The Daily Journal*, Wednesday, September 30, 1730, and Thursday, October 8, 1730.

35. *The Daily Journal*, Thursday, October 8, 1730.

36. Ibid.

37. It must be remembered that the translator, or linguist, in these negotiations was Ludovick Grant, a trader based in Great Tellico, who, therefore, had reason to promote the importance of the leader of his Town.

38. *The Daily Journal*, Wednesday, September 30, 1730.

39. Ibid.

40. Ibid.

41. Ibid.

42. Ibid.

43. Colonel George Chicken was father to the George Chicken who later accompanied Cumming.

44. "Colonel Chicken's Journal to the Cherokee, 1725"; Mereness, *Travels in the American Colonies*, 101.

45. Ludovick Grant described Cumming's "crown" as a "cap worn by beloved men which 'resembles a wig and is made of Possum's Hair Dyed Red or Yellow.' " Grant, *Historical Relation*, 57.

46. *The Daily Journal*, Wednesday, September 30, 1730.

47. *The Daily Journal*, Thursday, October 8, 1730.

48. Ibid.

49. Grant, *Historical Relation*, 57.

50. *The Daily Journal*, Wednesday, September 30, 1730.

51. Cumming's Manuscript, Ayer MS 204, Newberry Library, Chicago, pp. 22 and 26.

52. Cumming reports that the "King, who had been just then made at Ookunny" was the same person as the "King of Keowee," *The Daily Journal*, Wednesday, September 30, 1730.

Interlude

Diagramming Worlds

Nancy Shoemaker

Diagrams are a useful way to expose the fundamentals of an argument or problem, and for the topic of worlds, Euler Diagrams, also known as Euler Circles, seem the ideal medium. When I first began formulating my ideas for this interlude, I thought the rough sketches I was constructing were Venn Diagrams, a mistake that grew out of some vague childhood memory of exercises in elementary set theory. But as I read up on Venn Diagrams, I realized that my crude and imperfect diagrams bore greater resemblance to those originally devised by Leonhard Euler in the mid-eighteenth century as a system to graphically represent the logic of syllogisms. More than one hundred years later, John Venn revised Euler's circles to eliminate some of their logical insufficiencies, but for my purposes the simpler and yet still visually effective Euler Diagrams will do.[1]

Modeling the past with Euler Diagrams has virtues and pitfalls. Such charts can usefully extract the fundamentals from life's complexities—life's white noise. And yet they are also so completely reductionist; we have to keep reminding ourselves that they are conceptual tools and not depictions of reality. Indeed, a circle can misrepresent reality in many ways. As a designation for a culture, nation, people, or world (which is the application ethnohistorians would find most pertinent), a circle implies a crisply bounded and uniform entity. Naming amorphous groups of people the "Cherokee Nation" or the "British Empire" also implies uniformity within and sharp distinctions between these categories, but words do not seem as definite in their implications as two circles sharing space in a rectangle. However, as scholars, we have to reduce to understand and explain, and so instead of dismissing reductionism as poor scholarship, we can embrace reductionist models while remaining self-conscious about their limits and problems. For those readers still averse to graphic depictions as oversimplification, they could consider the parallels between Euler Diagrams and eighteenth-century southeastern Indian-produced maps of the eighteenth century, both of which feature the circle prominently as an emblem denoting ethnic and national entities such as the Catawba, Chickasaw, and Alabama.[2] Both my diagrams and these eighteenth-century maps are schematics by which perspectives on how people relate to each other can be easily conveyed through graphic representation.

My first Euler Diagram (Figure 1) attempts to combine the three preceding essays into a single depiction of eastern North America in the seventeenth and eighteenth centuries. It is a mess. And it would be even messier if I tried to make it more representative of eastern North America by adding circles for the Dutch and the Delaware, the Spanish and the Shawnee, and so on, or if I tried to incorporate more nuance and ambiguity in my model or to accommodate change over time. To make sense of the region, ethnohistorians have no choice but to limit their analyses to a single question and a few peoples. Most ethnohistoric analyses examine the relationship between Indians and Europeans, as these three articles do, but

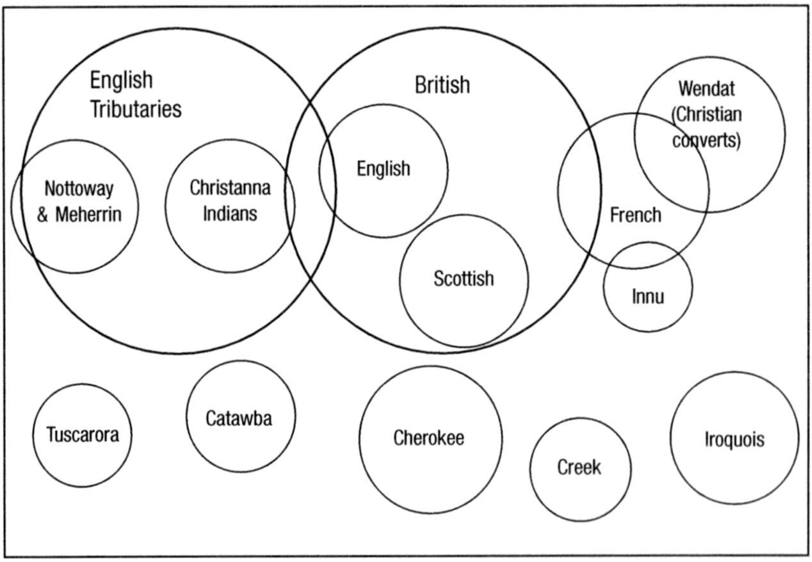

Figure 1. Euler Diagram of Eastern North America as Suggested by the Three Preceding Essays.

Europeans do not have to be featured as major players in every history of North America.[3]

Because historians do not try to capture the world in all its complexities but instead isolate patterns and themes for close analysis, they can dramatize their theses efficiently with Euler Diagrams much simpler in form than the dense and intricate Figure 1. Figure 2, for instance, schematizes Richard White's popular and influential argument in *The Middle Ground* (1991).[4] His minute examination of the political and cultural exchanges between the French and the native peoples of the Great Lakes region, whom he labels "Algonquins," has at its core an elegantly simple and easily diagrammed explanation of their relationship. Confused and stymied by their cultural differences, the French and the Algonquins constructed a "middle ground," built out of aspects of both cultures, that briefly flourished as a site for communication and action, a distinct cultural space that was neither fully French nor Algonquin but incorporated elements of both in an invention of new cultural practices. My own book on the eighteenth-century European and Indian cultural encounter, *A Strange Likeness* (2004), can just as easily be diagrammed to capture my main point—that Indians and Europeans had much in common, despite cultural differences, largely because of a shared cognitive approach to making sense of the world around them (Figure 3).[5]

Primary sources can also yield insights when their viewpoints are diagrammed. Each of the previous three essays features a man with a vision for the colonization of North America (Figure 4, page 91). As Kathryn Magee Labelle shows to great effect, the French Jesuit priest Jean de Brébeuf

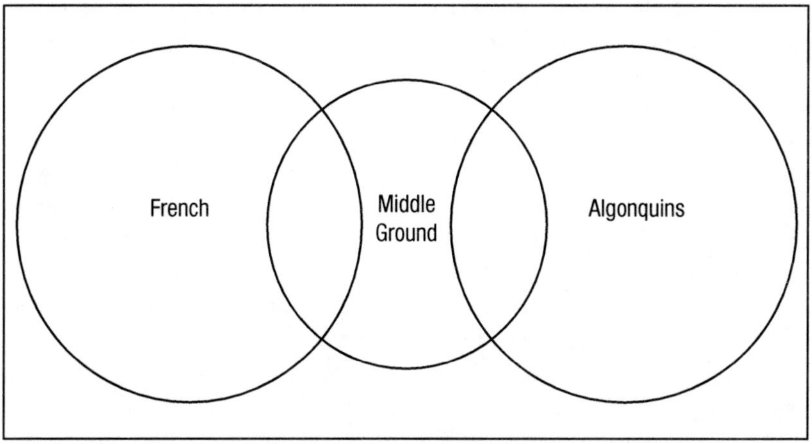

Figure 2. Euler Diagram of Richard White's *The Middle Ground.*

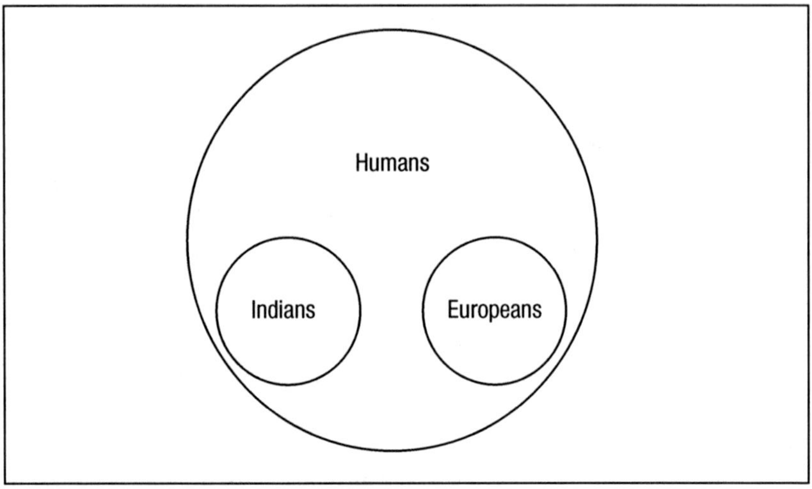

Figure 3. Euler Diagram of Nancy Shoemaker's *A Strange Likeness.*

expressed his belief that Indians and Europeans belonged to the same world by holding up to the Wendat (Huron) a small globe that he had brought with him to New France: "And when we preach to them of one God, Creator of Heaven and earth, and of all things, and even when we talk to them of Hell and Paradise and of our other mysteries, the headstrong savages reply that this is good for our Country and not for theirs; that every Country has its own fashions. But having pointed out to them, by means of a little globe that we had brought, that there is only one world, they remain without reply."[6] In early eighteenth-century Virginia, Lieutenant Governor Alexander Spotswood also envisioned a world of the future that would incorporate Indians in it, albeit refashioned to become Christian, literate, and more like Europeans in their manners and customs although remaining residents of separate Indian communities at the border of English settlements. Alexander Cumming, in his brief foray into Cherokee country in 1730, thought he had achieved incorporation of the Cherokee Nation into the British Empire, by demanding their consent to accept the sovereignty of the King in a ceremony of subordination that likely confused the Cherokees as much as Brébeuf's globe bemused the Wendat.

From the evidence that Kathryn Magee Labelle, Kristalyn Shefveland, and Ian Chambers present, it is striking how feasible one world seemed in the minds of these three colonizers; however, this is my own reading of

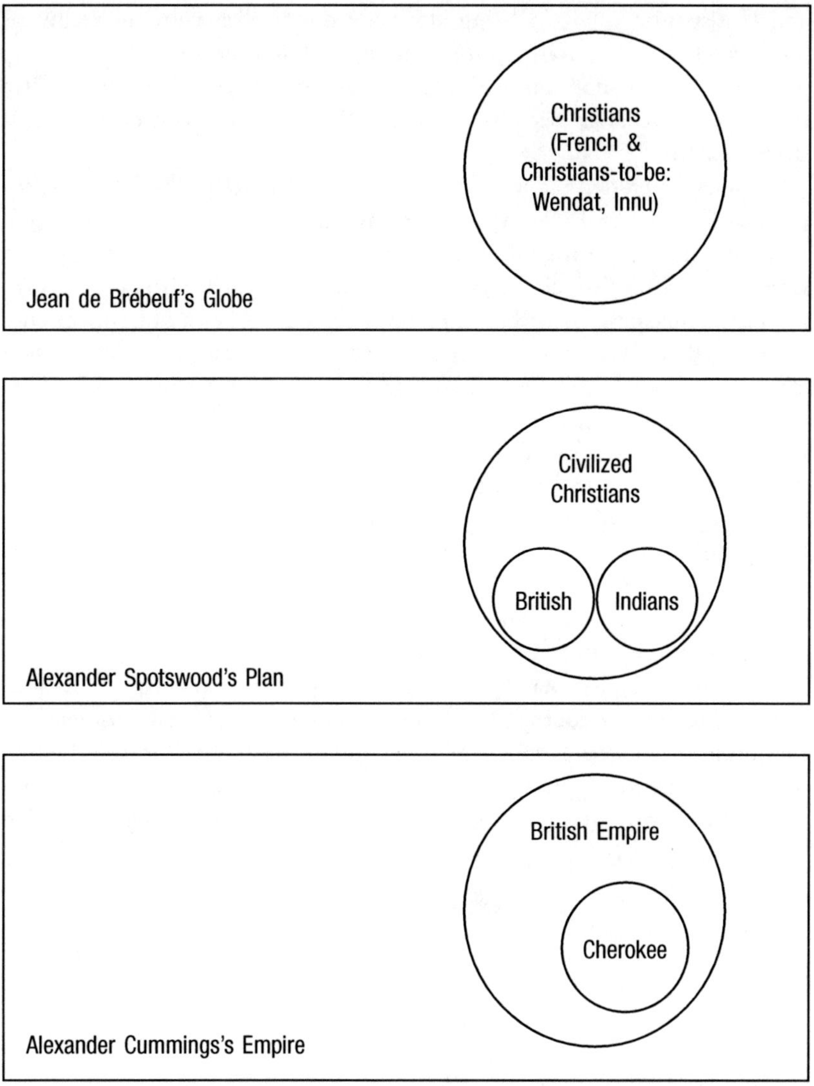

Figure 4. Euler Diagram Comparing European Visions of Colonization.

their evidence and not these authors' own arguments. Labelle and Chambers both believe that Indians had a more holistic and welcoming culture than Europeans and that it was the Europeans who were two-world ideologues. Shefveland is interested in how Spotswood's imagined world of civilized and Christianized Indians living alongside the English failed in reality, as Spotswood's contemporaries John Fontaine and William Byrd II noted only piecemeal Indian adoption of European ways and described a hybrid world that could be characterized as more like Richard White's Middle Ground than Spotswood's Plan.

What interested me most about these three articles is how the authors push us "beyond two worlds" by pointing out that there are other alternatives open to historical study than simply the juxtaposition of Indians and Europeans, each of which can be demonstrated in a Euler Diagram. Returning to the metaphor of Brébeuf's globe at the end of her essay, Labelle suggests that Brébeuf should have brought two globes because Jesuit conversion efforts more closely reflected a two-worlds ideology by separating Christian converts from their pagan kin and by introducing to the Wendat (Huron) the concept of two worlds in the afterlife, Heaven and Hell. However, the Wendat appear to have had a sense of bifurcated worlds in their own belief system because they imagined two mirror-image worlds, one for the living and one for the dead (Figure 5). This is a powerful reminder of how, whether French or Wendat, the afterlife existed as a distinct world or set of worlds full of import and meaning—a world that historians usually ignore as a space where history can be made.

Shefveland and Chambers also add complexity to the usual juxtaposition of Indians and Europeans by illuminating a diverse and contentious European settler population with different understandings of how best to relate to Indians (Figure 6). Presumably, Spotswood and Cumming both rested their diplomatic initiatives on the prospect of enhancing the Indian

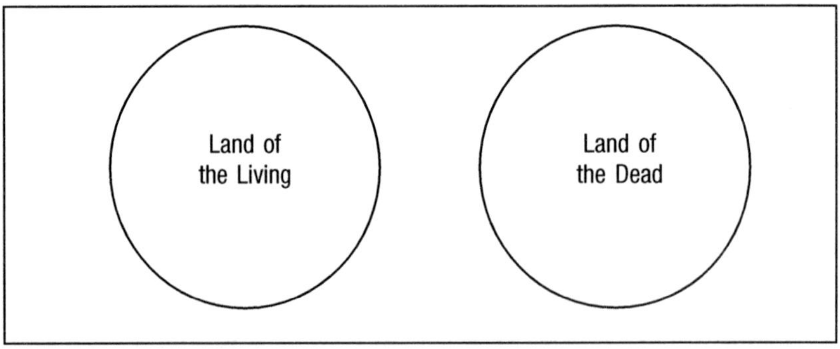

Figure 5. Euler Diagram of Wendat Worlds.

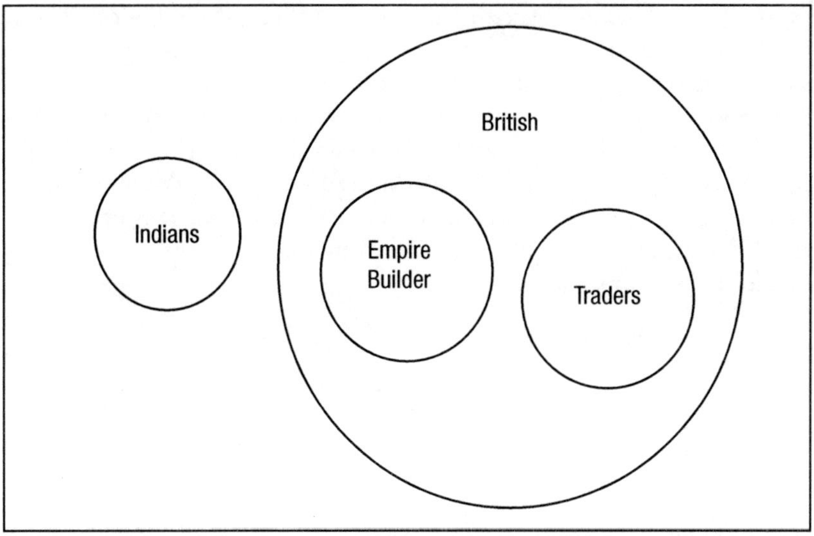

Figure 6. Euler Diagram of Indian-European Relations in the Eighteenth-Century Southeast.

trade, but they seem to have been guided more by an idealistic sense of imperial mission than just the material demands of trading. Shefveland distinguishes between the world of the imagined (Spotswood's vision) and the hybridized world that existed in reality (that is, the world that was observed by John Fontaine and William Byrd II), but these two worlds might also be thought of as that of the empire-builder and the trader. Cumming's romp through Cherokee Country, though assisted by those British most familiar with Cherokee language and customs—the traders—did engender trader animosity towards Cumming, because George Chicken, Ludovick Grant, and the other traders, knew that the Cherokees might interpret his brazen acts as insults and that they could all be killed as a consequence. Shefveland and Chambers do not pursue these differences within the European population, but they do incidentally point to how acknowledging some differences within a cultural group can help go beyond a two-worlds perspective without our becoming overwhelmed by complexity.

Thus, I do not believe that a two-worlds perspective is in itself a problem. Instead, it seems a natural offshoot of a human predilection for binary thought, as in self and other, us and them. Moreover, for people in the past as well as for scholars, conceiving of two worlds in relationship could serve as a useful analytical tool for making sense of chaos. The problem with two worlds seems to rest mainly with our dependence on the construct of an Indian world juxtaposed against a European world. While ethnohistorians have long lamented the paucity of scholarship that breaks up the paradigm of Europeans versus Indians to focus instead on Indian relationships with other Indians, these papers suggest to me that there are a range of alternative juxtapositions of worlds that could help scholars complicate the study of Indian-European relations.

Notes

1. I thank my Philosophy colleague Jc Beall for steering me toward clarity on this issue; however, my primitive discussion of Euler and Venn falls far short of how a logician would describe their differences. For more on Euler Diagrams, see Sun-Joo Shin and Oliver Lemon, "Diagrams" (3 September 2008), *Stanford Encyclopedia of Philosophy*, <http://plato.stanford.edu/entries/diagrams>/, accessed 16 February 2011; Eric Hammer and Sun-Joo Shin, "Euler's Visual Logic," *History and Philosophy of Logic* 19 (1998), 1–29.

2. Gregory A. Waselkov, "Indian Maps of the Colonial Southeast," in *Powhatan's Mantle: Indians in the Colonial Southeast*, eds. Peter H. Wood, Gregory A. Waselkov, and M. Thomas Hatley (Lincoln: University of Nebraska Press, 1989), 292–343.

3. The classic work on Indian-Indian relations history is Daniel K. Richter and James H. Merrell, eds., *Beyond the Covenant Chain: The Iroquois and Their Neighbors in Indian North America, 1600–1800* (Syracuse, NY: Syracuse University Press, 1987).

4. Richard White, *The Middle Ground: Indians, Empires, and Republics in the Great Lakes Region, 1650–1815* (New York: Cambridge University Press, 1991).

5. Nancy Shoemaker, *A Strange Likeness: Becoming Red and White in Eighteenth-Century North America* (New York: Oxford University Press, 2004).

6. "Relation of What Occurred Among the Hurons in the Year 1635, Sent to Kebec to Father le Jeune, by Father Brebouf," in Reuben Gold Thwaites, ed., *The Jesuit Relations and Allied Documents: Travels and Explorations of the Jesuit Missionaries in New France, 1610–1791*, Vol. 8 (Cleveland, OH: Burrows Brothers, 1897), 119.

II

The Real and the Imagined

4

Imagined Worlds and Archival Realities

The Patchwork World of Early Nineteenth-Century Indiana

James Joseph Buss

In 1834 Miami leaders in Indiana signed a treaty with the United States government that relinquished more than 200,000 acres of their "Big Reserve" in exchange for one dollar per acre and the payment of more than $50,000 in debts to American traders. President Andrew Jackson refused to sign the document, insisting that the goal of American Indian policy should be to encourage the permanent removal of Native communities, not facilitate smaller land cessions. American settlers in places like Indiana did not seem to care; they assumed that Miami departure was inevitable and that small land cessions ultimately would lead to more. An 1836 "Census of Indian Tribes" in the Great Lakes region might provide the most striking example of how Americans felt about the imminence of removal. The document contained two categories for counting Native people: "Number of Indians Emigrated" and "Number of Indians to Remove."[1] By the 1830s Americans in the lower Great Lakes clearly had constructed two imaginary worlds that came to define their spatial understanding of the region—one world belonging to themselves and one still occupied by Native people. Moreover, they believed that time would render one of those worlds invisible.

President Van Buren ultimately ratified the treaty in 1837 (after Jackson left office), and Miami leaders agreed the following year to additional land cessions. This time they requested more than $300,000 in payments, of which $150,000 would be used to settle tribal debts.[2] Such large monetary payments required mountains of paperwork. In order to protect both

Indians and the federal government from corruption, Congress formed commissions to validate the claims made by traders. Rather than confirm the existence of separate worlds, the commission reports have left behind evidence of an interdependent landscape comprised of Americans and Native Americans engaged in complex market relationships. When Miami chiefs ultimately agreed to sign a removal treaty, the resulting document should have offered additional evidence of the complicated patchwork world of early nineteenth-century Indiana, but Americans continued to insist that they and Native people resided in two separate spaces.

In November 1840, Miami chiefs privately drafted a removal treaty, wherein they voluntarily agreed to relinquish "the residue of the Big Reserve" and transfer the tribal government from Indiana to a new 500,000-acre reserve in present-day Kansas. Furthermore, they requested the United States pay $300,000 in debts that had been accumulated by the Miami community over the previous decades and pay the tribe an additional $250,000 in annual installments over the course of the subsequent twenty years. The treaty contained several special exemptions. Family members of principal chief Jean Baptiste Richardville and recently deceased former War Chief Francis Godfroy were given tracts of land in Indiana and permitted to stay. Furthermore, the U.S. government granted the extended families of both Richardville and Godfroy annual payments beyond those given to displaced Miami people. The treaties granted the Miami five years to complete the process.[3] Hence, while the tribal government moved west in the early 1840s, the families of former tribal leaders remained in the east. This partial removal, triumphed as the complete removal of the Miami by nineteenth-century Hoosiers, illustrates again the complexities of Miami–U.S. relations in this time period. Had the Miami been a homogenous and discernable group, removal could have been accomplished more easily, but trade, intermarriage, and personal friendships made a comprehensive removal of the Miami impossible.

Over the past 170 years, scholars, tribal members, and armchair historians have scrutinized the actions of whites and Indians associated with the treaties. In particular, those participants involved in drafting the 1840 treaty (especially Richardville and Godfroy) have been vilified, as historians conclude that they acted in their own self-interest to the detriment of their tribe. Richardville and Godfroy, so the story goes, abandoned the Miami, all the while profiting handsomely from greedy American agents who blatantly bribed and induced them to betray their people. Some scholars have gone so far as to dismiss the chiefs' role in the treaty as the actions of mixed-race individuals, who had adopted white customs and livelihoods and thus held looser connections to the rest of the Miami Nation. One scholar has even asked, were the two men, "who had adopted white customs and habits, degenerated or enlightened?"[4] Such questions rest upon a series of assumptions about nineteenth-century lower Great Lakes Indian history that are based on a two-worlds framework erected by nineteenth-century Americans who ignored the cross-cultural world around them in order to justify removal itself.

Historians have likewise stigmatized American traders using the bifurcated worlds of nineteenth-century Americans. Allen Hamilton (a close associate of Francis Godfroy and an Irish immigrant turned merchant) is often depicted as a land-hungry white trader, despite the fact that he played a key role in drafting the 1840 treaty and was named executor of both Godfroy's and Richardville's estates by those chiefs. An examination of private correspondence and commissioner reports reveals complex motives that scholars have long simplified as the actions of public individuals performing their role as American agents of settler colonialism. Viewing these individual actions in light of the larger market relationships that developed between whites and Native peoples in the region provides a deeper understanding of nineteenth-century Indiana as a complicated racialized landscape.

How might scholars reexamine these relationships? A different reading of understudied sources from the nineteenth century suggests exciting new interpretations. Letters exchanged between Miami chiefs and American traders, government reports issued by claims commissioners, and personal correspondence between American officials seriously question the writings of Hoosiers in nineteenth-century Indiana. A reexamination of these documents—available to historians but seldom used by them—points to a complex and intertwined reality for Americans and Miamis living in the region. Rather than resembling a landscape divided into two worlds, nineteenth-century Indiana consisted of a patchwork landscape within which whites and Indians lived side-by-side, often in reliance of one another. A deep rereading of these sources, in fact, reveals significant contradictions between the starkly divided landscape that white settlers described to outsiders and what they must have witnessed on a day-to-day basis. This chapter in *Beyond Two Worlds* examines three aspects of the two-worlds framework. First, it attempts to explore the origins of the framework in central Indiana in order to better understand how nineteenth-century Hoosiers used it to justify removal. Second, it proposes new ways of reexamining old sources that might reveal a different perspective on the region's history. And, finally, it argues that a deeper study of the very organization of archival materials might suggest new ways of understanding nineteenth-century Indiana.

Imagining Two Worlds

In 1829, the editor of the Democratic *Potawatomie and Miami Times* in Logansport, Indiana, wrote, "The crisis has arrived in which they [Indians in Indiana] are either to be *saved* or *lost*. The call of humanity is loud in their behalf; and justice demands for them, a last resting place for their feet."[5] A week earlier, he had opined that "ever since they became entitled to an annuity from the government, they have placed their dependence upon it for support, hence they have abandoned their habit of hunting, have become *lazy*, have lost their credit, and as the annuity is not sufficient to support them in their idleness, they consequently must suffer, or go where they can better their condition."[6] Accounts like these predicted a bleak future.

While the editor of the *Potawatomie and Miami Times* called upon readers to embrace removal as a benevolent act, writers in other newspaper columns argued that removal was necessary in order to ensure American progress. In 1834, the editor of the Logansport *Telegraph* argued that land held by the Miami in the Hoosier State would "no doubt retard the tide of emigration" and "check in some measure, the rapid progress of improvements." He concluded that "experience, the surest guide in all things" had "shewn [sic] that the red men" could "neither be happy, prosperous, nor contented, when surrounded by, and liable to the daily encroachment of the white population." The Miami in particular, he believed, were "ignorant of our language, averse to enduring the labor attending an agricultural life, deprived by our laws, of the rights of citizens" that had caused them to "sink into idleness, brutality, and intemperance."[7] Rather than suggest benevolence, this editor blamed Native people for their own predicament and scorned them for inhibiting white progress by abandoning agriculture.

Other writers agreed that the vision of two worlds best described the situation in Indiana, but they lamented its arrival. One writer in the *Cass County Times* claimed that the prospect of whites and Native Americans living side-by-side had passed. "There is no subject," he posited, "in which this country are so deeply interested, as the removal of the Indians. Everyday convinces us more and more of the necessity of their removal beyond the sentiments of the whites." The author attributed their destitution to the introduction of alcohol into the Miami community. "These people are not what they used to be," he concluded. "The time was when they were sober, honest and industrious; but since their intercourse with the whites, they have become dissipated, dishonest and idle. With few exceptions they have given up hunting, scillig [sic] or pawning their knives, guns and blankets for whiskey! . . . Justice to the citizens, and to the Indians themselves, requires that something should be done."[8]

Whether explaining it as benevolence, clearing an obstacle to progress, or lamenting the deleterious effects of alcohol among Native people, newspaper editors and writers concurred that Americans and Indians lived in two disparate worlds—one of Indian primitivism and another of American ingenuity and progress; one looking backward, the other forward. In attempting to justify Indian (and particularly Miami) Removal, American settlers constructed a bifurcated landscape within which individuals were judged by how well they functioned in their respective roles. Native people were supposed to remove themselves from the Hoosier landscape, while whites served as harbingers of progress who would remake it as their own.

Nathaniel West's Tangled World in Indiana

The United States government agreed to incur the debt of the Miami Nation through a series of treaties signed in the 1830s. In 1838, Nathaniel West arrived in Indianapolis to investigate claims made by traders against Indians in the region. As United States Commissioner for claims against the Miami, he was charged with protecting both the tribe and the federal government against abuses. Consequently, West posted notices in local newspapers inviting traders to submit the necessary paperwork before he undertook the tedious task of validating each claim. The commissioner took his job seriously and confided in American trader Allen Hamilton, "I feel that I have done strict justice to all; and if I have erred, it will be from want of capacity, and not of good intentions." He considered Hamilton a close friend of the Miami and an honest person, as he made allowances for all of Hamilton's claims. For the many individuals who filed false claims, West wrote, "I care not a fig for the rest, selfish men, who cannot judge correctly when their particular interests are involved." These men, he believed, would "as a matter of course complain," as would "men of desperate fortunes who look upon the Indians property dispensed under a Commission as a lottery in which they may draw a prize."[9]

Because West went through the arduous process of examining each claim, his reports reveal interesting insights into market transactions in early nineteenth-century Indiana and question the rigidity of the two worlds described in the pages of local newspapers. The first thing that he discovered was that the Miami had accumulated an incredible amount of debt. In fact, the commissioner admitted that it was nearly impossible to get Miami tribal members to testify about the validity of claims, because, in testifying, they would be forced to admit publicly their personal involvement in charging items and goods against the tribe's annuities. "Each individual for his extravagance had contributed to involve the whole," West wrote in the report, "was of course restrained from coming forward and in public, acknowledging his indebtedness, not only for fear of the censure, but perhaps, even the knife of the more economical." Instead, the Miami chiefs spoke on behalf of the nation during the testimonies. For several days, West believed that "nearly the whole nation" had descended upon the treaty grounds to witness the process and consult the chiefs about disputed affidavits.[10]

The deliberations revealed the extent of interaction between the Miami and their white neighbors. It quickly became clear that the Miami did more than simply purchase items from Americans in the region. One of the first disputed claims involved a charge by local handyman John Duquette. Duquette's written statement listed debts incurred by Miami chief John B. Richardville and his family for labor performed while building at least four homes and "digging a well and clearing four acres of land." Duquette claimed that the Richardville family had paid him $690 but still owed an additional $590. Richardville disputed the charge, arguing that he had paid the remaining balance. West ultimately disallowed the claim after Duquette refused to travel to the treaty grounds to testify. At first Duquette declared he was too ill to travel, but a later note from Francis Godfroy explained that Duquette "was busy planting hay" for the Miami chief near his home.[11]

We might posit several interpretations for Duquette's claim. First, on the surface, it illustrates the dependence of local white settlers on the Miami for wage labor, something that suggests a more complicated relationship than short and simple hand-to-hand commercial exchanges. Furthermore, a closer reading of West's report indicates that long-term relationships existed between whites and Indians. In the affidavit, Duquette admitted that he had worked for the Richardville family for more than a decade (1820–1838) and been paid for his work on at least five occasions by five different family members. Although the report does not chronicle extensively these commercial relationships, one might imagine what they entailed. The elder Richardville must have negotiated wages with Duquette and outlined his plans for the construction of multiple houses. Additionally, members of Richardville's household might have inspected Duquette's work to ensure that it was finished on schedule and to the satisfaction of the family. Finally, payment (and multiple payments in this case) required another moment of contact and conversation between white workers and Indian employers. It is not hard to imagine the numerous personal exchanges between the Richardville family and Duquette that are captured in the pages of the commissioner's report.

Additional affidavits point to additional (and more continuous) private exchanges between Miami community members and settlers. John Smith issued claims for $150 worth of baked goods. Smith testified that he and his father owned a bakery in Logansport, Indiana, where members of the Miami community "frequently credited at the shop" as they visited and purchased bread.[12] Smith's account of daily interaction between Americans and Indians corroborates earlier generalized accounts. In 1834, a letter to the Logansport *Times* claimed that "the red men, you know, are objects of curiosity, 'away down in old Virginia.' Not so here. They visit town daily: sometimes in great numbers, dressed fantastically in the finest broad cloth, and having their ears, noses, arms, &c, ornamented."[13] In a world described by most newspaper accounts as bifurcated and segregated, short testimonials bound within the claims commission report point to a different reality. Smith's testimony (corroborated by the letter to the newspaper) suggests that whites and Indians moved freely among one another in frontier Indiana. In fact, the documents suggest that it was commonplace for Miami tribal members to visit bustling canal towns, like Logansport or Delphi or Lafayette, to conduct routine business.

Contact and exchange between whites and Miami tribal members occurred in Indiana beyond the limits of frontier towns and trading posts. Fort Wayne tavern-keeper Zenas Henderson issued claims totaling more than $2,200 in charges made by Miami Indians for "provisions of all kinds, merchandize of various kinds, feeding and keeping." He argued that tribal members frequently visited his establishment in Fort Wayne and charged goods against the Miami account. Since the federal government refused to reimburse traders for alcohol, his personal records (not included in the claims commission report) must have included a number of items such as food and daily provisions. In any case, some of Henderson's claims came from purchases made outside of Fort Wayne. Henderson routinely traveled to the local treaty grounds (near the home of Richardville) and sold "gingerbread, pies, raisins, bread, etc." to the Miami. These debts demonstrate both Henderson's reliance on the Miami for income and his near daily exchange with members of the Miami community.[14]

Additional claims included in Henderson's affidavit reveal a prolonged relationship between the proprietor and other local tribesmen. Sometime prior to the 1836 treaty, a Miami man named Owl became sick at Henderson's inn. The tavern-keeper housed him for nearly three months during his recovery. Over the course of that time, Henderson fed and interacted with numerous Miami who came to visit the ailing Miami community member. Again, though scant on detail, these short passages in West's records indicate both prolonged and complicated relationships between whites and Indians.[15]

West's report provides abundant evidence that Indians routinely visited white towns and Americans likewise visited Miami communities. In the 1830s John Baccas delivered more than $900 worth of bread to the Miami and Potawatomi.[16] During that same period, John Miller, performed manual labor for the Miami chiefs and charged $264 for "clearing up land, fencing and ploughing land, and for a stolen horse."[17] Despite claims that the Miami had become docile people who refused to farm and adapt to American ways, Miami chiefs employed white neighbors to clear fields, fence pasturelands, and build impressive log homes. Essentially, they had become commercial farmers who hired white day-laborers. While West's report chronicles hundreds of face-to-face transactions and exchanges between whites and the Miami, personal correspondence between Miami chiefs and white traders alongside Miami trading-post ledgers provide additional evidence documenting the complex market economy of the lower Great Lakes.

As they attempted to impose American hegemony in the region and usher out Native Americans, whites became increasingly defensive about maintaining the illusion of a bifurcated two-worlded landscape. West's aversion toward fairness and justice ultimately threatened this version of the Hoosier imagination. In 1839, Congress again deployed Nathaniel West to Indiana to conduct an investigation of claims made against the Miami. During that investigation, West admitted that he faced a hostile environment. "Darkness is around me," he told Miami chief Francis Godfroy, "and I well know that I have *secret enemies* and *false friends* but with Gods [sic] help I will faithfully do my duty so that which is just and right so far as my poor ability will enable me to do so."[18] West understood that lucrative markets for fur, trade goods, and land provided opportunities for unscrupulous individuals to exploit the Miami, since they controlled access to area lands and resources. For their part, Miami leaders appeared deeply cognizant of the shifting political landscape around them, as evidenced in their correspondence with West.

A Patchwork World in a Market Economy

West was not the only American to write to Godfroy. In fact, the Miami chief's business papers include charges from local blacksmith shops, tailors, saddle makers, and a host of local laborers and field hands that further reveal the complex world of market exchanges and interpersonal relationships of

Indiana. Like the claims included in West's reports, these documents have long been overlooked due their brevity; most of them include little more than dated entries for purchases, sales, or charges. Still, within the terse statements long ago inked on the pages of Godfroy's ledger books, evidence abounds that likewise indicates a continuous interaction between the Miami community and their white American neighbors. For example, a single entry states that Francis Godfroy owed $22.45 to local blacksmith David Beggs for services rendered between December 1835 and August 1836. In an only slightly longer explanation of the charges, Godfroy recorded that Beggs performed at least seventeen separate jobs—from mending horseshoes to sharpening farm equipment.[19] Another entry from the first half of 1837 records twenty-one additional jobs that included shoeing horses and repairing equipment for the Miami mill for a total of $48.75.[20] While Beggs provided basic services to the Miami as a government-appointed blacksmith, his work also provides evidence of a multifaceted Miami history that included the rearing of livestock (shoeing), the raising of agricultural crops (sharpening of farm equipment), and the processing of grain at the Miami mills (maintenance of mill parts).

In addition, Godfroy's ledgers provide evidence that defies notions of nineteenth-century Indian primitiveness. Over the course of the 1830s, Francis Godfroy built numerous homes for himself and his extended family. In May 1837, he paid John Christman more than $663 to construct a two-story home measuring 28 by 18 feet. The home included paneled doors, cornicing, and paned windows.[21] The following year Christman returned to paint the home, build shutters for the windows, and erect a smokehouse.[22] By late March 1839, Godfroy hired additional workers to begin construction on a second large timber-framed home. This two-story building, which measured 35 by 20 feet and sat on a stone foundation, included tongue-and-grooved floors, paneled doors, corniced moldings, glass windows, and a shingled roof. In all, labor and materials totaled $1,037. More than 500 feet of shelving lined the walls of the lower floor, providing space for goods and supplies, as the home also served as a trading house for Miami chief.[23]

Godfroy's home and trading house were emblematic of the larger patchwork nature of central Indiana, where whites and Indians cohabited the region. The private reservations granted to Miami chiefs and families during the 1830s treaties were often sold to raise much needed capital, especially during the economic crises that affected both whites and Indians in the last half of the decade. Private land transactions between Miami chiefs and their white neighbors meant that the physical boundary between whites and Indians described by proponents of removal as a distinct frontier boundary rarely described the realities of life in Indiana, let alone the geographic separation of whites and Indians.[24] Instead, white settlements often neighbored Indian reserves or were surrounded by them. What's more, Miami leaders did not always confine themselves to traditional reservations. Jean B. Richardville built a stately Greek revival mansion near Fort Wayne in 1827 (costing more than $2,200) in addition to his large home and storehouse near the forks of the Wabash River. At Fort Wayne he hosted American officials and business leaders and participated in typical American frontier urban life.[25]

Despite being dead at the time that the 1840 treaty was signed, Francis Godfroy played an integral role in drafting the document. His close association with Allen Hamilton led to special exemptions for Godfroy's larger kin network. The two men were part of a larger network of traders and trading houses that stretched along the Wabash River from Fort Wayne, Indiana (in the northeast corner of the state) to the Ohio River (in the southwest corner). By the 1830s, when the two men started writing one another, the Wabash River had become a major thoroughfare for goods and people. Although they were both connected to the larger web of white and other Indian traders, Godfroy and Hamilton developed a special relationship that differed from the common interface between traders and Indians. Letters between the two men reveal a close and personal bond that extended beyond business (and beyond the relationships that they held with others in the area).[26] Although their public association began in the 1820s, when Hamilton began shipping goods to Godfroy, their closer personal connection appears to have begun in 1834 when Hamilton sent Godfroy a confidential letter informing him that American officials intended to conduct a treaty council among a limited number of Miami leaders. He urged Godfroy to attend.[27] It's difficult to surmise Hamilton's intentions in this early case, but the letter convinced Godfroy to travel to the meeting and prompted him to draft a petition to the Indiana State Legislature demanding they return a tract of land that had been granted him by an earlier treaty.

Over the following years, Hamilton helped Godfroy fight for those lands. The wealth that Godfroy accumulated as a result of these treaties has become the focus of those who castigate him as an ambitious mixed-race Indian who sought personal gain rather than tribal autonomy. It is true, the Miami leader had built a trading empire along the Wabash, including nearly 4,000 acres of land and an impressive home and trading post that eclipsed those of his white neighbors.[28] The letters between Godfroy and Hamilton portray complex motivations behind their actions. Godfroy was deeply concerned about the consequences of removal on his immediate and extended families. Like Richardville, Godfroy served as patriarch to an extraordinary number of kin that included hundreds of individuals living along the Wabash and Mississenewa Rivers. In fact, the Godfroy homestead and trading post, called Mount Pleasant, served as the center of a larger Miami kinship network. When he visited there in 1839, English painter George Winter remarked that that Mount Pleasant had been known as "head quarters for the Miamies of the neighboring villages."[29]

Godfroy's business papers, located in the Allen Hamilton collection at the Indiana State Library, demonstrate the war chief's importance within this network. Bills and receipts from across Indiana document the number of Miami individuals that were allowed to purchase goods using Godfroy's credit.[30] For much of the late 1830s, the nearly 350-pound Godfroy lay ill at his home in Mount Pleasant, while his family traveled about the state living comfortably under their father's care. But Godfroy's generosity and concern for family extended beyond his own children (from at least three wives). In 1838, Godfroy wrote Allen Hamilton, asking him for a personal favor. Approximately one year earlier, Godfroy's brother, Louis, who had also served as war chief, died. Louis had placed his estate in the hands of French trader Francois Comparet. But Francis Godfroy did not trust that Comparet was administering the estate in the best interest of his brother's family. He wanted Hamilton to intervene and instructed him to question Comparet's decision to sell Louis (sometimes spelled Lewis) Godfroy's land in order to settle his debts. Francis argued that the debts should have been paid as a result of a subsequent treaty, but if they weren't, the family should consider selling its lands near the St. Mary's River, rather than part with the more valuable lands near the Salamonie. "If necessary to have a lawyer," Godfroy wrote Hamilton, "employ one." If that didn't work, Godfroy offered to pay the debts himself.[31]

Godfroy's willingness to allow family members use of his credit, along with his personal fight to save the lands of his late brother, reveals an interdependent kinship system that linked scattered Miami villages across Indiana by the 1830s. Furthermore, the patchwork world of Indiana, which featured white settlements interspersed among the Miami villages, made it necessary for some Miami leaders to rely on white traders as intermediaries. As Godfroy languished in bed by the end of the 1830s, he relied more and more on Allen Hamilton to communicate with Principal Chief John B. Richardville. For much of 1838, 1839, and 1840, Hamilton passed messages about treaty proposals and land disputes between the two elderly chiefs. The letters that passed through Allen Hamilton's hands further reveal the patchwork nature of the region by demonstrating disconnections between the Miami villages. In 1838, Godfroy wrote Hamilton, asking him to resolve a land dispute involving tracts of the Miami leader's lands. It appeared to Godfroy, based on a new survey of all the Miami holdings in Indiana, that part of his improvements fell under Richardville's tract from a treaty negotiated earlier that year. Instead of dealing with the matter personally, Godfroy asked Hamilton to approach Richardville and resolve the conflict.[32]

Godfroy's trust in Hamilton is perhaps nowhere better illustrated than in the text of Francis Godfroy's will. Before he died in 1840, the Miami chief designated Hamilton and the elderly Jean B. Richardville executors of his estate—he must have been aware that Richardville, in his late 70s, would play only a minor role in executing the will, as he added a stipulation that if either Hamilton or Richardville died, the other would become sole administer. Godfroy entrusted the care of his extended family to Hamilton and asked that they be afforded private plats along the Wabash or Mississinewa Rivers—carved out of the larger Godfroy land holdings. Godfroy also anticipated that whites would try to gain access the lands once he died. In a final article of the incredibly detailed document, he ordered the executors of his estate "at the next treaty, use all proper influence to obtain for my family from the government . . . one section of land for each of my children and the same privileges in regard to the payments of their annuities and those of my wife as are now guaranteed to the family of Chief Richardville."[33] It was clear in the will that Godfroy had always intended on using his vast fortunes to secure the livelihoods of his large extended family. Even after the 1840 treaty, which took place a few months after he died, Godfroy's immense land holdings became a refugee camp for those Miami who did not want to remove. The 1840 treaty also revealed the complex web of Godfroy's kin whose personal fortunes were tied to his own. As part of the treaty, the government agreed to pay nearly $15,000 worth of debt that had been accumulated by Godfroy's family members on accounts across Indiana.[34]

Allen Hamilton played a crucial role in securing these items in the treaty. In fact, he acted as the sole American involved with drafting the original text of the document. Rumors spread to the nation's capital by September of that year suggesting that the Miami chiefs were willing to reconsider removal. Commissioner Crawford wrote Hamilton and told him, "although not authorized to hold a treaty," Hamilton should try and "reduce any agreement about it to writing."[35] What Crawford did not know was that Hamilton had already been working with Jean B. Richardville on drafting an agreement that reflected Godfroy's wishes. Hamilton's behind-the-scenes work on the document has often been "read" as the action of an ambitious land-hungry American looking to profit from the death of Godfroy and Miami removal in general. One historian, writing about the white traders of Indiana, describes them (including Hamilton) as "young products of the frontier and aggressive capitalists looking for the main chance."[36] As such, these scholars leave little latitude for understanding the actions of individuals in the removal period. But Hamilton's personal relationship with Francis Godfroy, rather than his public life as a merchant and trader, reveals how a reliance on a two-worlds framework has obscured our understanding of both Native and non-Native peoples.

Godfroy did not place his estate and the fate of his extended family in Hamilton's hands simply because Hamilton had performed well in negotiating land disputes. As early as 1838, Godfroy began sending his two youngest sons, William and Washington, to live with Hamilton at Fort Wayne, where they attended school with the young Hamilton children. In 1839, as Godfroy's sons prepared to join the Hamilton family in Fort Wayne, Allen Hamilton sent Godfroy a troublesome note: his own youngest daughter was ill and his wife distraught.[37] A few days later, before Godfroy could reply, a more foreboding message arrived at his door: Hamilton's daughter had died. Still, Hamilton told his good friend to send the boys anyway, and that the Hamilton family would "have them put to some good place," suggesting that they would find another appropriate family to house them while they grieved.[38] In response, the ailing Godfroy suggested that he personally make the 70-mile journey from Mount Pleasant to Fort Wayne to visit Hamilton and bring the boys. The journey was unusual as Godfroy rarely visited Fort Wayne, despite the fact that Miami Principal Chief Richardville lived there.[39]

The relationship between the Godfroy and Hamilton families shaped the way that other Miami leaders viewed Hamilton and his role in American westward expansion. Miami Principal Chief Jean B. Richardville also named Hamilton as executor of his estate, and when Richardville died in 1841, it became Hamilton's responsibility to ensure the livelihoods of both the Godfroy and Richardville families.[40] This began a new relationship between Hamilton and the Miami Indian villages, as Francis Godfroy's cousin Edward emerged as a leader among the Miami living around Mount Pleasant. In fact, Edward had long been a silent player in the relationship between his cousin and Hamilton. In the months leading up to Francis Godfroy's death, Edward's voice emerged, as the letters often contained two sections—one by Francis and another by Edward—both in the same hand.[41]

Francis Godfroy's legacy among the Miami can be seen today, as the descendants of his extended family continue to reside in the central part of

Indiana, near the same locations that Godfroy tried to secure over a century and a half ago. In 1847, it became clear just how much the late-Miami chief had meant (financially) to his descendants. After settling Godfroy's debts, Hamilton reported, and turned over to his descendants, an estate worth $30,701.68 (approximately $600,000 to $900,000 in today's purchasing power).[42] For his part, Hamilton went on to become a leader in the Fort Wayne community, helping found a local bank that financed the expansion of the city. Before he left Fort Wayne in the early 1860s (due to declining health), he was reportedly the richest man in the city.[43]

Godfroy, Richardville, and Hamilton's impressive wealth has long been used as ammunition by critics who wish to argue that the men spent the better part of the nineteenth century satiating their own greed at the expense of others. In 1830 Lewis Cass wrote Superintendent of Indian Affairs Thomas McKenney that Richardville was "an artful man, seeking his own interest, without much regard to that of the tribe."[44] Friends of the Miami attempted to convince officials that the Miami chiefs represented the best interests of the tribe. In 1837, Indian agent A. C. Pepper told Commissioner of Indian Affairs Thomas Hartley Crawford that Richardville was "remarkable over other Indians . . . in sagacity, skill, and wisdom." He also commented that the chief also displayed "a large fund of general intelligence and a thorough knowledge of the interest of his tribe."[45] In 1840, Samuel Milroy and Allen Hamilton wrote Commissioner Crawford that Richardville "has been a common benefactor to his people." Furthermore, they explained that a private reservation for the chief would "enable him to do justice to individuals of the tribe" who had not "received a due share of the money arising from former sales of their land."[46] Regardless, scholars of the twentieth century have fallen into the trap of judging these men based on their ability to conform to prescribed roles dictated nearly two centuries ago.[47]

The Historian's Tangled World in the Archives

Archives are peculiar places. They purport to preserve the collective knowledge of a community's past; yet most community members will never access their vaults, let alone their reading rooms. This is not due to inaccessibility. In fact, American archives are especially proud of their openness to the public—a by-product of an intensely democratic nation. In her enlightening examination of Dutch colonial archives, Ann Stoler argues that "inaccessibility has more to do with the principles that organize colonial governance and the 'common sense' that underwrote what were deemed political issues and how those issues traveled by paper through the bureaucratic pathways of the colonial administration."[48] According to Stoler, archival processes of taxonomy, categorization, and labeling have reflected colonial systems of classification and come to establish "foundational fictions"—stories of a community's creation and boundaries (spatial, racial, and otherwise)—that reinforced, and continue to reinforce, colonial categories of racial division.[49] Consequently, archival practices, just as much as archival contents, have proved to be highly influential in shaping a nation's interpretation of their past.

Despite their openness, American archives likewise have perpetuated a dated colonial system, especially in regard to archiving the history of Native people. The brevity of records pertaining to Native people has long swayed scholars in other directions, but, as I have tried to demonstrate, we might read deeper into these documents in order to challenge colonial categories and excavate the history of nineteenth-century American Indian history. It is true that American agents and commissioners seemed little interested in capturing the voices of Native speakers on the pages of official documents—many of the claims and affidavits are less than a page long, while some are only a few short sentences—still, much can be gleaned from these pithy documents. As suggested earlier, each record represents real personal contact and exchanges between Miami people and their white neighbors. Of course, reading beyond (let alone between) the lines requires historians and other scholars to do the uncomfortable (and for many, unthinkable) in being suggestive and speculative with our archival sources by supplementing them with oral histories and the work of scholars beyond our fields.

American archival practices still threaten to replicate nineteenth-century racial classifications. Scholars of the Miami may not be surprised to find a Francis Godfroy Collection housed in the manuscript department of the Indiana State Library, including three folders dedicated to the papers of the late war chief. Needless to say, I particularly was excited to glean these documents in conducting research for this chapter, if only to learn more about a man that has been only sporadically mentioned in the historical literature. I could have been disappointed, as I am sure many other historians were before me, when I found the folders filled with Photostat and Xeroxed copies of documents held elsewhere. Although some of Godfroy's personal papers appear in the collection, most of the letters are written to Godfroy from American Indian agents or traders (and even these are disappointingly scarce). In fact, the preponderance of letters were penned by Irish-immigrant-turned-American-trader, Allen Hamilton. But, when I looked into the Allen Hamilton Family collection at the same library I found something that seemed to disrupt the very framework that supposedly separated the men and their two worlds. Hundreds of documents, which include Francis Godfroy's business papers, personal correspondence, and his will, are interwoven with the business papers and personal correspondence of Hamilton—the papers of the two men comprise the 54-box Hamilton Family Papers.

On the surface (and in the online collection guide), Godfroy's papers are shrouded by an archival taxonomy that perpetuates colonial systems and power relationships. The collection (and the documents that capture Godfroy's life) is catalogued under Hamilton family's name, rather than retitled to reflect the diversity of contents in the collection. Only by browsing through the hundreds of folders that comprise the Hamilton Family Papers does one "discover" or "re-discover" the details of Godfroy's life and the rich history of an indigenous nineteenth-century Indiana landscape. These types of collections are precisely where a deconstruction of the two-worlds framework should begin. As Achille Mbembe reminds us, "The relationship between the archive and the state . . . rests on a paradox. On the one hand, there is no state without archives—without archives. On the other hand, the very existence of the archive constitutes a constant threat to the state."[50] For the people at the heart of this chapter, state and federal archives inadvertently preserved a window into the daily lives of Miami people in Indiana, particularly within official documents—claim commission files and the papers of leading businessmen—that were meant to support a narrative of settler colonialism and state building. Furthermore, some of these records capture the intimacy of colonialism that has long been overlooked.

The Godfroy and Hamilton letters, rarely mentioned in the historical literature, testify to a more complicated and integrated nineteenth-century world than a two-worlds framework allows. Within that older framework it has been easy to demonize Richardville and Godfroy as individuals who did not obey their cue and move westward. Or valorize them as crafty leaders who exempted their families from removal. Additionally, it has made it easy to generalize white traders as land-hungry villains looking to profit from Indian Removal. This chapter has suggested that historians, in particular, must do two important things to move beyond replicating the two-worlds framework. First, we must move beyond conventional methodologies and read beyond our sources. Second, we must approach archives in new ways that challenge the confining nature of archival classifications. In other words, we must stop allowing the past to dictate how we view historical actors in the present.

Notes

1. Logansport *Telegraph*, April 16, 1836. A third category, "Number of Indians of the Indigenot [sic] Tribes within Striking Distance of the Frontier," described Native communities west of the Great Lakes. Further reference to the Logansport *Telegraph* are indicated by *LT*.

2. Charles Kappler, ed., *Indian Affairs: Laws and Treaties* (Washington, DC: Government Printing Office, 1904); II: 250–51.

3. Kappler, 531–34.

4. Anson, 187.

5. Potawatomie and Miami Times, October 17, 1829.

6. Potawatomie and Miami Times, October 10, 1829.

7. *LT*, August 30, 1834.

8. Cass County Times, February 21, 1833.

9. Hamilton Papers, West to Hamilton, November 2, 1838, Box 5, folder 9.

10. "Report on Miami Claims, August 1, 1838–January 2, 1839," National Archives and Records Administration, Record Group 75, Records of the Bureau of Indian Affairs, General Records, Journals of Commissions, 1824–1839, Entry 106, Box 1.

11. Claim, 12.

12. Claim, 16.

13. *LT,* September 20, 1834.

14. Claim, 20.

15. Ibid.

16. Claim, 81.

17. Claim, 66.

18. Hamilton Papers, West to Godfroy, October 17, 1839.

19. Francis Godfroy Account with David Beggs, December 9, 1835 to August 20, 1836, Hamilton Family Papers, Box 3, folder 14.

20. Francis Godfroy Account with David Beggs, December 11, 1836 to June 2, 1837, Hamilton Family Papers, Box 1, folder 8.

21. Bill of Work for Francis Godfroys House, May 5, 1837, Hamilton Papers, Box 4, folder 7.

22. Poqua Godfroy House Bill with John Christman, December 1, 1838, Hamilton Papers, Box 5, folder 11.

23. Francis Godfroy House Bill (from John Gorrell), March 26, 1839 and Memorandum of Materials in Godfroys House (from P. Huling), March 27, 1839 both in Hamilton Family Papers, ISL, 4, 7. Also see Daniel Bearss to Francis Godfroy, August 17, 1839, Daniel Bearss Collection, Indiana Historical Society. Bearss settled part of the labor bill for the store house with William Healing.

24. Allen Hamilton conducted many of these land sales for men like Godfroy and Richardville. The details of these land exchanges can be found in the Hamilton Family Papers, Indiana State Library.

25. <www.fwhistorycenter.com/chiefRichardvilleHouse.html>.

26. Compare letters between Godfroy and Hamilton to those between Godfroy and the Ewing brothers, see William and Geroge Ewing to Francis Godfroy, August 17, 1830, Folder 1, Miami Collection, Indiana State Library, Indianapolis Indiana [hereafter referred to as ISL]; Ewings to Godfroy, April 4, 1831, ibid; Ewings to Godfroy, July 13, 1831, ibid.

27. Allen Hamilton to Francis Godfroy, 1834, ibid. The dispute was not resolved until several years later, and clearly Allen Hamilton was involved in the resolution, see Allen Hamilton to Francis Godfroy, January 4, 1837, ibid.

28. Sarah Cooke and Rachel Ramadhyani, eds., *Indians and a Changing Frontier: The Art of George Winter* (Indianapolis: Indiana Historical Society in Cooperation with the Tippecanoe County Historical Society, 1993), 121–23. The house at Mount Pleasant measured 35 feet long by 20 feet wide and was built only a short time before George Winter's visit, see Francis Godfroy House Bill, March 26, 1839, Box 4, folder 7, Hamilton Family Papers, ISL; Memorandum of Materials in Godfroy's House, March 27, 1839, ibid. The house cost $1,038.05 for supplies and labor. It was not the only large home at Mount Pleasant. Two years earlier, Godfory had a 28 feet by 18 feet two-story home built on the site for probably more than the 1839 house. The labor along for the 1837 building amounted to over $663.00—more than a 25 percent more than the later home. See Bill of Work for Francis Godfroy's House, May 5, 1837, ibid.

29. Cooke and Ramadyani, eds., *Indians and a Changing Frontier*, 121. In fact, Allen Hamilton was the person who convinced Godfroy to make Mount Pleasant as his home. Hamilton wrote Godfroy, "the late laws of the state are such that you can leave your property so that your children cannot sell it—the Mount Pleasant property of sections would make a delightful estate. See Allen Hamilton to Francis Godfroy, November 27, 1838, Miami Collection, ISL.

30. Godfroy's sons and extended family had charged food, clothing, lodging, and other goods to his account, see Francis Godfroy acct with JB Richardville, November 14, 1837, Box 4, folder 12, Hamilton Family Papers, ISL; Francis Godfroy acct with Hamilton, Gales and Co., Box 5, folder 1, ibid.; Francis Godfroy to Hill and Morreson, June 23, 1838 to November 2, 1838, Box 5, folder 9, ibid; and In Account of Francis Godfroy Purchase of Goods in 1839, Box 6, folder 5, ibid.

31. Francis Godfroy to Allen Hamilton, November 26, 1838, Box 5, folder 10, ibid.

32. Francis Godfroy to Allen Hamilton, January 14, 1839, Box 6, folder 1, Hamilton Family Papers, ISL.

33. Last Will and Testament of Francis Godfroy, February 26, 1840, Box 2, folder 14, ibid.

34. Kappler, *Indian Affairs*; and Rafert, 100.

35. T. Hartley to Allen Hamilton, September 18, 1840, Miami Indians, Box 26, folder 23, Allen County Fort Wayne Historical Society, Fort Wayne, Indiana [hereafter cited as ACFWHS].

36. Rafert, *The Miami Indians of Indiana*, 83.

37. Allen Hamilton to Francis Godfroy, January 2, 1838, Miami Collection, ISL.

38. Allen Hamitlon to Francis Godfroy, January 8, 1838, ibid.

39. Francis Godfroy to Allen Hamilton, January 14, 1839, Box 6, folder 1, Hamilton Family Papers, ISL.

40. Will of John B. Richardville (copy), 1841, Allen County Public Library Genealogy Center, Fort Wayne, Indiana. Another copy can be found in Miami Indians, Box 45, ACFWHS.

41. Edward Godfroy to Allen Hamilton, February 29, 1840, Box 7, folder 2, Hamilton Family Papers, ISL; Edward Godfroy to Allen Hamilton, March 11, 1840, Box 7, folder 3, ibid; Frances Godfroy to Allen Hamilton, March 19, 1839, Box 7, folder 4, ibid; Francis Godfroy to Allen Hamilton, April 13, 1840, Box 7, folder 5, ibid; and Edward Godfroy to Allen Hamilton, April 15, 1840, ibid.

42. Allen Hamilton acting as Executor . . . , November 8, 1847, Miami Collection, Box 3, ISL.

43. *Combination Atlas Map of Cass County, Indiana* (Kingman Brothers, 1878), 25–26.

44. Lewis Cass to Thomas McKenney, March 11, 1830, NARA, Letters Received by the Office of Indian Affairs, 1824–1881, Microcopy No 234, Roll 427, Michigan Superintendency Emigrations, 1830–1848 and Michigan Superintendency Reserves, 1837–1848.

45. A. C. Pepper to T. Hartley Crawford, November 6, 1838, NARA, Microcopy No. T 494, Documents Relating to the Negotiation of Ratified and Unratified Treaties with Various Tribes of Indians, 1801–1869, Roll 4, Ratified Treaties, 1838–1853.

46. Samuel Milroy and Allen Hamitlon to T. Hartley Crawford, November 28, 1840, ibid.

47. None of this is to suggest that Hamilton's actions were entirely altruistic; he profited greatly from his relationship with Miami leaders. Instead, this section suggests that relationships between individuals, like Godfory and Hamilton, are more complex and largely tied to the interdependent world of Indiana's market economy of the mid-nineteenth century. It is not, as some previous scholars and popular authors have suggested, merely a world where individuals can be categorized as "good guys" and/or "bad guys."

48. Ann Laura Stoler, *Along the Archival Grain: Epistemic Anxieties and Colonial Common Sense* (Princeton, NJ: Princeton University Press, 2009), 9. For similar arguments, see essays in Caroline Hamilton, Verne Harris, Jane Taylor, Graeme Reid, and Razia Saleh, eds., *Refiguring the Archive* (Norwell, MA: Kluwer Academic Publishing, 2002).

49. Doris Summer, *Foundational Fictions: The National Romances of Latin America* (Berkeley: University of Californian Press, 1991).

50. Achille Mbembe, "The Power of the Archive and its Limits," in *Refiguring the Archive*, 23.

5

The Indians' Capital City

Diplomatic Visits, Place, and Two-Worlds Discourse in Nineteenth-Century Washington, DC

C. Joseph Genetin-Pilawa

In 1978, Henry Old Coyote, a member of the Crow Nation and adviser to the Senate on federal Indian legislation, noted that Washington, DC, was a special place for American Indian people. "Indians love their country and this country is administered by the government so they tie the two of them together." Washington, he said, symbolized that government.[1] Indeed, of the approximately 370 treaties ratified between various Indian nations and the United States, roughly 20 percent were negotiated in the federal city, a significantly larger percentage than at any other single place.[2] Furthermore, for every delegation whose visit to the capital ended with the creation of a treaty, literally dozens more, either as authorized or unauthorized diplomatic envoys, made the trip in the nineteenth century. As Henry Old Coyote would echo decades later, diplomacy in the capital held critical meaning for Native people.

Washington City and the United States grew in tandem over the course of the nineteenth century, and one could argue, as art historian Vivien Green Fryd did, that the art, architecture, and public discourse in the former was designed specifically to justify and legitimate America's sense of Manifest Destiny. In *Art and Empire*, she asserted, "much of the sculpture and painting in the U.S. Capitol forms an iconographic program that outlines the course of North American empire by promoting and legitimizing the subjugation of the Native Americans."[3] To put it another way, taken as a whole, the public discourse of the capital reiterated spatially the evolving notion of "two worlds"—a normative, modern, urban, and superior world inhabited by whites, and a separate, pre-modern, and savage Indian world.

The process of "worlding"—imagining binary geographic, temporal, and cultural spaces, as well as assigning ethnic or racial groups to these separate "worlds"—was a critical component of both United States and European imperialism.[4] In the context of American Indian history, though, there were several corollary concepts that prove instructive here. In the nineteenth century, as the constructed landscape of the capital city took shape, most Americans came to believe that Indigenous people would soon vanish from the landscape altogether. In important ways this mindset shaped American colonial policy, as historian Brian Dippie argued, "belief in the Vanishing Indian was the ultimate cause of the Indian's vanishing." Robert Berkhofer suggested that the use of "traditional Indian imagery rationalized the needs of the United States in the continued push of Native Americans from lands desired by Whites."[5] If Vivien Green Fryd's argument that the built environment of the capital was designed to legitimate American colonialism is persuasive (and I believe it is), then we must take very seriously the manner in which the two-worlds framework functioned within the iconographic program she outlined, as well as within the broader public discourse of Washington, DC.[6]

In *Diplomats in Buckskins*, historian Herman Viola explained that the many Indian delegations who travelled to Washington, "generally underwent the same experiences—sightseeing, a round of social and diplomatic appointments, and interviews with high state officials."[7] This pattern, he argued, was designed to intimidate potentially hostile Indian leaders or to introduce them to the "superiority of civilized life compared to theirs."[8] The delegations, both authorized and unauthorized (or invited by the federal government and of their own volition) came to DC to negotiate treaties when negotiations in the field had failed; they came to quell intertribal warfare through mediation, or to declare peaceful intentions or friendship, or loyalty; they came to receive gifts from the federal government, many visited again and again. Some stayed.

Both Fryd and Viola present interesting and powerful arguments, but taken together, they also present a puzzling picture. If, as Viola suggested, a primary purpose from the perspective of policymakers, was to intimidate Indian delegations at worse, and introduce them to the wonders of non-Native society at best, then it would be necessary to convey these messages over and over to many Indian people in many separate delegations (as they did). But, if the purpose of the iconographic program and public discourse, approved of by U.S. policymakers, as Fryd suggested, was to justify and legitimate federal colonial policies of removal, segregation, and coercive assimilation, in part because of the inherent backwardness of Indian people, and because their numbers were supposedly dwindling rapidly, then the presence on a daily basis of many Indian people around the capital would certainly undermine that very purpose. In other words, if the policymakers' goals were effective, how could any Indian delegates view the federal city as a place of reverence, as Henry Old Coyote suggested?

This essay focuses upon the inconsistencies and contradictions in the historical record concerning the Indian experience in Washington, DC.[9] I hope, through a re-reading of this evidence, to present a more complex, and ultimately more accurate, picture of this experience. In the following sections I suggest that the public discourse, a term used to denote artwork, drama, newspaper rhetoric, and guidebook language, reiterated spatially, in the capital, the evolving notion of "two worlds," by presenting Indian people as primitive, mystified by "modern" (especially urban) life, and at a most basic level, curiosities to be beheld by an urbane and sophisticated audience. In this way I reiterate Coll Thrush's assertion in *Native Seattle*, that in both popular culture and academic scholarship, "Indians and cities—cannot coexist, and one must necessarily be eclipsed by the other."[10] The public discourse in the capital, due to the city's position as the seat of political, military, and even social life in the nation, provided legitimacy to this two-worlds framework. However, a closer reading of this record demonstrates that this framework hides a much more complex and more interesting history of Native people engaging with non-Native society in Washington City.

While the amount of evidence that exists to reconstruct the Native experience of nineteenth-century Washington, DC, is staggering, the following paragraphs focus first on visual representations of Indian people, then on symbolic and rhetorical portrayals, all the while calling attention to the ways actual Indigenous people engaged with the visual, symbolic, and language of the capital city. While non-Native Washingtonians attempted to shape and define a two-worlds framework, Native people in the capital, by their presence alone, and often more overtly, questioned the foundations of American colonialism.

Carved between 1825 and 1827, a large relief adorns each of the four directional doors in the Capitol Rotunda. The first (Figure 7), entitled *Preservation of Captain Smith by Pocahontas*, was carved by Antonio Capellano in 1825 and depicts that mythic scene of John Smith's rescue by the smitten Indian "princess." That same year, Enrico Causici carved the second relief (Figure 8) called *Landing of the Pilgrims,* which illustrates an Indian

Figure 7. Antonio Capellano, *Preservation of Captain Smith by Pocahontas.* (Courtesy of the Architect of the Capitol)

man offering corn to a smiling, newly arrived Separatist. Nicholas Gevelot carved a third (Figure 9), called *William Penn's Treaty with the Indians,* which memorializes the agreement between Penn and the Delaware. Finally, in 1827, Enrico Causici finished his second relief, the fourth in the group (Figure 10). Named the *Conflict of Daniel Boone and the Indians,* it depicts a mortal struggle between Boone and an anonymous Indian warrior, both of whom are standing atop a second, already defeated Indian warrior. These reliefs all portray a moment of initial contact within the colonial New World, and the overall message of the group is one of inevitable subjugation or assimilation for Native people. As Fryd found, these works played an

Figure 8. Enrico Causici, *Landing of the Pilgrims.* (Courtesy of the Architect of the Capitol)

important role in the public discourse of the capital and "present situations from the past that seem to condone the policies being contemporaneously formulated by Congress and the presidents."[11]

Countless Indian delegations viewed these reliefs in the Capitol Rotunda, but the tale most often told, particularly in nineteenth-century guidebooks for DC tourists, involved the Ho-Chunk delegation of 1837. The story originated in William Force's *Picture of Washington and its Vicinity.* The Indians, whose "faces were painted of various colors, . . . [with] their scalping knives and tomahawks, and . . . [and] their long iron looking bows and arrows," examined the first three reliefs, but stopped in front of

Figure 9. Nicholas Gevelot, *William Penn's Treaty with the Indians.* (Courtesy of the Architect of the Capitol)

Figure 10. Enrico Causici, *Conflict of Daniel Boone and the Indians.* (Courtesy of the Architect of the Capitol)

the Boone depiction. They "looked intently for some moments, scrutinizing and recognizing every part of the scene . . . [and then] suddenly, as of one impulse, they raised their dreadful war-cry and ran hurriedly from the hall."[12] Force offered no explanation and his reader was left to wonder if perhaps the Indians could not distinguish between sandstone and flesh and were therefore scared for their lives, or if they ran out to avenge the deaths of the depicted Indians, his message was clear—these men were not suited to life in the city.

In 1857, actors performed a play called *Fashions and Follies of Washington Life*, for a DC audience. The play's purpose, wrote author Henry Clay Preuss, was "to exhibit a panoramic view of characters and events, illustrative of Metropolitan life and society." Among the clerks, politicians, debutantes, and slaves in the drama, was Tonawaha, described as a "live Indian Chief." The author offered an advance apology for Tonawaha's "bad grammar," and in his most dramatic scene, the Indian accosts Emma, described as "A true woman," exclaiming his love for her but lamenting "squaw no love Indian . . . Indian ugly man. Squaw love great white chief." Moments later, Noall, a man who is described as a gentleman who quite literally "knows all about it," enters, and insults Tonawaha, calling him an "ill-bred savage." The Indian responds by choking Noall. Only at the last second is he spared when Emma convinces Tonawaha to release him. Much like the heavily armed Ho-Chunk delegation that ran screaming from the Capitol Rotunda, Tonawaha is unpredictable, potentially dangerous, and according to the author, ill-suited for the fashions and follies of Washington life.

The theme of potential Indian violence also seemed to run through much of the public discourse. In 1828, Margaret Bayard Smith, a chronicler of social life in the early capital, declared herself the "self constituted delegate from the young ladies of Washington" and begged Secretary of War Peter Porter to "use his authority and forbid the ferocious Winebagos from assaulting the girls in the manner they did." Although Smith had not witnessed or experienced this treatment herself, she claimed that the Indians ran "after several young ladies and others they have caught in their arms and kissed, till decent young women are nearly afraid to walk out." Lewis Cass, then Governor of Michigan Territory, overheard the discussion and defended the Indians. In a letter to her husband, though, Smith exclaimed, "You have no idea, what a general dread [these Indians] inspired."[13]

Washington newspapers often commented upon the numerous Indian delegations that visited the city; many of their columns lent credence to the notion that Indians were ill-prepared for existence in a "non-Native world." In 1828, the *Daily National Journal* warned that the Winnebago delegation "moving through our streets . . . will no doubt be much annoyed by the countless number of idle boys who will follow them; but we hope they will be promptly punished if they attempt playing any of the tricks which we have seen practiced upon straggling Indians from the north." The language employed here was quite telling, the reporter imagined "straggling Indians," not clearly defined diplomatic envoys visiting at the request of the federal government. He went further and imagined potential violence, stating that the Indians would not "brook their pranks, and a sense of personal danger should restrain them." Later in the same article, the columnist asked—playing upon expectations of Indian drunkenness—that no one give the Indians "ardent spirits . . . [because they were] already sufficiently ungovernable, and when excited cannot be controlled."[14]

When not warning of potential Indian violence, newspaper commentators frequently speculated about how overwhelming the experience of visiting the capital must have been for Indian delegates. An 1858 letter to the editor at the *Daily National Intelligencer* detailed an account of a sightseeing tour by a delegation of Pawnee, Ponca, Dakota, and Potawatomi representatives. At the end of the article, the author imagined that "there can be no doubt the events of the day will be long impressed on their memories." The writer read the moment as a clash of two worlds when he noted that the Pawnee, who saw fit to honor their hosts with a dance, had to be "informed that, owing to the difference in taste, they must, in deference to the white ladies present," remain fully dressed. Moreover, he suggested that these worlds were incompatible, as the Indians were "hampered at not being permitted on the occasion to dance themselves 'out of their clothes.' "[15]

Under the headline, "Arrival of Distinguished Scalp-Hunters," another writer recounted the first evening tour of the 1870 Sioux delegation that included (among others) Spotted Tail, Swift Bear, and Red Cloud. The reporter described with amusement how the "bewildered sons of the forest" wandered about Pennsylvania Avenue before retiring to their hotel rooms. Once there though, the mysteries of modern life continued to confuse them, he suggested: "not knowing the comfort of mattresses and sheets," the Indians clung "to their primitive notions of luxury by sleeping on the floor."[16] Another reporter concluded, after several days of meetings and sightseeing tours, that the Indians were "rather astonished at the sights which have met their visions in the civilized regions they have passed through" and that Spotted Tail had "already more to tell his people than twelve months time will allow."[17]

Washingtonians who read about the wild and exotic Indians visiting their city had ample opportunity to view them as well. In this case, though, it seems they felt most comfortable seeing them on canvas and wood, rather than in the flesh. For a twenty-year period in the early 1800s, Charles Bird King, a Washington artist whose studio was located nearby the War Department building, painted Indian delegates. Thomas L. McKenney, the long-time commissioner of Indian Affairs used government funds to purchase the nearly 150 portraits and arrayed them on the walls of the Indian Office. Indian leaders from John Ross to Keokuk, Black Hawk to Pushmataha graced the portrait gallery. For more than three decades, distinguished visitors—international and domestic—made their way to the Indian Office to visit them.[18]

Despite being lost in a fire at the Smithsonian, it is possible to gauge the public response to the portraits and the overall message of the gallery by examining the words of a few of its visitors. In his 1830 guidebook, Jonathan Elliot encouraged his readers to stop at the Indian Office. It "possesses much interest," he stated, "perhaps more than any other in the Government." The paintings, he wrote, were "not only fine specimens of the art, but . . . close resemblance to the originals, they are *perfect*." His following sentences, though, read almost like a phrenological assessment. He described the clarity with which the Indians' heads had been portrayed, paying special attention to the "central hemispheres," because it is there that the "governing powers that lift man so far above the lower order of beings, and . . . distinguish his relative grade, and characteristics of mind and intellect" reside. Special care, he noted, had also been "taken to preserve the costume of each tribe." The scientific tone to his description concluded by echoing the Vanishing Indian trope. Imaging that Indians eventually would cease to exist, Elliot stated, "our posterity would ask in vain—'*what sort of a looking being was the red man of this country?*' " Seemingly unaware of the irony in this statement, he reminded readers—referring to the portraits, not the delegates themselves—that Indians "must be *seen* to be known."[19]

In her response to McKenney's Indian portrait gallery, British travelogue author Francis Trollope focused upon expressions she imagined on the subjects' faces. "The countenances are full of expression," she wrote, "but the expression in most of them is extremely similar." She continued, "I should say that they have but two sorts of expression; the one is that of very noble and warlike daring, the other of a gentle and naive simplicity, that has no mixture of folly in it."[20] The noble savage. The childlike innocent of the wilderness. The vanishing Indian. None of these impressions suggests that the subjects of the portraits would fit well in the "non-Native world" of Washington City.

If all this evidence were to be accepted uncritically, it would seem that the interpretation holds true, that Indian delegates were primitive, that they were mystified by the vagaries of modern urban life. In short, that they were from a separate and inferior "world." Of course, a closer reading of the evidence illustrates a much more complex relationship between the Indian delegates, Washington society, and the public discourse of the national capital. In fact, evidence suggests that diplomatic travel to DC was actually a normative experience for many Indian leaders and that Indian people carved out their own specific place within DC society, perhaps not far from where whites gazed fancifully upon their images.

Native leaders who visited the theatre in Washington behaved quite differently than those depicted on the stage. In 1837, a delegation of Sioux, Iowa, Sauk, and Fox from the Missouri River found great amusement watching "Miss Nelson" portray a mountain sylph. So impressed by her agility and beauty, the men saluted her and gave her gifts, including several of their war caps and a white wolf-skin robe. Though this was completely unplanned, the actress, in a display of impromptu grace, thanked the men, saying, she would "ever regard them as friends and brethren" and gave each an ostrich plume from her costume as a return gift.[21] This display was a far cry from the potential violence portrayed in the *Fashions and Follies*.

A closer reading of the evidence also calls into question the implications in many newspapers that Indian delegates found the "foreignness" of urban life to be disorienting. The same Margaret Bayard Smith who feared the "ferocious Winebagos" and their depredations upon Washington, DC, ladies, wrote of an 1805 Osage delegation, "One would have supposed in a scene so novel and imposing as was . . . exhibited to these sons of the Forest, that some indication of curiosity or surprise might have been discovered in words, looks or gestures." On the contrary, she believed they were imperturbable. No one, Smith argued, "could have mistaken their imperturbability for stupidity."[22] Sir Augustus John Foster, a British diplomat who lived in the federal city for two extended periods between 1805 and the War of 1812, wrote in similar ways about Indian delegations in his travel narrative. Referring to a group of Sauk, Mandan, and Osage delegates at a dinner party, he found them to be "particularly observant not to commit the slightest impropriety and their manners were perhaps more gentlemenlike than those of the greater part" of the other guests.[23] Newspaper reporters, though likely to focus on the sensational, in fact, often commented upon the poise of the Indian diplomats. A *Daily National Journal* writer referred to a Choctaw delegation in 1824 as "young men of education and virtue, with talents to conduct the business of their nation."[24] Furthermore, despite all the discussion of potential Indian violence, it should be noted that there were no known instances of Indians harming anyone during their diplomatic travels to the capital city.

Indian delegations engaged in interesting ways with Thomas L. McKenney's portrait gallery as well. The Ho-Chunk delegation of 1828, according to Herman Viola, enjoyed viewing the paintings, although they spent less time considering the phrenological significance of the images or imagining the inherent nature of those portrayed. Instead, they took pleasure in recognizing friends and neighbors who had previously visited Washington City. Seeing these friendly faces probably eased any anxieties they may have felt during their visit. They requested that their portraits be made to hang in the gallery and even offered to donate their clothes and other belongings when it seemed that there were not sufficient funds to pay Charles Bird King for the work.[25]

It is difficult to gauge the extent to which Charles Bird King manipulated his Indian portraits to reflect the two-worlds public discourse of the capital, but some evidence does exist to suggest that one of his successors, the photographer Alexander Gardner, did just that. An early collaborator with Matthew Brady, Gardner rose to prominence photographing scenes from the Civil War, even though many of his images were misattributed to Brady himself. In 1863, Gardner opened a studio on Pennsylvania Avenue and throughout the 1860s photographed Indian delegations and treaty councils both in Washington, DC, and in the Plains. Thus, when the bulk of King's portrait gallery was lost in a fire at the Smithsonian Institution on January 24, 1865 (the gallery had been relocated there in the late-1850s), Gardner was well-positioned to document, visually, the visiting Indians. In the aftermath of the fire, Smithsonian Secretary Joseph Henry suggested that photographs be taken of all the delegations in DC to replace the artwork that had been destroyed. While Congress failed to provide the funding, a private investor, William Henry Blackmore, bankrolled the work and in 1872, Gardner became the official photographer for the Office of Indian Affairs.[26]

Gardner photographed over a hundred different Indian delegates in Washington City, and the portraits are both striking and beautiful. Rather than seeking a true-to-life image, though, it seems that Gardner engaged quite actively with the two-worlds discourse. The delegates often came to Washington dressed in suits, pants, skirts, and other "odds and ends of the white man's clothing." Perhaps influenced by pressure from his private investor or because to do otherwise made no sense, Gardner kept an assortment of "feathers and beads and tribal garments" as well as weapons in his studio. Consequently his photographs often depicted Indians as anachronistic and ill-prepared for modern, urban life.[27] Herman Viola suggested that wearing Euro-American clothing made the subjects "entirely unsuitable to the noble savage image the photographers wished to portray."[28] Gardner's career in Indian portraiture was short-lived, though, as Mrs. Gardner complained about the "smelly collection" of Indian items kept in her husband's studio. Ultimately, the "sittings were something of an ordeal for the Gardner family" and came to an end.[29]

While the agitated 1837 Ho-Chunk delegation (described in William Force's guidebook) was the most talked about group of Indians who engaged dramatically with the Capitol Rotunda reliefs, many other Indian people commented on those same pieces in significantly different ways. In Benjamin Perley Poore's two-volume *Reminiscences*, the author (a veteran Washington journalist) told a similar story about a Menominee chief named Grizzly Bear. After looking at the first three reliefs and noting that the Indians fed, saved, and gave land to Euro-Americans, Grizzly Bear turned to the Boone image and lamented, "There white man kill Ingen. Ugh!"[30] During one of his many diplomatic visits on behalf of the Tonawanda Seneca, Ely Parker stood in the center of the Rotunda and questioned the legacy of each of the moments depicted in sandstone. Looking at an Indian offering a Pilgrim corn, Parker asked, "Who now of the descendants of those illustrious pilgrims will give one morsel to the dying and starving Indian?" Viewing the scene of Pocahontas saving John Smith, he asked, who among Smith's descendants would "give his or her life for an Indian?" Finally, in his most dramatic tone, he compared the fate of Indian people to that of the two Indian warriors depicted in the Boone relief. "Such is the fate of the poor red man," he said, "his contest with the whites is hopeless, yet he is not permitted to live even in peace, nor are his last moments given him by his insulting foe to make his peace with his God." "Humbly we ask whether justice will always sleep and will not the oppressed go free," he finished.[31] Far from screaming and running from the Capitol building, these men engaged with the iconographic program and critiqued the hypocrisies erected by the two-worlds narrative. The very presence of these men and their overt challenge to American colonialism marks a dramatic departure from the imagined capital, whereby Indians are supposed to be bewildered or simply absent.

Perhaps one of the most dangerous interpretations to be gleaned from the two-worlds public discourse of the capital is that an Indian presence in the city was irregular or uncommon over the course of the nineteenth century. Quite the opposite seems true. Sir Augustus John Foster's travel narrative is filled with interesting anecdotes that reveal fascinating details about the multitribal experiences in the city. In December 1805, he met with a group of Osage diplomats who were lodging with several Sauk, Dakota, Mississagua, and Missouri leaders. Across the street from this full house, stayed a Cherokee delegation.[32] In 1807, he escorted a group of Mandan leaders to the theatre, where they were seated next to five Osage men, one Delaware diplomat, and several Native women and children.[33] From hotel lobbies to theatre audiences, Indians existed everywhere in the nation's capital.

For Native people, Washington had become more than the home of the "Great Father;" it had become a place of entertainment, the locus of official Indian business, even a tourist destination. In essence, it had also become the Indian's capital city. Indian agents often played key roles in facilitating these delegations, either as a way to expedite treaty negotiations or to impress upon the Indians the military might, industrial prowess, and sheer population size of the United States. The annual reports of the commissioner of Indian Affairs are quite revealing on this topic. In 1871, Thomas Lightfoot, the agent for the Sauk and Fox of Missouri, encouraged the Indian Office to invite a delegation to the capital because, "they will never agree to make arrangements or sign papers . . . elsewhere than at Washington."[34] William Mitchell, an Army captain and agent at the Warm Springs agency in Oregon, suggested "a visit by a portion of these people to the seat of government would be of incalculable benefit to them, as they would learn how insignificant their numbers are as compared to their more powerful neighbors, the whites."[35] Echoing this sentiment, the annual report of the commissioner of Indian Affairs for 1872 described in detail the "unusually large and important Indian delegations" that visited Washington City that year. It asserted that "the Indians of the plains have, up to a recent date, really believed that they outnumbered the whites . . . It has only been the concurrent testimony of many chiefs and braves, out of many bands and tribes, that . . . made him appreciate, as he is beginning to do, the power and resources of the whites."[36]

Sir Augustus John Foster also became particularly close to a young Sauk diplomat named Wa Pawni Ha. The two men traveled together and enjoyed many long conversations. In his memoir, Foster wrote about introducing the young man to a Lake Superior Ojibwe who had moved semi-permanently to Washington where he was "to be educated."[37] While it might seem strange that an Indian man from the Great Lakes decided to move to and live in the capital in the nineteenth century, it was not entirely uncommon.

Over the course of the nineteenth century, the Indian's Capital City became a place where Indians lived, died, and even married. While many Indian diplomats stayed for only brief periods, others lived there for considerable amounts of time and could be described as "resident delegates."[38] Beginning in the 1820s, fulltime Indian lobbyists, especially from the Cherokee, Creek, and Stockbridge-Munsee nations, as well as the Six Nations, established an important presence in the city.[39] It is tough to determine how many resident delegates might have been in DC at any given time, but, Herman Viola suggested that the "number . . . [was] far greater than one would imagine." In 1876, the commissioner of Indian affairs listed nearly twenty men from seven different nations as resident delegates.[40] Many notable individuals would fit within this description including John Ross, the Cherokee leader who spent a considerable amount of time in the capital and ultimately died there during the strained and tense post-Civil War era; William Adair, a Cherokee negotiator who made twelve diplomatic trips and died in DC in 1889; John W. Quinney, a Stockbridge-Munsee delegate made ten trips between 1823 and 1855; Red Cloud, the Oglala leader also made ten visits starting in the 1870, and Peter Pitchlynn, the Choctaw delegate lived in the Capital off and on in the mid-1800s, ultimately finding his eternal resting place in the congressional cemetery in 1874.[41]

The boundaries between the imagined two worlds of the public discourse blurred even further when issues of sex and marriage across racial lines surfaced. During his visit in 1870, Spotted Tail and the other Lakota delegates enjoyed watching the young women who worked at the Treasury Department. Spotted Tail himself wondered why President Grant would have only one wife when there were so many beautiful women in Washington.[42] According to Herman Viola, at least two delegates married white women in the capital, a Santee man in 1858 and an Ojibwe man in 1867. The newspapers, perhaps influenced by the two-worlds discourse, or perhaps attempting to maintain the imagined cultural gulf between Native and non-Native people through their columns, suggested that only "fallen" women would be interested in such affairs with Indigenous men and thus their brides must have been prostitutes. Other commentators offered a less lascivious explanation, claiming that the women simply worked at the hotels where the delegates stayed.[43]

In 1867, newspaper reporters devoted significant column space to the marriage between Tonawanda Seneca spokesman Ely Parker and the white debutante Minnie Sackett. The *New York Tribune*, reporting on the DC scene, noted that the "female portion of the community were exceedingly interested in the event, and . . . that not less than 5,000 of the fair sex visited the church."[44] The *New York Herald* called to mind another famous marriage that bridged two worlds, although in that case it was the Old and the New, when it stated, "A repetition of the grand matrimonial and spectacular drama of 'Pocahontas,' with the sexes reversed . . . Eli Parker, with his warrior's sash, plume and tribal trappings, leading his fair Caucasian bride to the alter, was a picture so seldom presented in these prosaic days that no wonder if sentimental fair ones in Washington flocked to witness the romantic event."[45] While the tone of these reports echoed the two-worlds discourse, it is important to note that none of the reporters condemned the marriage, nor did any violence or outrage surround the event itself. Instead, it seems that Parker, an Indian man and member of the DC community, proved to be an acceptable husband for an elite white wife.[46]

Some of the long-term Indian delegates boarded with Washington families, but most needed to find hotel accommodations for their short or lengthy stays. City residents, between 1837 and the Civil War, called the Union Hotel at 13½ St. and Pennsylvania, "Indian Headquarters," due to the regularity of Indian delegations boarding there. It was located only a short walk from the White House itself, and its proprietor, Jimmy Maher, had an interesting reputation. He was known, "to talk to the Indians in their native language . . . [and was willing] to accommodate every delegation, however large, with the most convenient quarters, where every attention will be paid to their comfort and convenience."[47] Maher had to remain vigilant, however, due to significant competition for the patronage of the Indian delegates. Since the Departments of War or Interior often covered the delegates' expenses, "rivalry among innkeepers, merchants, and other entrepreneurs who wished to feed at the federal trough spawned a host of abuses that were difficult to control." As was often the case when the Bureau of Indian Affairs got involved, "many government officials participated in the profiteering."[48]

Literary critic and screenwriter Greg Sarris has argued that "certain popular and critically accepted representatives of Indian selves created by non-Indian editors often establish a standard and become models for future textual representations on Indians' lives."[49] The creators of public discourse in nineteenth-century Washington, DC—newspaper reporters, guidebook authors, sculptors, painters, and playwrights—by focusing on the exotic, and imagining the capital city experience through Indian eyes, left a textual and visual record that masks more than it reveals. By presenting representations of Indians as primitive "sons of the forest," noble savages, childlike innocents from the wilderness, Vanishing Americans unfit for life in a "modern" urban environment, these writers and artists engaged in a national dialogue that drew arbitrary and often false lines between Native and non-Native experiences. In so doing, they also ignored a more complex and much more interesting local history that a closer reading of the evidence suggests. Washington, DC, was not always a seat of global power. It was a local place first—it became national, it became global. As the city evolved into the physical manifestation of the national imagination, images and words about Native peoples and histories, and more importantly Indigenous people themselves populated that landscape. Native experiences with the city shaped its process of becoming. Henry Old Coyote, whose words began this chapter, also said of Washington DC, "It's more like a shrine to the Indians . . . and they hold it as such and they feel that a certain reverence should be extended to the place."[50]

Notes

1. Herman J. Viola, *Diplomats in Buckskins: A History of Indian Delegates in Washington City* (Bluffton, SC: Rivilo Books, 1995 [1981]), 95. This quote and the one that ends the paper comes from an interview with Old Coyote on April 26, 1978. The transcript is held at the National Anthropological Archives, Smithsonian Institution.

2. Robert F. Berkhofer, *The White Man's Indian: Images of the American Indian from Columbus to the Present* (New York: Vintage Books, 1978), 171.

3. Vivien Green Fryd, *Art and Empire: The Politics of Ethnicity in the United States Capitol, 1815–1860* (Athens, OH: Ohio University Press, 2001 [1992]), 3.

4. It can also be understood as what colonization studies scholar, Ann Laura Stoler might call "a central colonial sorting technique," or a way that colonizers delineated who had access to which resources and rights, and who do not. See Gayatri Chakravorty Spivak, "Three Women's Texts and a Critique of Imperialism," *Critical Inquiry* 12, no. 1 (Autumn 1985): 243–61; and Ann Laura Stoler, "Intimidations of Empire: Predicaments of the Tactile and Unseen," in *Haunted by Empire: Geographies on Intimacy in North American History*, ed. Ann Laura Stoler (Durham, NC: Duke University Press, 2006.

5. Brian Dippie, *The Vanishing American: White Attitudes and U.S. Indian Policy* (Lawrence: University of Kansas Press, 1982), 71; and Robert Berkhofer, *The White Man's Indian: Images of the American Indian from Columbus to the Present* (New York: Vintage Books, 1978), 160.

6. In his recent book, *Hotel: An American History*, Andrew Sandoval-Strausz made an interesting and persuasive argument for studying the built environment. He wrote, "In short: talk is cheap; buildings are expensive. If we want to do scholarship 'from the bottom up,' we must take what people built as seriously as what they wrote down." See Andrew Sandoval-Strausz, *Hotel: An American History* (New Haven, CT: Yale University Press, 2007), 6.

7. Viola, *Diplomats in Buckskins*, 20.

8. Ibid., 28.

9. This essay is a preliminary exploration into a larger research project that examines the visual, symbolic, and actual presence of Native people in the nineteenth-century capital. Although I believe it can stand on its own, I also see it as a starting point for a much longer and larger study.

10. Coll Thrush, *Native Seattle: Histories from the Crossing-Over Place* (Seattle: University of Washington Press, 2007), 8. Political historian Kevin Bruyneel echoed and broadened the primitive/modern duality critique and suggested that "economic,

cultural, and political narratives . . . place temporal boundaries between an 'advancing' people and a 'static' people, locating the latter out of time . . . where they are unable to be modern, autonomous agents." See Kevin Bruyneel, *The Third Space of Sovereignty: The Postcolonial Politics of U.S.-Indigenous Relations* (Minneapolis: University of Minnesota Press, 2007), 2.

11. Fryd, *Art and Empire*, 40. There is a significant literature on the art and architecture of Washington, DC, much focusing on the Capitol building itself, however, Fryd's book is the only study that focuses specifically on Indian imagery. See also Charles E. Fairman, *Art and Artists of the Capitol of the United States of America* (Washington, DC: GPO, 1927); Ellwood Parry, *The Images of the Indian and the Black Man in American Art*, 1590–1900 (New York: George Braziller, 1974); Angela Miller, *The Empire of the Eye: Landscape Representation and American Cultural Politics, 1825–1875* (Ithaca, NY: Cornell University Press, 1993); Donald Kennon, ed., *The United States Capitol: Designing and Decorating a National Icon* (Athens, OH: Ohio University Press, 2000); William Dickinson, Dean Herrin, and Donald Kennon, eds., *Montgomery C. Meigs and the Building of the Nation's Capital* (Athens, OH: Ohio University Press, 2001); Donald Kennon and Thomas Somma, eds., *American Pantheon: Sculptural and Artistic Decoration of the United States Capitol* (Athens, OH: Ohio University Press, 2004); Cynthia Field, Isabelle Gournay, and Thomas Somma, eds., *Paris on the Potomac: The French Influence on the Architecture and Art of Washington DC* (Athens, OH: Ohio University Press, 2007).

12. William Q. Force, *Picture of Washington and its Vicinity, for 1848, with twenty embellishments on wood, by Gilbert & Gihon, and eighteen on steel, and an introduction by Rev. R. R. Gurley* (Washington, DC: William Q. Force, 1848), 57–61. This was a reprint edition that was remarkably similar to the 1845 edition. It was reprinted annually as new buildings and art installations were completed. In her Pulitzer Prize-winning book, *Washington: Village and Capital, 1800–1878*, Constance Green retold this story, noting "Negroes as well as whites doubtless relished telling of the fierce Winnebagos who were persuaded to enter the "Rotundo" of the Capitol and, upon seeing the frieze of Daniel Boone slaying a savage, suddenly uttered a dreadful war whoop and fled the building." (147) See Constance Green, *Washington: Village and Capital, 1800–1878* (Princeton, NJ: Princeton University Press, 1962).

13. Gaillard Hunt, ed., *The First Forty Years of Washington Society, in the Family Letters of Margaret Bayard Smith* (New York: Frederick Ungar Publishing, 1965 [1906]), 245. This episode is fully recounted in the letter from Margaret Smith to her husband, dated November 30, 1828, and reprinted in this collection.

14. "The Winnebago Visitors," *Daily National Journal* (Washington, DC), 24 October 1828.

15. "Indians at Washington," *National Daily Intelligencer*, 1 March 1858.

16. "Arrival of Distinguished Scalp-Hunters, "*New York Herald*, 25 May 1870. Article reprinted from Washington, DC.

17. "Disadvantage of Civilization," *New York Herald*, 26 May 1870. Article reprinted from Washington, DC.

18. Viola, *Diplomats in Buckskins*, 174–78.

19. Jonathan Elliot, *Historical Sketches of the Ten Miles Square Forming the District of Columbia; with a Picture of Washington, Describing Objects of General Interest or Curiosity at the Metropolis of the Union* (Washington, DC: J. Elliot Jr., 1830), 165–67.

20. Francis Trollope, *Domestic Manners of the Americans*, Vol. 1 (London: Gilbert and Rivington Printers, 1832), 314–15.

21. "The Indians Seeing the Play," *Daily National Intelligencer*, 4 October 1837.

22. Hunt, ed., *The First Forty Years*, 402.

23. Richard B. Davis, ed., *Jeffersonian America: Notes on the United States of America, Collected in the Years 1805–6–7 and 11–12 by Sir Augustus John Foster, Bart.* (San Marino, CA: The Huntington Library, 1954), 43.

24. "Choctaw Deputation," *Daily National Journal*, 2 November 1824.

25. Viola, *Diplomats in Buckskins*, 176.

26. For more on Gardner, see D. Mark Katz, *Witness to an Era: The Life and Photographs of Alexander Gardner, The Civil War, Lincoln, and the West* (New York: Viking Books, 1991), especially chapter 8, "The Indians." See also Raymond DeMallie, " 'Scenes in Indian Country': A Portfolio of Alexander Gardner's Stereographic Views of the 1868 Fort Laramie Treaty Council," *Montana: The Magazine of Western History* 31 (1981): 42–59.

27. Josephine Cobb, "Alexander Gardner," *Image: Journal of Photography and Motion Pictures of the George Eastman House* (June 1958): 124–36, 134.

28. Viola, *Diplomats in Buckskins*, 182.

29. Cobb, "Alexander Gardner," 134. Viola related a similar explanation. See Viola, *Diplomats in Buckskins*, 182.

30. Benjamin Perley Poore, *Perley's Reminiscences of Sixty Years in the National Metropolis* (Philadelphia: Hubbard Brothers, Publishers, 1886), 46.

31. Ely S. Parker, "Twenty-two pages of a diary with comments on . . . ," January 1–13, 1847, Box 2, 1846–1848, Ely S. Parker Papers, American Philosophical Society, Philadelphia, PA.

32. Davis, ed., *Jeffersonian America*, 32.

33. Ibid., 28.

34. *Annual Report of the Commissioner of Indian Affairs*, 1871: 873.

35. Ibid., 1869: 606.

36. Ibid., 1872: 486–87.

37. Davis, ed., *Jeffersonian America*, 35.

38. Herman Viola does just that in his book.

39. Viola, *Diplomats in Buckskins*, 85. Some of the more prominent "resident delegates" included Ely S. Parker (Seneca), John Quinney (Stockbridge-Munsee), John Ross (Cherokee), John C. Adams (Stockbridge-Munsee), and Peter Pitchlynn (Choctaw). For more on Pitchlynn, see "Peter Pitchlynn, Chief of the Choctaws," *Vermont Chronicle*, 23 April 1870.

40. Viola, *Diplomats in Buckskins*, 88. The list of resident delegates was compiled at the request of Congress.

41. Ibid., 79–91.

42. Ibid., 150–51.

43. Ibid., 145.

44. *The New York Daily Tribune*, December 25, 1867, p. 1.

45. "The Parker-Sackett Nuptials," *New York Herald*, December 25, 1867.

46. For more on this wedding ceremony, see C. Joseph Genetin-Pilawa, " 'All Intent on Seeing the White Women Married to the Red Man': The Parker/Sackett Affair and the Public Spectacle of Intermarriage," *Journal of Women's History* 20, no. 2 (Summer 2008): 57–85.

47. Ibid., 123. For Maher's advertising statement, see *Boyd's Washington and Georgetown Directory* (Washington, DC, 1860).

48. Viola, *Diplomats in Buckskins*, 54.

49. Greg Sarris, "American Indian Lives and Others' Selves: The Invention of Indian Selves in Autobiography" in *Thinking Bodies*, edited by Juliet Flower MacCannell and Laura Zakarin (Stanford, CA: Stanford University Press, 1994): 141–48, 144.

50. Viola, *Diplomats in Buckskins*, 95.

6

Under One Big Tent

Race, Resistance, and Community Building in Two Nineteenth-Century Circus Towns

Sakina M. Hughes

On June 17, 1905, the *Michigan Daily* reported that the best tenors in vaudeville were "Brown and Brown," two "Indian boys from Butler Indian School."[1] Interestingly, the "Brown Brothers" were neither related, nor Native American. Like other performers of the day, Brown and Brown chose to conceal their African-American roots, for what they believed to be safer and more lucrative performance identities. Five years later, Harry Brown, one of the "Indian" tenors, commented on professional race-shifting in the black newspaper, *The Indianapolis Freeman*: "There are lots of acts that . . . are daily changing their nationality—those that can. . . . Seven years ago I put Indian before or after my name, and it has been a savior for me."[2]

Perhaps surprising now, the Brown Brothers' story may have been representative of many successful turn-of-the-century artists of color who used American attitudes about race and ethnicity to their professional advantage. Musicians and artists toured the country in circuses, minstrel shows, Wild West shows, and other itinerant performance troupes that relied heavily on racial and ethnic stereotypes. This chapter argues that African Americans and American Indians at the end of the nineteenth century used circuses to build their careers and communities while manipulating meanings of race and shaping the traveling entertainment industry itself. An examination of two circus communities—The Wallace Shows in Miami County, Indiana, and The Sells Brothers Circus in Sellsville, Ohio—reveals how blacks and Indians were crucial actors in circus operations, local community formation, and extended professional networks.[3] This chapter will consider challenges for performers of color, explore how black and Native American employees used opportunities within circus towns to build careers and communities, and consider how they used race and color expectations to navigate through racially oppressive times.

Both the Sells Brothers and Wallace shows included blacks and Indians in most levels of their productions, from labor to performance and management.[4] In both communities, the local quarters and the traveling shows often shielded black and Indian employees from racial violence and offered alternative professional opportunities that facilitated the creation of relatively stable social and professional networks. Increased professional opportunities and institution-building in circus towns enabled some Native Americans and African Americans to break race-based labor and other social restrictions common to the era.

This window, of course, was veiled in irony. Post-Reconstruction circus managers may have inadvertently created spaces where employees could subvert the oppressive racial norms of the era. Knowing that a successful show, in part, depended on an increasingly diverse array of acts and performers, the Sells and Wallace managements took advantage of the multi-ethnic spaces they found in Ohio and Indiana and used these fertile grounds to plant seeds of even more ethnically, racially diverse work communities within communities. From a management perspective, this business model increased ticket sales to American audiences who were eager to view the exotic and reinforce current racial, class, and gender hierarchies.[5] Though they faced considerable race and class-based prejudices, Native American and African-American artists challenged white domination of the entertainment industry and popular culture. Their stories also provide a challenge to the two-worlds framework of American history.

Miami County, Indiana, and the Wallace Circus Quarters

The winter quarters of the Great Wallace Show and later the combined Hagenbeck-Wallace Show were located in Miami County, Indiana, first in the city of Peru and then in neighboring Butler Township. Between 1880 and 1910 the population of the county ranged from 24,083 to 29,350 people.[6] The area in the immediate vicinity of the winter quarters consisted primarily of farmland and private Miami reserves.

The ways Miami people utilized opportunities in the circuses reflected their history of strategic cultural exchange, economic transformation and survival.[7] In the eighteenth century, missionaries and government officials obsessed with racial hierarchies expressed difficulty ascertaining the lineage of members of the Miami villages. By the nineteenth century it was often impossible to distinguish between which Miami practices were Indigenous and which were European in origin.[8] In this multicultural landscape, some asserted that the entire tribe consisted of people of mixed lineage.[9]

A series of land session treaties from 1834 to 1840 considerably shrank Miami landholdings.[10] Though a large number of Miami people were forcibly removed to Kansas in 1846, others resisted removal with a range of strategies from asserting their whiteness to leveraging their vast fortunes and political ties.[11] Some families succeeded—such as those of Frances Slocum, wife of a deceased War Chief, Principal Chief Jean Baptiste Richardville, and War Chief Francis Godfroy—and were exempted from removal. These families formed private Miami reservations on lands across Indiana.[12] By 1850, the remaining Miami population combined with several forcibly removed families who had returned was over 250 in and around Peru.[13] Private reserves became refuge sites as reserve holders like the Godfroys used their lands to enable other Miami to remain or return. Gabriel Godfroy hired farm laborers to cultivate his land and, by 1870, was one of the most important farming teachers and advocates in the community.[14] Miami leadership met as a tribal council and handled the overall direction of the tribe. The Miami community school and many social events took place in the one-room Stony Point School house located on the Godfroy reserve.[15] The building hosted church services, Sunday school, spelling bees, vocal groups, and debate and literary societies. The original school building was condemned in 1881 and rebuilt with Butler Township funds.[16]

There were a few small black communities in nineteenth-century Miami County that experienced growth and development after the circus was established. Housing patterns were checkered, and most of the schools and churches were segregated—some were for Indians and whites only and others for blacks only. Blacks inside the Peru city limits congregated around South Broadway and Hood Street, Third and Tippecanoe Streets, and West Second and Lafayette Streets. These blocks housed the African Methodist Episcopal Church, barbershops, residences, and other black businesses.[17]

Another black community, Boxcar Town, was an offspring of the Peru Steel Casting works, located a mile west of Peru. At its opening in 1898, the plant imported a southern workforce, including over 150 black men and their families. The company purchased boxcars from the Lake Erie & Western Railway and renovated them first for white and then for black employees to rent as living quarters.[18] Black residents established The Beulah Mission

Church. Beulah's pastor, Reverend B. T. Harvey, was a graduate of Tuskegee College, held regular services, taught classes for children, and networked in the greater Peru community. Networking was a success to a certain extent, and the manager of the steel casting company as well as white and black ministers from across Peru attended the church's dedication ceremony.[19]

Three schools served African Americans in the area. The Beulah Mission Church doubled as a school for the Boxcar Town community.[20] Quakers established a school for blacks and non-local Indians five miles from Peru.[21] R. A. Edwards, a Peru banker, established a school at his residence that admitted black students.[22] Jane Moss, an African-American graduate of Oberlin College and a Peru hairdresser, taught in the Edwards' multiracial school.[23]

African Americans had a handful of options in regard to houses of worship. Black residents of Peru organized the African Methodist Episcopal Church in the early 1870s and temporarily held services led by Elder Patterson in a donated engine house.[24] In 1874, the congregation erected a small brick church at the corner of Third and Tippecanoe Streets with Reverend Robert Jeffries as their leader. In 1893 Reverend Zachariah Roberts became pastor of the less than a dozen members. The congregation grew as members came from the circus winter quarters and other communities around the county.[25] Other churches in the area served blacks that worked in nearby mines, railroad, and mills.[26]

One of the most significant developments impacting the communities in Miami County in the 1860s was its emergence as an important rail crossing for the Chesapeake and Ohio, Nickel Plate, and Wabash Railroads that intersected the town.[27] With the coming of the railroad, small traveling entertainment troupes began to stop off at small towns and rural areas in the Midwest. Usually held in public arenas, these shows featured dogs, ponies, and monkeys, and later grew into larger menageries and circuses. As in other small towns, these shows stopped in Peru due to easy rail access.

Benjamin Wallace, a local businessman, took advantage of the new opportunities the rails afforded him. By 1881, he advertised that he had the largest livery stable in Indiana. Wallace's stable became an overnight stop over for traveling performance troupes passing through Peru.[28] In 1882, Wallace bought a bankrupt circus and began to purchase wild animals. In 1884, he sold his livery stable and opened his own circus, which he put on the railroad in 1886. Wallace required a large amount of land to house the circus winter quarters and bought a large plot in the center of the Miami community.[29] The circus wintered there from November to April, then usually went on the road in April.

The growth of the circus industry had broad implications for the Miami community. By 1891, the circus outgrew its original quarters. Wallace purchased Gabriel Godfroy's 220-acre farm at the mouth of the Mississinewa River to use as the new, larger winter quarters.[30] The new winter quarters were a mile northwest of the old quarters in Butler Township and were in easy walking distance from local Miami communities. Men worked as animal feeders and laborers on the circus farm. Eventually, Miami men and women took performance roles. Despite lower agricultural prices and a drop in local land base going from 2,200 acres in 1880 to about 1,800 acres in 1890, the Miami in Butler Township fared relatively well due to circus jobs.[31] Circus work paid moderately well and employed an increasingly cosmopolitan mixture of outsiders, some of whom married into the Miami community. The circus also provided opportunities for intertribal interactions, as Indians from across the country came to Miami County and as Miami artists performed across state and the country.

Local African Americans were also attracted to circus work. For some, the circus provided familiar forms of labor in an alternative venue: they were farmhands and domestic workers, porters, and smiths. For others, the circus provided avenues away from manual labor and into music and performing arts careers. The ability to travel was also a large attraction. Housing was also an advantage of working for large circus operations. The maps of the winter quarters include homes that Wallace built for laborers and farmhands with no obvious lines of segregation.[32]

Columbus, Ohio, and the Sellsville Quarters

The Sells Brothers Circus winter quarters, or Sellsville, were located just outside of Columbus along the Olentangy River in Clinton Township, Ohio.[33] Clinton Township had a population range between 800 and 9,132 people at the time of the Sells Brothers Circus, and the neighborhood of Sellsville grew from 300 to 1,000.[34] At its peak, the circus employed approximately 332 laborers and 64 performers.[35]

In 1871, Peter, Ephraim, Lewis, and Allen Sells established a small-scale circus and traveling menagerie in Linworth, Ohio. As their operation grew, they moved their quarters to East Main Street between Washington and Grant Avenues in Columbus.[36] The Sells family was known in Columbus as businessmen and entrepreneurs who had interests in newspapers, real estate, transportation, and several other ventures. On Friday, March 8, 1872, the brothers announced in the *Ohio State Journal* that they were

> . . . determined to go into other business and wish to return thanks to their many patrons who have favored them during the last three years, and feel assured that they have the good wishes of their friends in the new enterprise in which they are about to embark. . . . In answer to many inquiries, we will state that our concern will be known as Sells Brothers' Quadruple Alliance, Museum, Menagerie, Caravan and Circus, which will take the road about April 20th, giving its first performance in this city.[37]

The *Ohio State Journal* gave a warm welcome to the Sells Brothers' endeavor. On April 26, 1872, the *Ohio State Journal* editors wrote, "We look for a decided sensation . . . on the inauguration of the Sells Brothers' QA in this city to-morrow, [The] Sells are well known in Columbus as industrious and energetic in whatever they undertake. . . ."[38] The *Ohio State Journal* seemed to welcome some circus workers as well. The paper ran an ad, "*Important to Showmen*: Showmen passing through Columbus can obtain at the State Journal Job Office: Date lines, gutter snipes, programmers, descriptive bills, three sheet posters, dodgers, streamers, etc, etc, etc. . . . Comly and Smith, Columbus"[39] Over the years, the Columbus-based *Ohio State Journal* followed the comings and goings of what it referred to often as a home-grown industry. The paper focused on the additions or deaths of exotic circus animals such as tigers and elephants, featured stories about injured acrobats and mauled lion trainers, highlighted the reception of audiences across the country, and chronicled the opening and closing of each season.

The Sells family was respected in Columbus and used that respect to construct the kind of circus town they desired. In October, at the end of their opening season, the Sells returned to a company town of their own design. In total they owned and leased over 1,000 acres to house workers, workers' families, circus animals, and equipment during the off-season.[40] Other businesses emerged to support the circus, its workers and their families. Circus-related businesses and their families remained in the neighborhood year round.[41] In 1896, the show and the quarters doubled in size when the Sells show combined with the already successful Adam Forepaugh Circus to create, The Adam Forepaugh–Sells Brothers Circus.

Remarkably, the Sells Brothers constructed a racially integrated winter quarters. Within the Sellsville neighborhood, blacks and whites lived next door to each other, intermarried, and raised families. Of the sixty-nine households in the immediate neighborhood, twenty-three were African American and perhaps two were multifamily homes shared by blacks and whites.[42] Furthermore, these homes were dispersed throughout the neighborhood among the homes and small businesses of whites. By 1900, Columbus and the area surrounding Sellsville were popular destinations for African-American emigrants from the South.[43] Despite their origins, it appears that these emigrants did not replicate the Jim Crow lifestyle they had experienced growing up. Based on the census of the neighborhood in 1880, 1900, and 1910, Southerners appear to have maintained the same intermixed housing patterns as other residents of Clinton Township. Integrated cooperation went beyond the family and home placement. Though the circus segregated its all-black sideshow band from it all-white main show band, members of the black band often played at integrated community events and at a local white-owned grocery store.[44]

The Sells family supported integrated institutions in the quarters. For instance, the Polkadot School was the only school serving the residents of Sellsville. It is believed to have gotten its name because the population of the school was almost always equally white and black.[45] In 1900, its two teachers, Katie Martin and Mary Drury, taught black and white children.[46] In a school photograph from that year, the children were clearly familiar with each other and mingled side by side.[47] Of the 57 children attending the school in 1900, about 25 were recorded as Negro or mulatto.[48] Benjamin Bowen, a mixed-race man whose family had lived in Clinton Township for over 100 years and had gained some prominence in the community, owned a transfer business and drove wagons for the Polkadot School.[49] The duty of driving the children to and from school was another example of interracial cooperation. Harley Hughes, recorded as mulatto, and Richard Cradic, recorded as white, shared this responsibility. The school closed around 1913, around the time of municipal redistricting.[50]

The Sells also worked with the community to establish an integrated neighborhood church. Like the Polkadot School, the Antioch Baptist Church was the sole institution of its kind serving Sellsville, and it continues to be an important local institution. In 1891 an integrated group of Christians held Sunday school in the Polkadot School. On May 18, 1893, eight integrated founders officially organized the Antioch Baptist Church, with Reverend Ovie O. Jones of London, Ohio, acting as moderator.[51] The first pastor was Reverend I. A. Thornton. The first-year members held camp meetings in the nearby Neil Woods to raise money to purchase two lots for a building site. The Sells family assisted the congregation by loaning tents and seats for the early meetings. A year later, the Sells family donated furniture to the congregation as the church laid its cornerstone.[52]

The circus quarters benefitted black families that were already established in Clinton Township. These opportunities provided support for individuals and an entire community of African Americans in the area. For instance, Sellsville employed two African-American United States Postal Service clerks, Joshua Ellsworth Fields and James Scurry.[53] James Scurry served as a mail carrier while attending Ohio State University.[54] The Bowen family had lived in the neighborhood for nearly 100 years by the time the circus opened. Census records reveal that members of the household included people identified as white, black, and mulatto.[55] Benjamin, whose mother was white and father was black, lived with his wife Katie, an African-American woman, and their four children—Minni, Della, Lottie, and Leslie. The family primarily farmed and, in 1900, they began a successful hauling business for the circus. Reverend George Walker, the fourth pastor of the Antioch Baptist Church, and his wife Laura, a teacher at the Polkadot School, lived in the circus cookhouse for several years. They stayed in the neighborhood year round to serve the community while the circus traveled the country. The son of an escaped slave, James Reynolds, owned one of the two successful blacksmith shops in Sellsville.[56] The income from shoeing horses for the Sells Brothers Circus enabled him to raise his four children in the area. Other local African Americans held jobs ranging from work at the local flourmill to driving wagons for area schools.

The remarkable integration of the community and the range of opportunities in the circus set Sellsville apart from most other Midwestern towns at the turn of the century. The Sells Brothers additionally recruited African Americans and Native Americans as performers, professional animal trainers, managers, musicians, and bandleaders. The Sells Brothers were the first to incorporate an all-black, black-managed sideshow. When it combined with the Forepaugh Show, the outfit was the first circus to include a Wild West Show with American Indian actors, hire black equestrian managers, and maintain a black-managed elephant training crew.

Challenges for Performers in the Circus Industry

Traveling circus life was difficult for all who chose it, but it posed special challenges for Native American and African-American employees. The American circus in the late nineteenth and early twentieth centuries reinforced many of the ugliest racial stereotypes of the times.[57] Employees of color faced demeaning racial depictions and performed to those expectations on a daily basis.[58] Native Americans and African Americans navigated through legal barriers such as Jim Crow laws and industry-imposed restrictions, and faced the threat of racial and mob violence as they traveled with their companies.

Circuses were notorious for the public unrest that they could stir, and people of color were especially vulnerable to violence.[59] The most infamous case of racial mob violence occurred in Duluth, Minnesota, in the summer of 1920. There, a white mob brutally beat, burned, shot, and hanged four black employees of the John Robinson Circus.[60] The Great Wallace Show took measures to avoid incidents of racial violence, but could not completely shield its employees. During the 1885 season the company opted to cancel evening shows and scheduled only morning performances in southern states. Management hoped to avoid violence against employees typical of evening shows in the South.[61] This strategy helped Wallace avoid a mob of sixteen armed men who aimed to harass circus employees at one southern venue.[62] In 1903, the Great Wallace Show encountered a race riot in Evansville, Indiana, and was not allowed to perform there. The citizens of Linton, Indiana, the next venue, announced that they would not allow the circus to perform if it employed blacks. Wallace left all of his black employees in a nearby city and secretly brought them back in the evening just before the trains left that town.[63]

The federal government and some assimilationist reformers took great measures to stop Native Americans from performing in Wild West and similar circus-based shows in the 1880s and 1890s. To discourage reservation residents from joining traveling circuses and Wild West Shows, the Commissioner of Indian Affairs warned that show Indians "must not look to this Office for favor or assistance."[64] This created a significant barrier for people living on reservations looking for employment in the industry. Show managers viewed this interference as a nearly insurmountable obstacle to continuing their operations.[65] Despite this challenge, some Native American performers retained their careers in circuses and Wild West shows. For instance, Native American employees in the Adam Forepaugh Show, one of the first circuses to include an almost all-Indian Wild West show, kept their positions. Other American Indians intent on breaking into the industry attempted to bypass the law. In 1886, several American Indians attempted to join the Sells Brothers Circus to create a Wild West Show. The Sells Brothers paid producer Pawnee Bill an advance for their transportation. The plan failed when an Indian agent discovered them and prosecuted Pawnee Bill.[66] The Indian Commissioner claimed that he was "opposed to Indians being taken from the reservation for any but educational purposes."[67] The Sells eventually bought Adam Forepaugh's show and with its Indian-cast Wild West show.

Circus managers also imposed race-based barriers around which employees navigated. None of the major nationally touring shows allowed blacks to perform under the main tent until the 1920s, though some did have specialty acts featuring other ethnic minorities.[68] Other companies that did employ blacks before the 1920s gave them the most labor-intensive positions. These laborers, called roustabouts, raised and lowered tents, cleaned, and performed all manual labor required by the company. They were expendable, easily exploitable, the last to eat, and responsible for their own sleeping arrangements. They often slept with the animals whose cars they cleaned, under the open sky, or sometimes under railcars to escape inclement weather. Additionally, the majority of black circus employees traveled in poorly maintained railcars. While Sells and Wallace stand out because of their willingness to work with black and Indian performers, give them higher wages, and in some cases provide better work conditions, both companies maintained a racial hierarchy. Neither company allowed black performers in the main show tent, instead African Americans performed only in the sideshow tent.[69]

Changes in ownership in the first two decades of the twentieth century created more challenges for employees of the Forepaugh-Sells and the Hagenbeck-Wallace circuses.[70] For African-American employees, new management often meant dealing with old attitudes of racial discrimination.[71] Changes in working conditions, pay cuts, bans on blacks holding leadership positions, and decreased job security were all issues that black employees faced under new leadership. In 1905, when the last Sells brother involved in the circus company died, Barnum and Bailey bought out the Forepaugh-Sells Show, and all fired blacks in leadership positions.[72]

Native Americans and African Americans Utilized Circus Opportunities in Their Neighborhoods and Abroad

The Sells Brothers Circus and the Great Wallace Show were some of the first to tap into the wealth of talented black and Indian performers and create windows of opportunity for these performers.[73] For years black minstrel shows included aerial acts, animal acts, magicians, jugglers, wirewalkers, and musicians.[74] When circus managers began hiring them for the sideshow tent, they first performed alongside so-called human oddities, acts such as the infamous fat ladies, human skeletons, and conjoined twins. Times did change. By 1910, one *Indianapolis Freeman* reporter wrote, "Have you noticed that nearly every circus on the road has a colored aggregation taking care of the side show? Dear colored performer, please take care of the opportunity given you and don't squabble yourself out of a job."[75] Black sideshows became an anticipated part of every large circus outfit.

Though they undoubtedly had their bottom line in mind, opportunities provided by circus owners to African-American and Native American employees opened doorways for many people of color. Those who decided to take the path of the circus life forged new economic paths, built educational foundations for entire communities, created beneficial social networks, and even devised ways to shift boundaries of race both inside and outside of the circus. For example, the African-American trainer, Ephraim Williams, became known as an "equestrian superstar" through his work in the John Robinson Circus from 1867 to 1878.[76] The Forepaugh Circus employed one of the most famous elephant trainers, Eph Thompson, and his all-black crew.[77] Thompson met success all over Europe and Northern Africa. In 1891, the Sells also hired Sol White to lead his all-black band for the sideshow tent.[78] And still later, the company maintained one of the most famous black sideshow bandleaders, P. G. Lowery.

During the 1891–1892 season, Wallace hired his show's first all-black sideshow band. From that season forward, Wallace maintained a black band and added other African-American acts, such as comedians, minstrels, clowns, and vocalists. Many of these acts followed the Wallace circuses for several seasons and enjoyed stable employment, national publicity, and relatively safe passage throughout the United States. The Black Hussar Band, for example, toured with Wallace from 1892 to 1897 and intermittently from 1897 to 1913.[79] As sideshow acts increased in popularity and size, Wallace turned their supervision over to black managers and bandleaders. These men advertised for new positions, trained artists, and mentored black circus leadership. They placed ads continuously in national black newspapers, including the *Indianapolis Freeman*, the *Chicago Defender*, and the *Kansas Herald*. Additionally, managers used race papers as a forum for reporting on their successes, failures, and the dramas of day-to-day life on the road.[80]

Of the African Americans who rose to prominence in the circus industry, the name that stands out among many is P. G. Lowery, distinguished bandleader, renowned variety show owner, and eminent professor of ragtime music. Lowery's lengthy career, in many ways, exemplified African-American ingenuity and perseverance inside of the circus industry. He both collaborated with circus managers and fought against their unfair policies. He built several successful and highly popular traveling sideshows. Most notably, he educated hundreds of black musicians while he kept multiracial audiences in awe of his expertise. His life is a window into black entertainers' experiences in the circus during this period. For several years Lowery divided his time between his own companies, the Sells Brothers Circus, and the

Great Wallace Shows. His fame spanned the nation. In 1910, the *Freeman* declared:

> The branch of colored show business known as circus minstrels and vaudeville had its beginnings with P. G. Lowery, the renowned cornetist and bandmaster . . . in 1899 . . . Since Lowery's initiative, . . . no less than fourteen white tents are giving employment to big colored companies. . . . Something like three hundred people—performers and musicians—are employed in this phase of the show business. The number promises to increase.[81]

The P. G. Lowery Band consisted of nearly two-dozen members and expanded for special engagements. They toured with the Sells Brothers Circus in the 1890s and with Wallace from 1905 through 1913. Lowery was pleased with this arrangement, saying of the collaboration, "good people, good treatment, and great show."[82] In fact, Lowery tended to speak very highly of the industry. In his early career he praised the circus life and the opportunities made available to African-American entertainers. Lowery asserted, "It is generally understood by the public at large that circus people have a tough time. I deny the assertion and will say for good treatment, equal justice and sure salary, give me the circus."[83] Lowery's band lived in Peru much of the time and his celebrity brought black artists and musicians from across the country to Peru. Many were musicians with whom Lowery had previously worked on minstrel and vaudeville circuits or during his schooling at the New England Conservatory.

By the 1913 season, Lowery was listed on the first page of the Hagenbeck-Wallace yearbook as "director of the sideshow tent" alongside other "Head of Departments." Other members of the "Executive" and "Business" staff included the equestrian director, the musical director, the general press agent, and the official announcer.[84] Eventually, the black sideshow band, accompanied by a comedy or variety act, was a staple in the Wallace shows. The Lowery Band was advertised on a larger-than-life canvas alongside the main entrance and advertisements for other "essential" acts such as the equestrian show.

As black sideshow acts increased, so did Lowery's popularity. In 1913, a *Freeman* correspondent noted, "P.G. always freely shares his schooling, which he paid very dearly for in Boston."[85] Lowery's traveling circus sideshow band had solidified its reputation as a traveling conservatory among black and white circus writers. One correspondent in Harrisburg, Pennsylvania, wrote, "The Barnum and Bailey show, also the 101 Ranch were in our city with colored companies . . . but as soon as Lowery's band played their first number one could see a vast difference in Lowery's band and the bands with other companies. . . . When hearing Lowery's band, one can easily tell they are from the Lowery school."[86] In 1916, The *Freeman* asserted that, "P. G. Lowery's band is known as the 'School of Music.' The best musicians in the profession are from the Lowery School."[87]

The most famous and successful networker in Peru, Indiana, was P. G. Lowery, having had experience in many types of show business. Just as he had done in Columbus, Lowery aided African-American residents of Miami County. One such aspiring musician was local Miami County resident, Sarah Byrd.[88] Lowery helped her to successfully audition for internationally touring musical companies. Byrd toured Europe with *Black Patti*, one of the most well-known contemporary women in black ragtime entertainment.[89]

Lowery also used the circus as a platform from which to build dissent and create better working conditions for black circus employees. Through his networking he strengthened black management by training young leaders. He protested the demeaning messages of the minstrel show with his own touring show called, "This is Not a Minstrel Show." Lowery formed a labor union with some of the foremost black show managers who aimed to protect African Americans "by demanding first-class accommodations and keeping the salaries up to standard."[90] Lowery even convinced the Sells Brothers management to provide him with his own railcars, which were especially useful when traveling through the segregated South. When Hagenbeck-Wallace management cut wages and benefits for its black workers, Lowery lead a strike of black performers that cut deep into the circus profits in the 1915 season. The strike ended when management gave in to the black performers' demands.[91] In 1920, P. G. Lowery's sideshow band broke the big tent race barrier and became the first African-American band to play under the main show tent in the Ringling Brothers Circus. Ringling had banned black performers up to that point.[92]

Black artists formed self-help alliances as well. Through their experiences in the Wallace circus, blacks created national and international networks, boosted their individual careers and served as safety nets for each other in difficult times. In 1906, Ernest Hogan said, "Salvation of the Negro race lies in the arts."[93] Hogan was an internationally famous black ragtime artist. When Peru members of Hogan's troupe, Bill Wilkins, Anna Brown, and Hummer Butler, ran into financial difficulties in Europe in 1900, Peru people helped to raise the money to bring them home.[94]

While Miami neighborhoods in the Butler Township private reserves were economically strengthened, African-American neighborhoods were created and increased in population in at least three parts of Miami County. Census data is often unreliable in this area. Many circus employees traveled with other entertainment troupes during the off-season and led nomadic lifestyles that were difficult for census takers to document.[95] However, circus yearbooks, community histories, and personal recollections fill in some gaps the census leaves blank. By 1913, black residential, business, and institutional enclaves were on Gabriel Godfroy's land in Butler Township, in Peru, and in Boxcar Town just outside the Peru city limits. Individuals from Boxcar Town commuted to and from the circus quarters on a bus that Wallace hired to transport workers.[96] African Americans who lived on Gabriel Godfroy's land lived close to both the private Miami reserves and the circus quarters.

Some blacks and Native Americans used their experiences in white-owned companies to raise capital for their own shows or launch new ones. In 1924, Lowery and his employees created the Lowery Brothers Circus in Cleveland, Ohio, to benefit the Cuyahoga Lodge #95, an African-American chapter of the fraternal order of Elks.[97] Ephraim Williams owned a circus from 1888 to 1902, and may have been the first black man to own a circus.[98] Eph Thompson, the elephant trainer from the Forepaugh-Sells Show, relocated to London, England, created his own show, and hired black aerialists and other performers.[99]

Native Americans in Miami County took advantage of circus employment for economic gain during otherwise difficult economic times. Miami people utilized circus employment to stabilize their community in the 1880s through a period of land loss and lowered agricultural prices.[100] Benjamin Wallace's decision to place both the original and the second, larger winter quarters in the center of the Miami community made it easy for Miami people to work for the circus. Men and women moved beyond labor and animal caretaking into performance careers. Circus employment was consistent, even if sometimes only seasonal.

In 1920, when Jerry Mugivan and his colleagues formed the American Circus Corporation, circus work became even more important to Miami people. The corporation bought a fleet of new railcars and hoped to overtake its main rival, the Ringling Brothers Circus. Around 100 to 150 people worked on the quarters, year-round. Miami people ran concession stands, worked on the circus farms, handled animals, and performed in preshow concerts, equestrian, and Wild West Shows.[101]

Local Miami man, LaMoine Marks, remembered the circus as a positive part of his community. He said, "They were good to them. They were a good thing for a town."[102] Marks, born in 1907, was a boy when the

Hagenbeck-Wallace Circus kept quarters nearby his Miami community.[103] He witnessed the devastating 1913 flood that killed many animals and led Wallace to sell his company. When the American Circus Corporation set up shop in nearby Peru, the young Marks did odd jobs for extra cash. He, like many other young men of his generation, worked concession stands selling hotdogs, candy, cotton candy, and ice cream, and helped to build and take down concession stands before and after shows. Marks went on to be a "candy butcher," managing his own concession stand. He did other work in the circus as well, such as taxidermy, and sometimes performed in equestrian shows. Other Miami people found work as elephant trainers, teamsters, and drivers.[104]

Miami people used circus opportunities to travel and make connections with a cosmopolitan mixture of people from across the country and around the world. LaMoine Marks remembered, "You could walk down the street on a Saturday night in Peru, because it was a Saturday night town, and you could hear French language, Italian, Greek, German, and many others. They even had a Russian group, Cossack riders. . . ."[105] Miami performers occasionally worked with some of America's top entertainers. LaMoine Marks worked with famed lion tamer, Clyde Beatty, and cowboy and film star, Tom Mix.[106] Sioux performers from Montana made seasonal trips to Miami County to participate in the circus equestrian shows.[107] Black and white Southerners, too, joined the company for seasonal labor.[108] European circus employees stayed in Peru for extended periods, giving Miami people further opportunities to meet and connect to diverse peoples and cultures from around the world.[109] Miami labor crews also worked with African-American stake drivers, cooks, porters, canvass men, farmers, animal trainers, and performers.[110] Indian people from other tribes, such as Sioux performers, came through Miami County as well.[111]

Miami built businesses and cultivated family opportunities within the circus. Local Miami children who grew up fascinated by circus life began careers in the business in their late teens.[112] Horse riding, breeding, and selling were important ways that local Miami connected to the circus. Horse breeders benefitted from the flow of non-native animals to the area and traded or bought a variety of animals.[113] LaMoine Marks put the advanced horse riding techniques he learned as a child to use when he performed in circus equestrian shows. He performed in the Western Concert, an equestrian showcase before the circus.[114] Several members of Marks's family worked for the circus, in fact. His brother-in-law trained elephants in the Hagenbeck-Wallace Circus before the 1913 flood and for the American Circus Corporation in the 1920s.[115] The Marks family ran refreshment stands for the Hagenbeck-Wallace Show as well as for Miami Muk-Koons-Kwa Company performances, a troupe that promoted Miami identity in north-central Indiana.[116] Concession stand businesses were very common among blacks and American Indians who traveled alongside the circus show. In some case,s companies hired them to sell their wares on the circus property. In other cases, African Americans and American Indians set up shop outside the circus entrance.

Other Miami families chose circus professions. Men and women of the Tucker family performed with and trained elephants. Very particular about the tools he used, Gabe Tucker began a business making bull hooks, an instrument used in training elephants. His sister, Mary Tucker rode elephants during the summer touring circus season, and was a schoolteacher in the winter. Gabe moved away and ran a business in Warsaw for several years. When he came back to Miami County after several years away, Tucker's brother-in-law, Cheerful Gardner, the head elephant man at the time, gave him a job training elephants. By this time, Mary Tucker performed a major act under the big top.[117] Sarah Tucker Weisenberger sewed costumes for performers, and Susie Tucker Mellinger worked as a cook. Many members of these families later traveled with the Muk-Koons-Kwa Company of Miami Indians.[118]

Manipulating the Spotlight

The Brown Brothers' story and Harry Brown's own ambivalence toward his professional decisions illustrate some of the complexities of race in nineteenth- and early twentieth-century popular entertainment. Traveling circuses and Wild West shows provided some of the first real opportunities for a wide range of black and Indian performers. However, systemic racism plagued every new vista in the industry.[119] Managers appeased white audiences by creating spaces to view black and Indian people without the alleged dangers of moving beyond racial hierarchies or colonial rhetoric. "Race" entertainers performed both in the main tent shows and the sideshows. Indiana Miami played roles of Indians, blacks, and Pacific Islanders. Countless other African Americans and Native Americans were hired on to play Indians, African tribesmen, and any other race for which they could pass in whatever Wild West show, biblical drama, tragedy, or comedy circus managers devised.[120]

This issue was not simply a matter of an exploiter and the exploited, or unenlightened entertainers. Performers of color sometimes used limited industry opportunities to turn the limitation of race on its head. Circus performers learned to use and manipulate white audience's feelings and expectations about race in order to succeed in a broader variety of careers than typically available to them. These artists understood what they were doing, played upon the fears and expectations of white audiences to meet their aims, and shaped what they saw as theirs to manipulate. Performers protected the racial identities of their coworkers.[121] They understood that maintaining certain illusions on and off the stage helped to advance careers.

Philip Deloria argued that, "Indian performers used expectations to gain entrée into positions in which they were able to participate in shaping the particular form of the modern."[122] Once in these positions, they played many roles, both positive and negative. These roles, Vine Deloria claimed, saved some Indians from undue pressures of farming and harsh treatment that many others faced. Many Indians used traveling entertainment to gain higher levels of freedom, to learn more about the rest of the nation and the world, and as a transnational educational device.[123] Joy Kasson argued that Sitting Bull, who performed frequently in Buffalo Bill's Wild West shows, would not have chosen the show over the hunting life. However, given the circumstances and the choice between entertainment and farming, Sitting Bull chose the former. This life afforded him opportunities that were not available elsewhere.[124] Within the circus, black and Indian artists created spaces where they performed "race" based on their own expectations and aims. In doing so, they subverted racial hierarchies and opened doors that were closed to people of color in other professions. Some historians have argued that the Wild West Show helped to preserve some aspects of Indian life and culture during an era of cultural reform and deprivation.[125] Al Wells, black performer and manager of a trapeze act said, "Colored novelty acts have never had the chance that our white brothers have had, nor do they get the salary." Wells could not get work for his black trapeze troupe until he changed the title to *Los Cubanos, The Three Garcia Brothers*. White audiences, it seemed, were fascinated by the opportunity to see "real" Cubans, and Wells's troupe worked steadily after the name change.[126]

Conclusion: Performers and Entertainers Push Racial Lines Beyond Two Worlds

The tidy, two-worlds framework neglects that African Americans had relationships with Native Americans. It denies the impact of these groups on each other and wider American popular culture. Communities of Native

American and African-American performers—through their decisions, career choices, and everyday lives—add a long overdue chapter in nineteenth-century America. While the circus represented the imperialist orientation characteristic of other nineteenth-century expositions, the circus town represented a possibility for American Indians and African Americans to resist racial and ethnic restrictions. American Indians and African Americans in Midwest circuses greatly impacted an industry constructed to demean them in a part of the country that largely sought to constrain them. The risks they took and the opportunities they found enabled them to build stronger tools and greater alliances to transcend those barriers. They constantly negotiated, strategized, created, and recreated themselves with the materials they possessed. The results are rich bodies of work and significant contributions to American popular and artistic culture.

Notes

1. *The Michigan Daily*, 17 June 1905.
2. *Indianapolis Freeman*, 1 October 1910.
3. This period covers incarnations of the Sells Brothers Circus and the combined Forepaugh-Sells Brothers Circus from 1872 to 1905, the Great Wallace Show and the combined Hagenbeck-Wallace Show from about 1881 to 1913, and the early years of the American Circus Corporation in the 1920s.
4. A few African-American newspapers ran regular columns that featured black entertainment news. The most prominent were the *Chicago Defender, The Eureka Herald,* and the *Indianapolis Freeman.* Additionally, *The Billboard*, established in 1894 also chronicled traveling entertainment troupes such as circuses and minstrel shows.
5. Davis, 10.
6. Tenth and Thirteenth Census of the United States, 1880 and 1910, Indiana, Miami County.
7. See Susan Sleeper-Smith, *Indian Women and French Men: Rethinking Cultural Encounter in the Western Great Lakes* (Amherst: University of Massachusetts Press, 2001) and Stewart Rafert, *The Miami Indians of Indiana: A Persistent People, 1654–1994* (Indianapolis: Indiana Historical Society, 1996).
8. James J. Buss, " 'They Found and Left Her an Indian' Gender, Race, and the Whitening of Young Bear," *Frontiers: A Journal of Women's Studies* 29, no. 2 & 3 (2008): 6; Sleeper-Smith, 128.
9. Bradley J. Birzer, "Jean Baptiste Richardville: Miami Metis," in *Enduring Nations: Native Americans in the Midwest*, ed. R. David Edmunds (Urbana and Chicago: University of Illinois Press, 2008), 94–95.
10. For a detailed discussion of this era's removal treaties and Miami people's persistence in the region, see Scott M. Shoemaker, "Trickster Skins: Narratives of

Landscape, Representation, and the Miami Nation" (Ph D diss., University of Minnesota 2011), 123–73.

11. Rafert, 166.

12. Susan Sleeper-Smith, "Resistance to Removal: The 'White Indian,' Frances Slocum," *Enduring Nations: Native Americans in the Midwest*, ed. R. David Edmunds, (Urbana: University of Illinois Press, 2008), 113; Rafert, 77–114.

13. Sleeper-Smith, "Resistance to Removal," 111; Rafert, 124.

14. Rafert, 162.

15. Melissa A. Rinehart, "Miami Indian Language Shift and Recovery" (PhD diss., Michigan State University 2006), 75. Stony Point was located in the center of the Miami reserves and Miami children accounted for over half of its enrollment.

16. Miami County Historical Society, *Stony Point School: The School With Many Names and an Historic Past* (Peru, IN: Miami County Historical Society, 1986), 3–4. In 1914 after the devastating flood, Stony Point was closed

17. *Encyclopedia of Miami County*, "Pioneer Negro Citizens of Peru, Indiana," 417–27; and John H. Stephens, *History of Miami County* (1896), 351.

18. "Pioneer Negroes of Peru, Indiana," 424. Boxcar living was not uncommon for blacks and whites alike, as several families lived in discarded railcars between the Wabash River and the towpath of the Wabash and Erie Canal.

19. Ibid.

20. Ibid., 424.

21. Rafert, 186.

22. Arthur Lawrence Bodurtha, *History of Miami County, Indiana: A Narrative account of its Historical Progress, Its People and Its Principal Interests* (Chicago: Lewis Publishing Company, 1914), 564; *Pioneer Negroes of Peru, Indiana*, 427.

23. Bodurtha, 563–65; "Pioneer Negroes of Peru, Indiana," 427. Jane Moss's husband, Alex Moss, eventually convinced the state legislature that the taxpaying blacks of Peru should be able to attend the public schools there.

24. John H. Stephens, *History of Miami County* (1896), 351–52.

25. *Peru Tribune*, "Wayman A. M. E. Church is Observing 100th anniversary this Sunday," (June 18, 1971).

26. Stephens, 352.

27. Gayle Thornbrough, *Indiana History* (Indianapolis: Indiana Historical Bureau, 1956).

28. Chalmer Condon, "B. E. Wallace," *Bandwagon* 8, no. 4 (Jul–Aug 1964): 3.

29. Ibid. See also, Will M. Hundley, *My Boyhood Among the Last Miami Indians* (Caldwell, ID: Caxton Printers, 1939). The quarters were adjacent to an area called "Squawtown," named for the Eel River Miami women who had taken refuge there since the middle of the century

30. Rafert, 166. Godfroy moved his household to his father's old trading house a half-mile away.

31. Ibid.

32. Winter Quarters of the Wallace Circus at Peru, Indiana (Indiana Historical Society Digital Library).

33. This area currently contains the Grandville Heights and Marble Cliffs neighborhoods.

34. United States Census, 1870: The Statistics of the Population of the United States . . . From the Original Returns of the Ninth Census Volume 1 by Francis A. Walker. Washington: Government Printing Office, 1872; and The Thirteenth Census of the United States Taken in the Year 1910: Population, Volume 3 by William C. Hunt. Washington: Government Printing Office, 1913.35. Carl Weisheimer, "Sellsville ca. 1900 [1971]," 109, Special Collections, Ohio Historical Society, Columbus.

36. Weisheimer, 109.

37. *Ohio State Journal* (Columbus), 27 April 1872.

38. Ibid.

39. *Ohio State Journal* (Columbus), 13 January 1872.

40. Fred D. Pfening, *Bandwagon* 8, no. 1 (Jan–Feb 1964): 7.

41. Ibid., 2.

42. Weisheimer, 4.

43. Himes, 134.

44. Weisheimer, 53, and *Sells Brothers Circus Yearbook 1900 [1900]*, p. 28, Sells Brothers Circus file, Circus World Museum.

45. Weisheimer, 50.

46. Ibid.

47. Weisheimer, 51.

48. Ibid.

49. Ibid.

50. J. S. Himes, "Forty Years of Negro Life in Columbus, Ohio," *The Journal of Negro History* 27 no. 2 (April, 1942): 130.

51. "Antioch Baptist Church History 1893–2001 [2001]," Antioch Baptist Church records, (Columbus).

52. Ibid.

53. Weisheimer, 53

54. Ibid., 40

55. Ibid., 63.

56. Ibid., 61.

57. See Janet Davis, *The Circus Age: Culture and Society Under the American Big Top* (Chapel Hill: University of North Carolina Press, 2002); Benjamin Reiss, *The Showman and the Slave: Race, Death, and Memory in Barnum's America* (Cambridge, MA: Harvard University Press, 2001); Gregory J. Renoff, *The Big Tent: The Traveling Circus in Georgia, 1820–1920* (Athens: University of Georgia Press, 2008).

58. Scholars of circus history have largely perpetuated this injustice by omitting serious discussions on the contributions of people of color in the industry. See Lynn Abbott and Doug Seroff, *Ragged But Right: Black Traveling Shows, "Coon Songs," and the Dark Pathway to Blues and Jazz* (Jackson: University of Mississippi Press, 2007).

59. Brawls between circus workers and local citizens were common occurrences. They were often fodder for local newspapers to write anti-circus diatribes that

accused the shows of introducing immorality to otherwise peaceful, God-fearing, small-town audiences. The *Billboard Magazine* ran a weekly column entitled, "Prudes on the Prowl" that chronicled, in a condescending and somewhat comical way, the fears and anti-circus sentiment found in local newspapers across small-town America.

60. *The Billboard,* July 1920.

61. Condon, 4.

62. Ibid.

63. Ibid.

64. Joy S. Kasson, *Buffalo Bill's Wild West: Celebrity, Memory, and Popular History* (New York: Hill and Wang: 2000), 184–85.

65. *The Billboard,* February 1900.

66. Weisheimer, 96.

67. *The Billboard,* February 1900.

68. While blacks were initially barred from performing under the main show tent, Arab, Greek, Chinese, and Japanese acts were common. See Davis, 197–98.

69. "Behind the Scenes: The Life of a Circus Employee as seen by a Herald Reporter," *The Carroll (Iowa) Herald,* 15 July 1885.

70. With the deaths of several of the industry's leading circus men between 1906 and 1929, the industry experienced drastic changes in management which posed new challenges for employees. Bailey bought the Forepaugh-Sells Circus after the death of the last Sells brother in 1906. Within a year Bailey died and Ringling went on to buy the Forepaugh-Sells Circus and the Barnum and Bailey Circus. He then combined his interests to form the Ringling Brothers and Barnum and Bailey Circus. After a devastating flood in 1913, Benjamin Wallace's circus came under ownership of Jerry Mugivan, Ed Ballard, and Bert Bowers. They formed the American Circus Corporation in 1921 in Peru. Between 1921 and 1929, the American Circus Corporation owned and managed several circuses including Hagenbeck-Wallace, Howes Great London Shows, Robinson's Famous Shows, Sells-Floto, Sparks Circus, and the Al G. Barnes Circus. By the 1929 season, the American Circus Corporation sent out five circuses on 145 rail cars. Their major competitor, the combined Ringling Brothers and Barnum & Bailey show, sent out ninety railcars. In about one generation, the circus industry changed from several companies with varying management styles to basically two large outfits that dominated the industry. See Helen Stoddart, *Rings of Desire: Circus History and Representation* (Manchester, IN: Manchester University Press, 2000); *Variety,* January 26, 1907; *Billboard,* April 11, 1942.

71. In contrast, these changes had more positive effects on people in Miami County, Indiana. The American Circus Corporation based its headquarters in Miami County—in Peru, Indiana, neighboring city to the Godfroy reserve. This, as will be discussed later, benefitted Miami families and other American Indians involved in circus work.

72. Davis, 70.

73. This includes the Forepaugh-Sells Show and the Hagenbeck-Wallace Show which were combination circuses born of mergers of the companies, but run by the Sells and Wallace, respectively

74. Abbott and Seroff, 158.

75. "The Parrot in the Theater Loft," *Indianapolis Freeman*, 14 May 1910.

76. Gregory Renoff, *The Big Tent: The Traveling Circus in Georgia, 1820–1930* (Athens: University of Georgia Press, 2008), 144.

77. Davis, 71.

78. *Indianapolis Freeman*, 9 May 1891.

79. Henry Sampson, *The Ghost Walks: A Chronological History of Blacks in Show Business, 1865–1910* (Metuchen, N J, and London: The Scarecrow Press, 1988), 127.

80. Abbott and Seroff, 14.

81. "P. G. Lowery, Originator," the *Indianapolis Freeman*, 9 July 1910.

82. *Indianapolis Freeman*, 10 June 1905.

83. Watkins, 59–60; *Indianapolis Freeman*, 10 June 1905; *Indianapolis Freeman*, 9 November 1901.

84. *Hagenbeck-Wallace Official Route Book 1913 [1913]*: 28, Hagenbeck Wallace Combined Show file, Circus World Museum.

85. "Lowery's Band, Orchestra, Minstrel Show and Other Attractions with The Wallace and Hagenbeck Show," *Indianapolis Freeman*, June 14, 1913

86. "Harrisburg, Pa., Lowery's Minstrels, the Best Under Canvas," *Indianapolis Freeman*, May 31, 1913.

87. "Stage," *Indianapolis Freeman*, 25 March 1916.

88. Ibid.

89. Black Patti was the stage name for soprano soloist, Matilda Sissieretta Joyner Jones. Black Patti had launched her international career on a six-month tour in the West Indies with J. R. Smith's Tennessee Jubilee Singers. The musicians returned in February 1889, and the *Indianapolis Freeman* published a series of interviews that chronicled the tour in June 15, 1889. See also Bernard L. Peterson, Jr., *A Century of Musicals in Black and White: An Encyclopedia of Musical Stage Works by, About, or Involving African Americans* (Westport, CT: Greenwood Press, 1993).

90. *Indianapolis Freeman*, 28 December 1907.

91. Watkins, 99.

92. Clifford E. Watkins, *The Showman and The Slave: The Life and Music of Perry George Lowery* (Jackson: University Press of Mississippi, 2003), 114.

93. *Indianapolis Freeman*, 7 November 1906.

94. *Encyclopedia of Miami County*, "Pioneer Negroes of Peru, Indiana," Indiana State Library, 421.

95. Davis, 74.

96. Rafert, 27; *Pioneer Negroes of Peru, Indiana*, 424. The Peru Steel Works plant closed soon after the turn of the century.

97. Watkins, 114 and 116.

98. *Freeman*, May 23, 1908; Abbott and Seroff, 309–310.

99. Davis, 71.

100. Rafert, 164.

101. LaMoine Marks, interview by Stewart Rafert, 11 October 1991, "Circus/Elephants," transcript, Indiana Historical Society, Indianapolis, IN.

102. Ibid.

103. Social Security Death Index, number 306-26-3905, Indiana State, <http://search.ancestrylibrary.com/cgi-bin/sse.dll?rank=1&gsfn=LaMoineMarks>, [1 November 2010].

104. LaMoine Marks, interview by Stewart Rafert, 11 May 1993, "Circus," transcript, Indiana Historical Society, Indianapolis, IN.

105. Ibid.

106. Rafert, 211; and LaMoine Marks interview (1991).

107. LaMoine Marks (1991).

108. Ibid.

109. Ibid.

110. Ibid.

111. Rafert 116; and LaMoine Marks (1991).

112. LaMoine Marks (1991).

113. LaMoine Marks (1991).

114. LaMoine Marks (1991).

115. Ibid.

116. For an exploration of the Muk-Koons-Kwa Company of Miami Indians, see chapter four, "Wiihsakacaakwa's Bloody Nose: Narrating Identity in Landscape," of Scott Shoemaker's dissertation. From about 1924 to 1937, Indiana Miami created and performed the Muk-Koons-Kwa Company, a traveling show displaying Indian culture and history. It depicted an interpretation of the Frances Slocum captivity narrative that asserted Miami identity and claimed north-central Indiana as a Miami landscape. This Miami institution educated non-Indians about Miami history and culture and contradicted the "dying Indian" myth. It also helped to unify the Miami community as it gained publicity and income for the tribe's lawyers and lobbyists in Washington, DC. The performance showcased some of the tribe's oldest storytellers, teachers, and leaders in the shows. Leaders such as Clarence Godfroy, John and Ross Bundy, and Anna Marks taught Miami children Miami language, history and culture while performing.

117. LaMoine Marks (1993).

118. Shoemaker, 175.

119. Abbott and Seroff, 3.

120. Joy S. Kasson, 213–17.

121. See Henry T. Sampson, *The Ghost Walks: A Chronological History of Blacks in Show Business, 1865–1910* (Metuchen: The Scarecrow Press, 1988), chapter eight.

122. Philip J. Deloria, *Indians in Unexpected Places* (Lawrence: University Press of Kansas, 2004), 14.

123. Vine Deloria, *The Indians*, in Brooklyn Museum, ed., *Buffalo Bill and the Wild West* (Brooklyn: The Brooklyn Museum, 1981).

124. Kasson, 171.

125. Ibid., 164.

126. Sampson, 531–32; Al Wells, "Negro Novelty Acts," *Indianapolis Freeman*, 26 August 1916.

Interlude

Of Two Worlds and Intimate Domains

SUSAN E. GRAY

This volume takes its title from a passage in *Custer Died for Your Sins: An Indian Manifesto* (1969) in which Vine Deloria, Jr,. roundly condemns anthropologists for attributing the "terrible crisis" facing American Indians, not to dire structural conditions on reservations over which they have little control, but to their tragic cultural position "BETWEEN TWO WORLDS." As colonized people, Indians are no longer authentically Indigenous, but neither can they fully adapt to white (and therefore modern) ways. Deloria attacks this argument by taking readers on a tour of what might be called the sites and circuitries of "two-worlds" knowledge production—the creation, in Foucauldian terms, of a technology of power. Changing the metaphor, we might also think of the scenario he depicts as a pernicious seasonal round.[1]

Deloria begins his tour in the summer, during which anthropologists visit Indian reservations to collect the observations that they will turn into books in the winter. This production is also the means of reproduction—of knowledge and anthropologists; graduate students will read the books and eventually themselves go to reservations to verify the original observations. In the meantime, summaries of the books appear as scholarly articles, prompting licensed anthropological practitioners to conduct their own fieldwork on reservations. "[C]ondensations" of the summaries are sent as reports to government agencies or private foundations to account for the grants that funded the previous summer's research and to apply for renewed support. These reports are too long for busy granting officials to read, so "secretaries" condense them into "slogans" ("administrative assistants" and "bullet points" in today's language) for easy circulation. The slogans become themes for conferences in early spring, where they engender disputes among opposing camps of anthropologists, thus setting the research agenda for the next summer's fieldwork. This agenda, in turn, determines the fresh round of "observations" made on reservations.

The end result of these scholarly endeavors is a "massive volume of useless knowledge . . . attempting to capture real Indians in a network of theories [which] have contributed substantially to the invisibility of Indian people today." As colonized people, they cannot be seen by whites to be participating as Indians in modern American society. Moreover, whites foist their "knowledge" of Indians onto Indigenous people themselves, who may adopt it in an attempt to communicate. The consequences are particularly damaging for young Indians, who are told in workshops run by well-meaning whites that all of their problems stem from being "BETWEEN TWO WORLDS."

What is striking to me about Deloria's tour of two-worlds knowledge production is the contrast that he draws between the stasis, boundedness, and abstraction of the two worlds—"never the twain shall meet" is his summary of the "anthropological message"—and the dynamic, place-specific network of social relations in which the knowledge is produced. This contrast has direct application today to the burgeoning global field of intimate colonialism, to which the work of Ann Laura Stoler is central. American scholars commonly approach the Stoler corpus through her 2001 essay in the *Journal of American History* calling for a rapprochement between post-colonial and North American studies. "Tense and Tender Ties"—an allusion to Sylvia Van Kirk's path breaking 1980 analysis of Indigenous women in the Canadian fur trade—led directly to a 2006 collection of essays edited by Stoler, *Haunted by Empire: The Geographies of Intimacy in North American History*, as well as a number of major monographs and special issues of journals.[2]

In Stoler's lexicon, a geography of intimacy constitutes a site for the enactment of colonial power relations central to which is racial classification intended to reinforce gender hierarchy. "Intimacy" refers to the bodies of both colonizer and colonized and to the "structures of feeling"—and "habits of heart and mind"—that make possible domination and subordination. What interests me here is the parallel between Deloria's acerbic depiction of culturally incompatible "worlds" that endlessly recreate the very asymmetrical power relations which they seek to explain and the disconnect between Stoler's own locational language and the relative lack of attention those who work within her framework pay to the physical spaces in which intimate connections occurred. In Stoler's case, the disconnect has two obvious sources: her enormous debt to Foucault and her own work on the Dutch East Indies and its imperial rule by the colonial bureaucracy of a distant metropolis.[3] Stoler-like arguments usually appear with respect to state regulation of racial categories as a means of control over colonial populations, and far less often to colonial relations on the ground. They are directed, in other words, toward the role of the state in the creation of racial others and the institutionalization of racial othering as a form of rule. Focused on the production and policing of the two worlds of colonizer and colonized, this analytical approach is not as well equipped to consider what happened when the twain did meet—on the ground and especially in settler societies.

This is not to say that domains of intimacy do not offer a significant lens for understanding colonial power relations. The question, instead, is how we might locate these domains in the messiness of everyday lived experience, in the shared spaces of colonizer and colonized, particularly those in which power was not consolidated but diffused. To answer this question, I will first consider Stoler's call to seek out domains of intimacy in the context of U.S. internal colonialism. I will then link this framework to the "frontier" historiography of the Old Northwest with particular respect to Indian-white relations. Here I will draw on geographer Denis Cosgrove's analysis of the idea of landscape and the ideological power of settlement as a landscape. Finally, I will show how geographer Doreen Massey's conception of place as a social network can help us to disentangle complicated and ambiguous colonial relations on the ground. Following Massey, in other words, I will recast the geography of intimacy as a geography of social relations. This turn will ultimately bring us back to Stoler who, in her introductory essay to *Haunted by Empire*, muses about "what counts as the intimate." She evokes "Heidegger's notion of 'nearness'—not something that can be measured by physical distance so much as degree of involvement, engagement, concern, attention one gives to it."[4] For this exploration of the spatiality of intimate domains, I will draw on my work on Old Wing Mission, a Protestant endeavor near present-day Holland, Michigan, resulting from the 1836 Treaty of Washington in which Odawa and Ojibwe peoples were compelled to cede to the federal government the western half of the Lower Peninsula north of the Grand River and the eastern half of the Upper Peninsula. My account of Old Wing is drawn from a larger, forthcoming biography of two families—one Odawa, the other white—who met as central actors in the affairs of the mission.[5]

Let me begin with Stoler's discussion of internal colonialism. In "Tense and Tender Ties" internal colonialism is one of four "moments" in U.S. history that she singles out for comparison with colonial circumstances in

Africa and Southeast Asia. Stoler's description of three of these moments is precise and straightforward: the "colonial period" before American independence, the antebellum plantation South, and the "conventionally defined 'age of American imperialism,' " beginning with the Spanish-American War. All such specificity vanishes in her explanation of the fourth moment "highlighted in the model of internal colonialism used to describe the contact zones of the Native American colonial encounter." Not only do global points of comparison fail Stoler, but she gropes to place the moment in time and space. Perhaps it refers to the "period from 1870 to 1920"; perhaps it occurred as early as the 1850s, or perhaps still earlier. The construct of internal colonialism describes everything from "the dislocations of Native Americans and the warpings of their domestic arrangements," to "modes of interaction between Mexican farm workers and Anglos in the copper towns of Arizona, and black sharecroppers and the dominant white culture of the South." The cloud of conceptual confusion does not lift in Stoler's subsequent edited volume, *Haunted by Empire.* Here internal, or domestic, colonialism is applied to a "swath of U.S. history," including "the post slavery conditions of African American populations . . . Native Americans, and border relations in southern states."[6]

My object here is neither to belittle Stoler's call for comparative histories of colonialism, nor to reject internal colonialism as a conceptual framework potentially applicable to a number of instances in U.S. history.[7] But it is to argue for greater geohistorical specificity in the deployment of this portmanteau term. It is also to argue that there is a logic behind the very vagueness of the term in its U.S. incarnations that speaks both to the national historiography of Indian-white relations and to the limitations of Stoler's own conception of colonialism for our understanding of those relations. Let me be clear, first, that by internal colonialism I refer to the enactment and enforcement of policies designed to render Indigenous communities perpetually subordinate as a form of nation-building. Although the Constitution conferred responsibility for relations between Indians and Americans on the federal government, the practice of internal colonialism extended far beyond federal policymakers and officials, particularly in certain times and places. Territorial, state, and local governments, as well as private citizens, as individuals and as members of voluntary associations, all played a role in the imposition of colonial relations on Native peoples.[8] In his essay in this volume, moreover, Joe Genetin-Pilawa explores political ramifications of Indigenous relations with nineteenth-century Washington, DC, far broader than encounters with federal officialdom.

Agents of several levels of opinion, authority, and power came together at Old Wing Mission, and more generally in Michigan and elsewhere in the Old Northwest, in the generation before the Civil War. In the Old Northwest, implementation of the federal policy of Indian removal occurred in tandem with the creation of new states from territory already cleared of Native title. Federal officials and white settlers alike saw elimination of Indigenous land claims as a necessary, early step in the formation of a commercial agrarian countryside, dotted with villages and towns linked by state-sponsored internal improvements to eastern markets, and benignly ruled by republican institutions. There is a matter-of-fact, taken-for-granted quality to accounts of settlement in the Old Northwest, both by contemporary and later commentators, including, until quite recently, most historians. But, in fact, settlement was hardly foreordained, and it was certainly not innocent. Just how unsettling settlement was can be seen by considering it not only as a process, but as a landscape.

To evoke the landscape of settlement is to bring together two terms, both dating from the sixteenth century, with a shared history in North America. As Denis Cosgrove has shown, the idea of landscape is fundamentally perspectival. As a way of seeing, it is also ideological. The idea of landscape as "prospect," he argues, emerged in the long transition from feudalism to capitalism, key to which was the shift in the value of land from status to property. In the same period, the term settlement became associated with occupation or dwelling, with colonization, and with the transformation of forest into farms. In the North American context, Cosgrove identifies settlement as a landscape in his discussion of the rectangular survey, brought into being by the Land Ordinance of 1785, the fruit of Jefferson's physiocratic commitment to land as the foundation of all value.[9] It is hard to see the grid system of the federal survey as a "prospect" except when looking down on a flat map or—an option unavailable to Jefferson's skeptical contemporaries—from the vantage point of an airplane window. But a prospect the rectangular survey is, nevertheless. It valorized landownership in severalty, linking the future of the republic to citizens' access to the public domain; and it imposed abstract uniformity over the most varied physiography. Less obviously, perhaps, it made settlement a landscape of futurity, seemingly without limit in its ability to expand through space over time. Well aware that settlement always entailed transition or becoming, nineteenth-century Americans spoke of going to "look land" or to "prospect" when selecting parcels of federal land for purchase.[10]

In the late eighteenth century and for at least a century thereafter, Americans entertained a remarkably consistent notion of what settlement looked like, of what followed when private citizens claimed a portion of the public domain for their own. Alexis de Tocqueville was so impressed by this consistency that he composed a generic description of settlement after touring Michigan Territory in 1831. "As all these settlements are exactly like one another, whether they are in the depths of Michigan or just close to New York," he writes in "Quinze Jours au Désert" ["A Fortnight in the Wilderness"], "I will try to describe them once and for all." The first signs of settlement, he continues, are audible—the bells of unfenced livestock and the ringing of the ax. Then appears evidence of the work of the ax—swatches of dead and dying girdled trees—followed by a patch of ground "more carefully cultivated than the rest . . . the trees hav[ing] been cut but not yet grubbed up." In a single-room cabin, without "interior partition or light," lives the settler-family, rough planks serving as their furniture, and an open fireplace providing their heat and light. Crude as it is, however, this dwelling signifies to its occupants not the deprivation of the present, but the plenty of the future. The cabin, Tocqueville marveled, was an "ark of civilization lost in an ocean of leaves."[11]

Faith that the plow followed the ax remained strong even in places not well-suited to agriculture, whose chief economic assets were extractable resources, such as the trees themselves. Thus, in 1876, a local booster in northern Michigan decried the "unfavorable" prospects for farming in Alpena when its "principal business . . . in those days of early settlement was the manufacture of lumber" and declared that "success . . . in the future depends . . . on the development of farming." Almost twenty years later, his counterpart in somewhat better endowed Oceana County expressed relief that the area had "passed from the critical lumber stage of existence" and was "now fairly entered upon the period of unsurpassed agricultural and horticultural prosperity."[12] As these examples suggest, a good deal of the persistent appeal of the landscape of settlement was its immense flexibility. Precisely because it was a landscape of futurity, it could absorb all manner of non-agricultural activities, including land speculation, while remaining faithful to the ideal of farms from forest.

Thus, the landscape of settlement provided the spatial referent for the narrative of progress, with its binary of savagery and civilization, which lay at the foundation of relations between nineteenth-century Americans and Native peoples. It was prima facie justification not only for the federal policy of Indian removal but, as James Buss demonstrates for the lower Great Lakes region in his essay in this volume and in his recent monograph, of removing Indians from the public discourse in places where they still lived.[13] The logic of this erasure was impeccable. Despite common American recognition of the regularity with which Indigenous people moved around well-defined homelands and their deep resistance to relocation, in contrast to the sometimes deplored, sometimes celebrated willingness of Americans repeatedly to pull up stakes, Indians could not be settlers. Henry Rowe Schoolcraft, architect of the 1836 Treaty of Washington, spelled out the twain that could not meet in Article 13, which gave Odawa and Ojibwe signatories occupancy rights to the ceded area until "the land is required for settlement."[14]

As Buss has shown, this logic of settlement was subsequently written into American history. It is very much with us today. It not only provides the story line for the "frontier" period of individual state histories, but it accounts for the relative lack until recently of scholarly attention to Native peoples in the Old Northwest after their loss of political autonomy, even though the process of removal was incomplete in Ohio, Indiana, and Illinois, and largely failed in Michigan and Wisconsin. The narrative acknowledges neither ongoing relations on the ground between Natives and newcomers, nor the role of other institutions besides the federal government in shaping those relations. Put another way, there is no room for the multiracial circus towns, safe havens for Native and African Americans alike, which are the subject of Sakina Hughes's essay in this volume.[15]

Which brings us back to Ann Laura Stoler's understanding of internal colonialism in various U.S. contexts. Her vagueness with respect to time and place is of a piece with the national historiography of Indian-white relations, which privileges the role of the federal government and tends to overlook contact zones that remained intact after Native conquest. But there is more going on here than the limiting effect of historiography on Stoler's understanding of U.S. history. As she herself has explained, students like her of European colonialisms have focused on the concept of race as a "central colonial sorting technique." They have primarily dwelt on the "sites and circuitries of racial classification," showing much less interest in "how these categories work on the ground."[16] Analysis of categories on the ground, however, requires a concept of place, something that Stoler's Foucauldian framework is ill-equipped to provide. As geographer Doreen Massey has argued, Foucault's is a "notion of space as only [original emphasis] systems of simultaneous relations," and she remarks on the "contrast" in his scheme "between temporal movement and . . . a notion of space as instantaneous connections between things at one moment." In other words, the sites and circuitries of colonial relations may change over time, but they lack spatial form and content except as part of a larger grid of relations at any one point in time.[17] This is exactly the scenario that Deloria describes to explain two-worlds knowledge production.

Colonial relations on the ground, however, cannot be gauged without considering their spatial form and content because they are by nature imbedded in place. In Massey's terms, a place arises from the "particular set of social relations which intersect at a particular location."[18] This unbounded conception of place, I contend, offers a useful way of thinking about internal colonialism. Because social networks overlap and intersect in space, one can determine connections among places on a scale from the local to the global. Because social networks evolve over time, one can specify the nature of change within and across places. Most importantly for my purposes here, Massey's conception of place as a geography of social relations offers a way of approaching colonial intimacies from the perspective of lived experience.

Let me now turn to Old Wing Mission, beginning with its origins in the 1836 Treaty of Washington. The original version of the treaty provided its Odawa and Ojibwe signatories with permanent reserves in Michigan. Before ratifying the treaty, however, the Senate made the reserves temporary, declaring that the Indians should prepare for removal within five years unless granted permission to remain in the state by the president. It fell to Henry Rowe Schoolcraft, Acting Michigan Superintendent of Indian Affairs and federal negotiator of the treaty, to convince the Odawas and Ojibwes, who had been highly reluctant to sell any of their land and were deeply disturbed by the Senate's alterations, to accept the revised treaty. This Schoolcraft did by arguing that the Indians would not miss the permanent reserves because the use-rights provision in Article 13 would allow them to pursue "indefinitely" their seasonal round of hunting, fishing, horticulture, and gathering.[19]

One of the Odawas present on Mackinac Island when Schoolcraft made his case to the Native signatories for accepting the Senate's amendments was a man named Ogemainne (chief man; Joseph Waukazoo), whose designation on the final treaty as a "second-class chief" indicates that he had considerable standing within his band, but was not yet a senior headman. Ogemainne was from Apahtuwaing, one of the villages of Wawgawnawkezee (L'Arbre Croche), the northern homeland of Odawas in Michigan, which stretched along the northeastern shore of Lake Michgian between present-day Petoskey and the Straits of Mackinac. He also had close relatives at Weekwitonsing, a new village which represented an Odawa effort to deal with the increasing American presence in northern Michigan following the War of 1812. At Weekwitonsing, the Odawas had intensified their horticultural production, welcomed a Catholic missionary, and sought schooling in English for their children. Ogemainne and members of his immediate family were baptized as Catholics in the 1820s, placing them among the Odawas who by 1836 had already come a good distance in preparing to live in the midst of white settlers. In fact, Ogemainne had already petitioned President

Andrew Jackson and the U.S. Congress, arguing that the reserves provided no security for his people because "we shall be obliged to sell them at some future time whether we wish it or not," and praying that Congress would instead deed him and his band "some land from which has been bought of the Indians."[20]

Ogemainne saw land ownership as a defense against removal because he understood that, for Americans, possession of real property established a claim to citizenship. At Old Wing, he and his band repeatedly demonstrated their understanding of this equation by the care that they took to pay state and local taxes on their lands and their successful negotiation and implementation of a government contract to build a road through the township where the mission was located. Ogemainne's petition itself evokes the landscape of settlement, declaring the Odawas' desire for "Schools, Churches, & Roads." Moreover, despite its address to the president and congress, a salutation typical of Indian remonstrances to the federal government, the form of the petition is that of a citizens' appeal. Sixty-eight American men from Allegan, a new lumbering town on the Kalamazoo River, signed Ogemainne's petition, attesting to his character and the worthiness of his request.

It would be a mistake, however, to conclude that Ogemainne saw disappearance into the landscape of settlement as the price of continued Odawa residence in Michigan. On the contrary, he viewed land ownership as a means of perpetuating the seasonal round by creating a permanent base from which his band could exercise their use-rights under Article 13. Playing on the trope of the wandering Indian, the petition asks that he may be granted a "home" where "he may lay his bones where . . . the bones of his descendants for ages to come will be"; in reality, it seeks legal title to a home that Odawas had long occupied. The location of the land the Ogemainne sought to claim was telling. Since acquisition of land was an urgent matter and the cession was unsurveyed public domain, he looked south of the Grand River. There lay his winter hunting grounds along the Kalamazoo River between Allegan and Lake Michigan.

There is no record of any response from president or congress to Ogemainne's petition, but he persisted in his determination to acquire land south of the Grand River. Because this area had been open to settlement since the late 1820s, Ogemainne needed to establish a different set of relations with whites than the federal connection embodied by Acting Superintendent Schoolcraft. Building on his petition to Washington, he found in Allegan the white allies who would make possible the establishment of Old Wing Mission on federal land purchased by the Odawas with treaty annuity monies: the Western Michigan Society to Benefit the Indians. The driving force in this evangelical Protestant voluntary association was John R. Kellogg, one of whose partners in the lumber business, not incidentally, was Henry Rowe Schoolcraft. The WMSBI formed part of the network of benevolence that had taken shape in Michigan at the same time, and for largely the same reason, that the Odawas and Ojibwes had been compelled to sell their lands: the rush of settlers from New England and upstate New York into the southern Lower Peninsula beginning in the early 1830s.[21] Article 6 of the Treaty of Washington also reflected the western reach of the network of benevolence by providing funds to church-related societies for the establishment of Protestant and Catholic missions among the Indians. Under this treaty provision, Old Wing Mission would receive an initial grant of $750 and funding for a teacher and a farmer after 1843.

In the late 1830s, it was never clear to either the Odawas or their white supporters whether the federal government intended missionary instruction of the Indians in "civilization" as preparation for their removal or for their permanent residence amid whites in Michigan. Until his own removal for gross mismanagement of his office, including nepotism, Schoolcraft argued for one position or the other depending on his correspondent. The WMSBI, however, apparently harbored no doubts about either the desirability of the Odawas' remaining in Michigan, or about their potential for "civilization." On the first point, the society was joined by many white settlers and long-established fur traders, who found dealing with the Indians useful and profitable, not least for the annual infusion of treaty monies into the cash-starved frontier economy.[22] Details about the WMSBI's role in promoting a program of civilization at Old Wing are sparse, but its intentions and the outlines of its activities are clear enough. The society intended that the Odawas would live the year round on their lands, learning to farm them in the manner of white settlers; they would also embrace the evangelical Protestant version of Christianity, and they would send their children to school. All of these aims would prove intensely divisive at Old Wing but, in 1838, when Ogemainne and his followers first approached the society, both sides had grounds for believing in a shared understanding of Old Wing's purpose. The Odawas from L'Arbre Croche had already demonstrated an interest in schooling for their children and, although at least nominal Catholics, they were willing to tolerate Protestant services. Despite their devotion to the seasonal round, they also had experience with intensified horticultural production. They were willing to accept a program of civilization, but on their own terms.

For its part, the society saw in Old Wing a heaven-sent opportunity to transform Indians into Yankees like themselves, so it provided the Odawas with logistical assistance in buying federal land, and raised funds for the mission through the network of benevolence that connected Calvinist churches in Michigan to their counterparts in the East. Central to both of these endeavors was the recruitment of the Reverend George Nelson Smith as a missionary. In 1838, when Smith first became involved in the affairs of the WMSBI, he was already a missionary, but for the American Home Missionary Society, a joint venture of the Presbyterian General Assembly and the Congregational Consociation of Connecticut to colonize the West with Calvinist churches by subsidizing clergymen in new settlements too poor to support ministers on their own.[23] For a man like Smith, who was only a few years removed from ordination, laboring for the AHMS was an obvious career path in a new country. Relying on his connections in the benevolent network, Smith had migrated to Michigan from Vermont in 1833, bringing with him a wife, young son, and a few years of part-time theological study under the direction of a Congregational clergyman in St. Albans. It took Smith two years of additional study, alternated with grinding manual labor, to be licensed and called to preach at Plainfield (later Plainwell), located east of Allegan on the Kalamazoo River. When he began work for the WMSBI, Smith drew on the same network of benevolence that had made possible his career in the ministry. He solicited funds from Calvinist churches throughout southwest Michigan. At many of these he had once preached, and they were now led by his colleagues, variously affiliated with the Congregational Association of Michigan, of which he was a founding member, the St. Joseph Presbytery, and the AHMS. He used all of these connections to solicit directly churches and women's charitable societies in the East for funds and supplies for the new mission.[24]

Smith spent most of his time, however, working with the Odawas to establish the mission. He went with them to L'Arbre Croche to collect treaty annuity monies and to the land office in Ionia to purchase some 1,200 acres of land near Black River a few miles inland from Lake Michigan. In the late summer of 1839, he and his family canoed down the Kalamazoo River to the tiny village of Saugatuck at it mouth on Lake Michigan. There Arvilla Smith and their now three children stayed while George moved to a site that he later purchased adjacent to the Indians' land. The site could only be reached by hiking more than a half dozen miles through heavy timber, or by sailing up Lake Michigan from Saugatuck and then trekking inland a few miles. Wherever possible, therefore, all visitors to Old Wing, Odawa and white, came by water. Thus isolated in the woods, Smith and a hired man built a simple cabin that would serve as the Smith family home and headquarters for the mission for the next seven years. Into this two-room dwelling, with its partial dirt floor, leaky roof, and entryway without a door, the Smiths and their meager possession moved in October. The mission family saw little of the Odawas—or anyone else—until December, when the "Chief," as the Smiths referred to Ogemainne, called on them. Ogemainne brought the family a welcome gift of venison; he addressed George as his "brother," and he told Arvilla that he would bring more venison once "they had understood the hunting better." He also promised the Smith that the Odawas would continue to visit them so that they did not "get lonesome" in the woods."[25]

This episode encapsulates social relations and their spatial expression at Old Wing. It attests, first, to the Odawas' commitment to the seasonal round. The mission was located in Ogemainne's hunting territory, so he and his followers did not appear at Old Wing until late autumn. Before 1849, when the mission moved north to the Leelanau Peninsula, near present-day Traverse City, the Odawas made little attempt to live on the year round and to farm the land that they had purchased near the mission house. Instead, they built lodges several miles away near the shore of Lake Michigan on land that they purchased collectively with the money they had earned from fulfilling the government road contract. From there, they traveled in the fall to collect cranberries and to gather reeds to make mats. In the spring, they moved to a nearby grove of maple trees to make sugar, which they sold at Grand Haven, the port at the mouth of the Grand River, or in Chicago, along with the berries and pelts they had harvested. When the days grew long and warm, they paddled their canoes north to visit their relations and friends at L'Arbre Croche. Moving the end-of-summer payments of treaty annuities from Mackinac to Grand Haven shortened these visits but did not end them.

Ogemainne's concern that the Smiths not become "lonesome in the woods" was a direct reference to the spatiality of the seasonal round in relation to Odawa social organization. During the winter, the band dispersed into small family groups for hunting. At Old Wing, many of these encampments were located on the properties owned by individual Odawas near the mission house, enabling the children to attend school. In warmer weather, however, the Odawas drew together at the village near the Lake Michigan, the center for them of social, political, economic, and—to the Smiths' dismay—religious life. Even after they had put at least some of their lands into production, they refused to live during the growing season on their farmsteads, contending that the woods made them "sick" as well as "lonesome." And, indeed, the woods did make people sick because they were full of malaria-bearing mosquitoes. From an American perspective, suffering the "ague" was the price of farm-making, as was physical isolation, both conditions testaments of commitment to the landscape of settlement. At Old Wing, it was the Smiths who became sick and lonesome in the woods.[26]

Despite this commitment to the woods, however, the mission family quickly became implicated in the seasonal round. Benevolent and federal support for the mission proved inadequate and erratic. The small donations from many sources on which Old Wing depended slowed during the depression following the Panic of 1837–1839. Much of the money set aside in Article 6 of the Treaty of Washington for missions had already been allocated by 1839. As a result, the Smiths not infrequently relied on Odawa generosity, and were therefore in no position to compel the Indians to make substantial changes to their lifeways. The Smiths found their teaching and preaching largely confined to the winter months. They traded clothing from the missionary barrels for Indian commodities.

Ogemainne's comment about "understanding the hunting" also suggests the complexity of social relations at Old Wing, because it points to the presence of other Indians in the areas besides the extended families from Apahtuwaing. The Grand River just north of Old Wing was home to a concentration of Odawa villages roughly comparable in size to those at Wawgawnawkezee and organized in much the same way around politically autonomous bands and their headmen. Old Wing Mission drew Odawa extended families to it from the Grand River Valley, and they challenged Ogemainne's leadership. The headman and his brother Pendunwan found themselves locked in rivalry with Maksabe and his sons, both sides pressing Smith for his allegiance. It is significant that Ogemainne referred to Smith as his equal—his brother—for it signals his intention of enfolding the missionary family in a web of mutual obligations through fictive kinship.

The political ramifications of such social relations were fraught. On the one hand, Smith's credibility as a missionary to federal officials and benevolent supporters depended on his ability to persuade them of Indian progress toward civilization. Yet he had no power to compel the Odawas to comply with white demands, except the threat to close the mission, which undermined his own investment in it. On the other hand, Smith's effectiveness among the Odawas depended on his ability to represent their needs to outside authorities. For their part, the Odawas proved extremely adept at pitting the various representatives of American authority—Smith, the executive committee of the WSMBI, and the Acting Superintendent of Indian Affairs in Detroit—against one another when anyone of them became too pressing in their demands. To this end they were also capable of exploiting the rivalry between Ogemainne and Maksabe which otherwise proved so poisonous for life at Old Wing.[27] There were bitter, continual negotiations over what the Odawas would and would not do in conformity to competing Native and American visions of the purpose of the mission: they would build houses on their lands near the mission, but they would not forsake their annual visit to Wawgawnawkezee; or, they would move the mission entirely to the lakeshore, if Smith would come with them; or, they would accept the assistance of a federally appointed farmer in clearing their land for planting, but only if he were a Catholic métis of their own choosing from Mackinac, and not a Presbyterian Yankee from Allegan; or, they would acquire livestock with federal funds, but would not fence in the animals. Over the years, the specific conflict changed, but the larger problem the ongoing turmoil represented was never resolved.

The center of Old Wing, this complicated place, so small and personal, yet so deeply enmeshed in external social networks and their attendant power relations, was the mission house, where Ogemainne visited the Smiths in late December of 1839. Indeed, for over two years, the dwelling was the only structure at the mission proper until the Odawas and members of the WMSBI built nearby a school that also served as a meeting house. The mission house was Old Wing's domain of intimacy. In it, the lines between public and private completely blurred. It provided living space for the Smiths, who displayed themselves to the Odawas as a model Christian family. It was a site of worship, sometimes for the family alone, and at others with Odawas in attendance. All sorts of mission business took place within its walls: exchanges of goods, feasts, and interminable discussions of mission politics. It was also a place where George, and particularly Arvilla, taught school, bringing together the Smith children with those of Ogemainne's extended family. There was no other space like it at the mission. The Smiths did occasionally make social calls on the Odawas in their lodges, and George attempted to preach and attended to the ill and dying there. But, in general, the life of the mission was the mission house; there the Odawa presence was palpable in a way that the Smiths' never were at the village by the lake.

For all the activity that occurred within its cramped confines, moreover, the mission house was also a gendered space, where unfolded a story of women barely visible within the documentary record of Old Wing. Life at the mission subjected Arvilla Smith to immense physical and psychological stress. She was often unwell, and George frequently left her and their children alone when he went off on business for the mission. In her first six years at Old Wing, she suffered a miscarriage and the deaths of two newborn infants and a toddler. In her diary, Arvilla referred again and again to God as her only friend. But she was less physically isolated than her diary and George's memoranda books suggest on first reading. For not only did she teach the children of Ogemainne, his brother Pendunwan, and sister Kinnequay, but she was constantly visited during her illnesses and in George's frequent absences by these children and Ogemainne's wife, mother, and sister. While she learned Anishinaabemowin, and they acquired more English, Arvilla communicated with the women through an interpreter, a métis woman named Mary Ann Willard, who lived with the Smiths. To the extent that relations between the Odawas at Old Wing and the mission family ever achieved the "nearness" on which Stoler has commented as an aspect of intimate domains, it was among women in the mission house. The women's prayer circle that Arvilla and Willard formed with Ogemainne's female relations were among the first Odawas that George baptized and among the founding members of the church that he subsequently organized on the Leelanau Peninsula.

The Odawa women, Arvilla complained in her diary, were "no company for me," but they did provide comfort, she admitted. She did not, as she had once envisioned, teach the women Yankee domestic skills, so much as she submitted to their ministrations during her illnesses, and she was grateful for their kindness. These intimate relations ultimately resulted in something completely unexpected, outside both Odawa and American purposes in establishing Old Wing. In 1851, two years after the mission's relocation on the Leelanau, the fictive kinship Ogemainne had posited between his family and the Smiths became a real relation when two of Arvilla's old students married: her daughter Mary Jane and Kinnequay's son, Payson Wolfe.

Notes

1. Here and what follows refer to Vine Deloria, *Custer Died for Your Sins: An Indian Manifesto* (Norman: University of Oklahoma Press, 1989 [1969]), 79–86.

2. Ann Laura Stoler, "Tense and Tender Ties: The Politics of Comparison in North American History and (Post) Colonial Studies," *Journal of American History*, 88, no. 3 (December 2001): 829–55; *Idem*, ed., *Haunted by Empire: The Geographies of Intimacy in North American History* (Durham, NC: Duke University Press, 2006. See also, *idem*, *Carnal Knowledge and Imperial Power: Race and the Intimate in Colonial Rule* (Berkeley: University of California Press, 2002); *Along the Archival Grain: Epistemic Anxieties and Colonial Common Sense* (Princeton, NJ: Princeton University Press, 2009). The title of Stoler's essay in the *Journal of American History* refers to Sylvia Van Kirk's *"Many Tender Ties": Women in Fur-Trade Soceity in Western Canada* (Winnipeg: Watson and Dwyer, 1980). For an appraisal of this germinal

work, see Robin Jarvis Brownless and Valerie J. Korinke, eds., *Finding a Way to the Heart: Feminist Writings on Aboriginal and Women's History in Canada* (Winnipeg: University of Manitoba Press, 2012). Major North American monographs influenced by Stoler include Cathleen D. Cahill, *Federal Fathers and Mothers: A Social History of the United States Indian Service, 1869–1933* (Chapel Hill: University of North Carolina Press, 2011); Sarah Carter, *Marriage and Nation-Building in Western Canada to 1915* (Edmonton: University of Alberta Press, 2008); Margaret D, Jacobs, *White Mothers to a Dark Race: Settler Colonialism, Maternalism, and the Removal of Indigenous Children in the American West and Australia, 1880–1940* (Lincoln: University of Nebraska Press, 2009); and Adele Perry, *On the Edge of Empire: Gender, Race, and the Making of British Columbia, 1849–1871* (Toronto: University of Toronto Press, 2001). See also two special issues of *Frontiers: A Journal of Women Studies*, "Domestic Frontiers: The Home and Colonization," 28, nos. 1–2 (2007); and "Intermarriage and North American Indians," 29, nos. 2–3 (2008).

3. On Stoler's debt to Foucault, see *Race and the Education of Desire: Foucault's History of Sexuality and the Colonial Order of Things* (Durham, NC: Duke University Press, 1995.)

4. Ann Laura Stoler, "Intimidations of Empire: Predicaments of the Tactile and Unseen," in *Haunted by Empire*, 15.

5. Susan E. Gray, *Lines of Descent: Family Stories from the North Country*, forthcoming, University of North Carolina Press.

6. "Tense and Tender Ties" is reprinted in Stoler, ed., *Haunted by Empire*, 23–70. Page numbers here refer to the reprint version: 32–37. The second quotation form *Haunted by Empire* comes from Stoler's introductory essay, "Intimidations of Empire," 12.

7. For a thoughtful review of these instances, see Linda Gordon, "Internal Colonialism and Gender," in *Haunted by Empire*, 427–51. Also useful are the essays in the special issue "Domestic Frontiers: The Home and Colonization," especially the "Introduction" by guest editors Victoria Haskins and Margaret Jacobs, in *Frontiers: A Journal of Women Studies*, 28, nos. 1–2 (2007): ix–xvi. For a discussion of the invention of the term "internal colonialism" by "Third World sociologists to account for the social realities of their country and region" (104) and its applications in various contexts of U.S. and Latin American history, see Walter D. Mignolo, *Local History/Global Designs: Coloniality, Subaltern Knowledges, and Border Thinking* (Princeton, NJ: Princeton University Press, 200), 102–05, 197–201.

8. Roger G. Kennedy, *Mr. Jefferson's Lost Cause: Land, Farmers, Slavery, and the Louisiana Purchase* (New York: Oxford University Press, 2003); Deborah Rosen, *American Indians and State Law: Sovereignty, Race, and Citizenship, 1790–1880* (Lincoln: University of Nebraska Press, 2008); Bethel Saler, "An Empire for Liberty, a State for Empire: The U.S. National State before and after the Revolution of 1800," in James Horn, et al, eds., *The Revolution of 1800: Democracy, Race, and the New Republic* (Charlottesville: University of Virginia Press, 2002); Anthony F. C. Wallace, *Jefferson and the Indians: The Tragic Fate of the First Americans* (Cambridge, MA: Belknap Press of Harvard University Press, 2001).

9. Denis E. Cosgrove, *Social Formation and Symbolic Landscape* (Madison: University of Wisconsin Press, 1998 [1984]), 161–88; on the etymology of landscape, see John Brinckerhoof Jackson, "The Word Itself," in John Brinckerhoff Jackson, *Landscape in Sight: Looking at America*, edited by Helen Lefkowitz Horowitz (New Haven: Yale University Press, 1997), 299–306; on the etymology of settlement, see Susan E. Gray, Rebuttal Report, 2005, on behalf of the Chippewa Otttawa Resource Authority, *U.S. v. Michigan*, 2007, 11–20.

10. On "prospecting," see Susan E. Gray, *The Yankee West: Community Life on the Michigan Frontier* (Chapel Hill: University of North Carolina Press, 1996), 17–41.

11. Alexis de Tocqueville, Excerpt from "A Fortnight in the Wilderness," in Justin L. Kestenbaum, ed., *The Making of Michigan, 1820–1860: A Pioneer Anthology* (Detroit: Wayne State University Press, 1990), 23–27.

12. William Bolton (in 1876), "Alpena County: History of Alpena County," *Michigan Pioneer and Historical Collections* 6 (1907): 181–82; Hon. Enoch T. Magford, "Reminiscences of Oceana County," *Michigan Pioneer and Historical Collections*, 22 (1894): 235–36.

13. James Joseph Buss, *Winning the West with Words: Language and Conquest in the Lower Great Lakes* (Norman: University of Oklahoma Press, 2011).

14. "Treaty with the Ottawa, etc., 1836" in Charles J. Kappler, ed., *Indian Treaties, 1778–1883,* vol. II (Washington, DC: Government Printing Office, 1904), 450–56.

15. For a transnational take on this argument, see Susan E. Gray, "Writing Michigan History from a Transborder Perspective," Special Issue on the Great Lakes Basin, 34, no. 1 (Spring 2008): 1–24. For recent examples of the settlement narrative in state histories, Andrew Cayton, *Frontier Indiana* (Bloomington: Indiana University Press, 1996); James E. Davis, *Frontier Illinois* (Bloomington: Indiana University Press, 1998); and R. Douglas Hurt, *The Ohio Frontiers: Crucible of the Old Northwest* (Bloomington: Indiana University Press, 1998). An overdue examination of the persistence of Indigenous peoples in the Old Northwest is R. David Edmunds, ed., *Enduring Nations: Native Americans in the Midwest* (Urbana: University of Illinois Press, 2008.)

16. Stoler, "Intimidations of Empire," in Stoler, ed., *Haunted by Empire,* 2.

17. Doreen Massey, *Space, Place, Gender* (Minneapolis: University of Minnesota Press, 1994), 264.

18. Massey, *Space, Place, Gender,* 168.

19. For an account of the negotiations, see Charles E. Cleland, *Faith in Paper: The Ethnohistory and Litigation of Upper Great Lakes Indian Treaties* (Ann Arbor: University of Michigan Press, 2011), 56–80. My account of Old Wing Mission is primarily drawn from two bodies of evidence: the annual memoranda books of the Reverend George N. Smith, 1838–1846 and 1848–1849, and the diaries of Smith (1843–1845) and his wife Arvilla, 1834–1845, with Reminiscence, 1808–1834. These personal narratives are located in the Michigan Historical Collections of the Bentley Historical Library at the University of Michigan. The second body of

evidence, contained in the National Archives is the correspondence of the Michigan Superintendent of Indian Affairs. Published transcriptions of most of the documents pertaining to the history of Old Wing Mission may be found in Robert P. Swierenga and William Van Appledorn, eds., *Old Wing Mission: Cultural Interchange as Chronicled by George and Arvilla Smith in Their Work with Chief Wakazoo's Ottawa Band on the West Michigan Frontier* (Grand Rapids, MI: William B. Eerdmans, 2008). All transcriptions in this essay are my own. Changes in punctuation for clarity are silent. Spelling is original.

20. Andrew J. Blackbird, *History of the Ottawa and Chippewa Indians of Michigan; a Grammar of Their Language and Personal and Family History of the Author* (Ypsilanti, MI: Ypsilanti Job Printing House, 1887; reprint Charleston, SC: Nabu, 2010), 24–52; James M. McClurken, *Gah-Bah-Jhgwah-Buk: The Way It Happened: A Visual Culture History of the Little Traverse Bay Bands of Odawa* (East Lansing: Michigan State University Press, 1991), 18–20. Joseph Wakazoo, "Petition to the President of the U.S. & the Senate and House of Representatives," April 29, 1836, NAM, RG75, MSMALR, M1, Roll 41, 486–88.

21. On Yankee migration to Michigan and elsewhere in the Upper Midwest in the generation before the Civil War, see Gray, *The Yankee West*; John C. Hudson, "Yankeeland in the Middle West," *Journal of Geography* 85 (Sept.–Oct. 1986): 195–200. The classic account is Lois K. Mathews, *The Expansion of New England* (Boston: Houghton Mifflin, 1909).

22. Susan E. Gray, "Limits and Possibilities: Indian-White Relations in Western Michigan in the Era of Removal," *Michigan Historical Review*, 20, no. 2 (Fall 1994): 71–92.

23. Gray, *The Yankee West*, 119–38; Colin Goodykootz, *Home Missions on the American Frontiers with Particular Reference to the American Home Missionary Society* (Caldwell, ID: Caxton Printers, 1939), 165–269; Frederick I. Kuhns, "The Operation of the American Home Missionary Society in the Old Northwest, 1826–61" (PhD diss.: University of Chicago, 1947).

24. A good discussion of how these connections worked in the East and the central role played by women's organizations is Carolyn J. Lawes, *Women and Reform in a New England Community, 1815–1860* (Lexington: University of Kentucky Press, 2000).

25. Arvilla (Powers) Smith, Diary, 1834–1845, and Reminiscences, 1808–1834 (Ann Arbor: Michigan Historical Collections, Bentley Historical Library, University of Michigan), unpaginated, December 22, 1839.

26. On the village, the seasonal round, and Anishinaabeg social organization, see Cary Miller, *Ogimaag: Anishinaabeg leadership, 1760–1845* (Lincoln: University of Nebraska Press, 2010), 21–64.

27. This interpretation of the rivalry between Ogemainne and Maksabe owes much to Rebecca Kugel's insights about the political advantages of factionalism in *To Be the Main Leaders of Our People: A History of Minnesota Ojibwe Politics, 1825–1898* (East Lansing: Michigan State University Press, 1998).

III

Consequences and Implications

7

nahi meehtohseeniwinki: iilinweeyankwi neehi iši meehtohseeniwiyankwi aatotamankwi

To Live Well: Our Language and Our Lives

George Ironstrack

> Wiihsakacaakwa sprang up. He shook all seven of the Manitou's heads. He failed to wake the Manitou up. And so then he opened a keg of gunpowder. He poured it out onto the Manitou's heads. And then he rubbed gunpowder into a rag. And he strung it out away from their heads, towards the door. Then he got out. He lit the fuse.[1]
>
> —Wiihsakacaakwa Aalhsoohkani Tawaahkwakinanka, late 1800s

"George, if you come from a couple of tribes, do you have to choose one?" The question was nearly drowned out by the noise of the Miami Tribe bus as it moved through the Oklahoma countryside. On the bus were about thirty Myaamia (Miami) youth and educational staff. We were all returning to the Miami Tribe of Oklahoma's Cultural Grounds, where the tribe holds its annual *Eewansaapita* youth education program. The group had been out traveling for the afternoon to a mining museum in Baxter Springs, Kansas, and observing the many mountainous chat piles that dot the landscape around Pitcher, Oklahoma. This was the summer following the devastating EF4 tornado that tore through northeast Oklahoma and western Missouri. As a result, Myaamia youth were exposed to both the terrible ongoing ecological damage produced by the remnants of lead and zinc mines (the metal infused chunks of gravel that formed the chat piles) and the dramatic after effects of *soowapinamwa* (tornado). The older youth, especially those who live in the vicinity of Pitcher, were quiet and reflective as the bus bounced its way along the gravel roads toward our shared home for the week. Despite the noise, the circumstances magnified the importance of the question: "do you have to choose?"

The Myaamia *ahkwaniswa* (young Miami woman) who posed the question was fourteen years old at the time and had been attending Myaamia education programs for four years. A generally quiet and observant youth, this young woman is from a multiethnic and multilingual background that includes both tribal and non-tribal peoples. Among Myaamia educators we often say "your knowledge isn't demonstrated by the questions you can answer, but the questions you can ask," and this young woman's softly spoken yet powerful question demonstrated that she had reached a new level of awareness of herself and her place within the communities to which she belongs. The timing of the question surprised me but not the question itself. It is the kind of question I dearly hope all of our youth eventually turn their minds toward. My answer was careful and as quietly spoken as her question. It went something like this, "In one way, yes, you do have to choose. Our politics requires that you can only be a voting member of one tribe. But outside of that, no you don't have to choose. If you can learn the language, kinship networks, and the responsibilities of each group, then it is possible to belong to all of the communities that your family connects you to." She nodded and sat back in her seat watching the dust kicked up by the bus as we neared our destination. Since that brief conversation, she has never broached the question again. She has taken on ever-greater responsibility among her relatives and is helping other young people explore what it means to be from our community.

Her question continues to be powerful for me, as it reflects one of the key efforts of Myaamia educators—to reinforce, and where necessary recreate, *Myaamionki* (the place of the Miami), which includes lands in Oklahoma, Kansas, and Indiana. In this place, our once silent language will fill the air and help shape the thoughts of Myaamia people. In this place, the wisdom derived from our people's collective and continuing experiences over many generations will be shared in a responsible manner.[2] However, it is my hope, and I believe the hope of many of my fellow Myaamia educators, that this reinforcement of our cultural and linguistic boundaries will lead to a revitalized *Myaamionki* that is fully enmeshed and interconnected with the communities all around us. Our history has taught us well what happens to a people who become ghettoized.

In our heritage language, Miami-Illinois, we call ourselves Myaamiaki (the downstream people) as well as *Mihtohseeniaki* (human beings or commonly translated as "the people"). We originally emerged as a distinct and different people in the northern Wabash River Valley in what is today the state of Indiana. Our people's experience was shaped in part by the physical forces brought to bear on us by settler groups: disease, invasion, war, settlement, division, and forced removals. The effect of this physical force was amplified over time by the settlers' constructions of a series of double binds wrapped around the poles of assimilation and authenticity.[3] Through the use all of these forces, settler societies produced an unprecedented fracturing of Myaamia cultural landscapes. We believe that our ancestors found ways to resist these pernicious influences, but the disruption eventually weakened us internally to the point that our heritage language passed into a period of dormancy in the 1960s.[4]

Beginning in the 1990s, Myaamia people engaged in an effort to reclaim, reawaken, and revitalize our language. These revitalization efforts center on two communities—the Miami Tribe of Oklahoma and the Miami Nation of Indiana. The existence of these two separate groups is partly the product of past fracturing, but this breaking has not been either permanent or absolute. Myaamia families, my own included, have moved unceasingly between the groups maintaining kinship connections and a sense of cultural unity. These connections are demonstrated by our work in language reclamation and revitalization. Members from the Indiana Myaamia community sparked the contemporary language revitalization effort and the flames of that fire spread quickly to members from the Oklahoma Myaamia community. Today, as a result of this mutually beneficial work, there are hundreds of Myaamia people who acknowledge the living presence of their language and many are learning to speak at various levels. For the first time in nearly 100 years, children are born into this world hearing our heritage language and are learning to speak it in infancy.[5]

We recognize this work as a long-term intergenerational effort that requires continued mending of the fabric of our society. It compels us to identify the false dichotomies we faced in the past. These stark "either-or" constructions relegated Myaamia language and culture to an uncivilized and unproductive past and presented settler languages and cultures as the means to a civilized and productive future. We have to acknowledge the impact that gross differences in power had on the choices our people made over time. To be successful we must help future generations of Myaamia people recognize and reinforce the place of their culture and their language in a world we share with a multitude of peoples, languages, and cultures. We believe that for our people, language and cultural revitalization requires an intergenerational focus on helping our youth to better understand and strengthen our collective sense of peoplehood and their own individual place within this group. We also firmly believe that our young people must seek an understanding, but not necessarily an acceptance, of outsider perceptions of our people.[6] Through this process we believe that our nation will enjoy a healthier future in which we thrive according to our own internal sense of a collective good life.

This is not to say that I believe that there is a single unchanging Myaamia sense of peoplehood and self. I understand that our sense of community constantly flexes with our ever-changing environment and that individual understandings of self are even more highly varied. Yet, within the flux of our lived experience, we do also find certain consistencies in our peoplehood over time. We seek to center our young people on these relatively constant features of being Myaamia, while providing them with experiences to understand how and why our community changes over time. We believe that this will allow future generations of our community to stand strong together upon these foundational features as Myaamia people. At the same time, this will allow them to make conscious decisions as individuals and as a community about how to alter behaviors in tune with both the constantly changing world and generations of Myaamia knowledge and experience.

The young woman's question remains significant to me because I believe it shows that she is beginning to recognize that she has choices and we as a community have the right to define the options. From my perspective, that is powerful. It is a Myaamia power, one built by interweaving an intense respect for individual choice with an equally intense sense of responsibility to our people through the generations. It is a power which, based on our historical experiences, should not have survived. But here we are. What follows is my personal understanding of my community's past experiences, an explanation of how those experiences affect my thinking about education within our community, and a few concrete examples of how these conceptions play out on the ground in Myaamia educational programs.

As much as possible, I will attempt to be clear about the line between my personal beliefs and what I perceive as communally held beliefs. The Myaamia are a small but diverse community and I hope my writings honor the diversity of viewpoints that help make us strong. In addition to the programs administered by the Miami Tribe of Oklahoma, there are educational initiatives administered by our relatives within the Miami Nation of Indians of Indiana, and family specific efforts that fall outside the purview of any governmental entity. All of these groups hold slightly different attitudes and beliefs, and each group uses educational practices unique to their situation. I do not speak for these groups or the individuals who head up their efforts. What follows are thoughts that have emerged from my role within the educational efforts of the Myaamia Project and the Miami Tribe of Oklahoma.

In the historical background section of this essay I have included references to sources that may help interested parties understand my perspective of our stories of the past. Much of my interpretation of our history is based on my personal experiences and is not necessarily reflected in the record as traditionally employed by trained historians. Nearly two decades of learning our heritage language has shifted my interpretative lens and dramatically altered my sense of our people's narratives. In sharing my perspectives of our past I am only seeking a "balance of stories."[7] I am not asking anyone to change his or her narratives, only to listen to ours with an open heart and mind.

A Story of Evolving Peoplehood: Disruption, Change, and Community Health

> Mihtami Myaamiaki nipinkonci saakaciweeciki.
> At first the Miamis came out the water.
>
> —Waapanaakikaapwa, 1914[8]

> Miisaahaki eehkwa peemhkawaaciki neeminki awiikawaanki oowaaha ašiihkiwi
> The prints of my ancestor's houses are everywhere to be seen here.
>
> —Mihšihkinaahkwa, 1795[9]

The shared history that forms one of the core elements of peoplehood for the Myaamia begins with the story "Where the Miami First Came From" and the emergence of the Myaamia from the water at *Saakiiweeyonki* (at the confluence near contemporary St. Joseph, Michigan).[10] Among Myaamia people there is a diversity of opinion on whether this story of emerging from the water is a story of migration or creation. Regardless, both interpretations tend to lead people to agree that the story marks our beginning as a distinct and different group.

In 1914, *Waapanaakikaapwa* shared this story in Miami-Illinois with the self-trained language enthusiast Jacob P. Dunn. *Waapanaakikaapwa*, also known as Gabriel Godfroy, established the communal veracity of his story by stating, "[t]his is how my mothers told me, my mother *Seekaahkweeta*, and her older sister *Waapankihkwa*" and that "[a]ll the old Indian men believed it." Statements such as these are absent from other stories that *Waapanaakikaapwa* shared as well as from stories shared by other storytellers. From my perspective these statements mark this story as a uniquely important foundational story. It teaches us much about our people's earliest perceptions of themselves and others.

At the beginning of this story, the group struggled to climb the riverbank at *Saakiiweeyonki*. They raised their voices together and implored each other to "Grab a hold of tree-limbs" and to pull their way out of the water. They then formed a town at this location. After an unstated amount of time, Myaamia people left the village. The narrative does not state where they went, but other stories describe Myaamia people settling numerous villages along the *Waapaahšiki Siipiiwi* (Wabash River) over an extended period of time.[11] After some time away, one Myaamia man returned to *Saakiiweeyonki*. In the next scene of the story we believe we observe how our ancestors perceived themselves and the multitude of peoples with whom we shared our homelands. This scene of the story includes the Miami-Illinois in order to facilitate a clearer intra-group understanding.

> *Kapootwe nkoti aapweeyaata.*
> After a while one returned.
> *Aapwe pyaata kwitakaki mihtohseeniaki neewaaciki Saakiiweeyonki.*
> When he came back he saw the other Indians at Coming Out Place.
> *Naahpa-'hsa naapi iilaataweeciki iilataaweeyaanki.*
> To our surprise, their language was just like our language
> *Neehi-'hsa weentaawaaci 'Mahtahkisenaakana', iilaaciki iina mihtohseeniaki.*
> He named them 'Old Moccasins'; that's what he called those Indians.
> *Moohci ninkihkeelimaahsoo weencinaakosiwaaci.*
> I don't know which tribe they belonged to.
> *Moohci aweeyaki kihkeelimaawaata eehi-'yaawaaci.*
> Nobody knew where they went.

In this moment of first meetings between two unfamiliar peoples I believe we see a deep expression of our peoplehood reflected in the means by which our ancestors perceived various groups of humans. At first glance, a non-speaker of Miami-Illinois might be misled by the fact that the English term "Indians" shows up two times in this passage. However, the term *mihtohseeniaki* that *Waapanaakikapwa* and Dunn, working collaboratively, translated as "Indian" is more commonly glossed as "human beings." Technically, there was originally no term for "Indian" in the language. This term, which has a literal translation of "one who walks bare," originally applied to all humans. In its oldest form, this story outlines how our ancestors differentiated other groups of humans: by the language they spoke and the place from which they came.[12]

In this story, there is a collectively voiced surprise that this unfamiliar group of humans spoke in the same manner as the Myaamia. I understand this surprise to be indicative of linguistic diversity that existed among our neighbors. To encounter an unfamiliar group who spoke in the most familiar manner possible was a rare occurrence. Linguistic similarity paralleled a sense of relatedness between Myaamia people and their neighbors. The *Inoka*, or Illinois people, spoke the same language as the Myaamia and they were referred to collectively as our "younger siblings." Groups like the *Acipwia* (Ojibwa), *Wahoonaha* (Potawatomi), and *Taawaawa* (Ottawa) spoke related languages that were not mutually intelligible, but shared many common words and structures. These groups were all referred to as "elder brothers." For much of our history, peaceful discourse and reciprocal exchange has structured the relations among these younger and elder siblings.[13]

In general, regional groups who spoke non-Algonquian languages could be brought into the kinship network, avoided, or warred against. Prior to the end of the eighteenth century, this status tended to be consistent with Central Algonquian-speaking groups sharing kin status and Iroquoian speaking and Siouan speaking groups treated as enemies. A prominent exception was the Wyandot, an Iroquoian speaking group, who were considered kin prior to the time of contact with the French.[14]

After establishing a linguistic affinity between this new group of humans and our people, the story then sets them apart as different. This difference is based on place. The Myaamia man in this story cannot connect these humans to a place in his known landscape. He does not know their point of origin or their ultimate destination. Once again, the English gloss does not make this distinction clear. *Waapanaakikapwa* used the word *weencinaakosiwaaci*, which literally translates to "he is from a place." Dunn and *Waapanaakikapwa* glossed this word as "tribe," but its original meaning is purely place-based. Only following contact with Europeans did the meaning shift to include the European concept of tribe. It is our belief that the concept of "tribe" is one that evolved through contact with Europeans, as did the concept of an "Indian," and solidified into its current form through the treaty years (1795–1871). In the pre-contact period, this passage would have likely been understood to indicate only that this Myaamia observer knew neither where these people came from nor where they went. Though they spoke the same language, these humans, whom he named "Old Moccasins," were a mystery to Myaamia people then and remain unknown to us today.[15]

This story of emergence provides us with the outlines of the earliest sense of our peoplehood. Myaamia people spoke the same language and were connected to the same point of origin, *Saakiiweeyonki*. Untold generations lived in interconnected networks of villages along *Waapaahšiki Siipiiwi* (the Wabash River) and its many feeder streams. According to *Meehcikilita* (Le Gros) and *Pinšiwa* (J. B. Richardville), Myaamia people moved from *Saakiiweeyonki* to settle a village where the *Kohciisa Siipiwi* (St. Joseph River) and the *Maameewa Siipiiwa* (St. Marys River) join to form the *Taawaawa Siipiiwi* (Maumee River). This village eventually came to be called *Kiihkayonki* in our heritage language, though it has been known by many other names in its past.[16] Today it is the location of the city of Ft. Wayne, Indiana. This location provided excellent bottomland for farming and was one end of a strategic portage linking the peoples of northeastern North America with those living in the south and west.

As the village at *Kiihkayonki* grew too large to support its population, groups split off and formed new villages downstream on the *Waapaahšiki Siipiiwi* (Wabash River) and its feeder streams.[17] For most of our history, our peoplehood was centered on these villages. The villages spoke the same language, shared many of the same stories, followed a similar ecologically based and cyclical lunar calendar, and hunted and farmed in nearly identical ways. Yet, each individual village governed itself and was not bound to any larger entity. These villages would often join together to address large issues that affected the kin group, like war and peace, but disagreement and conflict between villages did occur from time to time. In chaotic periods, like the ensuing conflicts that followed the arrival of Europeans, some of these related villages even came to violent blows.[18]

Within Myaamia villages, group identity was divided and balanced by the interweaving of clans. Originally, there may have been ten or more clans, which were often named for animals, birds, weather phenomena, and celestial bodies. Because marriage within one's own clan was taboo, new marriages produced links between clans that may have helped maintain communication and compromise between villages. During times of discord, villages may have found the means to settle disputes through the intervillage families of clans. At some point during the early to mid-1800s, these systems of intra-village organization ceased to function as Myaamia people transitioned to a non-clan lineage organizational system.[19]

A Myaamia individual was born into a society where the household was controlled by their mother or another female relative. This was a flexible system, but in general children lived with their birth mother and were surrounded by their close female relatives: all those that they called *ninkya* (birth mother and her sisters). All of these women's children were referred to as siblings in addition to all the children of *noohsaki*, one's close male relatives (birth father and all his brothers). An individual's self-understanding was very much shaped by a sense of belonging and responsibility to a large family. Close male relatives were often absent from the village while hunting or engaging in acts of war. When they were in the village, however, close male relatives took an active role in the education and training of their many children. Parents' lessons emphasized a heavy of sense of group responsibility, especially to one's close relatives, but they also engendered a powerful sense of individuality.[20]

Within village, clan, and home the division of gender roles and responsibilities also shaped an individual's sense of self. Adult men were responsible for hunting, making war, and negotiating peace, which included the ritual exchanges later called "trade." Adult women were responsible for the construction and maintenance of the home dwelling; care of the children; farming and the processing and storage of produce; meat and hide processing; and the cooking of meals.

Following a separation between a married couple, the former husband would leave taking only his clothing, hunting equipment, and weapons with him. The mother maintained control of the house and the children. Foodstuffs produced through agriculture and the processing of the results of a hunt were also a part of the household and therefore controlled by the women. Men received nourishment and shelter from women as a part of a reciprocal exchange in which women received the results of successful hunts, protection from external violence, and specialized goods from other group's homelands. Ideally, this exchange maintained an equitable balance between the two groups. There were historical moments when this system broke down and abuse became sadly commonplace, but the equitable balance seems to have nearly always reemerged.[21]

Like most of the cultural norms within a village, gender roles were highly flexible. Men often worked in the farm fields and women commonly accompanied men on hunting trips. There were also exceptional individuals in the community who were born sexually male and lived most of their lives in a woman's gender role. The reverse was also true. Some of these exceptional individuals moved back and forth between gender roles throughout their lifetimes. The flexibility that was inherent to Myaamia gender roles reflected a cultural norm of intense respect for an individual's right to choose their own path in life.[22]

One of the key historic practices that highlights this sense of individuality is the training in fasting and dreaming that a young person sought out. As soon as one was physically capable, an individual would fast and spend time alone outside the village. This practice would continue intermittently until an individual successfully acquired a dream that provided significant insight into the direction one's life should take. Through this process an individual acquired a dream "guardian" that would ideally provide a sense of direction for the rest of an individual's life. This process was a significant cornerstone in the lives of young people. The French Jesuits recognized dreaming as significant to the culture and made concerted efforts to destroy this important creative process as a first step in "disabusing" the youth of their "superstitions."[23]

New dreams and a new direction in life could be sought out at any point that an individual thought it necessary, and these later dreams were often accepted with as much regard as the dreams of adolescents. Many times dreams and dream messages were the vehicles through which individuals challenged group norms. One *Aacimooni* (historical narrative) centers on a woman whose dream caused her to lead a successful war party against the Seneca. War parties were usually a male enterprise, but in this case the warriors of the village followed her on account of her dream. She led the war party by carrying the group's collective war bundle and provided the strategy for the successful attack. In an even more dramatic sense, dreams could also lead to a change in an entire community's long-term behaviors.[24]

Historically, this intense respect for individual freedom was paralleled by the lack of a fixed hierarchy within a village community. Civil leaders were attended to because of their abilities in mediation and oration, but they could not command. Leaders who tried to give orders were usually ignored and if their behavior continued, they quickly found themselves no longer in the position to represent the community. A village community was not held together by the forceful will of a strong leader, but by the sense of community created by the interweaving of close and extended family.

There were, of course, limits to individual freedom. Individual freedom was always situated within the context of community responsibility. An individual who committed destructive acts and failed to atone for those acts could be asked to leave the community. Only in cases of murder was punishing retribution sought. This *lex talionis* style of atonement could be avoided if the murderer were to attempt restitution through other means, usually ritual gift giving.[25]

Ideally, a healthy village community was produced from the blending of a strong sense of collective responsibility with an intense respect for individual beliefs, perspectives, and actions. Striving to maintain a healthy community was an ongoing process, one that required continual adjustment to the natural flux within the community, within the village's environment, and among the communities of other groups (be they relatives, friends, or foreigners). There are many examples of Myaamia villages in various stages of ill health, and we believe these moments have much to teach us about what happens when we make poor choices as a community or when the field of choices becomes constricted by others in a manner that does not allow us to strive to be healthy in our own way.[26] These examples also have much to teach us about how our ancestors recovered from serious disruptions.

It was the arrival of numerous radically new groups of people into our ancestors' homelands that began a three-hundred-year period of decline in our ability to determine our own present, and thereby, our future.[27] Each new group usually shared a common homeland and they often shared a common language. Today, we know that each of these groups—French, English, Spanish, and German—had high levels of regional diversity in both place and language in their respective homelands. However, we do not know if our ancestors fully recognized the internal diversity of these groups. It is possible that they perceived each new group as a people, in that they came originally from an unknown shared homeland and spoke the same language. Perhaps they would have assumed that each of these groups had many relatively independent villages in their homeland and that they too could come together during times of requirement. Our ancestors may have recognized the potential for independent-minded subgroups. What we do know of our ancestors' perceptions of these new peoples is stored in the remaining stories of these encounters and the terminology they created to describe each new group.

These new peoples were recognized as unique in a multitude of ways and our ancestors' names for these groups reflect this. The *Meehtikoošiaki*, the wooden boat people, were one of the first of these new groups our ancestors encountered. This group's homeland in Western Europe was unknown to our ancestors, so our external identification of the group centered on their unique watercraft. Our own stories say that we likely first encountered the *Meehtikoošia* (French) prior to the series of disruptions usually called the Beaver Wars. *Aakalaahšima* was a name "borrowed" from the English language, the language in common of the often multilingual Scottish, Irish, and English with whom Myaamia people interacted. The *Meeleewaatawiaki* (Germans), the bad speakers, were identified by an apparent pattern of speech. The *Iihpaawala* (Spanish) were named for their place of origin or the language that they spoke. *Iihpaawala* was either borrowed directly from the French "Espagnol" or indirectly through another Algonquian speaking group.[28]

Over time, as these new "families" grew in size and spawned siblings, speakers of Miami-Illinois continued to recognize new distinctive group features and named them accordingly. Most prominent among the younger siblings descended from the early settlers of North American were the *Mihši-maalhsa*, the big knives. This name was first applied to the English-speaking settlers of lands to the east of our homelands, which the *Mihši-maalhsa* called Virginia. By the time of the American Revolution against the British, the *Mihši-maalhsa* began to migrate west along the southern edge of the *Kaanseenseepiiwi* (Ohio River) into what became the state of Kentucky. This migration initiated a continuous series of physical and cultural conflicts that endured for over one hundred years.

It is important to note that none of the names for all of these "new" groups drew on conceptions of race. These groups were recognized as unique based on the languages they spoke, the technologies they possessed, or the behaviors they engaged in. The vocabulary for commenting on skin color or other physical features existed and was used, but it did not become the primary means by which Myaamia people dealt with the unique groups they encountered.

In addition to unique languages, technologies, diseases, and animal species, settlers also carried unique ideas with them. One such conceptual construct carried into our homelands in the 1600s was the idea of "the tribe." As stated above, unity among peoples called Miami and Illinois by European groups was experienced through common language, shared landscape, shared history, and similar lifeways. Beginning in the 1600s, European settlers attempted to interact with speakers of Miami-Illinois, with a greater degree of formality and rigidity. As a tribe, the Miami were seen as including all the villages of Wabash River Valley, including the *Waayaahtanwa* (Wea) and *Peeyankihšia* (Piankashaw). From a European perspective, most of the villages to the west of the Wabash that spoke Miami-Illinois were referred to as "Illinois." Europeans employed this concept in attempting to create coalitions among tribes that could be used to make wars, create peace, and sustain trade networks. Over a period of two hundred years Euro-American expectations of tribal cohesion, especially in terms of leadership, led to structural changes in the way speakers of Miami-Illinois organized themselves.

From the Beaver Wars (mid-1600s) until the Removal Era (1840s), speakers of Miami-Illinois altered the way they organized themselves in response to the demands and expectations of outsiders. Change is a natural part of life and we can point to many examples of change brought about by our people through reflection and consensus. However, as the settler groups grew increasingly powerful, Miami-Illinois speaking communities were often forced to make choices out of desperation—choices that did not allow for meaningful compromise; did not take into account long term consequences; and did not allow the groups to base their decisions, at least in part, on their own lived experiences and knowledge systems.

As "the tribe" grew in strength, the influence of individual villages declined. Prior to sustained contact with Europeans there was no means of coercing an individual village to accept a group decision. Village independence could reduce internal strife among related villages by either producing compromises necessary to create consensus or allowing a village to go its own way. European peace treaties and American land treaties carried the expectation that an agreement bound the entire tribe and the entire tribe would be held responsible for violations committed by independent-minded villages. For the Americans, tribal nations provided the bounded legal entities that could negotiate away the title to land and thereby create a "legitimate" context for American settlement of Indigenous lands. The creation of tribes as bounded entities divided speakers of Miami-Illinois initially into two groups—the Miami and the Illinois—and increased strife among these siblings.[29]

In part, division and strife increased because of the demands placed on related village communities to make decisions for the entire "tribe." At first, Miami-Illinois speaking communities accomplished this goal by selecting individuals or small groups of leaders to speak on behalf of the group. These men, called *maawikima* (Council Chief or Principal Chief), were skilled orators and ambassadors who merely represented the decisions of the group. Between 1650 and 1840, the role of the *maawikima* shifted from that of temporarily selected orator to that of a more permanent representative of all Myaamia people. The *maawikima* was still responsible for attempting to generate consensus and representing the desires of the people of the community. However, the increase in the importance of the Principal Chief led to a corresponding decrease in the importance of village leaders.[30] In addition, time constraints imposed by outsiders, especially the Americans, often did not allow the *maawikima* an opportunity to engage in the time consuming discussions so vital to the production of consensus. These pressured decisions often left individual villages bound to decisions that were not to their benefit and understandably produced resentment.[31]

This is not to say that these newer tribal entities lost all of the original flexibility of group membership. Following forced removal, the *Waayaahtanwa* (Wea) and *Peeyankihšia* (Piankashaw) merged with two remaining subgroups of the Illinois, the *Peewaalia* (Peoria) and *Kaahkaahkia* (Kaskaskia), in the west. Together they formed the Confederated Peoria Tribe of Oklahoma. As described above, the *Waayaahtanwa* and *Peeyankihšia* villages were originally considered a part of the Myaamia family but as having the closest connections to their Illinois siblings. As they were moved west during the removal era and found each other living as even nearer neighbors, it should not be surprising that they found strength in joining together as family under a tribal-national banner. For a brief period, the Myaamia even considered joining under the same banner, but for reasons not wholly understood, chose to maintain a separate tribal nation.[32]

This transition from village/community focused decision making to tribal/national decision-making was paralleled by a gradual shift in Myaamia understandings of place. During the treaty period (1795–1871), place transitioned from a culturally defined landscape controlled and used by each village, to a cartographically delineated land base owned by the tribal nation, to individually owned parcels defined by legal titles. During this period, outsiders saw collective land use as a sign of wasteful tribal backwardness. Our near neighbors never respected the legal boundaries of tribal lands, as defined by Euro-American treaties. It is my belief that Myaamia people were presented with a choice: maintain a collective land base and face having our resources taken from us through extra-legal means or adopt individual family land holdings and have the supposed ability to protect property through the American legal system.[33]

This three-stage transition took place in less than one hundred years. By the 1870s, some Myaamia people arrived in the northeast corner of Indian Territory (Oklahoma) and were provided lands that were already individually allotted or divided shortly after arrival. By this time as well, the families who remained in the states of Kansas and Indiana also held individual parcels of lands.[34]

This transition did not completely sever Myaamia people from *Myaamionki*. Myaamia people continued to visit many of the important sites that were now controlled by others. Yet, continuance of these collective cultural connections to place without rights of access or control was challenging in the legalistic land-as-commodity society that surrounded our people.

Individual land ownership produced a change in Myaamia family dynamics as well. For at least one generation after allotment, Myaamia residency patterns tended to be organized around intra-group conceptions of family: multigenerational extended families. Over the following generation, parcels of land were lost due to illegal taxation and rising debts. Myaamia families were quickly broken up into nuclear families as people dispersed throughout the surrounding states to seek work. Big economic disasters, like the Great Depression, tended to scatter Myaamia people even more widely as the quest to survive within an economic system not of our design became nearly all consuming. In some cases, intergenerational living patterns continued, especially among those families who were able to stay in Oklahoma, Kansas, and Indiana during these lean years. In general, extended families were no longer able to support themselves while living together in one home.

The breakup of the intergenerational extended family had dire consequences for the natural transmission of language and culture to children. Without the presence of many grandmothers, grandfathers, mothers, fathers, aunts, and uncles, young children lost much of the immersive environment through which they learned how to speak and how to behave through observation.

The negative impact of this disintegration was magnified by the impact of the boarding schools. Many of the first generation of Myaamia people to attend boarding schools retained their fluency and a deep sense of individual identity as Myaamia. Their language and their identity could not be beaten or shamed out of them, but the desire to teach their children could. Numerous elders, born just after the turn of the century, tell stories of observing their relatives joyfully speaking Myaamia outside the home. Most of these elders report that they asked their relatives to teach them to speak and the reply was usually some derivation of "you don't need to speak it, learning it will only hurt you."

In a healthy multigenerational extended family household, this phenomenon might not have had as dramatic an effect. In a healthy context, children would have been surrounded by conversation and activity. But in the context of an isolated nuclear family, the conscious decision of one parent not to speak to his or her children in their heritage language and not to require them to speak it back to them had powerful ramifications.

The relative cultural isolation that came with allotment and the boarding school experience was accompanied by a new level of immersion in a foreign conceptual category: "the Indian." On a continent that once held three hundred or more distinct language groups and many times that number of distinct cultural groups, settlers had gradually formed one racialized category in which to place all Indigenous North Americans. Government agents and interested traders understood much of the complexities that differentiated tribal-nations from each other. They could not successfully negotiate with these groups without that recognition. But the vast majority of the American settler populace had no such understanding. To the majority of the populace our ancestors were simply "Indians."

Our experience with this construct tells me that "Indians" were perceived as: poor, lazy, uneducated, alcoholic, and vanishing. Indians were viewed as a people of the past, not a people with much of a present—and certainly not a people with a future. As a racialized category, Indians were also believed to have one particular appearance. By the late 1800s, this appearance was defined by the settlers' imagining of the plains horse culture peoples: dark skinned, twin braids, draped in eagle feathers, astride a bareback horse, and carrying a weapon. Obviously, this imagining flew in the face of the vast differences inherent in Indigenous North American phenotypes, clothes, hairstyles, dwellings, means of sustenance, and modes of transport. Indigenous groups that met the stereotype suffered from the negative attributes that the settlers' believed plagued the Indian. Those that did not meet the stereotype were considered to no longer be authentically Indian.

This was, and continues to be, one of the most vicious of the cultural traps created by the settler society. To survive and to eventually thrive again, all groups need space and time to change according to their own community predilections. Often, groups that find the wherewithal to change in a healthy manner and begin to thrive again, face accusations of no longer being "Indian." The perniciousness of this double bind is magnified because many of the legal rights that Indigenous groups have maintained through the treaty process require that the group be recognized as culturally distinct. For most of the American populace, distinctiveness is tied to their imagining of the "Indian." In the eyes of most Americans the exercise of sovereign rights requires that a group remain authentically unchanged, and by extension mired in negative circumstances, or risk facing an assault on those rights based on the argument that the group is "no longer Indian."[35]

Legally, this concept extended into the debate over the worthiness of Indians for American citizenship. Up until the 1924 Indian Citizenship Act, a citizen of an Indian tribal-nation could not also be a citizen of the United States. Fully competent Indians, as defined by the settler society, could choose to become U.S. citizens, but to do so they had to renounce their tribal citizenship. For citizens of Indigenous tribal-nations, the pre-1924 United States was a ghettoized world. For my people, it is important to note that nearly all of our collective and individual land was lost to us by the time it become possible to be both "Indian" and a U.S. citizen. This is not to imply that the ghettoization of "Indian" peoples ended in 1924. In some ways we as a people are still dealing with this reality today.

Often in human history, the racialized negative categories created by settler societies are inverted, mediated, and used by the trapped for their own benefit. The concept of the "Indian" is no different. For Myaamia people, we found that there were certain "Indian" behaviors and attributes that were deemed acceptable and even desired by our settler neighbors. Perceived as authentic people of the past, Myaamia people were often called upon to perform this authenticity publically and provide the settler groups with a sense of connectedness to a place that was relatively new to them. These performances usually involved public singing, dancing, and short narrative plays. By the early 1900s, the Myaamia were small in number and deemed nonthreatening, and so these performances were perceived as quaint representations of the past.[36]

Myaamia healing practices also became a cultural commodity in the late 1800s and early 1900s. Local settlers would often seek out elder Myaamia women for homeopathic cures that drew on their knowledge of local plants. These women were usually paid for their knowledge and the medicines they crafted. As "authentic Indians," these grandmotherly women had a knowledge base that was exotically in touch with nature. This exotic knowledge could be used to benefit non-Indians and required compensation, but it did not necessarily change the overall settler attitude regarding "Indians." For example, an elder related one poignant, painful, and emblematic story of how a settler man came to his grandmother's house seeking a cure for a painful malady. When she wanted to inspect his infected wound, the man pulled his head roughly away from her and refused to allow the "dirty Indian" to touch him. Yet, he maintained his respect for her knowledge of plants and accepted her curative poultice. This combination of exotic regard and visceral distain is an attitude that is sadly quite familiar to Myaamia people born at the turn of the twentieth century.

Indigenous peoples most directly mediated and transformed the foreign concept of the "Indian" through the creation of the Pan-Indian cultural arena. There are well-established examples of Pan-Indian groupings that trace from the Beaver Wars of the 1600s through the 1790s. At other times, the Myaamia resisted Pan-Indian groupings, especially when they were not reflective of our familial means of bringing groups together.[37] From my individual perspective, I believe that Pan-Indian networks took on new importance with our arrival west of the Mississippi after forced removal. Following our second removal from Kansas to Oklahoma, Pan-Indian networks allowed our people to stabilize and find the means to adapt to yet another set of circumstances.

Prior to the 1800s, we had little in common with the Cherokee, Quapaw, and Osage. In fact, at various points in our past they were all considered enemy groups. However, in Indian Territory (Oklahoma) they became our near neighbors. Other new neighbors included members of the extended "family" alliance system that preceded removal (Peoria, Ottawa, Eastern Shawnee, Wyandotte, and Seneca-Cayuga). By the late 1800s, all of these communities shared a similar experience of loss, multiple forced removals, and oppression. It comes as no surprise to me that they developed a sense of camaraderie.

This shared experience of life along the Neosho River in what became Northeastern Oklahoma has produced a lively intertribal network that includes shared political, economic, and cultural activities. Without a doubt, the Pan-Indian network of northeastern Oklahoma benefits Myaamia people. Our population is too small to engage in many of these enterprises alone, and the collective effort allows us to strengthen our nation in ways that would be impossible, or too time consuming, to be considered feasible. Despite these successes, there is a hidden risk in our increasing participation in Pan-Indian events.

As a people, we have been able to maintain group cohesion and distinctiveness for nearly forty years after our language went dormant. A fluent speaking Myaamia family surrounded the generation born in the early twentieth century, and this last generation of speakers continued to behave in definably Myaamia ways. Though they refused to actively pass on some of this knowledge to their children and grandchildren, many of these young people learned as children always had: through observation. The next generation, born in the middle of the twentieth century, was not so lucky. Their parents and grandparents possessed fragmented knowledge. More importantly, the context of Myaamia-speaking group interaction had begun to wither. Many Myaamia ways persisted, but many of our songs, dances, stories, and games ceased to be practiced at the communal level. As a result, a clear group understanding of the boundaries of Myaamia peoplehood deteriorated significantly. This missing generation began to fill these cultural voids with the actions and beliefs they encountered in Pan-Indian events.[38]

Beginning in the late 1980s and extending into the early 1990s, the children of this missing generation began to ask questions about their people's historical experiences and reflect on the answers that they found. From this reflection many in this generation began to acknowledge what had been lost and took the first concrete steps that initiated our current revitalization efforts.[39]

I recognize that this is not true for all Indigenous groups who participate in intertribal community events and who have experienced or are experiencing language loss. Many of our near neighbors in Ottawa County participate in their own community's events and intertribal events with no loss of intra-community cohesiveness or distinctiveness. Identity, after all, is not necessarily a zero-sum game.

Within the population of young people with which I interact at tribal education programs I see that we have reached a dangerous tipping point. Many of these young people talk and write about "Indian ways" and the "Indian language." Commonly, I hear some variation of "my grandmother/grandfather was an Indian." These "Indians," grandparents or not, are described as "they" and "them." Comments such as these are troubling because they demonstrate how some of our young people neither see themselves as members of the community nor have a sense of our community's distinctiveness as Myaamia. This is not true of all of our young people, but I have witnessed it enough to be concerned. As an educator, I see these failings as the interrelated results of the double binds that have slowly strangled our community since the 1800s. The real perniciousness of these traps is that it took nearly two hundred years for our community to wake up to the reality of what was happening to us.

Since beginning to awaken, our community has embarked on a huge undertaking. This effort, which began with reclaiming and revitalizing our heritage language, is now best defined as community revitalization. Our heritage language and our unique ways of knowing and being have a community context that needs to be restored for these behaviors to thrive again. Our challenge, as a community with many cross-cultural connections, is to strengthen the core of the group. If the next generation of young people understands what binds all Myaamia together as a distinct people, we will be another step closer to rebuilding a healthy communal context. With a strong community core, each individual will be able to draw on generations of Myaamia knowledge and experience, maintain group cohesiveness, and all the while dream of his or her own unique way of walking through this diverse world.

Lighting the Fuse—Myaamia Youth Education Programs

Our realization of the size and scope of this endeavor grows daily, but after fifteen years of dedicated work on language and community revitalization we have begun to see the outlines of our story. Those of us who work as Myaamia educators have a fuller understanding of the traps of the past and the present and a sense for how to prepare our young people to avoid those pitfalls as well as the unknown obstacles of the future. The young woman who asked the powerful question that opened this essay is an example of what can come from the educative conditions we have tried our best to create. We recognize that we cannot control what our young people will think or do. All we can do is create the "conditions under which they will begin to flourish" and hope that they will return some of this flourishing energy back to their community.[40]

The foundation of this community revitalization is formed from the relatively constant and definably Myaamia behaviors, attitudes, beliefs, and knowledge that endured and in a few cases thrived through the twentieth century. Much of the groundwork for this effort was laid by interviewing the generation of elders born at the turn of the twentieth century. In some cases individual elder knowledge was fragmented into areas of expertise. As each elder contributed his or her experiences, the sum total base of group knowledge became more substantial. In addition to this elder knowledge, our own understanding of the cultural lessons embedded in our heritage language expanded in an unexpected synergy with what the eldest among us were sharing.

Much of what we learned has led us to conclude that Myaamia ways of being and knowing are deeply connected to our sense of place, which links us to our homelands in Oklahoma, Kansas, and Indiana, and our sense of relatedness, which links us to each other. These two foundational elements are then woven together through the stories that have continued to be told and are reworked and rewoven through stories that we have reclaimed or newly crafted.

The traditional Myaamia names that we give to our children are often directly connected to both place and story. The giving of traditional names is one of the ways that the use of our heritage language has continued uninterrupted. To merely say a child's name often opens a pathway to stories and through these stories to family and place. Imbedded in these narratives, and by extension in our places and in our families, are unique Myaamia ways of being and knowing. These include an intense understanding that one must strive one's entire life to learn and that "there is no getting something for nothing." That generosity must define our relationship to each other and our people's relationships with other groups.[41] Our stories also serve as continual reminder of how a healthy Myaamia sense of humor holds the community together.

In our education programs we strive to connect our young people with this foundational core of Myaamia ways of being and knowing. Some of this work involves introducing individuals to concepts that are brand new to them. Some of the work involves awakening them to a new understanding about behaviors and beliefs that are ongoing around them in their family. With some young people, our effort is centered on reinforcing the Myaamia ways of being and knowing that they are actively observing and learning at home, though young people of this type are currently in the minority.

Within the context of a specific program, each of these individuals is seeking a different level of knowledge, but it is a seeking that occurs in a context of responsibility to the group. In the context of a particular program, the group is explicitly defined as including all the program participants (elders, staff, and students). By implication, much of our discussion of group dynamics, behaviors, and knowledge is extended to incorporate all Myaamia people. By the end of a typical program it is our hope that many of the young participants will extend their sense of group responsibility beyond the setting of the program, to their families back home, and eventually to their large extended Myaamia family.

Without exception, these young people are referred to as Myaamia by program staff. All of the language, both in Miami-Illinois and English, references "us," "we," "you," and "I." Even when discussing the distant past, our people are described in the first person. The word "Indian" is rarely, if ever, used in our programs. In our discussions, our community is described explicitly as Myaamia and the accoutrements of our community are often prefaced with Myaamia as an adjective, as in "Myaamia miiciona" (Myaamia foods).

By the end of a typical weeklong program, I believe we have planted some important seeds in the minds of these young people. After two or three years of working with these same individuals, I personally have witnessed a shift in their expressions of their self-understanding and in their descriptions of the community. Instead of the "Indian language," which is spoken by some third party, our youth say they speak "the Myaamia language." Our youth identify "us" as Myaamia and they self-identify as Myaamia. Most importantly, from my perspective, they have a nascent sense of what being Myaamia means, of how our group is unique.

The potential of our educational programs to build community and reinforce individual self-understanding is perhaps best highlighted through a concrete example. During the 2009–2010 academic year, the staff of the Myaamia Project—Daryl Baldwin, Andrew Strack, and myself—led a course designed specifically for the eighteen Myaamia students attending Miami University. The course's title was *iši neenkiki ašiihkiwi, iši meehtohseeniwiyankwi aatotamankwi* (How We See the Land, How We Talk about How We Live).

The goal of this course was to build and or reinforce a sense of awareness of the world around us that we felt was distinctively Myaamia. From our perspective, this awareness is inherently bound to *Myaamionki* (the place of the Myaamia) and is best taught through the use of story. From an external academic perspective, this class was a hybrid that combined history and ecology. From our perspective, the class was an exploration of our people's awareness of the world around them that connected both past and present into a continuum of a larger ongoing communal story.

Late in the summer of 2009, each participant in the class chose one feature to concentrate their observations on over the course of nine lunar months. These features included plants, trees, animals, birds, weather phenomena, celestial bodies, and constellations. They were asked to focus intently on this one feature, but to stay constantly aware of the larger context. Each individual then observed as they saw fit. They were asked to report regularly to the rest of the class community about what they were observing and to try and make connections between their separate experiences. These conversations were interspersed with discussions and readings of stories of our past and present as well as through the recounting of *Aalhsoohkana* (Winter Stories) during the winter months. Weather permitting, the class was usually held outside so that participants could learn to identify features and name them using our heritage language.

At first, the group found much of the work of observation extremely challenging. Many of our college students do not live the out-of-doors life of their grandparents' generation, and as a result they lack many of the basic skills of tree, plant, and animal identification. By narrowly focusing on just one feature, these young adults were able to develop and practice observational skills that they then could apply to the broader environment. Over the course of the first few lunar months, most of the group reported an increase in their awareness of the changes going on all around them.

These young adults were free to conduct their observations in whatever manner they considered useful. Some focused on one representation of their feature, like a specific individual tree. Others chose to observe many different examples of the same species. Some students took it upon themselves to do additional research on the specific ecology of their feature. Other students chose to rely solely on their personal observations even when they knew their experiences might not reflect the generalizations that scientific texts list as "facts" about a particular species.

The individually driven experience of observing was continually balanced by the reminders of the staff, and at times other participants, that everyone was responsible for sharing their observations with the group. Only by combining our observational efforts could the group create an interconnected conceptual web that would allow us to respond to the changes going on in the world around us. The timing of the activities of the group—harvesting plants and nuts, canoeing, winter storytelling, maple sugaring, and lacrosse—were made dependent on when the network of our observations indicated that the moment was right. In this manner, beneficial group activities were dependent on individual responsibility to the effort. Without being explicit, we successfully cultivated a sense of group responsibility while maintaining respect for an individual's right to find his or her own way.

When the weather was not conducive to being outside, we engaged in storytelling. Some of these stories were *Aalhsoohkana* (Winter Stories). These are stories of animals, tricksters, and other-than-human beings. Other stories we shared were *Aacimoona* (narratives) about our past as a people. Through these stories we discussed our people's past experiences in *Myamiamionki* and how our people adjusted to the rapid changes that accompanied the arrivals of settler groups. Together we wrestled with the impact of division, dislocation, and removal on the historic ecological practices of our ancestors. Through both *Aalhsoohkana* and *Aacimooni* we identified beliefs, values, and practices that our people have maintained with slight natural changes over time. From both of these story forms we also identified attitudes and behaviors that have fallen dormant among our people. Through story we were able to reawaken community memories and create the possibility of reclamation and revitalization of community activities.

Moving from remembering to doing requires that one or more of these young people take an interest in responsibly seeking a change in community behavior. For generations untold, young Myaamia people brought forward their dreams and inspired change. The potential is no less with this generation.

We brought the class to a close with two interrelated activities. In the first activity, each individual compiled his or her observations in written form. These essays were then published in a community blog, so that their experience could be shared with their Myaamia relatives.[42] This activity was both an opportunity to reflect and summarize for themselves and to demonstrate a sense of responsibility to their Myaamia relatives. In this manner, an increase in individual knowledge is always accompanied by a parallel increase in responsibility to the group.

In the second closing activity, we asked each member of the group to contribute a personal story of his or her own from the year to the pool of historical narratives that the group had immersed ourselves in throughout the year. From that moment, their stories became Myaamia history in the same way that the individual stories of their ancestors formed the history that we discussed throughout the year.

The resolution of this experience was powerful for me as a Myaamia educator and more simply as *mihtohseenia* (a human being). This year of observing and telling stories brought the group of young adults together as a healthy community. The stories, observations, and behaviors of the group were in a multitude of ways uniquely Myaamia, but in many ways what transpired was simply the humdrum daily life of community. Those simple patterns, which exist in many small communities, bind us together in just as powerful ways as our stories of creation, emergence, and other than human beings. I recognize that this experience was limited to the context of twenty Myaamia people on a college campus in Ohio, but it gave me a practical sense of hope for what we as a Nation can accomplish if we continue to strive for change.

Aapooši Aahkwaapawaayankwi
Once Again We Are Dreaming

Conclusions are always brief in Myaamia stories. I believe this practice recognizes an ending as an arbitrary breaking point, and that the narrative can be picked up and moved forward in numerous unknowable ways by numerous unknowable storytellers. This has taught me to recognize that the future is unknown. It can be influenced, but it cannot be controlled. I have reasons to hope that the collective efforts of all Myaamia people will continue to influence the revitalization of healthy Myaamia communities, but I cannot say for sure how this story will be moved forward. And so I will break this story off with two voices of hope regarding the choices that we all face. One is from a non-Myaamia man who is indigenous to a continent halfway around the world. The other is from one of our own youth, who has grown up speaking our heritage language.

> I can see no situation in which I will be presented with a Draconic choice between English and Igbo. For me, no either/or; I insist on both. Which, you might say, makes my life rather difficult and even a little untidy. But I prefer it that way.
>
> —Chinua Achebe[43]

ceeleelintamaani niišwi iilaataweenkia. myaamia neehi english

I like having two languages. Miami and English

—myaamia kwiiwhsa

Eehinki . . . (to there).

Notes

1. Originally recounted by *Tawaahkwakinanka*—George Washington Finley from David Costa, ed., *myaamia neehi peewaalia aacimoona neehi aalhsoohkana—Myaamia and Peoria Narratives and Winter Stories* (Miami; Ohio: Miami Tribe of Oklahoma and the Peoria Tribe of Oklahoma, 2011), 13–15.

2. This is our concept of Myaamia *Neepwaantiinki* (Myaamia Education) as outlined by the Myaamia Project: "Myaamia neepwaantiinki is the responsible sharing of knowledge and wisdom derived from our people's collective and continuing experiences over many generations."

3. Jessica Cattelino discusses this concept's relationship with sovereignty and economic development for the Seminoles of Florida. Jessica R. Cattelino, *High Stakes: Florida Seminole Gaming and Sovereignty* (Durham, NC: Duke University Press, 2008), 100.

4. Wesley Y. Leonard, "When is an 'Extinct Language' Not Extinct? Miami, a Formerly Sleeping Language," in Kendra A. King, et al., *Sustaining Linguistic Diversity: Endangered and Minority Languages and Language Varieties* (Washington DC: Georgetown University Press, 2008), 23–33.

5. For an outline of these efforts see Daryl Baldwin and Julie Olds "Miami Indian Language and Cultural Research at Miami University," in Daniel M. Cobb and Loretta Fowler, *Beyond Red Power: American Indian Politics and Activism Since 1900* (Santa Fe, NM: School for Advanced Research, 2007), 280–90.

6. Rogers Brubaker and Frederick Cooper, "Beyond 'Identity,'" *Theory and Society* 29 (2000). Brubaker and Cooper argue that outsider perceptions are best labeled with the terminology "identification and categorization." This is what most researchers unknowingly write about when discussing Myaamia identity. It is my belief that they misunderstand it for "self-understanding" and "groupness" (which I call peoplehood in this essay). Professor Tom Holt introduced me to Brubaker and Cooper's excellent and challenging essay and I thank him and my colleagues in his graduate seminar for critiquing my as yet imperfect response to Brubaker and Cooper's challenge. For more on peoplehood see Tom Holm, J. Diane Pearson, and Ben Chavis, "Peoplehood: A Model for the Extension of Sovereignty in American Indian Studies," *Wicazo Sa Review* 18, no. 1 (2003): 1–15.

7. A request made by Chinua Achebe in his essay "Today, the Balance of Stories" in *Home and Exile* (New York: Oxford University Press, 2000), 73–105. Reiterated by Chimamanda Ngozi Adichie in her talk at TEDGlobal 2009 <http://www.ted.com/talks/chimamanda_adichie_the_danger_of_a_single_story.html>.

8. *Waapanaakikapwa*—Gabriel Godfroy in Costa, *myaamia neehi peewaalia aacimoona neehi aalhsoohkana*, 52–53.

9. *Waapanaakikapwa*—Gabriel Godfroy back-translated a part of the speech of *Mihšihkinaahkwa* (Little Turtle) at the Treaty of Greenville (1795) from English into Myaamia. Collections of the Myaamia Project.

10. Holm, et al., "Peoplehood," 1–15. According to the authors, peoplehood is defined as consisting of four elements: place, language, sacred history, and

ceremonial cycle. A Myaamia peoplehood matrix consists of: place, language, story, governance, and habitual behaviors.

11. Charles C. Trowbridge, and W. Vernon Kinietz, *Meearmeear Traditions* (Ann Arbor, MI: University of Michigan Press, 1938), 7–13.

12. *Waapanaakikapwa*—Gabriel Godfroy in Costa, *myaamia neehi peewaalia aacimoona neehi aalhsoohkana*, 52–53.

13. Trowbridge, *Meearmeear Traditions*, 12–13.

14. The Wyandot have long been considered kin even though they are Iroquoian linguistically.See Trowbridge, *Meearmeear Traditions*, 12–13. The Haudenosaunee became kin in the 1740s see Samuel Hazard et al., *Pennsylvania Colonial Records*, Vol. 5 (Philadelphia: Published by the State; Printed by J. Severns, 1851), 308–17.

15. David J. Costa, "Miami-Illinois Tribe Names" in *Papers of the Thirty-First Algonquian Conference*, John D. Nichols, ed. (University of Manitoba Press, 2000), 30–53.

16. Michael McCafferty, *Native American Places Names in Indiana* (Urbana: University of Illinois Press, 2008), 69–87.

17. Trowbridge, *Meearmeear Traditions*, 7–13. Helen Hornbeck Tanner and Miklos Pinther, *Atlas of Great Lakes Indian History*, 1st ed., *Civilization of the American Indian Series; V. 174.* (Norman: Published for the Newberry Library by the University of Oklahoma Press, 1987), 40–41, 58–59.

18. This is especially true during the Beaver Wars when Myaamia villages and Inoka villages engaged in violent conflict with each other. Following the Great Peace of Montreal in 1701, Myaamia villages began to organize more effectively to eliminate conflict among all the villages that spoke Miami-Illinois. Richard White, *The Middle Ground: Indians, Empires, and Republics in the Great Lakes Region, 1650–1815*, *Cambridge Studies in North American Indian History* (Cambridge, MA; New York: Cambridge University Press, 1991), 1–49.

19. For more on Myaamia clans see Trowbridge, *Meearmeear Traditions*, 13.

20. On lectures and a parent's lack of power of their children see Trowbridge, *Meearmeear Traditions*, 39–40.

21. Trowbridge, *Meearmeear Traditions*, 13–15, 19–30, 46–48, 68–69. Deliette on violence against women see the Deliette/De Gannes Journal in Theodore Calvin Pease and Raymond Clarence Werner, *The French Foundations, 1680–1693* (Springfield, IL: Illinois State Historical Library), 334–37.

22. Trowbridge, *Meearmeear Traditions*, 68.

23. On fasting as a youth see Trowbridge, *Meearmeear Traditions*, 56. On Jesuit attitudes regarding dreaming see Jacob Piatt Dunn and G. W. H. Kemper, *Indiana and Indianans: A History of Aboriginal and Territorial Indiana and the Century of Statehood* (Chicago and New York: The American Historical Society, 1919) 72.

24. For the story of the woman war leader see Trowbridge, *Meearmeear Traditions*, 26. On both the start and the end of the man-eater societies see 88–90.

25. Trowbridge, *Meearmeear Traditions*, 16–17.

26. The oft-cited example of the Miami village near Green Bay, Wisconsin is a classic example of an unhealthy situation. The village was too large, by the preceding cultural standards, and the militancy of the time led to other temporary changes in behavior that were unhealthy by these standards. See Perrot's account in Louise Phelps Kellogg, *Early Narratives of the Northwest: 1634–1699* (New York: Barnes & Noble, 1945), 83–88.

27. Krauss writes that of the 300 plus languages indigenous to North America only two-thirds are still spoken. Michael Krauss "Status of Native American Language Endangerment," at *Stabilizing Indigenous Languages/Teaching Indigenous Languages* <http://www2.nau.edu/jar/SIL/Krauss.pdf>, 15.

28. *Aakalaahšima* appears to be a loan from the English, "Englishman." David Costa in email communication February 8, 2011.

29. During the "Beaver Wars" of the 1600s Myaamia and Inoka people briefly warred with each other. See White, *Middle Ground*, 29. In the early 1700s multiple conflicts erupted among related tribes see Bert Anson, *The Miami Indians*, 1st ed. (Norman: University of Oklahoma Press, 1970), 39–42.

30. This loss was probably greatest among women, who organized and represented their voice in the community through village councils. Trowbridge outlines a historic balance between male leadership positions and female leadership positions. He also describes a village council, which consisted of the male leadership of a particular village. He does not mention a parallel women's council, but it seems likely that there was one. Women have continued to gather formally and informally among Myaamia people of today. Trowbridge, *Meearmeear Traditions*, 16.

31. The best example of this discord is connected to the Treaty of Fort Wayne in 1809 and the removal of *Mihšihkinaahkwa* from the position of *maawikima*. See Stewart Rafert, *The Miami Indians of Indiana: A Persistent People, 1654–1994* (Indianapolis, IN: Indiana Historical Society, 1996), 71–73.

32. Anson, *The Miami Indians*, 236–42.

33. The dialogue around the Treaty of the Mississinewa 1826 highlights this clash of perspectives. John Tipton, Glen Arthur Blackburn, Nellie Armstrong Robertson, Dorothy Lois Riker, and Indiana Historical Bureau. *The John Tipton Papers*. Vol. I (Indianapolis: The Indiana Historical Bureau, 1942), 577–92.

34. On allotments in Kansas and Oklahoma see Anson, *The Miami Indians*, 239–44, 255–60. For the last allotment in Indiana see Rafert, *The Miami Indians of Indiana*, 139–48.

35. For examples of this double bind at work with the Seminole Nation of Florida, see Cattelino, *High Stakes*, 100.

36. See Scott Shoemaker, "Trickster Skins: Narratives of Landscape, Representations, and the Miami Nation," (University of Minnesota: PhD diss., 2011) for more on Miami Indian pageants in Indiana as well as Rafert, *The Miami Indians of Indiana*, 212.

37. Myaamia people participated prominently in Pan-Indian alliances during the Beaver Wars of the middle to late seventeenth century and in the system of

alliances that resisted three invasions by the U.S. Army in 1790, 1791, and 1794. Participation in the Pan-Indian alliance created by Tenskwatawa and Tecumseh divided Myaamia people as many were uncomfortable with the cultural and political changes demanded by the brothers' revitalization movement. Gregory Evans Dowd, *A Spirited Resistance: The North American Indian Struggle for Unity, 1745–1815* (Baltimore: Johns Hopkins University Press, 1993), 129, 138–143. Alfred A. Cave, *Prophets of the Great Spirit: Native American Revitalization Movement in Eastern North America* (Lincoln: University of Nebraska Press, 2006), 45–140.

38. Hammel stresses that indigenous identity is not a zero-sum game with Pan-Indian culture competing with community-specific culture. James F. Hamill, *Going Indian* (Urbana: University of Illinois Press, 2006). For a specific example of a group that participates in Pan-Indian networks while maintaining a strong sense of individual distinctiveness see Jason Baird Jackson, *Yuchi Ceremonial Life: Performance, Meaning, and Tradition in a Contemporary American Indian Community* (Lincoln: University of Nebraska Press, 2003), 133–39. Jackson references Howard as an example of the argument that Pan-Indian culture is a threat to community-specific culture and is one step removed from complete loss of cultural distinctiveness. James H. Howard, "Pan-Indian Culture of Oklahoma," *The Scientific Monthly*, Vol. 81, No. 5 (Nov., 1955), 215–20.

39. For more on the beginning of these efforts see Daryl Baldwin and Julie Olds, "Miami Indian Language and Culture Research at Miami University," in Daniel M Cobb and Loretta Fowler. 2007. *Beyond Red Power: American Indian Politics and Activism Since 1900* (Santa Fe, NM: School for Advanced Research, 2007), 280–90.

40. Ken Robinson (2010). *Bring on the learning revolution!* [Video] Retrieved October 20, 2010, from <http://www.ted.com/talks/lang/eng/sir_ken_robinson_bring_on_the_revolution.html>.

41. Waapanaakikaapwa said to Dunn that the central tenet of the Myaamia belief was "there is no getting something for nothing." See Dunn, *Indiana and the Indianians*, Vol. I.

42. Student essays and other class materials are archived on the Myaamia community blog: <http://myaamiahistory.wordpress.com/myaamia-ecological-perspectives-history/>.

43. Chinua Achebe, "The Writer and His Community," in *Hopes and Impediments: Selected Essays* (New York: Doubleday, 1989), 61.

8

Moving in Multiple Worlds

Native Indian Service Employees

CATHLEEN D. CAHILL

In 1930 Lucy Jobin, a matron in the federal Indian Service serving at the Chin Lee School on the Navajo reservation in Arizona, asked for travel leave to take "one of the personally conducted tours" of Europe.[1] Perhaps Jobin, a woman of mixed Chippewa and French descent, wanted to see one of her ancestral homelands, perhaps she wanted to experience the foreign cultures of European nations, or perhaps she believed it was something middle-class Americans should do at one point in their lives.[2] Like thousands of other countrymen and women, Jobin went with a tour group, like the famous Cook's Tours, which were especially aimed at the middle class and emphasized uplift through economical travel. Indeed, Cook's Tours were specifically timed to accommodate "teachers and those engaged in Educational Work," during their summer vacations.[3]

As this incident indicates, Lucy Jobin moved within multiple worlds, none of which is easy to categorize. She was of Chippewa-French heritage, but appears to have been unmoored from a tribal community or even family. Nonetheless, the federal government categorized her as "Indian" for the purposes of employment. She never married or had children of her own, but cared for thousands of Native children over the course of her career. In 1930 she was working among the Navajo, but Jobin had been stationed at six different posts among multiple tribal communities during her thirty-one-year tenure in the Indian Service. Her superiors described her in various ways ranging from excellent employee to rebellious insubordinate. She was Catholic and middle class; a Chilocco Indian School alumna who was friends with Natives and non-Natives alike. She liked to travel and enjoyed reading popular fiction and historical works.[4]

Nor was Jobin unique. At Navajo she was part of a small community of metís, people of mixed Native and European heritage, mostly Ho-Chunk (Winnebago) and French.[5] These employees at Navajo were part of a larger cohort of Indigenous and mixed-heritage people employed by the federal Indian Service, the workforce of the Office of Indian Affairs, in the years before the preferential hiring policies of the Indian Reorganization Act (1934). Regardless of their mixed heritage, the Indian Office labeled them as "Indian" employees. Their experiences offer a good place to test assumptions about people who might be "caught" between two worlds, Indian and white. When people of Indigenous or mixed heritage take part in the colonial apparatus, they are often derided as collaborators or mimics or lauded as cultural brokers, but rarely portrayed as complex individuals building their lives out of the constraints of circumstance. Many, but not all, Native Indian Service employees were of mixed heritage and they did work within the colonial bureaucracy of the United States. Moreover, the government had hired them in the hopes that they would help further the cultural and political destruction of Native nations. But, at the same time, like Jobin, they identified themselves in a multitude of ways that were not solely based on race. These complex individuals were members of many communities, real and imagined, which must be recognized in order to begin moving beyond a binary framework for exploring Native lives at the turn of the century.

This group of Indian Service employees, which comprised the first generation of Native professional and white-collar workers, were navigating a new world. As Phil Deloria has argued, the turn of the twentieth century was an historical moment in which "some Indian people . . . leapt quickly into modernity" and began to participate in the building of modern America. Deloria primarily focuses on Native people's engagement in "representational acts," but employees of the Indian service were also a part of this modern cohort. While they may have "performed assimilation" in some instances, in others, the faces they chose to present to the world were not always a performance. Many of them were of mixed heritage and valued both their Indigenous and European ancestry, but many had also experienced the wrenching disassociation of colonialism, either in the shattering of tribal ties in a single blow or the slow peeling away over generations. But they did not live their lives paralyzed by a stark choice between Indian and white worlds. Instead, they saw themselves as moving forward, making their own way in the world, attempting to do the best for themselves and often their families and sometimes wider communities. They often used the very structures of colonization to recreate ties with Native communities and individual Indian people. A close examination of their lives reveals what Deloria reminds us: that a close examination of their lives reveals the "complex lineaments of personal and cultural identity that can never be captured by dichotomies built around crude notions of difference and assimilation, white and Indian, primitive and advanced" and offers the chance of "a reimagining of the contours of modernity itself."[6]

Federal Hiring Policies

The southwestern desert country of Dinétah, or the Navajo homeland, stands in stark contrast to the lush green lake regions of the upper Midwest, home of Ho-Chunk (Winnebago) and other Indigenous people. But in the second decade of the twentieth century, a small community of metís made their homes in the area of Fort Defiance, Chin Lee, and St. Michaels, Arizona on the Navajo Reservation. How this community came into being, but more importantly, how it overlapped and intertwined with other communities, leads us from the employment policies of the federal Indian Office through the legacy and family history of a metís clan, before returning to the changing and challenging world of Indian Country at the turn of the twentieth century.

At the fin de siécle, the federal Indian Service was composed of a highly unusual group of personnel for its time. It employed large numbers of Native people, women and men, making it both racially and sexually diverse. There were generally two reasons for this distinctive employment pattern: the government's use of the nuclear family model, and its emphasis on the pedagogical possibilities of work within assimilation policy. Policymakers believed that the federal government's goal of bringing Indians into the nation as productive citizens required replacing their "tribal relations" with nineteenth-century middle-class households and their gendered division of labor. To achieve this, the Indian Office focused on land distribution and education policies. It was in education that female employees became most essential. In 1882, the Indian Office created the Indian School Service and began building a network of schools across the West. In an insidious effort to disrupt the affective bonds between Native children and their parents, the Indian schools, especially boarding schools, tried to substitute Indian Service employees as surrogate parents for an entire generation of Indian children. For this the service needed both male and female employees. By the 1890s, roughly 60 percent of the School Service personnel were female.[7]

The Indian Office also had a policy of hiring American Indians to fill positions. Administrators hoped that employment would inculcate work discipline and the desire for accumulation, but they also saw employment as instructive, a way to teach specific skills, as an incentive to keep educated Indians from "returning to the blanket," and as undermining tribal authority.[8] Native labor was also cheaper. Indeed the Indian Office often hired Indians in assistant positions that paid less for the same work. By 1880, the government had a specific policy of hiring Indians if possible. The regulations stated, "[N]o work must be given to white men which can be done by Indians."[9] By 1895 the Civil Service rules were amended so that "Indians employed in the Service at large" could be appointed without a Civil Service examination and those seeking regular positions such as teacher, matron, clerk, seamstress, or farmer were only required to pass a noncompetitive Civil Service exam.[10]

As a result of these policies the percentage of Native employees in the Indian Service climbed steadily throughout the last two decades of the nineteenth century. While most of the statistics are available only for the School Service portion of the Indian Service,[11] they are nonetheless suggestive. In 1888, the commissioner of Indian affairs reported that Indian employees constituted 15 percent of the School Service; by 1895 that proportion had risen to 25 percent.[12] In 1912, the commissioner of Indian affairs reported that Indian employees made up 30 percent of the 6,000 employees in the entire Indian Service (school and agency service) and one historian has estimated that 20 percent of them were white-collar workers.[13]

One of the results of these federal hiring policies was the development of a metís community in Arizona. The Ho-Chunk-French Paquette family was at the core of the community. Wisconsinite Peter Paquette began a seventeen-year term as superintendent at the Fort Defiance School and Agency in 1908.[14] The next year his sister, Mary Paquette, joined him in Arizona as matron at the Chin Lee School, remaining there until 1916. The Paquettes were third-generation government employees. Their grandfather, Pierre, a fur trader for the American Fur Company in Portage, Wisconsin, had served as an interpreter for both government officials and missionaries to the Winnebago. His son, Moses, Peter and Mary's father, also worked as federal interpreter for the Winnebago for many years.[15] It is not surprising, then, that Peter and Mary both chose to work for the Indian Service. The family's work history reflects changes in federal Indian policy. Between 1834 and the Civil War, only 253 Indians worked for the government, most as interpreters, like the Paquettes, or blacksmiths and teachers. The advent of assimilation policy and subsequent growth of federal Indian education in the 1870s and 1880s meant that the number of employees skyrocketed and Indians began to be employed in many different positions.[16]

Peter began his career at the Lac du Flambeau Indian School in Wisconsin in 1895 in the positions of farmer and industrial teacher. Mary joined her brother the following year after graduating from high school in Black River Falls, Wisconsin. In 1902, Ruben Perry, the white superintendent at the school, resigned, and Peter was appointed acting superintendent. While he hoped to replace Perry permanently, the Indian Office appointed another white man to take the position. Paquette appears to have remained on at the school for a few years before being transferred to the Navajo Agency as assistant superintendent. He transferred again in 1907 to the Arapaho Training School in Darlington, Oklahoma, also as assistant superintendent. In 1908, with the strong support of Father Anselm Weber, the Catholic missionary at St. Michaels, Arizona, the Indian Office appointed Paquette as superintendent at Fort Defiance on the Navajo Reservation. Father Weber explained, "It appears his Indian heritage has hindered his promotion so far."[17] Indeed, the Indian Office was hesitant to promote its "Indian" employees to high-ranking positions. It also preferred to have Indians unmoored from their homelands where they might have personal, or more importantly political, connections. Thus, when Peter Paquette ultimately received a superintendency, the highest ranking service position on a reservation, it was not in Wisconsin, but in Arizona.

Mary Paquette ran into similar resistance in her requests to be stationed closer to home. In 1907, the year her brother moved to the Arapaho School in Oklahoma, she requested a transfer as field matron to Black River Falls, Wisconsin, where her family lived. The commissioner of Indian affairs denied her request, noting: "[E]xperience has shown that employees of Indian blood usually succeed better among Indians who are *not* of their own tribe. Relatives, friends and tribal affiliations are more likely to be embarrassing than helpful."[18] Frustrated in her attempt to move closer to her family in Wisconsin, Mary then asked to be transferred to the Navajo Reservation, where her brother had just been appointed as superintendent.[19]

Family ties were important for both Mary and Peter, and they defined family in expansive terms that encompassed a wide range of kin and fictive kin. For example, Mary continued to return to Black River Falls in Wisconsin to visit family, especially her parents, and, according to her obituary, she "remained [there] with them in their declining years."[20] Also, many of the siblings' relatives moved to the Southwest to join them and take positions in the Indian Service. Looking at which relatives came to Arizona offers an intriguing example of how Indigenous people and people of mixed-

Indigenous heritage used extended kinship as an important survival strategy. Peter had no biological children, but served as a father figure for many, and not just symbolically in his role as superintendent in the Indian Service. In 1891, at his brother Solomon's request, Peter became the legal guardian of his nephews, Samuel and Abraham, and his niece, Dora Paquette. In 1898, while employed at the Lac du Flambeau School he became the guardian of another niece, his sister's daughter, Domitilla (Tillie) O'Connell.[21] Also, while at Lac du Flambeau, Peter became the legal protector of the Devine children, a family of mixed-Chippewa and Irish ancestry.[22] It is clear that Peter had some qualities that led other family members as well as acquaintances to see him as a stable, possibly economically equipped provider and guardian for their children. That he agreed to take on these duties indicates that he felt family and personal obligations strongly.

Many of his wards followed Peter into the Indian Service. Like their sister, Lizzie, who worked at the Chin Lee School from 1904 to 1916, several other Devine children worked temporarily at the school during those years. In 1909, Peter and Mary's nephew, Samuel Moses Paquette, moved to the area and began working for the government at Fort Defiance as a laborer and farmer in the Indian Service before going into private business as an Indian trader at St. Michaels.[23] He was followed south a few years later by his sister, Dora Winifred "Winnie" Paquette. By 1914, their cousin, Tillie (Domatilla) O'Connell, had moved to the area and was serving as a nurse at the Fort Defiance Hospital.[24] All of those family members were also Peter's legal wards. While many of Peter and Mary's relatives remained in Wisconsin, kinship had clearly created a strong pull between the Midwest and the Southwest. Nor were they the only Midwesterners or the only metís to live in the region. Lucy Jobin (Chippewa and French), worked at the Chin Lee School with Mary Paquette until 1915 and became a friend of the family. Julia DeCora (Winnebago and French) was also briefly under Peter Paquette's supervision when she worked as an assistant matron at Jicarilla.[25]

In addition to maintaining and reinforcing their webs of kinship, the Paquettes, Lizzie Devine, and Lucy Jobin also maintained their religious ties through the Catholic Church. As historian Susan Sleeper-Smith has demonstrated, Catholicism provided the Pottawatomie people of Michigan and their Native and French kin with the option of "accommodation rather than transformation."[26] She describes this as a legacy of the Catholic fur trade communities in which "kinship, Catholicism, and trade" were "inextricably interwined."[27] The Winnebago and Ho-Chunk had a similar relationship with Catholicism, and many of the families of mixed heritage remained Catholic, as did the Paquettes. Like the families Sleeper-Smith studied, kinship mattered a great deal to them as demonstrated by Peter's willingness to care for a wide range of relatives. It is also possible that the spiritual bonds of godparenting had joined with legal and kinship ties in his role as guardian to various relations. Moreover, the connections those relatives had to the Indian Service and later the Indian trading posts in the Southwest strongly suggest that this family helped each other find work in familiar industries. While Sleeper-Smith ends her study in the 1830s and was focused on a different upper Midwest tribe, the Paquettes demonstrate that Catholicism remained an important binding agent for people of Indigenous and mixed heritage during the period of assimilation in the late nineteenth century as well.

The Catholic Church offered them another kind of community, another world within which they found meaning and support. As Catholics, they were members of the worldwide communion of saints.[28] Father Weber rejoiced when Peter Paquette was appointed superintendent: "It appears that little by little, Fort Defiance is becoming Indian and Catholic. A Sioux, two Chippewa, two Navajo, and two Pueblo Indians—all Catholic—are now employed there. Aside from that two shop owners there are Catholic."[29] Thus Catholicism helped create bonds across Indigenous identities as well as race.

The Church offered an important site of community-building and status for the Catholics at the Navajo Agency. For example, in 1914, the dedication of the new chapel at Fort Defiance (to which the Paquettes and Lizzie Devine had donated) took place at Thanksgiving, and was a major event for the community. The Rt. Rev. Bishop, H. Granjon made the long trip from Tuscon, Arizona, to preside over the service, which was linked with the sacrament of confirmation for the "neophytes [t]here, at St. Michaels, and Chin Lee." A choir of Catholic students from the Fort Defiance Indian School sang the "Mass of the Angel Guardian" for the occasion. Catholics from throughout the area attended, including, "neighboring clergy, secular and regular . . . all the Catholic pupils of the Fort Defiance school, and the employees of the school and Agency, some of the Sisters and a number of the pupils from [the] St. Michaels Mission school, even representatives of Gallup, New Mexico." After the mass, Peter Paquette hosted the bishop, the clergy, and the Catholic employees to "a sumptuous turkey-dinner, prepared by some of the Catholic ladies of Fort Defiance."[30] In 1916 *The Catholic Missions of the Southwest* reported on a similarly exciting event, the first Catholic marriage "Catholics, Non-Catholics and heathens attended." Superintendent Paquette again hosted the banquet to which "all the 53 Government employees" were invited.[31]

As an agent for the federal government, Peter Paquette was one of the most powerful men in the area. His standing gave him the opportunity to host important guests like the bishops, but he reinforced his position with generous hospitality. Hospitality was certainly a trait emphasized in Ho-Chunk culture, but it was also an important Catholic virtue. Indeed, Paquette's Catholicism was closely bound to the family's French heritage. At another banquet celebrating the sacraments of Baptisms and First Communion, Paquette again hosted the bishop to a "sumptuous dinner" and "entertained the Rt. Rev. Bishop in his own mother tongue—in French."[32]

Religion offered this group a powerful identity that transcended the racial dichotomy that historians have privileged. Through their shared faith they formed bonds across race and tribe, celebrating important religious events with Navajo, Pueblo, and Winnebago, French, Anglo, and, most likely, Hispanic people. Moreover, the Catholic Church did not just bring neophytes together in marriage. Lizzie Devine's future husband, B. H. Dooley, was also a member of the church at Fort Defiance. And it appears that the man Mary Paquette would marry, Buris N. Barnes, was too. Both of the men in these relationships were white, but it was most likely their Catholic identity that mattered to their prospective spouses as much or more than their race.[33]

This group of people in the Southwest were not just bound together by a community of faith, many were also members of a shared profession, employees of the federal Indian Service. For Peter and Mary Paquette, as well as their family and wards, working for the federal government was a family tradition, but it also reinforced ties with other employees beyond kinship. Many of the Native employees of the Indian Service had attended federal Indian Schools and had begun to develop close connections with pupils from other tribes as well as Indian Service employees while they were students. Lizzie Devine, for instance, attended the Haskell Institute in Lawrence, Kansas, while Lucy Jobin attended the Chilocco Indian School until tenth grade and then graduated from Arkansas City High School.[34] After school, these ties of association and friendship deepened as many of them became personnel in the Indian Schools.

Regular employees who spent years in the Service, were often transferred throughout the national system and came to know many other coworkers as well as the Native people among whom they worked in the numerous locations. Lucy Jobin, for example, worked at six different posts, including Morris, Minnesota, Wind River, Wyoming, Fort Defiance and Chin Lee in Arizona, Black Rock at Zuni, New Mexico, and the Canton Asylum for Indians in Nebraska. Nor was she unusual. The retirement records of nine female Native employees who served for thirty years or more demonstrate that, on average, the women worked at more than six different locations throughout their careers.[35] This exposure to the Service as a national system gave them an increased sense of themselves as a larger cohort of professional civil servants.

The development of a national community of government workers was greatly facilitated by the periodicals that were printed in many of the larger boarding schools. They included *The Indian Leader: A Periodical Printed by and for Indians* from the Haskell Institute, *The Indian School Journal* published out of Chilocco Indian School, *The Native American* from the Phoenix Indian School, and *The Carlisle Arrow: A Weekly Letter to Our People.* While primarily meant for alumni (many of whom worked in the Indian Service), the journals also included information about personnel such as reports about distant schools and other employees. These journals extended Service workers' sense of who their colleagues were beyond the particular school or agency where they were stationed, to include the entire national reach of the Indian Service. The papers tied this community together by shrinking the distance between them; as *The Indian School Journal* implored its readers: "No employee in the Indian Service knows it all; all though, know some things well. You are one of them. Tell *The Journal* readers about it."[36]

Through the periodicals, employees were kept abreast of the important news in their colleague's lives. Some of these papers printed "Official Report of Indian Service Changes" including the name, position, and salary of new appointees, as well as information regarding reinstatements, transfers, and resignations.[37] Many also included more informal sections such as *The Native American*'s 1914 "News of our Neighbors and Co-Workers," or its 1916 "From Other Schools and Agencies." *The Carlisle Arrow* had a column titled "General News Notes" in which friendly gossip about different Service posts appeared. These sections included professional information about employee transfers, promotions, or resignations, and also highlighted the employees' personal lives noting weddings, anniversaries, births, illness, injuries, or deaths. They described school holiday parties and visits from other employees or Indian Service officials, as well as detailing information about where employees were spending their vacations.[38] Through the papers,[39] people learned about friends with whom they may once have worked, attended school, or perhaps had met at one of the Indian Service summer teaching institutes.[40]

For example, in the January 10, 1914, edition of *The Native American*, a correspondent from Fort Defiance described the Christmas "cantata." They informed readers that the Athletic Club had hosted a New Year's Eve banquette, noted that Superintendent Paquette "gave a turkey supper and smoker for the gentlemen, at his residence New Year's night," mentioned that the agency doctor and his wife had celebrated their twelfth wedding anniversary, and reported that the physician at Chin Lee had accepted a transfer to Cherokee, North Carolina, while the school nurse had been appointed to fill the vacancy left by the transfer of another employee to Dulce, New Mexico. The correspondent also added, "with a day school to be built at Lukai Chukai, a dormitory at Chin Lee, a hospital at Tohatchi and a sanatorium here, Superintendent Paquette will be kept busy for the next six months. However, if this work can be finished, Mr. Paquette is the man to do it."[41]

The Haskell Institute's *The Indian Leader*'s "Notes of Interest" were not tied to specific schools or agencies but informed the reader about the doings of former Haskell students or employees who had been connected with the school. That was certainly the case in 1916 when the paper reported: "Mrs. Elizabeth Devine Dooley spent July 29 and 30 here on her way from Fort Defiance, Ariz., where her husband is chief clerk, to her old home in Papoose, Wis. Mrs. Devine was a pupil here several years leaving 12 years ago. She has been employed nearly ever since as a seamstress or matron at Fort Defiance."[42] Such reports bound employees together as a cohort of colleagues who shared professional and social lives across vast distances.

While those bonds between coworkers could reinforce the intertribal connections established at Indian schools, they also transcended race. Lucy Jobin, for instance, was close friends with many of her non-Native female colleagues. They remembered her as fun and spontaneous. The daughter of one of her former coworkers for example, wrote that upon the occasion of her mother's wedding to her stepfather, "[s]ome of their friends decided a short camping trip would make a nice honeymoon and all would go along. Lucy Jobin and another teacher, Lottie Glenn, were full of mischief and the instigators of the camping trip idea. They took along lots of mosquito netting and fashioned a bridal veil for Mother. The bride carried a bouquet of sagebrush, and they staged a mock wedding. It was lots of fun for all to remember." Jobin also indulged her love of travel and interest in culture with white friends. For example, at one point she attended the Hopi Snake Dance with several colleagues.[43] These interracial ties were formed on the basis of both shared professional experiences and a shared middle-class culture.

If the Paquette family can be taken as somewhat representative (though few Native men reached the post of superintendent, and fewer still had tenures as long as Paquette's)[44] many of the Native people who worked for the Indian Service moved in multiple worlds. The Paquettes had retained tight bonds of kinship with their extended family, and Peter Paquette reinforced those ties and formed new ones using the system of legal guardianship (and possibly godparenting). The Catholic Church offered them another important site of fellowship and identity. Finally, their work also endowed them with identity in a particular cohort, as long-time employees in the Indian Service, part of a professional group of federal employees, many with ties to other Native people.

Despite these complex arrays of identity and loyalty, a strict dichotomy of race continued to shape their lives, often as a result of their employment in the Indian Service.[45] The Indian Office's project of assimilation required that it hire Indians, and its hiring policies required that it identify who was and who was not an Indian. Rather than recognize a long history of interracial encounters that had resulted in a wide variety of mixed heritages, the Indian Office policies structured its discourse into biracial terms of white and Indian. The Office identified its employees as either white or Indian, no matter how much or how little Indigenous heritage an employee might have. It then often acted on the basis of that classification; thus the category came to matter a great deal in its employees' lives.

Moreover, even as white policymakers sought to employ Indians as a way to assimilate them, they were wary of Native personnel. They based these fears on an idea of a unified "Indian" racial identity, worrying that Native employees would not have the ability to carry out the work of assimilation efficiently, or, more sinisterly, that they would be deliberately disloyal to the government. Responding to Native employees through this lens heightened the significance of race in the Indian Service.

In 1911, for example, a visiting inspector reported that Superintendent Paquette had hired too many of his family members and that this was causing disruption with the other employees at Fort Defiance and Chin Lee. On the surface, the resulting bureaucratic discussions and investigations were not so different from those involving white employees, who were also chastised for hiring family members. But they were shot through with assumptions about Native employees, especially Native women, which reveal the Indian Office's conflicting messages and ambiguous position on hiring Indian employees. After a lengthy debate of the situation, the commissioner sought to transfer Lizzie Devine, Paquette's niece and ward, and offered her a position at her alma mater, the Lac du Flambeau School in Wisconsin. This was unusual, because the office normally resisted sending employees to their own communities, but perhaps the commissioner was trying to sweeten the deal to encourage her acceptance of the transfer. In any case, he was foiled by Superintendent Sickels at Lac Du Flambeau who protested vigorously. The superintendent's concerns echoed those of many other superiors who complained that Native employees played favorites, were not motherly enough, or generally not good. "Lizzie Devine is a member of this tribe of Indians, formerly a pupil in this school," he wrote. "I do not believe it wise to place her in a responsible position of authority over her own relations." He went on to add that he preferred a white woman because "it is a hard responsible position, very confining and requires a good disciplinarian and motherly person. . . ." He concluded that as a "young, rather good looking" person, Lizzie Devine would "not be content to devote her time entirely to the work of this position."[46] While this initially seems specific to Devine, similar reasons appear almost word for word in the files of other Native women whose superintendents asserted that they were not maternal enough to fill matron or teaching positions in the schools and called for their demotion to support positions such as laundress or cook and their replacement by white women. This line of reasoning was consistent with the Indian Office's overall view of Native women that was embedded in the philosophy of assimilation. As Margaret Jacobs has demonstrated, the federal government had attacked Native women's very ability to be mothers in order to justify removing their children to boarding schools.[47] If they were not good enough to care for their own children whom the government had to remove to save, it was counterintuitive to many that Native women could serve in maternal positions in the schools to those same children.

Administrators also fretted about the loyalty of Native employees. As we saw with the accusations of favoritism above in Lizzie Devine's situation, they worried that tribal members employed among their own communities would work not for the good of the government, but for the good of their tribes. While policymakers claimed that this was the fault of the employees for playing favorites—"Relatives, friends, and tribal affiliations are more likely to be embarrassing than helpful"—they clearly feared tribal bureaucrats who might undermine federal authority from within. In dealing with these "local agitators," many administrators suggested transfers to reservations where they had no personal, or more importantly tribal, stake in governance.[48] While the Indian Office was too dependent on local Indian labor to completely end such hiring, especially for temporary jobs, it did try to enforce a policy of moving the better-educated regular employees away from their home communities. By 1912, the School Service's "Indian Application for Employment" form officially specified "it is not considered to be for the interest of the Service or the applicants to assign him to a position among his own people. Therefore the Indian Office looks with disfavor upon applications for appointment at home schools."[49] Administrators preferred to have Indian employees unmoored from their tribal identities so that they could avoid having a group of educated tribal bureaucrats who could challenge them.

This transfer policy created a new concern: that Native employees might form connections between their Indigenous coworkers or the tribe(s) among whom they worked. Having assigned all people of Native heritage to a single racial category, white administrators feared that Indian personnel would place their allegedly unitary racial interests ahead of their responsibilities to the federal government, thus subverting the goals of assimilation. Non-Native administrators rarely understood that people from different tribes (or different classes and statuses) did not automatically get along. Those administrators tended to blame all discontent on race loyalty rather than legitimate concerns, sometimes creating self-fulfilling prophecies in which their actions did lead Native people and people of mixed heritage to band together on the basis of race.

Administrators frequently questioned the loyalty of Native employees and repeatedly used particular phrases to signal their fears that the employees were being insubordinate. These accusations and phrases became a sort of racial code because they were rarely applied to white employees in the same way. The files of Native personnel are littered with charges of disloyalty that arose most often when employees disagreed with their superiors. Any behavior that was perceived as undermining the authority of the government or its representative, the superintendent or agent, was closely scrutinized through the lens of race and often labeled disloyal. When white administrators chastised Native personnel, they used phrases that ascribed racial politics to the employees' statements and actions. Key phrases that non-Native supervisors repeated in the efficiency reports of Indian personnel included "troublemaker," "too political," and forming part of an "Indian clique."[50] These terms signaled a fear that Indian employees regardless of tribe or "blood" would band together on the basis of race.

Lucy Jobin's principal at Chin Lee, for example, charged that she was "disregarding many of the rules and regulations laid down by officials and publicly criticizing and denouncing officials of the Indian Service."[51] Another administrator described Jobin as "[v]ery independent, as many Indian employees are," and concluded that this "sometimes interferes with her efficiency."[52] In 1918, Jobin received an efficiency report from the assistant superintendent of Indian schools who described her as a "trouble maker" and claimed that "[s]he causes factions in school . . . She was apparently forming a clique of Indian employees to work against the principal and white employees." The official concluded with a sarcastic final statement that reveals his concerns that Indian employees had the ability to undermine white authority: "If the Office wishes to keep her there [Chin Lee] I would suggest that all the white employees be transferred elsewhere and employ all Indians at this place. This would suit Supt. Paquette," he grumped.[53]

Like many Native employees, Jobin protested this stereotype of herself as a troublesome Indian employee. In this case, she suggested that her superintendent was prejudiced. "I am very much astounded to think that such ungrounded charges should be made against me. I emphatically deny that I have been disloyal to Mr. Garber. I have performed my duties in a loyal and faithful manner despite the fact that Mr. Garber has shown prejudice towards me since the time of his arrival here. He is also prejudice[d] against all Indian employees, and has shown and expressed himself openly in the matter."[54] Superintendent Paquette also disagreed with the report, but concluded that in his opinion, the principal's wife was at fault. The local Catholic priest, Father Weber (who had helped get Peter Paquette his appointment), also wrote in support of Jobin. He noted, "[o]f late, it seems, if I write in favor of any employee, it is for some Indian . . . An unfair treatment, not intentional, of course, on the part of the Indian Office towards Indian employees seems more likely to happen than towards others who have no prejudices from other employees to overcome."[55] His somewhat weak recognition of prejudice nonetheless hints at the difficulties Native employees confronted from the very people who were supposed to be working for their benefit.

Although the participants in this conversation framed their discussion in terms of race, Father Weber's support of Jobin also discloses another source of tension—the struggles between Catholics and Protestants. At the same time that he was championing Jobin, Father Weber was defending Peter Paquette from what he believed were religiously motivated attacks on the superintendent. A flurry of letters from the priest to his superiors in 1919 detailed his concern that Protestants were falsely accusing Paquette in hopes of forcing him out and gaining control of his position. Paquette, Weber insisted, "has tried to be fair to us and to favor neither us nor the Presbyterian ministers, but since he could not and would not accede to their bigoted demands, they have been calling him our 'slave' and have reported him a number of times to the Indian Office, and have tried ever since 1911 to have him removed."[56] This twist again reminds us that these employees were not living lives solely defined by race. But we cannot dismiss the enormous power it held in their lives; race was a significant category that could be deployed by many people in many ways.

Native people and people of mixed heritage understood the complexity of their positions and tried to use their identity in flexible ways as means to an end. As we have seen, the Indian Office both wanted to employ Native people, but also worried about the effect they might have on tribal communities. Applicants, who had their own agendas, often appealed to the government's ideas about race. Some tried to use their tribal connection as an advantage, but they were clearly aware that such a strategy could also work against them. Hoping to be appointed as a field matron at her home in Black River Falls, Wisconsin, in 1907, Mary Paquette initially highlighted her connections to the community writing, "I am a member of the Winnebago tribe and would like to work among my own people." When the commissioner of Indian affairs informed her that the Service did not station Native people with their own tribes, she disavowed her initial claims of tribal affiliation, responding: "I have no relatives among the Winnebagos. I have no friends among them and I have not and never have had any tribal affiliations with them." Her mother was white, she explained, and she was only one-sixteenth Indian blood. "I was brought up as a white girl" she insisted, adding, "I have never been a camp Indian."[57] Clearly, for Paquette, the important thing was landing the position in her home at Black River Falls. She was happy to let the government think of her in whatever category it liked, as long as it helped her reach that goal. When Lizzie Devine was requesting reinstatement in 1919, she wrote: "I am a Chippewa Indian, but not one of those knocking the Service."[58] She thus claimed a Native identity, but disavowed the stereotype of troublesome Indian employee.

Despite the ability of people of Native heritage to think about their identities in very complex ways, most of their non-Native colleagues did not. Some were better than others. Gertrude Golden, a sympathetic white teacher who worked under Peter Paquette on the Navajo reservation wrote, "I well remember hearing Superintendent Peter Paquette telling of the slights and ignominy which he and his sisters had to endure from their prejudiced school fellows and of the numerous fist-fights he was obliged to stage in order to defend their racial pride and dignity. And he was only a quarter-breed at that."[59] But employees with Native heritage of any amount often encountered intense racial animosity among their non-Native colleagues who were supposed to be working on behalf of Indian people. While the Indian Office had high hopes for the character of its white employees, many of those it hired to serve Indians were at best ignorant of separate tribal cultures and history and at worst blatantly prejudiced. For example, in 1923 the commissioner of Indian affairs reprimanded Mr. Earl Place for addressing Miss Lucie Jobin "in insolent and profane terms." Apparently Place defended himself with the claim that his "language was meant for 'squaws collectively,'" an explanation that the commissioner deemed a "very lame excuse." But instead of firing him, the commissioner counseled, "you will be expected hereafter to refrain from cursing employees associated with you" as "the work of our Service should be free from coarse or harsh methods and the influence of its personnel should be refining and exemplary, especially so because we are in contact with a race whose moral and social elevation depends largely upon the guidance we furnish."[60] For Native and mixed-heritage employees, the continual encounters with whites who insisted that they shared a race did help solidify ideas of a shared intertribal identity.

Their experiences working with people of different tribes combined with the non-Native tendency to lump them into a single category and facilitated the development of intertribal ties. For employees who had lost their tribal connections (and many Native employees had lost ties to their home communities or came from families of mixed heritage), employment in the Service offered them a way to reclaim or maintain links with Native communities. Lucy Jobin, for example, described herself as an Indian, but does not seem to have had a tribal affiliation (though her superiors and the federal census labeled her Chippewa). She never requested to be stationed in a particular place and her permanent address shifted as she changed jobs. In a poignant request for transfer back to the Chin Lee School where she had worked for several years she confessed, "that she never was so homesick in her life as she is now, and she thinks so often and so much of the Navahos (sic) that she sometimes feels as if she were a Navaho." Other Native Indian Service personnel often formed similar intertribal ties through marriages to their fellow employees.[61] These reconnections to other Native people and communities flew in the face of the federal government's goal of fragmenting tribal and community identity and replacing it with an individualistic ethic of citizenship disconnected from tribal politics or place.

Peter Paquette also formed intertribal ties with the Navajo people among whom he worked. Although it is hard to know how Navajo people felt about Paquette, small hints suggest that his mixed heritage made him more sympathetic to their concerns than non-Native administrators and that many appreciated his efforts. Father Weber, the Catholic missionary who was well-respected by many Navajos, believed that the Diné people liked Paquette and thought he was fair. Weber asserted that they thought that he was "the best superintendent they had since their return from Ft Sumner in 1868." During the 1913 Beautiful Mountain "uprising," Father Weber, Peter Paquette, and Chee Dodge all worked together to negotiate between Superintendent Shelton of the Shiprock Agency and a group of Navajos accused of polygamy. When Superintendent Shelton could not find Hatot-cli-yazzie, the accused husband, he arrested the three women he believed to be his wives instead. Hatot-cli-yazzie, along with his father, Be-zho-she, and several other men went to Shiprock and took the women back to Beautiful Mountain. An enraged Superintendent Shelton called in the U.S. Army. Weber, Paquette, and Dodge all worked feverishly as negotiators between the groups to solve the problem peacefully. In an interview with Paquette and Weber about the incident, Be-zho-she spoke to Paquette saying, "[M]y brother, I thought this would be straightened out here." Though Paquette stated that he unfortunately had no jurisdiction in the matter, it seems as though the Navajo men believed that he would be fairer than Shelton whom they described as "mean." "He stands out ready to jump on us," they complained. "We are like small birds hiding among the rocks to keep him from picking us."[62] They clearly saw Paquette in a different light.[63] Historians have also noted that when Paquette took the Navajo census of 1915, he was clearly cognizant and respectful of Navajo culture. He very carefully recorded the clan names for each man, woman, and child, something white administrators rarely, if ever, did. Marsha Weisiger has argued that the census was "a remarkable project, unusual in its cultural insight . . . as ethnographically astute as anything written up to that time. . . ."[64] Both examples suggest that Paquette's mixed heritage and his long family tradition of cultural brokering made him more sensitive to the concerns of Navajo people. Historian Peter Iverson has noted, the Navajos "wanted administrators and ministers to demonstrate qualities that they valued among themselves," and some administrators could earn their admiration, as Paquette seems to have done.[65]

Perhaps most revealing of the development of intertribal ties between Paquette and Navajo people was their deployment of fictive kinship. Just as he served as legal guardian for many of his own nieces and nephews, Paquette also became guardian to several Navajo children. For example, a young Navajo boy named George Peshlakai claimed that Paquette had adopted him "as his son."[66] In 1915, a wealthy white trader, Curt Cronemeyer, was murdered. Na Gee Bah,[67] a Navajo woman who had two children, Hoskay Yee Chee Nea and Che Che Bah, with Cronemeyer, requested that Paquette be made legal guardian of them, which he was. In that position he spent almost ten years involved in the court cases over their estates, often traveling the 125 miles between Fort Defiance and the county seat of St. Johns, Arizona, to attend court on their behalf. Sometimes the children and their mother traveled with him. Hoskay Yee Chee Nea and Che Che Bah were enrolled at his school at Fort Defiance where he would have seen them on a regular basis. Also, when the executors of their estates sought to have the children removed to the Riverside Indian School in California, Paquette protested and urged that the children remain at Fort Defiance. In full legalese Paquette argued: "it is for the best interests both moral and educational that said minor remain in said school and within said state of Arizona where it may be visited at stated intervals by its mother." This was the right course of action, he argued, because ". . . placing of said child in a strange school and among strange environments and persons that on account of tender years of said minor . . . a change will retard the said minor in school work." Although he used the language of education and morality that policymakers would have appreciated, he also indicated his concern for the relationship between Na Gee Bah and her children and recognized the importance of place and community to them.[68] The latter were considerations that non-Native administrators were actively seeking to undermine through the government's assimilation policies.

Although the exact nature of Paquette's relationship to these Navajo wards is unknown, it seems to have been a positive one. After all, Paquette used the same strategy of legal guardianship to help his own relatives. He looked after a number of nieces and nephews who were also his legal wards. They apparently appreciated him since several moved from Wisconsin to Arizona to live near him. He also appears to have helped them get jobs in the Indian Service. He likewise appears to have used legal guardianship to keep Che Che Bah and Hoskay Yee Chee Nea[69] close to their mother and to look after their interests. It is possible that Na Gee Bah requested his appointment as guardian because he was a respected figure in the community who also held significant power as an agent of the federal government.[70]

The Paquette family's relationships at Fort Defiance complicate many of the stories we tell ourselves. Race is certainly a key part of their story. The federal government hoped that by employing Native people in the Indian Service it could hasten assimilation and the disappearance of tribal identities, both cultural and political. Federal bureaucrats and other whites made race the number one attribute in their calculations and, as such, it structured the experiences of the Paquettes and other Indigenous people in significant ways. Even though many of the Indian Service's regular Indian employees had embraced many aspects of white middle-class culture, they knew the power of racial identity; they powerfully experienced race prejudice from childhood taunts to limits on their careers. Moreover, they understood how race shaped the colonial project. They watched non-Natives try to remove Native children from their parents or redirect wealth from Native to white communities. They witnessed administrators threaten to call in the U.S. Army over marital disputes on the reservation and weathered racial slurs.

Many of these experiences and policies did contribute to the congealing of racial categories around a binary of Native and non-Native, Indian and white worlds. In particular, we have seen how employment in the federal Indian Service, a colonial bureaucracy, contributed to the hardening of racial categories. Assimilation policy itself turned on ideas about racial attributes, and those ideas therefore structured the workforce hired to implement that policy. This, in turn, made Indian office officials acutely aware of racial categories. They used race to structure the federal agency, insisted on seeing it as the organizing factor in a person's life, and, as a result, feared allowing tribal employees to work in their own communities. By developing a bureaucracy in which race held such power, officials reduced individuals to an identity based on genetic makeup rather than behavior. This binary thinking often confined individuals of mixed heritage even as they sought to widen their opportunities. But such racialized thinking also helped create ties between people from widely different tribal, class, and regional backgrounds. As Native employees transferred through many different tribal communities and interacted with people from multiple cultures, the government in essence gave them a crash course in Native American studies. As they grew to know each other, especially as coworkers, Native people learned to appreciate other cultures and in some cases reconnect with an Indigenous identity in direct contrast to the government's goals of destroying it. Moreover, their employment kept them in Indian Country and engaged with the political issues facing Indian people.

As historians, we have to understand the terrible power that this racial project had in constraining people's lives, but we also have to do justice to individuals whose experiences cannot be reduced to a binary. People moved in multiple worlds and their racial identity (those they chose and those that others projected onto them) articulated with other categories in complex ways. They thought of themselves as members of extended families and communities of faith, as coworkers who shared frustrations or friends who celebrated joys and sorrows. For the Paquette family, these affiliations strongly shaped their lives and experiences and perhaps more importantly, were the ones they chose. Their family retained close ties of kinship across generations, supporting each other in many ways and even extending those ties through the fictive kin systems of legal guardianship. Their religious affiliation with the Catholic Church provided them with a worldwide community of believers, while also bridging local racial, ethnic, and national identities at Fort Defiance, where the Catholic community encompassed people who were Ho-Chunk, Irish, Navajo, French, and Pueblo. In the same way, their employment in the federal Indian Service gave them a professional identity that, while structured by race, also in many cases transcended it. As federal employees, they were part of a cohort of modern professionals. They participated in a national system that spanned many locations through its administration apparatus as well as the physical movement of employees. Their membership in this group often held great personal, professional, and perhaps patriotic significance for them. Domatilla O'Connell Showalter kept the names and contact information of friends she met in Service in her address book for years after they worked together. Likewise, Peter Paquette had among his possessions at the end of his life the certificate he received from the Department of the Interior upon his retirement. It recognized his twenty-nine years of "faithful services to his Government."[71]

For the Paquettes and other mixed-heritage people, the turn of the century was a moment of great promise and possibility even as they encountered great constraint. In a recent reflection on that moment in time, Phil Deloria mused that there "lies an interesting and as-yet-unexplored cast of historical characters" who might reveal "an incredibly complex Indian world." To find them, we should look in the "unexpected places" that he has suggested, but when we find them, we must also look at their lives in unexpected ways.[72] The racial binary of two worlds will be there, but if we listen to them, we may learn about their other communities and concerns that also shaped their experiences. These affiliations allowed them to live vibrant lives in multiple worlds.

Notes

1. I want to acknowledge the generosity of Cheryll Blevins and Linda King who shared their family history and research with me, and Sr. Kathleen Kajer. SBS of the St. Michael's Indian School and Linda Waggoner for their help as well. Letter, 7 June 1930, from A. G. Wilson Principal Clerk In Charge, Personnel File [hereafter PF], Lucy Jobin, National Personnel Record Center, St. Louis, MO [hereafter NPRC]. In identifying people by tribal heritage, I have used their own language from correspondence, if available. If that is unavailable, I have generally used their superior's assertions or census data, though it needs to be acknowledged that the latter two are often inaccurate.

2. A few years later, Agnes Fredette, a Sioux woman allotted at the Standing Rock Reservation, but teaching in the Indian Service at Pine Ridge also spent her vacation in Europe. See Personnel File, Agness Fredette, NPRC.

3. Harvey A. Levenstien, *Seductive Journey: American Tourists in France from Jefferson to the Jazz Age*, (Chicago: University of Chicago, 1998), 160. See also 158–61, and 182.

4. See Personnel File, Lucy Jobin, NPRC. See also, Mary Jeanette Kennedy, *Tales of a Trader's Wife: Life on the Navajo Indian Reservation, 1913–1938* (Albuquerque: Valliant Co., 1965) 33, 35; and Jean and Bill Cousins, *Tales from Wide Ruins: Jean and Bill Cousins, Traders*, ed. Mary Tate Engels, (Lubbock: Texas Tech University Press, 1996), 24, 26.

5. *"Neither White Men nor Indians": Affidavits from the Winnebago Mixed-blood Claims Commissions*, ed. Linda M. Waggoner (Roseville, MN: Park Genealogical Books, 2002), 1–2.

6. Philip J. Deloria, *Indians in Unexpected Places*, (Lawrence: University Press of Kanses), 14.

7. *Annual Report of the Commissioner of Indian Affairs* (Washington, Government Printing Office, 1890) [hereafter ARCIA], Appendix: Employees of Indian Schools, 334; Paul Stuart, *The Indian Office: Growth & Development of American Institution, 1865–1900* (Ann Arbor, MI, 1979), 130–31. Despite his emphasis on the growth of educational programs, Stuart does not discuss the sex ratios of the employees or their racial identity. For brief discussions of the female teaching force, see Adams, *Education for Extinction,* 82–94 and Patricia A. Carter, "'Completely Discouraged': Women Teachers' Resistance in the Bureau of Indian Affairs Schools, 1900–1910," *Frontiers* 15 (1995).

8. For example, in describing the Indian police forces, a source of employment for many Indian men on the reservations, the commissioner of Indian affairs noted that federal employment "makes the Indian himself the representative of the power and majesty of the Government of the United States." ARCIA 1880–81, xviii. On the role of the police forces, see William T. Hagan, *Indian Police and Judges: Experiments in Acculturation and Control* (Lincoln: University of Nebraska Press, [1980] 1966). On hiring see Wilbert H. Ahern, "An Experiment Aborted: Returned Indian Students in the Indian Service, 1881–1908," *Ethnohistory* 1997 44(2): 263–304; Steven J. Novak, "The Real Takeover of the BIA: The Preferential Hiring of Indians," *Journal of Economic History* 1990 50(3): 639–54; and Cathleen D. Cahill, *Federal Fathers & Mothers: A Social History of the United States Indian Service, 1869–1933* (Chapel Hill: University of North Carolina Press, 2011).

9. Quoted in Steven J. Novak, "The Real Takeover of the BIA: The Preferential Hiring of Indians" *The Journal of Economic History* 50 (Fall 1990): 646. See also Wilbert Ahern, "An Experiment Aborted: Returned Indian Students in the Indian School Service" in *Ethnohistory* 44 (Spring 1997): 263–304.

10. Schmeckebier, *The Office of Indian Affairs*, 293–94 and Jon Allen Ryhner and Jeanne Eder, *American Indian Education: A History* (Norman: University of Oklahoma Press, 2004), 138.

11. The Indian Service was made up of the Agency Service, the School Service, and the Washington, DC, Office.

12. ARCIA Appendix Employees of Indian Schools, 1888 and 1895. 1888 is the first year that the numbers are broken down by race and unfortunately only for the employees in the School Service. There were at least as many and possibly more Native people employed in non-school service positions that included the Indian police forces and temporary laborer positions, both a major source of employment for Indian men.

13. Novak, "The Real Takeover of the BIA," 647.

14. Rose Mitchell, *Tall Woman: The Life Story of Rose Mitchell, a Navajo Woman, c. 1874–1977.* Charlotte Frisbie. She notes Paquette's tenure was 1908–1925 (355).

15. Joan M. Jensen, *Calling this Place Home: Women on the Wisconsin Frontier, 1850–1925* (St. Paul: Minnesota Historical Society Press, 2006), 392; and "Mrs. Buris N. Barnes" *The Banner Journal*, Black River Falls, Wisconsin, 3 July 1929, clippings file, Historical Society, Jackson County, Wisconsin. Thank you to Linda King for sharing her copy of this file with me.

16. Novak, "The Real Takeover of the BIA: The Preferential Hiring of Indians" *The Journal of Economic History* 50 (Fall 1990): 646. Novak demonstrates that this idea had a long history. It was first implemented in Section 9 of the 1834 Reorganization Act, but left to the discretion of local Indian agents, it appears that it was not heavily used.

17. Howard M. Bahr, *The Navajo as Seen by the Franciscans, 1898–1921: A sourcebook*, (Lanham, MD: Scarecrow Press, 2004), 208.

18. 12 October 1907, Acting Commission of Indian Affairs [hereafter CIA] to Agent PF Mary Paquette, NPRC.

19. The Superintendent of Indian Schools, Estelle Reel wrote on her behalf. Letter, 14 August 1908, PF Mary Paquette, NPRC.

20. "Mrs. Buris N. Barnes" *The Banner Journal*, Black River Falls, Wisconsin, 3 July 1929, clippings file, Historical Society, Jackson County, Wisconsin.

21. According to Peter and Mary's great-niece, Cheryll Blevins [nee Bowlin], these cousins were all raised together at their grandparent's house in Black River Falls. Domatilla O'Connell's mother, Domatilla (or Domatille) Paquette died in childbirth on March 16, 1886. Author's correspondence with Cheryll Blevins, July 22, 2013. In 1918, Miss O'Connell was working as a trained nurse in charge of the Fort Defiance Hospital on the Navajo Reservation under the supervision of her guardian, Peter Paquette. *The Franciscan Missions of the Southwest: An Annual Published in the Interest of the Franciscan Branch (Cincinnati Province) of the Preservation Society*, (The Franciscan Fathers: Saint Michaels, AZ) Ninth Number, 1921, 38.

22. Lizzie Devine had received her Indian Service appointment on the Navajo Reservation in 1904 after graduation from the Haskell Institute. It is possible that Peter found out about the position there through her. Efficiency Report 23, June 1911, PF Lizzie Devine, NPRC. According to Cheryll Blevins, Lizzie and her future husband, B. H. Dooley, kept in touch with Peter Paquette even after moving back to Wisconsin. Author's correspondence with Cheryll Blevins, July 22, 2013.

23. Peter also invested in The Wide Ruins Trading Post, at Pueblo Grande (Kin Teel in Navajo). He co-owned it with Spencer Balcomb and Wallace Sanders.

It was near the Cronemeyer trading post and perhaps how Peter knew his family. See *The Indian Traders*, 274–75.

24. Author's correspondence with Cheryll Blevins, July 22, 2013, including a copy of Domatilla O'Connell Showalter's work record. She had trained at the Chicago Hospital Training School for Nurses.

25. PF Julia DeCora Lukecart, NPRC.

26. Susan Sleeper-Smith, *Indian Women and French Men: Rethinking Cultural Encounter in the Western Great Lakes* (Amherst, MA: University of Massachusetts Press, 2001), 102.

27. Sleeper-Smith, *Indian Women and French Men*, 98.

28. In 1914 they donated money for the chapel at Fort Defiance in the following amounts: Peter Paquette donated $100. Elis. Divine (sic) $30, Mr. and Mrs. B. N. Barnes (nee Mary Paquette) $45, and B. H. Dooley (Lizzie Devine's future husband) $30. A number of other contributors from Fort Defiance and St. Michaels are listed as well. See *The Franciscan Missions of the Southwest: An Annual Published in the Interest of the Franciscan Branch (Cincinnati Province) of the Preservation Society*, (The Franciscan Fathers: Saint Michaels, AZ) Second Number, 1914, 42. An S. M. Paquette (probably Peter and Mary's nephew, Samuel Moses) also donated money. He was a trader at St. Michaels. See his advertisement in the end papers of *The Franciscan Missions of the Southwest: An Annual Published in the Interest of the Franciscan Branch (Cincinnati Province) of the Preservation Society*, (The Franciscan Fathers: Saint Michaels, AZ) First Number, 1913.

29. Bahr, *The Navajo as Seen by the Franciscans*, 208.

30. See *The Franciscan Missions of the Southwest: An Annual Published in the Interest of the Franciscan Branch (Cincinnati Province) of the Preservation Society*, (The Franciscan Fathers: Saint Michaels, AZ) Fourth Number, 1916, 46–48.

31. Ibid., 19–20. Sacraments were an important occasion for the Catholic community to come together. Paquette and the teachers and pupils from Ft. Defiance traveled to St. Michaels, eight miles away, for Baptism and First Communion ceremonies. See also *The Franciscan Missions of the Southwest: An Annual Published in the Interest of the Franciscan Branch (Cincinnati Province) of the Preservation Society*, (The Franciscan Fathers: Saint Michaels, AZ) Third Number, 1915, 19–20. Cheryll Blevins shared that Peter and Mary Paquette left a large number of serving dishes, cut glass, and chafing dishes to their relatives upon their death, dishes they probably used for entertaining at similar events. Author's correspondence with Cheryll Blevins, July 22, 2013

32. *The Franciscan Missions of the Southwest: An Annual Published in the Interest of the Franciscan Branch (Cincinnati Province) of the Preservation Society*, (The Franciscan Fathers: Saint Michaels, AZ) Third Number, 1915, 12–16. See also Grant Arndt "Ho-Chunk 'Indian Powwows' of the Early Twentieth Century" in *Powwow* by Clyde Ellis, Luke E. Lassiter, Gary H. Dunham (Lincoln: University of Nebraska Press, 2005), 46–67.

33. *The Franciscan Missions*, Second Number, 1914, 42.

34. Personal Record, June 6, 1911, PF Elizabeth Devine, NPRC and Efficiency Report, March 1928, PF Lucy Jobin, NPRC.

35. The median number of positions was also four and the median number of locations was five. The number of locations varied from a low of one school to a high of fifteen over the course of a career. The small number may a sample factor as the names were drawn from employees in 1905 while Native employees did not qualify for retirement pensions until 1929. See Cahill, *Federal Fathers & Mothers*, 123–24.

36. *The Indian School Journal*, Vol. 7 No. 6, April, 1907, 23.

37. Ibid., 31 and 36–40.

38. *The Native American* (Phoenix Indian School), May 27, 1916, 199. *The Carlisle Arrow* (Carlisle Indian School), Sept 22, 1916, 6. *The Indian School Journal* printed a section entitled "In and Out of the School Service." *The Indian School Journal* (Chilocco Indian Agricultural School), Vol. 7 No. 6 April 1907, 31. Sometimes this took the form of official articles about a specific school, see Superintendent John Flinn, "The Lac du Flambeau School," in *The Indian School Journal*, 17.

39. The efficiency reports required employees to list books and periodicals they read. Many often listed these newsletters.

40. For more information on the teaching institutes, see Cathleen D. Cahill, *Federal Fathers and Mothers*, 269–73.

41. *The Native American*, January 10, 1914, 21–22 and January 31, 1914, 61. Because of proximity, *The Native American* had many reports, especially on Peter Paquette who often went to Phoenix on business. See also *The Native American* Vol. 21, 1920, 23 and 56

42. *The Indian Leader* (Haskell Institute) Vol. XX No. 1 September 8, 1916, 6. See also Vol. XX No. 35, May 4, 1917, 4.

43. Jean Cousins, and Bill Cousins, *Tales from Wide Ruins: Jean and Bill Cousins, Traders*, ed. Mary Tate Engels, (Lubbock: Texas Tech University Press, 1996), 26; and Mary Jeanette Kennedy, *Tales of a Trader's Wife: Life on the Navajo Indian Reservation, 1913–1938* (Albuquerque: Valliant Co., 1965) 33, 35.

44. See Cahill, *Federal Fathers & Mothers*, 130–31.

45. In the lists of employees in the *Annual Reports of the Commissioner of Indian Affairs*, the overwhelming majority of employees were classified as either "Indian" or "White." This dichotomy tended to flatten what were more complexly mixed identities by ascribing the identity of "Indian" to all people of Native heritage, no matter how little or how much. Only in a few rare instances were employees listed as "H" (for "Half-blood"), but never consistently, and most people of mixed heritage were not identified as such in the statistics. There were also a few employees listed in one of three other racial categories: African Americans (classified as "N" for Negro), Mexicans ("M") or Chinese ("C"). Federal Indian law has had a similar effect of structuring the discourse into the biracial terms of "Indian" and "white." See Thomas Biolsi, *Deadliest Enemies: Law and the Making of Race Relations on and off Rosebud Reservation* (Oakland: University of California Press, 2001. Many regular Native employees had been trained in the federal school system and often subscribed to ideas of class based on Anglo standards, which differed from traditional tribal ways of assessing status. This often fell out along phenotypical lines. See Devon

A. Mihesuah, *Indigenous American Women: Decolonization, Empowerment, Activism* (Lincoln: University of Nebraska Press, 2003) and Devon A. Mihesuah, *Cultivating the Rosebuds: The Education of Native Women at the Cherokee Female Seminary, 1851–1909* (Champaign: University of Illinois Press, 1997).

46. Supt Sickles to CIA, 20 November 1912, PF Lizzie Devine, NPRC.

47. For other examples, see Margaret D. Jacobs, *White Mother to a Dark Race: Settler Colonialism, Maternalism, and the Removal of Indigenous Children in the American West and Australia, 1880–1940* (Lincoln: University of Nebraska Press, 2009).

48. PF Mary Paquette, letter, 12 October 1907, NPRC. See also PF, Naomi Dawson Pacheco, Efficiency Report 17 January 1914; letter, 7 August 1918; letter, 7 August 1918; Efficiency Report, 1 May 1918 and Efficiency Report, 24 July 1919, NPRC.

49. PF Nellie Santeo, Application for Appointment, 14 March 1912, NPRC.

50. These stereotypes appear to have been codified into the official Indian Office rules of 1929, which stated: "An attitude on the part of any employee of continuous fault-finding or grumbling . . . or a disposition to become a troublemaker will be deemed sufficient cause for separating the employee from the service." *Regulations of Indian Service*, 1929, 5

51. Efficiency Report 1 May 1917. See also Efficiency Report 15 November 1916 both in PF Lucy Jobin, NPRC.

52. Efficiency Report, 1 November 1910, PF Lucy Jobin, NPRC.

53. Efficiency Report, 13 May 1918, PF Lucy Jobin, NPRC.

54. Jobin to CIA, 14 June 1917, PF Lucy Jobin, NPRC.

55. Fr. Weber, O.F.M. to Charles Lusk, 27 January 1918, PF Lucy Jobin, NPRC.

56. *The Navajo as Seen by the Franciscans*, 474, 478.

57. Mary Paquette to CIA, 7 October 1907 and MP to CIA, 21 October 1907 in PF Mary Paquette, NPRC. See also CIA to U.S. Indian Agent, La Pointe Agency, WI, 12 October 1907, PF Mary Paquette, NPRC. These records illustrate why it is hard to know for sure how people may have identified. She was corresponding with the Indian Office in order to get a job and was most likely willing to tell them whatever they wanted to hear in order to do so. Certainly Mary was more than $^1/_{16}$, Linda King, a Paquette family genealogist, states that she and Peter were at least $^1/_8$ Winnebago and possibly $^1/_{16}$ Sac and Fox. Correspondence with Linda King, December 15, 2010. Mary's mother, Madeline LaRiviere of Paririe du Chien, was of French descent and may have emphasized that heritage, but Domitilla O'Conner Showalter testified in an affidavit that her grandmother, Madeline, was ¼ Sac Fox. Notarized affidavit, 7 May 1935, Fort Defiance. Thank you to Cheryll Blevins for sharing this source.

58. Letters CIA to Agent, 12 October 1907, and MP to CIA, 21 October 1907, NPRC, PF Mary Paquette, NPRC. See also Ada Rice, 16 July 1908, PF Ada Rice, NPRC. LD to CIA, 30 June 1919, PF Lizzie Devine, NPRC.

59. Gertrude Golden, *Red Moon Called Me: Memoirs of a Schoolteacher in the Government Indian Service* (San Antonio, TX: Naylor Company, 1954), 210–11.

Other members of the Paquette family had similar experiences. Domatilla O'Conner Showalter's granddaughter recalls family stories about her grandmother (Peter and Mary's niece) being taunted on the playground in Black River Falls. Author's correspondence with Cheryll Blevins, July 22, 2013.

60. CIA, 21 February 1923, PF Lucy Jobin, NPRC.

61. Fr. Leopold, OFM to Mr. Endicott 9 April 1920, PF, Lucy Jobin, NPRC.

62. Quoted in *"For Our Navajo People": Diné letters, speeches & petitions, 1900–1960.* Ed Peter Iverson (Albuquerque: University of New Mexico Press, 2002), 127. See also 123–28.

63. The headline for one of Paquette's obituaries read "Navajos Mourn Paquette as 'Friend,' Whites Hail Him as First New Dealer" and cited Sam Ayoo-Nalh-K'neezi, "one of the old time medicine men," as saying "Old Navajos lost awful good friend . . . he was one man who really understood us." Clipping, August 1939. Thanks to Cheryll Blevins for sharing this with me.

64. Marsha Weisiger, *Dreaming of Sheep in Navajo Country* (Seattle: University of Washington Press, 2009), 95.

65. Peter Iverson, and Monty Roessel, *Diné: A History of the Navajos,* (Albuquerque: University of New Mexico Press, 2002), 110–14. Notwithstanding his sensitivity, Paquette readily administered federal assimilation programs including the anti-polygamy ban and stock reduction efforts.

66. Bahr, *The Navajo as Seen by the Franciscans, 1898–1921: A Sourcebook,* 478.

67. The court records are slightly unclear on her name (indicative of how little she mattered in the proceedings). Paquette clearly edited several documents to read Na Gee Bah, adding "sometimes known as Ya Nip Bah." She also appears as Na Gee [Gle?] Nez Bah.

68. See Petition for letters of Guardianship, December 15, 1916, in Probate #9; Amended Petition for appointment of guardian of estates, April 5, 1916, Probate #10; and Reply to Petition to Place said minor in Riverside Indian School, August 2, 1920, Probate #10, all in Superior Court of Apache County, State of Arizona. See also McNitt, Frank *The Indian Traders,* (Norman: University of Oklahoma Press, 1962), 330–31.

69. It is unclear what happened to Che Che Bah, but Hoskay Yee Chee Nea, also known as Hoskie Cronemeyer, went on to become a member of the Navajo Catholic Council in 1949 as well as a member of the Navajo tribal council in the 1950s. *Navaho Saga: Franciscan Golden Jubilee*, ed. Thomas Shiya (Franciscan Fathers, St. Michaels, AZ, 1949), n.p., and *The Navajo Yearbook* for 1957, 1958, and 1961.

70. The estate of the two children was substantial and it is possible that Paquette was motivated by economic concerns, but his previous use of legal wardship seems to suggest otherwise. He was also never awarded guardianship of the estate, though he did petition for it a few years after he became guardian of the children. Again, this can be read as a desire to get his hands on the money, or an

attempt to shield the estate from misuse by its white guardians who were loaning the money out in large sums.

71. Author's correspondence with Cheryll Blevins, July 22, 2013.

72. Philip J. Deloria, "Four Thousand Invitations," Joint Special Issue, *Studies in American Indian Literatures*, Vol. 25 No. 2 (Summer 2013) and *American Indian Quarterly*, Vol. 37 No. 3 (Summer 2013), 39; and Deloria, *Indians in Unexpected Places.*

Interlude

Working and *Between-ness*

Brian Hosmer

I've been thinking and writing (more thinking than writing) about Indigenous communities and economic change for quite a number of years. In that time, scholarship has undergone tremendous, perhaps even seismic, change. Where not too long ago we typically dismissed the significance of wage laboring in the unfolding of American Indian histories, stories of Native participation in labor markets are quite familiar. Where many once regarded capitalism as an existential threat to Indigenous cultural values, we now understand economic change in the context of modern *tribal* nations as active participants in local and global marketplaces. In fact, many Indigenous communities use business ventures to revitalize cultural practices and more fully articulate sovereignty. Actions taken by courageous and far-sighted Native peoples have challenged historians to develop new scholarly approaches and revisit old certainties. So where once upon a time we separated Indians from work, just as we considered "traditionalism" antithetical to "modernity," we are now rightly skeptical of such artificial, static, and limiting binaries. At any given moment in history, some Native people work while others do not; some are wealthy while others want for basic necessities. Indians can be successful, or not.

It is with this in mind that I submit the following passage from a 1937 edition of *The Wyoming Indian*. Tom Shakespeare, Northern Arapaho rancher, farmer, tribal leader and participant in New Deal work relief programs then operating on the Wind River Indian Reservation wrote the essay. I discovered the piece a few years ago and ever since it has challenged me to think freshly about the ways Natives engage with the workplace, how they describe those experiences, and why scholars (no less, the general public) interpret those activities as we do. Even more directly, as Shakespeare asks us to consider relationships between labor and Indian identity, I want to ask what "working Indians" communicate about "living in two worlds."[1]

Human Success—Be Somebody—Do Something Useful

Worthwhile folks don't just happen. You aren't born worthwhile;
you are born only with the possibilities of becoming worthwhile.
Your job is to discover and develop the man or woman you ought to be;
sooner or later we sit down to the banquet of consequences.
Thousands of plume little seeds of worthwhile things and shy ambitious
little growths toward worthwhile achievements wither and die from neglect;
every generation has a good crop or human fizzles, but it's the human success
of each generation that moves life forward.

We Have Many Wants

It takes head work to organize them. We find in ourselves all sorts of wants,
some of them were born in us, some have been acquired by family
and friends. It's human to select soft, lazy, selfish, shortsighted ways
of living; it is also human to select big, generous, beautiful,
comfortable-in-the-long run ways of living; it is even more human to
select those better ways other wise we would still be savages fighting,
day by day, battles in the forest.[2]

"Be Somebody—Do Something Useful" reads as an unremarkable example of that genre of Indian writing focused on self-improvement through self-realization, the discovery of individuality presumably suppressed tribalism. John Collier's Indian Office valued these stories no less than its predecessors, or successors. People like Tom Shakespeare represented the promise of improved lives and the amelioration of desperate reservation conditions, often by internalizing the values and perspectives of the majority culture. Shakespeare succeeded as he came to resemble his white neighbors, and in the process imagined as moving between two worlds.

We know this story, and we also understand its implications. Like *Indians at Work*, Collier's famous New Deal newsletter, *The Wyoming Indian* advertised the Indian New Deal to multiple audiences: Indian and non-Indian, Arapaho and Shoshone, critics and supporters from Lander and Riverton, to Cheyenne, Washington, and maybe even Tulsa. Some readers undoubtedly recognized the voice of the assimilated Indian, imploring friends and relatives to cast off the shackles of tradition for industry and prosperity. Others may see hidden transcripts, weapons of the weak, and the faint glimmer of resurgent tribalism. Can reading this Shakespeare mean searching for the colonialist ventriloquist hiding behind the Indian face, or his typewriter? Is this a story of alienation, masked as empowerment?

I want to suggest that the Shakespeare who reaches through time challenges us to reconsider the impact of wage laboring upon Native individuals and the communities they build and sustain. We might direct this exegesis of Shakespeare's remarks toward a fresh consideration of this concept of "living between worlds," or perhaps the condition of *in between-ness*, by linking it with discussion of Indian engagements with capitalism and wage laboring. By this I do not simply intend to understand *in between-ness* as a companion of the working Indian, or a condition of capitalism's impact upon Indigenous communities, values, behaviors, and persons. Rather, I aim to reflect upon my own intellectual journey as a way of assessing how scholars have linked capitalism with *in between-ness*, where living between two worlds becomes shorthand for external evaluations of economic change for Indigenous communities. Here, we might shorten our inquiry: Are economic change and *in between-ness* two aspects of the same phenomenon? Why should we assume so?

There is much to recommend this approach. Even as we now accept the reality of Indian participation in capitalist marketplaces, we still wonder about the effects of capitalism upon "the Indian." In *High Stakes*, Jessica Cattelino remarks at how frequently she was asked if—really how much—gaming undermines Seminole culture. This despite the fact that Seminoles "never . . . claim that their casinos reflect something particularly Seminole; to the contrary, people often asserted that casinos are their business, not their culture."[3] But such misperceptions persist, as in journalist Jeff Benedict's harsh questioning of the authenticity of Connecticut's gaming tribes, or Ian Frazier's devastatingly superficial portrayal of reservation life on the northern plains.[4] In other words, even as scholars seek to contest dichotomies between traditional and modern Indian alongside work, we remain tempted to see Native engagements with capitalism as signaling cultural loss, however defined. So while we recognize Indian entrepreneurs, tribal capitalism, and Natives in the work force, we struggle to understand the effects of economic change, without presuming that capitalism requires Indian people to live between two worlds.

Let us be clear. Capitalism places immense demands upon individuals and communities. It rewards competitive individualism over cooperative communalism and reorients social relations and cultural values as it reorganizes economic principles and practices. The introduction of capitalism, often through the instrument of wage laboring, can be transformational in the sense that participation in marketplaces rewards some behaviors over others, and asks participants (willing or not) to reconcile divergent sets of principles. Just as importantly, working, or not, conditions external assessments of American Indian cultural identity. In this sense, it may be logical to associate wage laboring, and the incorporation of Indigenous peoples into market capitalism, with the condition of *in between-ness*. Or, to invert the equation, perhaps Indian workers live between two worlds, naturally and inevitably.

When I initiated conversations with members of the Eastern Shoshone and Northern Arapaho tribes, co-residents of the Wind River Indian Reservation, I was struck by how frequently questions about work prompted reflections upon broader issues. For example, why working was important, or just how having a job—or not—defined one's experiences, and perspectives on work. Often, questions about a particular working experience, a job or project, led to ruminations on laboring more generally, and in ways that seemed like shorthand for cultural, political, or social values. Or at least it seemed so to me. These interviews focused my attention upon ways individuals remember, describe, and interpret their experiences, for themselves and for outsiders like me.

Embedded in those conversations were all sorts of references to the meaning of work, what I took to be articulations of "work ethic," however conceived. My essay on New Deal work relief programs suggested that the concept of "work" resonates powerfully in Indian communities like Wind River. For instance Leo Cottonoir (Eastern Shoshone) tellingly described a lifetime spent working as "we just worked . . . the only thing I know is work." Ralph Kniffen (Fort Hall Shoshone) reminded me that work relief "was where we learned how to work . . . It was a lifesaver for a lot of us kids."[5] Their memories echo voices from Shakespeare's time, like John Little (Northern Arapaho), manager of the Trout Creek CCC camp. In a 1935 status report, Little practically gushed over the social impact of work relief. "Gone is the 'hang dog' look from faces, instead is the will to show the white people and their own people that they can do a job and do it as well as any other race of people." Decades before I met him, Leo Cottonoir managed a CCC camp and won an award for an essay on "What the I.E.C.W. has done for the Indian." According to Cottonoir, relief provided workers with a "new hold and outlook on life. He has gained a new confidence. He has shown he can do good work and in turn our government has shown it is striving to help the Indians get ahead, to boost him when he deserves it."[6]

Northern Arapaho Ben Warren, Jr. offered a similar assessment—but with a gesture toward *in between-ness*, and its consequences. "There is one thing wrong with us Indians, why we don't get ahead is that we are forever picking on those who are trying to do well, we are very fond of finding fault—we should from now on practice a more kindly respect toward everyone and pull together. If we will still do this we'll be on the road to Prosperity."[7] Decades later, Alfred "Sonny" Portwood (Northern Arapaho) still felt the sting of alienation that accompanied holding a position of authority in the workplace, when he recalled telling a "couple kids that had grown up away from me . . . to do something." Those kids, he recalled, "said something about an ornery old man . . . trying to make us work too hard." While "they did this in Arapaho," a pointed reference to Portwood's 'mixed' heritage, "I understood what they were saying . . . I let them get all through and . . . I said all right, here's your chores." So too for Lloyd Dewey who remembered work relief as simply a job. "There was no incentive of any kind . . . there was no way you could learn any more than what they had there." While a few "did learn how to run their crappy equipment," and "adapted pretty easily, some of us didn't."[8]

Do these narratives support this association of *between-ness* and wage laboring? Maybe. But if conversations about work reach in a variety of directions, from ways Indian people evaluate the importance of working (or idleness) upon their lives and communities, to how non-Natives understand Indian interactions with the world of work. They offer some sense of "what happens" when we place *Indian* and *work* in the same sentence.

Americans have had long practice with evaluating the nature and meaning of Indian work, and Indian idleness. Puritans cast Natives as indolent savages. Missionaries, policymakers, and even casual observers of the Indian condition (sometimes the Indian problem) designed all manner of programs to impress upon Indigenous peoples the value of work and dignity of labor, as if traditional Native people knew little of either. Its proponents cast allotment as a means to inculcate work ethic, even (as the late Melissa Meyer observed long ago) implementation of that program systematically deprived Indian workers of resources and opportunity.[9] More recently, programs from the New Deal to the War on Poverty focused on job training as much as job creation, with their creators secure in the conviction that poverty mitigation was as much about behavior modification as opportunity. But implicit in all of this was the conviction that successful participation in the marketplace required some reorientation of cultural values, imagined as movement between or betwixt divergent worlds.[10]

Ethnohistorians are grappling with these very issues. In *Indian Work* (2009) Daniel Usner decried our "unfortunate discourse" that "conceals how dynamic and durable societies actually blend tradition with innovation."

Colleen O'Neill identified the damage produced by casting tradition and modernity as binary opposites. Jessica Cattelino argued that when "poverty symbolically and materially structures indigeneity" native efforts to engage capitalism creatively are judged—negatively—against standards of cultural authenticity. Elizabeth Povinelli offers similar assessments for Australia, as do the Comaroffs for South Africa, all attesting to a growing interest in framing Indigenous intersections with capitalism as "settler colonial" phenomena. As Cattelino reminds us, casino gaming reveals colonialism's "double bind," (another manifestation of *in between-ness*?) where Indian assertions of economic competence undermine claims for cultural and political sovereignty.[11]

Examining the implications of Indians operating in "unexpected places," or the consequences of an imposed (but sometimes internalized) "authenticity," scholars working in this small corner of the ethnohistorical project seek not just to document Indian engagement with multiple workplaces but to examine the cultural framing of those very activities.[12] Alexandra Harmon explores the multiple and manifold meanings of wealth and success in and around Indian contexts, situating Indian people within multiple economic and social strata, thereby challenging static notions of cultural authenticity. Harmon, O'Neill, and historian Paul Rosier draw attention to "interwoven economic histories" of Indian and capitalist America, where a growing body of scholarship reminds us of "what should be obvious: indigenous Americans have always worked for a living." If "working Indians" interpreted these activities as adaptations to changed circumstances, shaped and understood through cultural values, they also battled against the reality, or perception, that capitalism brought disruption, anomie, and between ness. In this context, casting Indians merely as victims of change, defined via poverty or dependence upon government remediation, "without including tales of adaptation to the market capitalist economy leaves the readers with no basis for understanding the economic practices and status of twenty-first-century Indians."[13]

Writing more than three decades ago, Canadian labor historian Rolf Knight challenged scholars to revisit prevailing assumptions "that ongoing traditional values somehow limited Indian capacities to deal with new industries." In ways that anticipated Harmon and Usner, O'Neill, Rosier, Raibmon and Deloria, Knight argued that the erasure of Indigenous workers from histories of British Columbia salmon canneries and railroad crews, commercial fishing fleets and logging camps, amounted to a misreading of the past. Even more, this self-induced myopia cemented Indians to a preindustrial past, hamstrung by unchangeable cultural values. Indians could not be workers because they were traditional; workers could not be truly Indian because they embraced modernity.[14]

Little noticed and soon out of print (my first copy was a pirated photocopy courtesy of my mentor), Knight's *Indians at Work* is rightly identified as a seminal study of Native peoples and labor markets. At one level, Knight challenges scholars to remove conceptual blinders separating Indians from the world of work. Rather than regarding the Indian worker as unique, or unusual, Knight saw Indian labor as a commonplace feature of industrializing economies across North America.

But as much as Knight anticipated current assessments of Indians and work, he also emphasized dramatic changes associated with colonialism and capitalism. Taking issue with "unregenerate romantics" who "see Indian labour in logging as akin to 'woodcraft,' " finding "no difference between the occasional tree felling of aboriginal time and the maze of skids, spring boards, steam donkeys, and bull blocks used in commercial logging," Knight saw ruptures in time, behavior, and practice. "[T]here was little similarity between indigenous woodworking and the requirements of commercial logging," he argued. "Native loggers were loggers, Indian longshoremen were longshoremen, Indian cannery workers were cannery workers."[15]

Knight cast Indian workers as budding proletarians, where material conditions determined worldviews, perhaps even cultural values. His Marxism may seem quaint, even simplistic, but warrants reconsideration in light of our concern with the consequences of *in between-ness*. If Knight is to be understood, Indian workers were both laborers and Indigenous, of a sort anyway. For while he argued that "ongoing traditional values" in no fashion "limited Indian capacities to deal with new industries," Knight insisted that wage labor changed Indian culture.[16] Does this mean working Indians differ, in condition or perspective, from those who did not exchange their labor for wages? If Knight left unexamined the impact of laboring on personhood, are we left to ask whether Indian workers operate between worlds, by necessity. If relationships of power structure the exercise of agency, and material conditions define perspective, were Indian workers *either* simple proletarians exhibiting a nascent class-consciousness, *or* living between two worlds?

Cultural anthropologists offer some assistance. In several studies rightly considered foundational to ethnohistory, Loretta Fowler identified the conceptual trap inherent in plotting cultural change along some sort of imagined continuum, with "traditional" located at one end point and "modern" at its opposite end. As Fowler explained, " 'the extent to which people have lost Indian culture and accepted a white-oriented way of life,' relies upon 'arbitrarily selected cultural traits,' that came to signify 'the meaning of particular behaviors.' " Instead, she directed us toward thinking about cultural change as a series of individual negotiations taking place in the context of cultural values, where innovations were interpreted through cultural values, which were reinterpreted in turn.[17]

Patricia Albers similarly challenged scholars to consider "the cultural constructs that express and give agency to a people's economic activity." By this she meant steering a careful course between "the tendency toward a culturalist exoticism that "misinterprets the cultural cues that govern labor efforts and their associated exchanges," and an equally myopic preoccupation with "the larger conditions under which labor unfolds and the structures within which it operates." The trick, she famously observed, amounted to persuading "construction and condition, agency and cause, the subject and its object, to properly dance with each other without overstepping the other."[18]

These sets of observations influenced my thinking about Indians, work, and their implications. I once ruminated on this question in a short, largely forgotten, essay focusing on the activities of two Menominee "entrepreneurs" who lived in the decades on either side of 1900. At that moment I wanted to revisit Mitchell Oshkenaniew and Reginald Oshkosh, central figures in my first book, in light of "cultural brokerage," a concept we might consider as roughly congruent with "between two worlds." Cultural brokerage offered a powerful tool for recovering Native agency amidst change by demonstrating, the capacity of individuals to operate across dissimilar social and cultural settings. These 150% men, as Malcolm McFee famously described brokers, served as intermediaries, drawing Natives and colonialists together, sharing words, concepts, foods, clothing, friendships and the like.[19]

That effort urged more nuanced applications of "brokerage" with careful attention to lived experiences of historical figures. Oshkenaniew and Oshkosh were intimately associated with development of a tribally controlled logging enterprise, a process that forced them to negotiate spaces in, around, and between Menominee cultural practices and the world of capitalism. As I argued then, a rough "combination of personality, message and heritage," structured their experiences, which meant that scholars seeking to understand "cultural brokers" would be well advised to "ground our evaluations firmly in local conditions, cultural practices, and expectations"—Indian and non-Indian, historical actor and historian.[20]

Upon further reflection, I am less certain I fully appreciated both the temptations and limitations of assessing Native accommodations to capitalism through brokerage. Participation in capitalist marketplaces, as workers and entrepreneurs, must have structured whatever *between-ness* Oshkenaniew and Oshkosh experienced. Fair enough as both men certainly negotiated Menominee accommodations with wage labor, entrepreneurialism, and capitalism. In this sense they may be considered "brokers." But it is difficult to see where, and how, either truly lived between or betwixt worlds. They were Menominee leaders, sometimes allies other times adversaries. They managed changing times and sought to preserve Menominee independence through creative engagement with capitalist marketplaces. We may interpret their experiences as living between two worlds, effectively or not. At the same time, Oshkosh and Oshkenaniew may have operated in a particular place, and time, where coordinating Menominee and capitalist values and practices had become part of everyday life for many such people. This was *a world* of Menominee capitalists and workers, who could be traditional and modern (as if that dichotomy is useful). That was *the world* they knew.

Stepping back another step, my interpretation of Menominee broker/entrepreneurs drew upon the revolution in scholarship on fur trade communities that partly culminated with the "middle ground," both in the sense of Richard White's magisterial work, and the metaphor it partly (though not entirely) spawned. If "middle grounds" are quintessentially between places, locations where we might find cultural brokers, and historical moments when divergent "worlds" come into contact, they are also deeply implicated with these economic transformations. Anthropologist Charles Bishop saw this in his groundbreaking analysis of the subarctic fur trade decades ago. So too did successive generations of ethnohistorians from Jennifer S. H. Brown and Jacqueline Peterson to Susan Sleeper-Smith, Lucy Murphy, and Carolyn Podruchny.[21] It makes great sense to see fur trade communities as economic meeting places and cultural middle grounds. Trade, entrepreneurism, capitalism, and wage laboring shaped those converging worlds, and often gave them rise in the first instance. Moreover, those "people in between," "new people," and progeny of "Indian women and French men" were products of, and frequently participants in, the emergent proto-capitalist worlds of the Great Lakes region—and beyond.

On the Northwest Coast for instance, a series of Tsimshian leaders known as Leg'eex (anglicized as Legaic), exploited the trade to enhance their circumstances, promoted intermarriage, and in the end saw their worlds refashioned by capitalism and wage labor.[22] The racially mixed, emergent capitalist, Creek nationalist Alexander McGillivray encapsulated the dilemmas and potentials inherent in encounters between worlds. Clearly McGillivray mediated between communities and races, just as he conversed in several languages and through divergent sets of cultural values. He was a trader and a politician; emergent capitalism shaped his middle ground, such as it was, and perhaps conditioned his *in between-ness*. But was McGillivray a liminal figure, or just one of many individuals negotiating the ever-shifting currents in the stream that was his world (single, not plural)?[23]

Those shifting streams could be treacherous, where the introduction of capitalism produced dispossession as often as opportunity. Colonialism, as Ned Blackhawk reminds us, is fundamentally violent; and middle grounds are places of oppression and marginalization.[24] This is important as we seek to understand that negotiation lies at the core of intersections between Indian and work, and account for relationships between capitalism and Indigenous cultural values, not to mention power and agency more generally. *American Indians in the Marketplace* attempted to consider Native accommodations to economic change largely as series of cultural negotiations. Conceived in the wake of ethnohistory's embrace of World Systems and other theories positing "the development of underdevelopment," that project argued in favor of native capacity to manage presumed contradictions between communalism and individual entrepreneurship.[25] More than that, it suggested economic change could, under some circumstances, foster cultural independence. The book's most frequently quoted phrase, where I argued Indians "chose economic modernization as the best possible way to preserve, not abandon, distinctive identities," reveals some discomfort, on my part, with emphasizing success over failure, or possibilities alongside the more familiar stories of failure and victimhood.[26]

Individuals stood at the center of the story I wanted to tell. Mitchell Oshkenaniew and Reginald Oshkosh at Menominee, Metlakatla Tsimshians David Leask, Wellington Clah, and (later) Edward Marsden, lived in, and with, those seeming contradictions. They balanced the evident appeal of wage laboring with Native communalism thus implying, if not establishing, structural links between capitalism and *in between-ness*. "My" entrepreneurs all occupied in between spaces, which they helped construct. Over time, this form of cultural mediation may account for the development of tribal capitalism, as when Menominee accommodations to gaming echoed their adjustments to a logging/lumbering economy of a century before. I wanted to argue that "Indian people—Menominees and others—have a long history of creative engagement with 'the market' and it is through these experiences that they devise certain strategies do deal with economic change." But in asserting that "far from finding participation on the marketplace 'toxic' to cultural values, Indian peoples . . . found that participation in the market might provide opportunity to preserve who, and what, they are," was I ignoring (or affirming) this convenient association of in between ness with Indigenous wage laboring?"[27]

I think I stand by that assessment, where cultural mediation and participation in marketplaces go hand-in-hand. Indeed, cultural mediation may be foundational to the development of tribal capitalism. But I am less certain about *in between-ness* as a condition of (or conditioned by) Indian engagements with capitalism. Even if we argue that Indigenous people engage the marketplace in multiple ways, and by referencing cultural values that are constantly in motion (as Albers reminds us), and even as we argue in favor of dynamic constructions of tradition and modernity, are we still seeing wage labor and *between-ness* as two aspects of the same phenomenon? If so, what about non-Indians living in between lives? People like Samuel D. Hinman, the Episcopal missionary who accompanied refugee Dakotas from Minnesota to Nebraska, or William Duncan of the two Metlakatlas? Both operated in spaces "in between" and shaped by intersections of capitalism and indigenous cultural life. If they were "fictive kin" in the sense that Gary Clayton Anderson offered, were they too operating in two worlds, acting as cultural brokers, experiencing *in between-ness*?[28] Perhaps not, since our distinctions follow our understanding of structural power and colonialism. But still, if (when?) we presume linkages between economic change and *in between-ness*, are we thinking about the lives Indigenous people led, and lead, or really referencing American (and settler colonial) anxieties over the effects of capitalism upon community, generally? Scholars working in settler colonial studies suggest as much,[29] and so those of us working in this small corner of the ethnohistorical enterprise should take heed. In other words, is in between ness about historical actors, or about historians?

Notes

1. I explored some of these ideas in, Brian Hosmer, "'Dollar a Day and Glad to Have It': Work Relief on the Wind River Indian Reservation as Memory," in *Native Pathways: American Indian Culture and Economic Development in the Twentieth Century*, Brian Hosmer and Colleen O'Neill, eds. (Boulder: University Press of Colorado, 2004), 282–307.

2. Tom Shakespeare, "Human Success—Be Somebody—Do Something Useful." *The Wyoming Indian*, Vol. II, No. 3 (March 31, 1937, p. 5. NARA, RG 75, Records of the Civilian Conservation Corps—Indian Division. File 58886-36-Shoshone-346).

3. Jessica Cattelino, *High Stakes: Florida Seminole Gaming and Sovereignty.* (Durham. NC: Duke University Press, 2008), 30.

4. Jeff Benedict, *Without Reservation: The Making of America's Most Powerful Indian Tribe and Foxwoods the World's Largest Casino* (New York: Harper, 2000); Ian Frazier, *On the Rez* (New York: Picador, 2000).

5. Quoted in Hosmer, "Dollar a Day," *Native Pathways*, 290, 298.

6. John Little to R. G. Pankey, "Monthly Report, September 1935." NARA, RG 75, CCC-ID, file 21338-39-Shoshone-344; "What the I.E.C.W. Has Done for the Indian," *The Tattler*, 15 November 1935. NARA, Rocky Mountain Branch, RG 75, General Correspondence Files, 1890–1960. Wind River Agency. Box 79, Decimal 01-A-1.

7. *The Tattler*, 15 February 1936. NARA, RMB, RG 75, General Correspondence Files, 1890–1960. Box 79, Folder 011-A-1.

8. Quoted in Hosmer, "Dollar a Day," 299–300.

9. Melissa Meyer, *The White Earth Tragedy: Ethnicity and Dispossession at a Minnesota Anishinaabe Reservation, 1889–1920* (Lincoln: University of Nebraska Press, 1994).

10. Tressa Berman writes powerfully about this topic. See Tressa Berman, " 'All We Needed Was Our Gardens:' Women's Work and Welfare Reform in the Reservation Economy." *Native Pathways*, 133–55; Berman, *Circle of Goods: Women, Work, and Welfare in a Reservation Community* (Albany: State University of New York Press, 2003). See also Kathleen Pickering, *Lakota Culture, World Economy* (Lincoln: University of Nebraska Press, 2000).

11. Daniel Usner, *Indian Work: Language and Livelihood in Native American History* (Cambridge, MA: Harvard University Press, 2009); Colleen O'Neill, from *Native Pathways*; John and Jean Comaroff, *Ethnography and the Historical Imagination* (Boulder, CO: Westview, 1992); Cattelino, *High Stakes*, 100, 196. For comparisons see, Elizabeth Povinelli, *The Cunning of Recognition: Indigenous Alterities and the Making of Australian Multiculturalism* (Durham, NC: University of North Carolina Press, 2002); and, Annie E. Coombs, ed., *Rethinking Settler Colonialism: History and Memory in Australia, Canada, Aotearoa, New Zealand and South Africa.* (Manchester, UK: Manchester University Press, 2006).

12. Philip J. Deloria, *Indians in Unexpected Places* (Lawrence: University Press of Kansas, 2004); Paige Raibmon, *Authentic Indians: Episodes of Encounters from the Late-Nineteenth Century Northwest Coast* (Durham, NC: Duke University Press, 2006). Other example of this rich literature include John Troutman, *Indian Blues: American Indians and the Politics of Music, 1879–1934* (Norman: University of Oklahoma Press, 2009); Elizabeth Hutchinson, *The Indian Craze: Primitivism, Modernism, and Transculturation in American Art, 1890–1915* (Durham, NC: Duke University Press, 2009); David Samuel, *Putting a Song On Top of It: Expression and Identity on the San Carlos Apache Reservation* (Tucson: University of Arizona Press, 2004); Erika Bsumek, *Indian Made: Navajo Culture in the Marketplace, 1868–1940* (Lawrence: University Press of Kansas, 2008).

13. Alexandra Harmon, Colleen O'Neill, and Paul C. Rosier, "Interwoven Economic Histories; American Indians in a Capitalist America," *Journal of American History*, December 2011, 709, 711, 717.

14. Rolf Knight, *Indians at Work: An Informal History of Native Labour in British Columbia, 1858–1930* (Vancouver: New Star Books, 1974), 6.

15. Knight, *Indians at Work*, 14–15.

16. Knight, *Indians at Work*, 6.

17. Loretta Fowler, *Shared Symbols, Contested Meanings: Gros Ventre Culture and History, 1778–1984* (Ithaca, NY: Cornell University Press, 1987), 6; Brian Hosmer, *American Indians in the Marketplace, Persistence and Innovation Among the Menominees and Metlakatlans, 1870–1920*, (Lawrence: University Press of Kansas, 1999), 7. See also, Loretta Fowler, *Tribal Sovereignty and the Historical Imagination: Cheyenne-Arapaho Politics* (Norman: University of Oklahoma Press, 2002)

18. Patricia C. Albers, "Marxism and Historical Materialism in American Indian History," in Nancy Shoemaker, ed., *Clearing a Path; Theorizing the Past in Native American Studies* (New York: Routledge, 2002), 107–08.

19. Malcolm McFee, "The 150% Man: A Product of Blackfoot Acculturation," *American Anthropologist*, 70 (1968), 1096–1107. See also, Margaret Connell Szasz, *Between Indian and White Worlds: The Cultural Broker* (Norman: University of Oklahoma Press, 1984); Irving A. Hallowell, "American Indians, White and Black: The Phenomenon of Transculturation, *Current Anthropology* 4 (1963), 519–29.

20. Brian C. Hosmer, "Reflections on Indian Cultural 'Brokers': Reginald Oshkosh, Mitchell Oshkenaniew, and the Politics of Menominee Lumbering." *Ethnohistory* 44:3 (Summer 1997), 493–509.

21. Richard White, *The Middle Ground: Indians, Empires, and Republics in the Great Lakes Region, 1650–1815* (New York; Cambridge University Press, 1991). The literature on the Indian fur trade is vast, which means that this footnote is hopelessly inadequate as anything other than a reference for ideas directly relevant to this discussion. See Charles A. Bishop, *The Northern Ojibwa and the Fur Trade: An Historical and Ecological Study* (Toronto: Holt, Rinehart and Winston of Canada, 1974); Sylvia van Kirk, *Many Tender Ties: Women in Fur Trade Society, 1670–1870* (Norman: University of Oklahoma Press, 1980); Jennifer S. H. Brown, *Strangers in Blood: Fur Trade Company Families in Indian Country* (Norman: University of Oklahoma Press, 1996. University of British Columbia Press, 1980); Jacqueline Peterson, "The People in Between: Indian-White Marriage and the Genesis of Metis Society and Culture in the Great Lakes Region, 1680–1830" (PhD diss., University of Illinois, Chicago Circle, 1981); Jacqueline Peterson, Jennifer S. H. Brown, eds, *The New Peoples: Being and Becoming Metis in North America* (Winnipeg: University of Manitoba Press, 1996); Susan Sleeper-Smith, *Indian Women and French Men: Rethinking Cultural Encounter in the Western Great Lakes* (Amherst: University of Massachusetts Press, 2001); Lucy Eldersveld Murphy, *A Gathering of Rivers: Indians, Metis, and Mining in the Western Great Lakes, 1737–1832* (Lincoln: University of Nebraska Press, 2000); Carolyn Podruchny, *Gathering Places: Aboriginal and Fur Trade Histories* (Vancouver: University of British Columbia Press, 2010).

22. Hosmer, *American Indians in the Marketplace*; Jonathan Dean, "'Rich Men,' 'Big Powers,' and Wastelands: The Tlingit-Tsimshian Border of the Northern Pacific Littoral, 1799 to 1867," (PhD dis., Univerity of Chicago, 1993). My gratitude as well to Michael Harkin's *The Helitsuks: Dialogues of Culture and History on the Northwest Coast* (Lincoln: University of Nebraska Press, 1997).

23. Michael D. Green, *The Politics of Indian Removal: Creek Government and Society in Crisis* (Lincoln: University of Nebraska Press, 1982); Claudio Saunt, *A New Order of Things: Property, Power and the Transformation of the Creek Indians,*

1733–1816 (New York: Cambridge University Press, 1999); James Taylor Carson offers a Choctaw example. See Carson, *Searching for the Bright Path; The Mississippi Choctaws from Prehistory to Removal* (Lincoln: University of Nebraska Press, 1999).

24. Ned Blackhawk, *Violence over the Land: Indians and Empires in the Early American West* (Cambridge, MA: Harvard University Press, 2006).

25. For critiques, see Colleen O'Neill, "Rethinking Modernity and the Discourse of Development in American Indian History, an introduction, in Hosmer and O'Neill, eds, *Native Pathways*, 1–24; Colleen O'Neill, *Working the Navajo Way: Labor and Culture in the Twentieth Century* (Lawrence: University Press of Kansas, 2005); Erika Bsumek, *Indian Made*; David Arnold, "Work and Culture in Southeastern Alaska: Tlingits and the Salmon Fisheries, in Hosmer and O'Neill, *Native Pathways*, 156–82; Hosmer, *American Indians in the Marketplace,* introduction. See also William J. Bauer, Jr., *We were all like migrant workers here: Work, Community and Memory on California's Round Valley Reservation, 1850–1941* (Chapel Hill: University of North Carolina Press, 2009), introduction; John W. Heaton, *The Shoshone-Bannocks: Culture and Commerce at Fort Hall, 1870–1940* (Lawrence: University Press of Kansas, 2005), introduction.

26. The literature on World Systems Theories is vast. For a sampling see Richard White, *The Roots of Dependency: Subsistence, Environment, and Social Change among the Choctaws, Pawnees and Navajos* (Lincoln: University of Nebraska Press, 1983); *The Cheyenne Nation: A Social and Demographic History*, (Lincoln: University of Nebraska Press, 1987); Joseph Jorgensen, "A Century of Political Economic Effects on American Indian Society, 1880–1980," *Journal of Ethnic Studies*, 6 (1978), 1–82; Hosmer, *American Indians in the Marketplace*, 1–18. Like many scholars of my generation, I was influenced by Eric Wolf's monumental studies. See in particular, *Europe and the People without History* (Berkeley: University of California Press, 1982). Quote is from: Hosmer, *American Indians in the Marketplace*, 224.

27. Brian Hosmer, "Blackjack and Lumberjack: Economic Development and Cultural Identity in Menominee County," in R. David Edmunds, ed., *Enduring Nations: Native Americans in the Midwest* (Urbana: University of Illinois Press, 2008), 234–35.

28. Gary Clayton Anderson, *Kinsmen of Another Kind: Dakota-White Relations in the Upper Mississippi Valley, 1650–1862* (Lincoln: University of Nebraska Press, 1984); Hosmer, *American Indians in the Marketplace*, 109–210; Brian C. Hosmer, "Hinman v. Hare: A Case Study of Conflict and Change in the Episcopal Mission to the Santee Sioux, 1859–1887," MA thesis, University of Texas at Austin, 1986.

29. See Harmon, *Rich Indians*, and Harmon, O'Neill, and Rosier, "Interwoven Economic Histories; American Indians in a Capitalist America," for insightful discussions of this phenomenon.

IV

Beyond Two Worlds

9

"born in the opposition"

D'Arcy McNickle, Ethnobiographically

Daniel M. Cobb,[1] Kyle D. Fields, and Joseph Cheatle

Although it continues to be a popular narrative device, the "search for an identity between Indian and white worlds" obscures as much as it reveals about the lived experiences of Native people. Recent scholarship has shown that the two-word binary reifies problematic expectations about what it means to be American Indian, establishes false dichotomies between authenticity and inauthenticity, and rests at the heart of what historian Paige Raibmon aptly terms "colonialism's Catch-22."[2] Nowhere can this be seen more clearly than in the life of Flathead author-activist D'Arcy McNickle (1904–1977). An evaluation of the conventional wisdom sheds light on how scholars arrived at a problematic "telling" of his life story.[3] Ethnobiography offers a fundamentally different approach. Focusing on oft-neglected diary entries from the period between 1932 and 1935, an economically perilous time in which McNickle attempted a carve out a place for himself and his family as an aspiring writer in New York City, we discern a man less concerned with being caught between two worlds than with making ends meet—a person much more anxious about political economy, democracy, and human dignity than culture and authenticity.[4] No insular matter, this re-visioning of one moment in one person's life offers a fundamental critique of deep-seated assumptions that remain far too prevalent in the field of American Indian biography.

D'Arcy, Understood

Born on the Flathead Reservation in 1904, D'Arcy McNickle played a prominent role in the Native Rights movement for more than three decades.

In 1936, he published *The Surrounded*, a novel that presaged a literary renaissance, and began working for John Collier to promote tribal self-government via the Indian New Deal. During the 1940s and 1950s, he helped found the National Congress of American Indians, launched American Indian Development (AID), and proposed a Point IV program for Native America, the latter inspired by U.S. assistance to nations emerging from colonialism. By the 1960s, a summer institute sponsored by AID catalyzed a generation of young people, including members of the National Indian Youth Council, and McNickle not only produced the initial draft of the "Declaration of Indian Purpose" but also chaired the steering committee for the 1961 American Indian Chicago Conference. From 1972 to 1977, the last five years of his life, he served as program director for today's D'Arcy McNickle Center for American Indian and Indigenous Studies at the Newberry Library.[5]

Literary scholars have done the most to shape our understanding of McNickle's life. As one might guess, they have focused on his writings, from short stories to novels, such as *The Surrounded, Runner in the Sun* (1954), and *Wind from an Enemy Sky* (1978).[6] With one exception, there appears to be unanimity around the idea that D'Arcy McNickle intended the words of his novels to be read autobiographically—as his innermost thoughts on the page. According to this interpretation, the characters' voices represent McNickle's voice; their feelings encapsulate McNickle's feelings. This explains why so much emphasis has been placed on the revisions he made to "The Hungry Generations," a handwritten early draft of *The Surrounded*, during the 1930s. The general consensus holds that they speak volumes about his search for an Indian identity.[7] According to this logic, the original manuscript featured an assimilationist trajectory for Archilde, the novel's protagonist, because McNickle believed in assimilation. Once he accepted his Indian identity, however, McNickle revised the story so that Archilde, too, embraced his Salish heritage.[8]

These analyses hinge on the idea that McNickle spent much of his life consciously negotiating an existence "between two worlds." Consider, for instance, the late Louis Owens's insistence on categorizing McNickle not as a Native author but as a "mixed blood" author so self-conscious about his inability to prove his "bloodedness" that he decided to "*forge* his own identity through his work."[9] For Owens, the tragic conclusions to both *The Surrounded* and *Wind from an Enemy Sky* demonstrate "that meaningful communication—the communication necessary to survival—is an impossibility between Indian and white worlds." He wanted us to believe that McNickle discerned two roads before Native people and that the "red road" led "to nowhere."[10,11] How far has this been taken? After reading

Dorothy R. Parker's biography of McNickle, one reviewer concluded that *The Surrounded* and *Wind from an Enemy Sky* represent nothing less than "therapeutic re-encounters with a tragic past."[12]

D'Arcy Understood

D'Arcy McNickle's diary fundamentally alters this narrative. Ironically, literary scholars have all but ignored it. As a former director of the McNickle Center once explained to me, many people have come away from reading it with the sense that "there's nothing there." It would be fair to describe it as something less than a page-turner, and the inscrutability of his handwriting would prevent a quick read even if that were not the case. And yet there is a lot of something to the supposed nothing that is there. To access these critical insights, however, required a theoretical and methodological approach attuned to the everday-ness of the entries. The search for one led to anthropologist Ray Fogelson's crucial distinction between "individualism" and "personhood," James Clifford's penetrating essay on ethnobiography, the anthropological literature on life stories, and Luke Lassiter's discussion of collaborative ethnography.[13]

Extending the spirit of "collaborative ethnography," an approach rooted in fieldwork, to textual sources proved particularly important. Approaching the diary in a deliberately collaborative and reciprocal mode—to imagine oneself reading and interpreting "alongside" rather than "over the shoulder of" McNickle—opened a range of interpretive possibilities.[14] It created a context in which one could imagine McNickle "speaking" through the diary and saying, in effect, "I know this is how others have made sense of my novels, but here is another way you might read them" or "I understand how others have arrived at the predominant narrative of my life, but consider the narrative that I constructed for myself." Historians do, of course, enter into conversation with their texts and attempt to understand them on their own terms, but how often do they approach them as one would an ethnographic interview?

This interpretive stance cast new light on one of Clifford's essential observations. While there exists "a diachronic strand running through any life, the thread of an identity forming and reforming itself," he noted, "[t]he most difficult task of biography is synchronic, the task of rendering personality as an experiential world." If in the pages of his diary McNickle narrated a story of *becoming*, in other words, he also narrated a story about *being*.[15] This idea made the premise that his life boils down to a search for an Indian identity more problematic. It simply does not appear as a salient theme in the entries, nor does the supposed dilemma of being "caught between two worlds." Authenticity—another slippery concept—does not show up either, suggesting that perhaps it only bothered him when someone else made it an issue.

What can be found in the diary is a person who loved classical music, good food, and fine wine; who reveled in seeing Babe Ruth play his last game as a Yankee and wrote detailed accounts of World Series games and presidential elections; who worried frequently about money and tried to stay in a marriage despite falling in love with someone else; who had a profound sense of place and home; who traveled incessantly and worked to the point of exhaustion; who believed in the integrity of Indigenous communities, the promise of young people, and in the necessity of change; who spent more time thinking about power and justice and the dynamics of social relations than what Comanche activist LaDonna Harris aptly (though perhaps indelicately) referred to as " 'two worlds' bullshit."[16]

To better grasp this final point, risk imagining yourself alongside McNickle and looking over his shoulder as he penned the three diary entries that follow. A conscious decision has been made to use long excerpts to emphasize the idea that approached ethnographically the text might speak—and that the written word might be heard as if it were spoken in the context of an interview. We begin in September 1933, move backward in time to May of that same year, and end in August 1932. Keep in mind that McNickle wrote each one while revising "The Hungry Generations," which scholars treat as the defining moment in his search for an Indian identity.

"I felt a terrific sense of emotion" (13 September 1933)

On Thursday, 13 September 1933, the day D'Arcy McNickle wrote the first entry, he had been living in New York City for more than seven years. Born and raised in Montana, he spent four years at a federal boarding school in Chemawa, Oregon, and another two in Langley, Washington, as a teenager. Soon after turning twenty-one, he sold his allotment on the Flathead Reservation to fund a year of study at Oxford University in England. Things did not work out as planned, and McNickle ultimately decided to remain in Oxford from September through December 1925. At that point, he moved to France, where he stayed until May 1926.

Rather than returning to Montana to complete his undergraduate training, McNickle remained in the East and convinced his college sweetheart, Joran Birkeland, to relocate to New York City so they could marry.

Despite a worsening economic crisis, McNickle made a decent salary as an assistant to the managing editor at a publishing house and together they earned enough to afford the rent on a quaint apartment in Greenwich Village. Besides, there was much to celebrate, for in May they learned they would be having a baby.

As Joran entered the last trimester of her pregnancy, D'Arcy found time away from several ongoing writing projects to set down these words:

> Yesterday I had a holiday from the office due to the NRA parade. I was up at the library at noon and worked for two hours just as the parade was getting under way. The excitement was intense: 42d St. had been cleared of traffic and people walked in the middle of the street in county-fair mood. It was impossible to get anywhere near the avenue. After coming home and eating lunch I went up 9th St. to Fifth Avenue and watched the parade for upward of an hour. The psychology is inexplicable. Several times, while watching simple, ill-dressed, unshaved self-conscious working men marching along I felt a terrific sense of emotion and tears came to my eyes. The people who marched were equally inexplicable. Some joined their groups early in the morning and did not join the march until three or four in the afternoon. The actual marching time, from the lower end of the avenue up to 72nd St. must have occupied a couple of hours. They seemed to enjoy it.

McNickle referred here to witnessing a mammoth parade promoting the National Industrial Recovery Act. The spectacle celebrated the centerpiece of President Franklin Delano Roosevelt's New Deal and intended to demonstrate American resolve in the face of the Great Depression. Imagine what D'Arcy would have seen. An estimated 1.5 million spectators crowded along Fifth Avenue from Washington Square to Central Park to watch a parade featuring more than 200 marching bands and nearly a quarter million representatives from ninety industrial and trade units. For more than nine hours, this "broad river of humanity" flowed between tall buildings made resplendent by a sea of American flags and colorful banners featuring the NRA's blue eagle. Waves of confetti showered down on marchers and on-lookers alike and seventy military aircraft filled the sky above them.[17]

And D'Arcy was moved to tears. Not by the awe-inspiring grandeur of the spectacle, but by the faces of ordinary people. "I felt a terrific sense of emotion and tears came to my eyes," he tells us, when he saw "simple, ill-dressed, unshaved self-conscious working men marching along. . . ." How do we explain this outpouring of feeling from a person known for being intensely private and not given to public displays of emotion? What accounts for his empathy with the working class? A second diary entry, written four months earlier, offers insight.

"He is effecting the revolution" (25 May 1933)

In the spring of 1933, the New Deal had only begun. Still in the midst of the "First Hundred Days," FDR and Congress set in motion a dizzying array of economic reform initiatives. McNickle avidly followed the news. Though initially leery of Roosevelt, McNickle wrote approvingly of his administration's progress. On March 4, D'Arcy reported on an "eventful and exciting week" that included praise for the "courage and clear vision" of the president's inaugural address. No less important, McNickle reported that after multiple rejections a press seemed to extend "their promise to publish 'The Hungry Generations'" after a final round of revisions (a promise not kept). His diary entry for 25 May 1933 reads:

> In Washington, everything is happening. It rather looks as if Char. E. Mitchell, one of the biggest of the stuffed shirts, will be convicted for income tax evasion.
>
> At the moment the archangel J. P. Morgan, no less, is on the carpet and it transpires that neither he nor any of his partners have paid income taxes since 1930. "Capital losses." All quite legal. I have paid more income tax than twenty of the richest, if not the powerfullest, men in America. A very pleasant state of affairs.
>
> At Muscle Shoals, operation of which has been finally authorized, a terrific scandal is about to break. The Hoover regime seemed bent on wrecking the project and two power companies were defrauding the government of money and abusing its property.
>
> A controlled economy, partly voluntary on the part of industries, and partly supervised by the gov't, is about to be enacted.
>
> Watching the oncoming of events these days is like riding in a car on a high mountain grade, in foggy weather, with no brakes, on a slippery roadbed. Time after time a desperate prospect looms ahead, there is nothing to do but hold on—then at the last moment the fog opens to reveal a straight stretch ahead.

> Roosevelt, by this time, has confounded all his detractors (my ill-informed judgment included: I, who [purport] to have no judgments) and amazed his warmest friends. He is effecting the revolution that no one else in America, individual or group, could have imagined. . . .
>
> If Roosevelt fails it should be because the system is incapable of the required modifications to meet a new world, not because of any lack of energy or courage or intelligence on his part.

This passage clarifies that McNickle's feeling of solidarity with common people grew, in part, out of deep antipathies for concentrated wealth and an economic system that seemed to enrich a few at the expense of everyone else. And initially, he did not think FDR had the wherewithal do anything about it. "There is no real distinction between the parties," McNickle wrote in late October. "Roosevelt is no radical. It is a question even whether he is a liberal." Being able to applaud the president for "effecting the revolution," then, must have come as a most welcome surprise. But was the position McNickle took regarding the role of the government in the economy a reaction to the recent collapse, as conventional wisdom holds, or did it represent a longstanding skepticism toward *laissez faire*?[18]

"Born in the Opposition" (11 August 1932)

A remarkable entry written nine months earlier—during the summer of 1932—provides an answer. These were hard times. D'Arcy and Joran married young—perhaps, they agreed, too young. They were in their early twenties when they took their vows, the first six years of their marriage proved rocky, and something seems to have driven their relationship to a new low. Not only that, but in the space of two terrible days in June, Harcourt Brace rejected "The Hungry Generations" manuscript for a third time and D'Arcy's employer instituted an unannounced 10 percent salary cut. On 11 August 1932, with the national unemployment rate at 25 percent, Hoover still in office, and no end to the economy's downward spiral in sight, McNickle penned the following:

> I have been a long time intending to make a brief record of these New York years, and now that I have some spare time on my hands (on vacation) I should make the effort.
>
> Naturally the first years were confusion. Scorning, instinctively, the ways of the prudent and worldly-wise, I had no

substitute for worldly wisdom. The instinct which led me away from the one path was not competent to stumble upon another. I knew that I wanted to write and that I did not want to return to the scene from which I had fled. What exactly was in my mind on that May morning 1926 when I returned from Paris, I cannot now recall. For one thing, I know that fear was present, rather apprehension. I was such an [undesigned], unaccountable, unwitting accident in the laws of causation. It was part of every constitution to stand at the ship's rail and perceive vaguely, in mist, the vision of the harbor and looming city. The vaguely defined scene could not have stood clearly forth in blinding sunlight, in the state of my vision. . . .

However it happened I cannot explain, but the fact is that I had been born in the opposition and I would not then, and feel that I never shall be able to, accomadate [sic] myself to the exigencies of a world capitalistically regimented. . . .

In my first job, selling automobiles [in Philadelphia], I went through a seven-months' daily betrayal of my birthright in opposition. Everything I was called upon to do was a violation of instinct and desire. I continued the effort under the impression that my instincts and desires were untutored and therefore probably in error: I could see nothing in prospect by following them, whereas the only safety seemed to lie in abandoning them. I was probably right and would undoubtedly be justified in feeling the same way today—but I should have learned this: instincts, right or wrong, cannot be abandoned without seriously impairing integrity, out of which rise self-possession, confidence, the very ability to act and think. In all reason, it must be better to have the wrong instincts—wrong in the sense of one's ability to accommodate oneself to the world—to which one is faithful, than to attempt to go counter to any instinct, right or wrong.

What were my instincts, and how were they wrong?

It was a distrust of capitalism—but no virtue save brevity is served in using labels. At that time I was probably not sure what the term meant, although I had had courses in economics. The distrust was real enough, however. It was directed against "high pressure" selling, which was unintelligent, wasteful, ruthless, animal, intent on driving every vestige of individual preferences in matters of taste, manner of living, and cultural pursuits out of existence; it was directed against the prevailing business morality which had advanced to the high estate of a religion[,] ideas of loyalty to a boss, of being on time, of "boosting" God, country, and company, of wearing a smile, of being "regular," of eschewing all mental activity that did not have to do with "getting ahead" in short the platitudes of a society bent on exploiting every inch, every microscopic entity, of the known world in the interests of money; during a seven months' sojourn in Philadelphia, I discovered it to be against that kind of intellectual prostitution which is known as applied industrial science, in whose name the cheap, money-making motive was allied with humanitarian doctrines of progress, betterment, enlightenment; it was against "enlightened self-interest" which was a ruse to evade the proper and unexorbitant demands of labor by offering stock ownership and petty concessions—a garden for every laborer, or a cow, or sick benefits, first aid cabinets, "pep" meetings, company magazines with "human interest" stories about the "stenos" in the assembling dept., etc., etc.—tactics which had no other purpose than to mislead the workers, executed with a magnanimous flourish and so successfully that even seemingly intelligent people were convinced that our captains of industry were about to create an age of industrial well-being and universal happiness such as the world had never known.

These things I distrusted, I could not see how the soulless corporation was to sire a renascence of humanitarian interests and cultural achievement that high-pressure selling should result in new creativeness in living, seemed to be sheer nonsense. Yet many persons in the public way predicted just such developments.

So long as "things were in the saddle," and in '28 when I went to Philadelphia it did seem as if the world had found its master, and that no force in nature no calamity devisable by man, could alter the least bit the forward drive—so long as the world continued as it was, my distrust, my instinctive opposition, was clearly in the wrong, and I was born out of my time.

But who could have predicted the events of '29–'30–'31–'32 which were to shake the world to its depths . . . and in an hour of black panic reveal our captains of industry, one and all, for what they really were—plundering opportunists, welchers, babbling panderers, senile optimists, contemptible bluffers? The world cracked before my eyes. The impossible became the accomplished fact. A predicted era was a last year's [rag], an outmoded style.

> As with Henry Adams so with me it is a question of education. Through long repetition, I had been led to assume that only the practical, the engineer-trained, the extrovert, the "smart," the super-salesmen, had any chance or any right to survive; the rest of us, if we could not die, had our futures cut out for us—which was to fill the roles of poor relations, and bad-tempered, crabbing, neurotic relations to boot; knowing that we should never be taken seriously, and that it was not even possible to rebel, for by our own constitutional infirmities we would never expect to agree with each other long enough to show a united front.
>
> Having been led to assume that such was the cast of our times, and having begun to adjust myself to such a function of insignificance, I now learn that it was all no more than a salesman's dream (if those unimaginative fellows ever dream), and the lessons which the world had presumed to back were no more than the muck of a propaganda-doctored text book.

If we take McNickle at his word, the answer to the question about his intellectual commitments to the working class and against *laissez faire* are clear. There was nothing new about them. "[T]he fact is," he tells us, "that I had been *born in the opposition* and I would not then, and feel that I never shall be able to, accommodate myself to the exigencies of a world capitalistically regimented." He possessed, in other words, an enduring "distrust of capitalism" and its guiding principles, which ran counter to every fiber of his being. He likened trying to live by its dictates to a "kind of intellectual prostitution" and believed the crash and depression confirmed his "instinctive opposition" rather than being somehow revelatory.

Juxtapositions and Tellings

Why, then, have his life and literary works been described so narrowly as "therapeutic," an "exploration of self," and the "resolution of his inner conflict about his own identity?"[19] As with so much of the scholarship on Native America, these narrative constructions tell us more about the writers than the lives of the people being written about. Their staying power confirms Philip Deloria's observation that we need to examine "how we came to certain kinds of tellings and not others."[20] With respect to McNickle, it is as if scholars created an interpretive funnel and began pouring every dimension of his life into it. Perhaps they simply disregarded as anomalous any elements that could not be forced through. In any event, they fashioned a telling defined by a series of diachronic transformations, epiphanies, and revelatory moments regarding his sense of identity. Compare this rendering with what Philip Deloria determined in regard to whether his grandfather saw himself foremost as an athlete, Christian, or Indian. The distinctions were false, he reasoned, because his grandfather "never parsed his life so neatly." So too with D'Arcy McNickle.[21]

This is why the diary is so important. It introduces new stories, but in a more fundamental sense it suggests the need for a different kind of *telling*. D'Arcy left Montana and did not want to return—but what was he leaving? D'Arcy seems to have struggled with feelings of insecurity—but what was he insecure about? D'Arcy did not wear his "Indianness" on his sleeve—but what does that *mean* exactly and why might it have made a lot of sense for him *not* to? We might also ask what McNickle intended *The Surrounded* to be about. Is it to be read as a meditation on his own identity, or might it be seen as a critique of concentrated power, religious hypocrisy, racism, inequality, and injustice?

D'Arcy McNickle's diary also serves as a window on James Clifford's notion of the "synchronic." The fact of the matter is that between August 1932 and September 1933 McNickle did not know that he would spend the remainder of his life at the forefront of the Indian Rights movement. Nonetheless, finding an answer to the question "How did he get there?" has become many a scholar's *raison d'être*. The finishing point of his career has taken so imperious a hold that his life is narrated with only that in mind.

But what of this latter-day nation builder's own state of mind in 1932 and 1933? What happens when we approach the diary in the spirit of collaborative ethnography, as an ethnographic interview in which McNickle helps us to understand how he conceived of his own life "in time" as opposed to "over time?" To be sure, the diary represents a constructed narrative in its own right and needs to be approached critically. But that does nothing to alter its value as a means of inspiring us to think about personhood "as an experiential world"—as not only a state of becoming but also a state of being.

In *Everything You Know About Indians Is Wrong,* Paul Chaat Smith argues that when it comes to thinking about Native America, there exists a dire need for invention rather than just revision—that we need to attend to "the unexpected, the improbable, and even the impossible."[22] "Worlding," to draw upon Spivak's term, prevents scholars from doing that. Rather than extending our vision, it occludes. How could it do otherwise? With origins in Europe's desire to dominate the globe's non-white peoples, worlding offered simple dichotomies—between civilized and savage, Christian and pagan, advanced and backward, modern and traditional—that served as the handmaidens of colonialism.[23] In the nineteenth and twentieth centuries, the same binaries produced the destructive policies of allotment, assimilation, and termination. How, then, can scholars conceivably claim to have captured the actual texture of lived experience through such a lens? Ethnobiography offers an alternative by allowing for the unexpected, improbable, and impossible. If it enables us to risk imagining that a Flathead tribal member in 1930's New York might have seen himself as a writer, husband, and expectant father "born in the opposition" instead of "walking between two worlds," it might also lead us to create more compelling portraits of other Native lives.

Notes

1. This chapter is the product of several years' worth of working with and thinking about the D'Arcy McNickle Diary, a document to which I was first introduced during my tenure as Assistant Director of the McNickle Center at the Newberry Library from 2003 to 2004. In the spring of 2005, my second semester as a faculty member at Miami University in Oxford, Ohio, the library agreed to acquire a microfilm copy. From that grew a senior capstone in which students transcribed and annotated the entries from late 1960 to early 1962. In the summer of 2009, I had the good fortune of working with Kyle Fields as my undergraduate associate. In addition to serving as my teaching assistant for a summer course, he spent hours digitizing the microfilm with me. This sparked his interest, and we devised an independent study for the fall of 2009 in which he transcribed an early portion of the diary. We continued the project in the spring of 2010 and added Joseph Cheatle, a talented graduate student from the English department, to our group via independent study. By the end of the semester, we had all contributed to drafting a complete transcript of the years 1930 through 1935. Nearly every week we gathered to discuss what we had learned and to check, double-check, and triple-check each other's transcriptions. Kyle and Joey also spent considerable time writing out from the diaries, using a conference paper I had given at the American Society for Ethnohistory in 2009 as a starting place. My departure for the University of North Carolina at Chapel Hill and Kyle's graduation prevented us from collaborating further. And while the writing in this essay is my own, it would not have been possible without the extraordinary work done by and exciting conversations with Kyle and Joey. It gives me great pleasure to acknowledge their tremendous contributions by listing them as co-authors.

2. Philip J. Deloria, *Indians in Unexpected Places* (Lawrence: University Press of Kansas, 2004); Paige Raibmon, *Authentic Indians: Episodes of Encounter from the Late-Nineteenth-Century Northwest Coast* (Durham, NC: Duke University Press, 2005).

3. The term "telling," discussed in greater depth in succeeding paragraphs, is from Deloria, *Indians in Unexpected Places*, 7.

4. D'Arcy McNickle Diaries, D'Arcy McNickle Papers, The Newberry Library, Chicago, Illinois.

5. McNickle, Academic Record, Folder 241, Box 31, McNickle Papers; D'Arcy to Helen, 28 October 1957, Folder 11, Box 1, Dorothy R. Parker D'Arcy McNickle Research Papers, The Newberry Library, Chicago, Illinois; American Indian Development Report, attached to D'Arcy McNickle to Roger Baldwin, 8 December 1952, Folder 13, Box 1130, American Civil Liberties Union Records, Seeley G. Mudd Manuscript Library, Princeton University, Princeton, NJ; Dorothy R. Parker, *Singing an Indian Song: A Biography of D'Arcy McNickle* (Lincoln: University of Nebraska Press, 1992), viii, 84–85, 126–136; D'Arcy McNickle and Harold Fey, *Indians and Other Americans: Two Ways of Life Meet* (New York: Harper, 1959), 197–200; Daniel M. Cobb, *Native Activism in Cold War America: The Struggle for Sovereignty* (Lawrence: University Press of Kansas, 2008), 8–13, 30–79.

6. D'Arcy McNickle, *The Hawk is Hungry and Other Stories*, Birgit Hans, ed. (Tucson: University of Arizona Press, 1992); D'Arcy McNickle, *The Surrounded* (New York: Dodd, Mead, 1936; Albuquerque: University of New Mexico Press, 1978); D'Arcy McNickle, *Runner in the Sun* (New York: Holt, Rinehart, and Winston, 1954; Albuquerque: University of New Mexico Press, 1987); D'Arcy McNickle, *Wind from an Enemy Sky* (New York: Harper and Row, 1978; Albuquerque: University of New Mexico Press, 1988). McNickle also wrote several historical works, including *They Came Here First* (Philadelphia: J. B. Lippincott Co., 1949); with Harold Fey, *Indians and Other Americans* (New York: Harper and Brothers, 1959); *The Indian Tribes of the United States* (London: Oxford University Press, 1962); and *Indian Man: The Life of Oliver LaFarge* (Bloomington: Indian University Press, 1971).

7. Brian C. Hosmer, Review of John Lloyd Purdy's *The Legacy of D'Arcy McNickle: Writer, Historian, Activist*, in *Montana: The Magazine of Western History* 49, no. 1 (spring 1999): 82. Three refreshing exceptions are Shari M Huhndorf and Scott L. Pratt, "Cultural Cartographies: The Logic of Domination and Native Cultural Survival," *Journal of Speculative Philosophy* 14, no. 4 (2001): 268–285; Alicia Kent, "'You can't run away nowadays': Redefining Modernity in D'Arcy McNickle's *The Surrounded*," *SAIL* 20, no. 2 (summer 2008): 22–46; and Lori Burlingame, "Empowerment Through 'Retroactive Prophecy' in D'Arcy McNickle's *Runner in the Sun: A Story of Indian Maize*, James Welch's *Fool's Crow*, and Leslie Marmon Silko's *Ceremony*, *American Indian Quarterly* 24, no. 1 (winter 2000): 1–18.

8. Louis Owens, Review of John Lloyd Purdy's *Word Ways: The Novels of D'Arcy McNickle*, *American Indian Quarterly* 15, no. 4 (Autumn 1991): 557–558; Louis Owens, "The Red Road to Nowhere: D'Arcy McNickle's *The Surrounded*, and "The Hungry Generations," *American Indian Quarterly* 13, no. 3 (summer 1989): 239; Gerald Vizenor, "The Ruins of Representation: Shadow Survivance and the Literature of Domination," *American Indian Quarterly* 17, no. 1 (winter 1993): 16, 27–28; John Lloyd Purdy, ed., *The Legacy of D'Arcy McNickle: Writer,*

Historian, Activist (Norman: University of Oklahoma Press, 1996; John Lloyd Purdy, *Word Ways: The Novels of D'Arcy McNickle* (Tucson: University of Arizona Press, 1990); Dorothy R. Parker, *Singing an Indian Song: A Biography of D'Arcy McNickle* (Lincoln: University of Nebraska Press, 1992); Birgit Hans, ed., *D'Arcy McNickle's* "The Hungry Generations": *The Evolution of a Novel* (Albuquerque: University of New Mexico Press, 2007; Phillip E. Doss, Review of Dorothy R. Parker, *Singing an Indian Song: A Biography of D'Arcy McNickle*, *Western Historical Quarterly* 25, no. 4 (winter 1994): 521.

9. Louis Owens, Review of John Lloyd Purdy's *Word Ways: The Novels of D'Arcy McNickle*, *American Indian Quarterly* 15, no. 4 (Autumn 1991): 557–558; Louis Owens, "The Red Road to Nowhere: D'Arcy McNickle's *The Surrounded*, and "The Hungry Generations," *American Indian Quarterly* 13, no. 3 (summer 1989): 239. I have added the italics to the word "forged" to underscore it as an at once instructive and problematic term, given that it might be seen here to work as a double entendre. Elizabeth Cook-Lynn took a stance different from Owens, arguing "that D'Arcy McNickle, even though he spent much of his professional life in Washington, D.C., and Chicago, and other cities of America, refused the imagination of the exile position and remained, in his own image, a tribal person in touch with his tribal compatriots." Even when literary scholars differ over how to read McNickle, however, they appear to do so without challenging the dichotomous two-worlds paradigm. Elizabeth Cook-Lynn, *The Notebooks of Elizabeth Cook-Lynn*, vol. 59, Sun Tracks: An American Indian Literary Series (Tucson: University of Arizona Press, 2007), 89. Also see Gerald Vizenor, "The Ruins of Representation: Shadow Survivance and the Literature of Domination," *American Indian Quarterly* 17, no. 1 (winter 1993): 16, 27–28.

10. Louis Owens, "The 'Map of the Mind': D'Arcy McNickle and the American Indian Novel," *Western American Literature* 19 (February 1985): 283. For a similar reading, see Robert F. Gish, Review of D'Arcy McNickle, *Wind from an Enemy Sky*; James Ruppert's *D'Arcy McNickle*; and John Joseph Mathew's *Sundown*, *American Indian Quarterly* 14, no. 3 (summer 1990): 336–338 and Sean Teuton, "The Callout: Writing American Indian Politics," in *Reasoning Together: The Native Critics Collective*, Craig S. Womack, Daniel Heath Justice, and Christopher B. Teuton, eds. (Norman: University of Oklahoma Press, 2007), 111.

11. More optimistic readings do not question whether McNickle wrote into his novels his own deeply felt convictions regarding the existence of two seemingly irreconcilable worlds. Rather, they suggest that he retained hope that common ground could be found. John Lloyd Purdy, ed., *The Legacy of D'Arcy McNickle: Writer, Historian, Activist* (Norman: University of Oklahoma Press, 1996; John Lloyd Purdy, *Word Ways: The Novels of D'Arcy McNickle* (Tucson: University of Arizona Press, 1990); Dorothy R. Parker, *Singing an Indian Song: A Biography of D'Arcy McNickle* (Lincoln: University of Nebraska Press, 1992).

12. "Choosing an Indian Identity," the title Dorothy Parker chose for the dissertation version of her biography, underscores this theme. For the quote, see Ruth Rosenberg, Review of Dorothy R. Parker, *Singing an Indian Song: A Biography of*

D'Arcy McNickle, *MELUS* 20, no. 2 (summer 1995): 168. For a much more sensitive appraisal that explores issues such as implied author, plot, characters, and implied reader, see James Ruppert, "Textual Perspectives and the Reader in *The Surrounded*," in *Narrative Chance: Postmodern Discourse on Native American Indian Literatures,* Gerald Vizenor, ed. (Albuquerque: University of New Mexico Press, 1989), 91–100.

13. Raymond D. Fogelson, "Night Thoughts on Native American Social History," in *D'Arcy McNickle Center for American Indian History Occasional Papers in Curriculum*, no. 3, *The Impact of Indian History on the Teaching of United States History* (Chicago: The Newberry Library, 1985): 82; Julie Cruikshank, *Life Lived Like a Story: Life Stories of Three Yukon Native Elders* (Lincoln: University of Nebraska Press, 1991); Eric Luke Lassiter, *The Chicago Guide to Collaborative Ethnography* (Chicago: University of Chicago Press, 2005); Jeffrey Anderson, *One Hundred Years of Old Man Sage: An Arapaho Life* (Lincoln: University of Nebraska Press, 2003). Another example is Raymond J. DeMallie's treaty of the George Sword narrative in "'These have no ears': Narrative and the Ethnohistorical Method," *Ethnohistory* 40, no. 4 (Autumn 1993): 515–538. See also the recent AHR Roundtable, "Historians and Biography," *American Historical Review* 114, no. 3 (June 2009): 573–661.

14. The allusion to "over the shoulder" refers to the work of symbolic interactionist Clifford Geertz. Lassiter, *Chicago Guide to Collaborative Ethnography*, xi, 3–16, 69–72, 98–116.

15. Clifford, "'Hanging Up Looking Glasses,'" 51.

16. Fred R. Harris and LaDonna Harris, interview by Daniel M. Cobb, tape recording, Bernalillo, NM, 14 May 2001.

17. These details are drawn from articles appearing in the *New York Times* between 10 September and 14 September 1933.

18. McNickle Diary, 31 October 1932, The Newberry Library. See also McNickle Diary, 10 November 1932 and 12 March 1933, The Newberry Library.

19. Parker, *Singing*, 39, 44; Hans, *The Hawk is Hungry*, xx

20. Deloria, *Indians in Unexpected Places*, 7.

21. Deloria, *Indians in Unexpected Places*, 112.

22. Paul Chaat Smith, *Everything You Know about Indians is Wrong* (Minneapolis: University of Minnesota Press, 2009), 52, 177.

23. Gayatri Chakravorty Spivak, "Three Women's Texts and a Critique of Imperialism," *Critical Inquiry* 12, no. 1 (autumn 1985): 243–261. For a brilliant summation of these binaries, see Raibmon, *Authentic Indians*, 7.

10

To Come to a Better Understanding

Complicating the "Two-Worlds" Trope

Sande Garner

" 'Culturcide' began in Indian country," announced the website *Indianz.com* on November 16, 2009. Lakota journalist Tim Giago shared a vignette about an encounter between Tatanka Iyotanka (Sitting Bull) and a Christian minister who arrived at Tatanka Iyotanka's home to inform him that he must rid himself of one of his two wives. The chief responded:

> "Well, there they are. Now you tell them which one has to leave."
>
> Which of these Lakota women would you deprive of a loving home? It was an answer based on plain Lakota logic. But then Lakota logic had baffled the white man for a century. And well it should because it was logic based on centuries of cultural beliefs totally unknown to the European settlers . . .
>
> Lakota logic and European logic did not blend. It was like trying to mix water and oil.

According to Giago, the cultural logics of Native and non-Native peoples are so disparate that they cannot "blend." Or, to use Giago's metaphor, they are akin to mixing "water and oil." The division between Christianity and Native cultural practices is one site where Giago believes that the repellent nature of these two incongruent cultural logics is clearly visible. While he correctly highlights the role of Christianity in the colonization of Indian people, Giago later argues that those "who acculturated and converted to Christianity" abandoned "their culture and traditions." The message offered by Giago is that Natives cannot embrace both Christianity *and* Native culture.

In 2007, the public policy think-tank Public Agenda published a report based on a qualitative study designed to determine how Native and non-Native people think about each other. One of the six key points read, "Between Two Worlds: Many Indians we spoke with felt torn between their traditional cultures and modern-day America. But non-Indians seemed oblivious to the conflicting pressures Indians feel."[1]

According to the report, the sense of being caught "between two worlds" was a product of "the powerful tides of assimilation into modern America," harmful stereotypes, and a lack of historical understanding by non-Native people.[2] As a result, the report concluded, Native people feel invisible in mainstream America and experience a profound sense of cultural loss. The solution, according to the authors, can be found in education. In this case, Native peoples are betwixt and between: torn between two cultures unable to fully engage either.

The "two-worlds" trope can also be seen in academia, where a proliferation of analyses regarding the life and motivation of Nicholas Black Elk has emerged in relation to the famous text, *Black Elk Speaks*. Scholars tend to follow one of two related, "two worlds," trajectories. The first centers on issues of authorship. Whose voice is really speaking in the text? Was the account the fictive inventions of Neihardt? Or, is Black Elk's voice present? The second trajectory centers on questions of Black Elk's religious loyalties. Black Elk held a prominent role as catechist in the Catholic Church. Did this association undermine, diminish, or shape his understanding of Lakota worldview and shape the story that he told Neihardt? Or, had Lakota religion remained the center of his understanding of the world? In all of these assessments we are left with an either/or alternative. Either *Black Elk Speaks* is the voice of Black Elk *or* Neihardt. Black Elk was either a Christian *or* a Lakota religious specialist.[3]

In each of the above cases, the binary "two-worlds" trope signals what postcolonial theorist and historian of religion Charles Long refers to as a "dynamics of concealment."[4] Long argues that in cases of "conquest and cultural contact" there is a "creation of discourses of power that prevent the meaning of *what really happened* from becoming a part of the cultural languages of the national community."[5] The "two-worlds" trope is such a discourse and as such it presents a conundrum for interpreting Native experience. In the example presented by Giago, those Indian people who have embraced Christianity, are viewed as traitors to Native cultures. Concealed are the many Native peoples who self-identify as *both* Christian and Native.

In the case of Public Agenda's findings, Native peoples exist in a liminal space unable to function as a Native person in modernity. Obscured are the lived material realities of Native people who are functional in modern American society while maintaining Native cultural practices and identifying as Indian. In the Black Elk case, this approach not only produces a one-dimensional and flattened portrayal of both the historical context and Black Elk, but it denies a reading of Black Elk as an active agent in the production of *Black Elk Speaks* while it also severely limits our ability to understand Black Elk as a whole, complex, real person.

The "two-worlds" trope conceals a rich and diverse Native experience, engagement, and agency in the contact zone and if we take the "two-worlds" trope seriously it further severely limits our ability to imagine Native American futures. In this essay I argue that when we are attentive to the complexity of colonialist interactions of particular historical moments and the "complex personhood" of the historical actors we are able escape the conundrum presented by the "two-worlds" trope and imagine Native futures as this sort of approach uncovers lived experience—contradictions, recognitions, misrecognitions, being stuck, and being transformed.[6] It also demonstrates what Robert Warrior refers to as a rich Native American intellectual tradition, from which we can draw.[7]

In the remainder of this essay, attentive to the complexity of colonialist interactions and complex personhood, I examine two case studies to illustrate one way to go "beyond two worlds." Although the two cases are very different, each represents situations that have been obfuscated by the "two-worlds" trope. The first considers dialogues from the Medicine Men's Association (MMA) meetings, which took place on the Rosebud Reservation between 1973 and 1978. The contributions of the MMA have been concealed by the focus on the activities of the American Indian Movement (AIM), a potent producer of the "two-worlds" trope during the same historical moment. With great frequency the medicine men gave accounts of the colonial conquest of their people and in particular the role played by the Catholic Church and education in this process, yet the large majority identified themselves *both* as Christians and medicine men. For these practitioners there was no disjunction of worldviews, they did not express tension in their multiple subject positions. The participants in this dialogue frequently stated that the reason they participated was "to come to a better understanding."[8] I argue that an approach attentive to complexities rather than drawing on the binary "two-worlds" trope helps us "to come to a better understanding" of the diverse strategies, negotiations, and ways of making sense of the world employed by Native peoples.

The second case study involves Lakota informant George Sword, who is arguably one of the most influential contributors to contemporary understandings of Lakota religious thought and practice. As an informant his input was critical to the production of knowledge for James R. Walker (Sun Dance) and James Mooney (Ghost Dance). Sword offers a different sort of example as neither he nor a multitude of scholars who draw on his contributions clearly evoke the "two-worlds" trope. Yet, the Sword case study provides an informative example of the trope in two senses. First, Sword seems to have internalized the trope to an extreme in order to fully step into modernity. Second, findings about the extent to which Sword aligned himself with Western culture present an uncomfortable dilemma for scholars who want to approach Native choices with respect. As a result the roles he played as army scout, reservation police chief, and friend to the many agents who oversaw the Pine Ridge Agency during the early reservation period are frequently obscured and Sword's self-professed role as a religious authority of Lakota thought and practice goes unquestioned. And, as we shall see, challenges to the content of Sword's contribution, such as those offered by Ella Deloria, are further concealed and rendered invisible.

Medicine Men's Association: It's not the Thought, It's the Action

On the evening of February 27, 1973, members of the American Indian Movement (AIM) and a group of grassroots reservation activists (Oglala Sioux Civil Rights Organization) met at Calico Hall in Pine Ridge, South Dakota, to discuss strategies for bringing change to the volatile political situation on the Pine Ridge Indian Reservation. This meeting may well have gone unnoticed had it not culminated in the decision to enter and occupy the hamlet at Wounded Knee, site of the infamous massacre that took place eighty-two years earlier. Native scholars Robert Warrior and Paul Chaat Smith note that the occupation "received more attention during its first week than the entire previous decade of Indian activism combined"; it "completely penetrated the national consciousness."[9]

Two weeks prior to this meeting (and one hundred miles away on the neighboring Rosebud Indian Reservation) another meeting took place, one which represented a different approach toward social, political, and religious activism. Prior to the meeting, a group of medicine men had come together to form the Medicine Men's Association (MMA). These men, their wives, and associates met regularly to discuss a number of pressing community issues. The group was involved in several activities, not the least of which was a five-year-long dialogue with priests and their associates from the St. Francis Mission, referred to as the Medicine Men and Pastors Meetings (MMPM). Both groups agreed that the purpose of the dialogues was "to work to a better understanding."[10]

From the first meeting it was clear that the priests and medicine men intended something very different when they mentioned "understanding." While the priests were concerned with understanding how God sent "his" message in different ways to different people, the medicine men were concerned with persuading the priests to understand the values of their worldview and practice. Father William Stolzman, who chaired the MMPM, opened the first meeting with the following explanation:

> We are gathered here tonight to talk about the things of God. This is a holy assembly, and we want to speak about the holy things, which God has revealed to his people. God has spoken to all peoples throughout the history of the world. He has spoken to them in different ways . . . by further talk and discussion we will learn more about the truth and things that God has given to us. It is only by talking and sharing, that we really can come to *understand* the revelations that God has given to us. (Emphasis added.)[11]

Medicine man Arthur Running Horse seconded Stolzman's appeal to this understanding, but changed the meaning.[12] Ben Black Bear, Jr. interpreted and summarized Running Horse's speech. "So he expresses the fact that he is happy about this meeting; that from this meeting we can start to understand each other and that we could return with something concrete and significant."[13] Running Horse was clear; he expected that a "better understanding" of Lakota worldview would result in changes in the material, or lived reality, of the Lakota.

The two meetings held that February in 1973 took place on reservations that were not only in close proximity to one another, but shared multiple familial relationships. They also shared a common history of colonial repression, the excesses of which continued to negatively impact their communities. The impulse to engage in social, political, and religious activism was shaped by a transformational historical moment. Perceptions about American Indians were changing on multiple registers: institutionally, in popular culture, and amongst Indian people. The meetings shared another similarity—they grounded their activist approach in a conceptual frame that located Lakota religious thought and practice at the center. Robert Warrior argues that connections to Indian religion made Native political and social activism unique among the contemporary minority social movements of the 1970s.[14]

The group who met at Pine Ridge chose militant and often violent activism as their strategy. Warrior and Paul Chaat Smith note that the "[t]wo faces of the Wounded Knee occupation, the sacred and profane, were present from the first moments of the takeover."[15] However, the group at Rosebud chose to tell their stories and it is clear that they felt this approach would result in practical and concrete changes within their community. Folklorist Joann Bromberg argues, "By telling personal stories we build our social identity; by exchanging or withholding our stories we manage our social relationships; and through story exchanges we construe and even change, society."[16] Bromberg's argument is quite similar to that made by N. Scott Momaday four decades earlier during the same era of AIM and the MMPM. In his address to the First Convocation of American Indian Scholars in 1970, Momaday famously argued, "we are all made of words; that our most essential being consists in language. It is the element in which we think and dream and act, in which we live our daily lives."[17] The contemporary emphasis on the activities of AIM and stories employed by them obscures a long history of social, political, and religious activism; it also conceals alternative storytelling strategies deployed by other Native people, such as the MMA, to evoke change.

Relatively little has been written about the MMPM.[18] The transcripts of the dialogues offer a rich resource for examining Lakota religious thought and practice as more than forty different medicine men participated at some point during five years of meetings. A number of the medicine men were elders who had performed the role of Lakota ritual specialist for many years. That there were this many experienced medicine men on the Rosebud Reservation during the early- to mid-1970s suggests that Lakota religious practices had a stronger presence in the Rosebud community than previously thought and that Lakota thought and practice, albeit repressed, had not been lost.

At the time of the first MMPM, the Catholic Church had maintained an active presence on the Rosebud and Pine Ridge Reservations for ninety years. Initial establishment had not been an easy task as Catholic missionaries were banned from the agency under policies instituted by President Grant in the 1870s.[19] In part, due to the pressure exerted by Sinte Gleska—Chief Spotted Tail—President Rutherford B. Hayes lifted the ban. In an 1877 meeting with the President, Sinte Gleska reportedly said:

> I would like to say something about a teacher. My children, all of them, would like to learn how to talk English. They would

> like to learn how to read and write. We have teachers there, but all they teach us is to talk Lakota, and to write Lakota, and that is not necessary. I would like to get Catholic priests. Those who wear black dresses. These men will teach us how to read and write English.[20]

By 1885 the first Catholic mission building was constructed. Within a year the St. Francis Mission School was in operation and the Society of Jesuits was involved in the project of "civilizing" Lakota.

Anthropologist Harvey Markowitz argues that understanding the Catholic mission is critical to any meaningful comprehension of the history of Native and Catholic relations.[21] The early mission efforts were shaped by a directive to help Indian peoples advance according to a developmental model of social Darwinism. "From the day of their arrival these religious rigorously pressed forward the government's assimilationist policies. They hoped that by following a stringent regimen the Oglalas and Brules could be advanced from 'savagery' to 'civilization' in one or two generations"[22] via a process of "cultural replacement."[23]

Fr. Robert Hilbert, S.J., who first arrived on the Rosebud Reservation in 1973 when the first MMPM began, notes that "when Saint Francis Mission was founded, it was common in missionary circles to speak of 'Christianizing and civilizing' non-European peoples."[24] Lakota belief and practice was viewed as "in opposition to Christianity."[25]

A strong argument could be made that the "two-worlds" trope emerged from non-Native perceptions of Native cultural practices. For instance, in 1881 Major John Bourke was sent to the Pine Ridge agency in order to study the Sun Dance and write a report for the United States government. Bourke's diary provides insight into his perception of the 1881 Sun Dance. Almost every person on the Pine Ridge agency was in attendance that year, as well as Sioux from other agencies and a number of non-Indian spectators. There were twenty-seven dancers including one woman, Pretty Enemy (reportedly the daughter of Little Wound). Bourke noted that he and McGillycuddy, the government's agent at Pine Ridge, were given tremendous access and even allowed to walk around inside the dance enclosure. Bourke recalled that Bull Man danced while pierced to a tree for over an hour and fainted four times. Six women offered their own flesh so that Bull Man's suffering would end. The Oglala worked to explain the Sun Dance to Bourke. In one exchange from the Bourke journals, Red Dog told Bourke during the piercing, "My friend, this is the way we have been raised. Do not think it strange. All men are different. Our grandfathers taught us to do this. Write it down on the paper." Bourke apparently disagreed calling the event a "bloody drama" and "a glimpse into a "Red-hot Hell."[26]

The experience of Lakota people, resulting from the mission directive, was told in a number of stories offered by medicine men during the meetings. Henry Crow Dog recalled that he tried to learn about Catholicism but was driven away because of his involvement with peyote and the Native American church. One winter evening in 1934 while camped outside of Saint Francis, Crow Dog and another Lakota singer were drumming and singing Lakota songs in an effort to doctor Crow Dog's two-year-old son, who was sick at the time. Missionaries thought Crow Dog was having a peyote meeting and sent the tribal police to arrest him. Driven from town, Crow Dog tried to make it to his allotment. Mary Gertrude, Crow Dog's wife recalled the night in great detail.

> So Henry packed up. He took down the tent that was our home and fixed up the wagon, hitched up his team. He loaded up everything we owned and put us all in the wagon. There was a blizzard. You couldn't see your hand before your eyes. And it was so cold! So Henry drove the team all the way to our allotment, with the snow and icy wind in his face. It was dark and you couldn't see. The horses were all iced over. There was hardly any road. It was slow going. And somewhere between Saint Francis and our land, our little boy died.[27]

The priests refused to bury the infant, Earl Edward, in the church cemetery, which they claimed "was for 'good Christians only.'"[28] Forty years later, the wound was still fresh for Crow Dog when he spoke at one of the early MMPMs.

> I was beginning to go to Holy Communion and pray to the Great Spirit, in Christ in that big church in St. Francis. About that time I was ordered to get off St. Francis grounds because I am a peyote man. At the same time I had [a] sick child and had to go to one of the Catholic houses but the roads were all blocked and so I took my baby home and he died there; after that I quit the Catholic Church and no more.[29]

Another medicine man recalled an incident from 1929. He joined the church and served as an altar boy. He thought he had a good relationship with one priest in particular, recalling that they had talked and laughed together. One Sunday a group of people entered the church late and Father Gall motioned to him to get a bench for the group. As the group went to sit they knocked over the bench, which made a loud noise when it hit the ground interrupting the service. "Fr. Gall came up and slapped me across the face and told me that I wasn't to interrupt him in his worship."[30] The humiliation of the episode was still felt four decades later.

> To this day I never forget that incident. A holy man, the Father who handles the body of Christ or whatever, slapped me across the face on account of the bench falling down. After that the Holy Family church was closed and nobody went there. It is still closed. That is one experience in my life that I will never forget, when I see a father then I am scared of them. I don't want nothing to do with them. Now I am getting over it and that is why I am here. [sic][31]

For some, such as Crow Dog and the unknown speaker above, negative experiences with Catholic ritual specialists caused them to break ties with the church.

At one point during the meetings Stolzman justified the Catholic approach as he remarked that this sort of treatment was directed by God. "At the turn of the century, 75 years ago the Lord directed the Missionaries to be quite stern and quite hard on the people to bring them closer to the Catholic practices," he argued.[32]

However, the majority of medicine men involved with the MMPMs, such as Charles Kills Enemy, continued to associate with the church in spite of such episodes and most identified themselves as *both* Catholic and medicine men. Kills Enemy, who was baptized in both the Episcopal and Catholic churches, frequently told the story of his excommunication from the Catholic Church. As a young man he had married in the church, but after a failed marriage began living with another woman. According to the church this co-habitation amounted to living in sin and Kills Enemy was excommunicated. Twenty-five years later, when his first wife died, he was finally able to marry the woman he had been living with and was welcomed back into the church.

> My belief is that I am a Catholic and I don't know how good a Catholic I am, but I try to be a good Catholic and I was excommunicated for twenty-five years but still I go to church and stay right there in my church. I didn't pout or anything and

> I didn't go away. I stayed right in my church. Prayed with the pipe and also took peyote. I go [to] that Native American church too . . . Now today I have a wife, we got married in church.[33]

For most of the Lakota ritual specialists, the Catholic Church and Lakota religion were not in opposition. These cultural transmitters clearly rejected the "two-worlds" trope. Rather, they took the position that the similarities between the two belief systems were such that aspects of Catholicism could be incorporated into Lakota ritual practices.[34] Translating for his father, Ben Black Bear, Jr. noted:

> The Indians before Christ prayed to God. After the coming of the Christians, the priests; their teachings were accepted into the Lakota religion as evidence into the Sun Dance. The Sun Dance symbolism, for instance they have a cross and they put up a sacred pole and the cross. The pole symbolized the cross . . . he said that he is not comparing one religion against another but rather taking them both. As being true . . . the peace of the Catholic Church is that they accept it in the Indian way.[35]

The medicine men did not find the theological underpinnings of Lakota thought and Christianity at odds. For them, the broader social concerns were related to dominant society's approach to the world. One issue cited specifically was that many members of dominant culture did not practice the teachings of Christianity.[36] The majority of medicine men expressed no opposition to the teachings of Christianity. Their complaint was that the teachings were not put into practice.

In January of 1974, John "Fire" Lame Deer launched a tirade at the majority meeting that critiqued the dominant society's practice of instant gratification, "instant steaks, instant pork chops, instant squaw."[37] He went on to observe, "The white man has a good book but who practices? That is our trouble."[38] A story told by Picket Pin, which was translated by Big Crow, dramatically illustrated Lame Deer's critiques.

> Mr. Picket Pin . . . told the story about some big shot coming down here. He was smoking the peace pipe with the Indians. So they sit in a circle and the chief lit the pipe and passed down to this big shot. He was not an Indian. And when it came to him, well he took his handkerchief and wiped off the stem. Then he started smoking it. So when he passed it to the next Indian,

> he didn't like this. You talk about brotherhood and sharing and there he was wiping off everything. When he passed it to the next Indian, [he] carried a knife in those days, so he reached in there and pulled out one of his little knives and cut the stem off all together.[39]

This story carried a great deal of potency and was remembered and re-told during another meeting by a different storyteller. The values of brotherhood, such as sharing with your relatives, were not being practiced by the "big shot." Wiping off the stem of the pipe before smoking it was taken as an affront by the Lakota. This faux pas was amplified and mirrored back when the next Indian in rotation to smoke the pipe took out his knife and cut off the stem sending a powerful message that an important form of etiquette had been breached. For the medicine men Christian thought was not the problem, but un-Christian actions were.

George Sword: Uncomfortable Findings Obscured

James R. Walker's *The Sun Dance and Other Ceremonies of the Oglala Division of the Teton Dakota* (1917) remains, nearly a century later, *the* canonical text on the Siouan Sun Dance. Anthropologist Raymond DeMallie observes, "Walker's *Sun Dance* has become a classic, a key work for understanding the traditional Lakota way of life."[40] While some have critiqued the processes deployed by Walker and challenged the validity of its data, *The Sun Dance and Other Ceremonies of the Oglala Division of the Teton Dakota* remains the primary source on the Sun Dance, Lakota religious concepts, and Lakota myth.[41] Walker was agency physician at the Pine Ridge Reservation for eighteen years (1896–1914) and during that time amassed considerable materials about "almost every facet of the old Lakota way of life."[42] He synthesized these for his book.

Critical to Walker's endeavor was the information given to him by a number of Oglala. In his introduction, Walker names "Little-Wound, American-horse, Bad-wound, Short-bull, No-flesh, Ringing-shield, Tyon, and Sword," as resources for information.[43] In the introduction, Walker focused most on Sword, about which he wrote:

> Sword was a man of marked ability with a philosophical trend far beyond the average Oglala. He could neither write nor speak English, but wrote much in old Lakota and the translations of

> his texts have been used in preparation of this paper. As but few Oglala can, he was able to talk interestingly of the former habits and conduct of his people, so as to give distinct ideas of their daily lives. He began an autobiography which promised to be of historical value, but died before completing it.[44]

Who was Sword, a man who garnered the longest acknowledgement in Walker's text? What did he contribute to the work? Walker's text provides very few clues. His composite description of the Sun Dance ritual does not cite specific contributors and in only a few instances does he credit a specific storyteller as the source for key concepts, terms, and narratives (myths and legends).

It was not until 1978, under the direction of DeMallie and Elaine Jahner, that Walker's primary materials from numerous sources were gathered together to produce three volumes: *Lakota Belief and Ritual* (1980, editors, DeMallie and Jahner), *Lakota Society* (1982, editor, DeMallie), and *Lakota Myth* (1983, editor, Jahner). Although Walker is credited as author for each volume, specific attention and detail is paid to individual Lakota informants. Of the informants, Sword takes center stage—so much so that a fourth volume that focuses specifically on the Sword material is forthcoming.[45]

Sword is one of the most perplexing historical actors of the early reservation era as he seemingly embraced dominant culture more than most. For contemporary scholars a tension emerges as a result of the uncomfortable accounts of Sword's alliances and his service to the U.S. government. Jahner suggests that the recovery work of contemporary scholars, such as herself and DeMallie, "distort the roles of people, such as Sword, who remained at the sidelines."[46] I would argue that Sword was not a marginal person during the early reservation years. He traveled extensively, was a member of several delegations of Lakota to Washington, DC, and held powerful positions during the early days of the Pine Ridge Reservation. So much so, that he warranted mention in Charles Eastman's autobiography, *From the Deep Woods to Civilization.* He also is mentioned by name in a number of *New York Times* articles published during his lifetime. One article written by schoolteacher Emma Sickels about the "Rival Chiefs" Red Cloud and Little Wound included a drawn sketch of the man. Furthermore, he was an informant par excellence for other works about the Oglala written by non-Native peoples. During his lifetime, Sword was both an influential and powerful man on the Pine Ridge agency, especially among the Oglala.

Jahner is correct however, in the sense that Sword's role and individual identity certainly would have drifted into obscurity had it not been for the materials compiled and published by the team. Whereas prior to this collection, references to Lakota thought, myth, and ritual cited Walker; today specific concepts are credited to Sword. For example, in the recently published text by David Martínez, a description of ceremonial offerings is credited to Sword and Martínez even cites Sword as ancestor of a "Dakota/Lakota/Nakota intellectual tradition."[47]

During Sword's lifetime, the Lakota underwent tremendous change and faced enormous challenges as they were forced to give up a way of life and submit to reservation living. As Jahner notes, "Sword lived through fundamental social and cultural changes. During his lifetime, the United States forced the Oglala to move from their traditional, seminomadic culture to reservation living."[48] His life provides an extreme example of *one* way of negotiating those changes. Sword's choices, the roles he assumed during the transitional processes and their implications, are disturbing as Sword appears to have internalized the "two-worlds" trope. Historian, Jeffrey Ostler notes, "Though many Lakota leaders advocated selective adoption of American ways of life, Sword went farther in the direction of acculturation than most. From his position as semipermanent head of the Indian police (he was not a band leader), he assisted in the suppression of Lakota religious practices and was a strong advocate of farming and allotment."[49]

Accounts from the period, such as that offered by Nebraska rancher Edgar Beecher Bronson, focus on Sword's allegiance to reservation agent Dr. Valentine McGillycuddy. One chapter in his reminiscences, "McGillycuddy's Sword," describes a tense situation where Sword, with a handful of men, put himself between several hundred angry "bucks" and McGillycuddy in order to protect the latter. This sort of allegiance was so unusual that in a letter Bronson wrote to McGillicuddy decades later, he asked "Was there really a Sword?"[50] These sorts of vignettes have been discounted as "slanted and prejudiced."[51] But there are a number of them from various sources. A strong case can be made that Sword consistently acted in the interest of the colonizer and nurtured these relationships.

Distinguishing the details of Sword's life is a messy project. He appears in many sources in the historical record but also provided various, often conflicting, details about his life to a number of non-Native ethnographers. Complicating the issue is that Sword had a brother, who also went by the name Sword before his death around 1876. We know that Sword was born sometime around 1847, but there are only two accounts from Sword's young adult life. In an interview with Eli Ricker he purported that he took part in the Fetterman Fight, which occurred in 1866, as well as the Wagon Box Fight the following year (Sword would have been barely twenty years old at the time of the former).

We also know that Sword was not his birth name. In fact, at different times during his life he gave dissimilar accounts about how he acquired the name. He told Eli Ricker that his name previously was Chase the Animal, but upon his brother's death, he took his brother's name, Sword.[52] The explanation he gave Walker had to do with an epiphany during his first trip to Washington, DC. "I went to Washington and to other large cities, and that showed me that the white people dug in the ground and built houses that could not be moved. Then I knew that when they came they could not be driven away. For this reason I took a new name, the name of Sword, because the leaders of the white solders wore swords."[53] There is a third telling of the name that comes from Billy Garnett in the Ricker interviews. "Garnett says Sword did not have the name of Sword until . . . he went to the Custer battlefield with Generals Sheridan and Crook (summer of 1877); that his name, as he recollects, was *Hunts the Enemy*."[54] Jahner, provides a fourth telling. Drawing on Ella Deloria's translation of the Sword ledger book, Jahner states that the original name was Enemy Bait, which he still went by in 1877.[55]

Little is known about Sword's life until the spring of 1879, when Dr. Valentine McGillycuddy arrived to take the position of agent in charge at Pine Ridge.[56] McGillycuddy possessed "strong opinions on how to guide the Oglalas along the white man's path."[57] Foremost among his plans was to break the hold of influence exerted by the traditional chiefs, such as Red Cloud, and one way to accomplish this task was through the creation of an Indian police force. Historian Robert Utley observes, "The chiefs rightly viewed the Indian police force as a menace to their supremacy."[58]

Most accounts credit Young Man Afraid of His Horses with McGillycuddy's choice of Sword to head up the reservation Indian police force on Pine Ridge agency.[59] This put Sword in direct opposition to Red Cloud, who strongly opposed both the plan and the choice of Sword. Julia McGillycuddy, second wife of the agent, wrote about the tension as Sword set about to recruit fifty young warriors to serve in the police force and Red Cloud exerted pressure to prevent participation. She recalls an incident when Sword proposed to hold a barbecue for potential recruits, but the event was disrupted when members of Red Cloud's band "swooped upon them, seized the roasting beef, and devoured it."[60] Sword eventually persuaded fifty young men to join and the police force was established with Sword at the helm. With the police force in place, they turned their attention to providing a vehicle for trials and punishment. On Pine Ridge this issue was resolved with the organization of "a Board of Councilmen to regulate Indian conduct and punish offenders. The one hundred councilmen, elected from different camps at Pine Ridge, selected Young Man Afraid of His Horses as president, with George Sword as secretary."[61] Bronson astutely observes in his recollection of the time that for Sword, "it not only gave an important command to a man then only a warrior, but also gave him, as executor of the agent's orders, general authority over even the elders and chiefs of the tribe. And little did the tribe like it, old or young."[62] At approximately thirty years old, Sword was a very powerful man in the new order of life on the reservation.

Sword's allegiance was tested early and frequently. One instance recalled by Bronson involved a number of men who had arrived at the agency in order to study the Sun Dance. The group, which included Bronson, McGillycuddy, Lieutenants Waite and Goldman, and Major John Bourke, were gathered in McGillycuddy's office. They were preparing to travel to the site of that year's Sun Dance (1881). A band of several hundred Brulé from the adjoining Rosebud agency arrived to attend the Sun Dance and descended upon the agent's office demanding food, which McGillycuddy refused. According to Bronson, the chief of the group then threatened to "kill every white man on this reservation" and McGillycuddy physically threw the chief out of the office.[63] The anxiety of the situation is palpable in Bronson's account written decades later. The group feared for their lives, a fear that was compounded when Sword and his men left the office. I quote at length from Bronson:

> Down we all dropped behind the fence wall, rifles cocked and leveled, and we were barely down when up over the bluff, not thirty yards distant, charging us at mad speed, came a sure-enough war party. Keen eyes sought sights and fingers were already pressing triggers when Changro [the translator] shouted:
>
> "No shoot! Sword he come!"
>
> It was indeed our trusty Sword, with every manjack of his youngsters!
>
> Reining in at the gate, Sword quietly led his men behind—to the north of—the office, left the ponies in charge of a few horse holders, and then lined his men along the wall beside us—honest Sword! Ready to come to death grips with his own flesh and blood in defence of his white chief!
>
> Dr. McGillicuddy may have known a prouder and happier moment than this, but I doubt it.[64]

The presence of Sword and his men had, according to Bronson, averted a potential disaster. After a heated exchange among the Brulé, they turned and headed toward the Sun Dance grounds, leaving the group unharmed.

Sword offered a performative challenge to the Sun Dance camp that year as well. After the incident with the Brulé, McGillycuddy and Bourke were uncertain whether or not to visit the dance and feared repercussions. However Bronson recalled that, "both agreed a bold front was likely to permanently settle the Brules's grouch and the Ogallalas' resentment of the doctor's police organization, more likely than to stay tight at the Agency, and leave them suspicious we were afraid of them."[65] The group set out from the agency with Sword's police in tow as protection.

> When well within the circle, Sword asked the doctor to stop the ambulances a few minutes. He then proceeded to put his police through a mounted company drill of no mean accuracy, good enough to command the commendation of Major Bourke and Lieutenants Waite and Goldman.
>
> The drill finished, and without the least hint to us of his purpose, Sword suddenly broke his cavalry formation and, at the head of his men, started a mad charge, in disordered savage mass, straight at the nearest point of the line of tepees to the west; and, come within twenty yards of the line, reined to the left parallel to the line, and so charge round the entire circle, his men shouting their war-cries and shooting as fast as they could load and fire over the heads of their people, sometimes actually through the tops of the lodges.
>
> It was Sword's challenge to the tribe! One hundred challenging twelve thousand! . . .
>
> Altogether it made about the most uncomfortable ten or fifteen minutes I ever passed, for we had nothing to do but sit idly in our ambulances, awaiting whatever row this mad freak might stir.
>
> At length, the circuit finished, Sword drew up proudly before us and saluted, his horses heaving of flank and dripping of sides, and spoke to Changro . . .
>
> "Sword he say now Sioux be good Injun—no bother police any more!"[66]

While Sun Dances were held yearly from the earliest period on the reservation; the government targeted the ceremony as a serious detriment to the civilization project. Early on McGillycuddy decided to ban the Sun

Dance, but it took until 1884 for him to accomplish his goal and required the use of agency police to enforce his decision. Sword and Young Man Afraid of His Horses cautioned against an approach that would result in an outright ban as they feared it would result in considerable bloodshed. They offered another alternative—threaten to withhold rations for the entire family if anyone from the family participated in the ceremony.[67] Red Cloud was outraged and reportedly said that "neither by treaty [n]or otherwise have they relinquished their right of participation in the practice."[68] But, the advice garnered from the two Lakota combined with other strategies worked and a public Sun Dance was not held that year.

By the time Walker arrived at the agency in 1896, Sword was no longer the head of the Indian police. However, he still held a powerful position as judge. Walker and Sword began a relationship that spanned fourteen years until Sword's death in 1910. The two men were approximately the same age—Sword was forty-nine and Walker forty-seven—and both men's life experiences were shaped by dramatic events and a radically shifting American dynamic. Walker had lived through the Civil War, Sword the Indian Wars. Both men were government employees and it is likely that they met soon after Walker's arrival. Only six weeks after coming to Pine Ridge, Walker had already conducted his first interview with Sword.[69]

DeMallie and Jahner write, "The medical needs at Pine Ridge Reservation motivated Walker's efforts to learn the ways of the traditional holy men."[70] In a letter dated in 1906 Walker described the rise of tuberculosis on the reservation and noted that the Oglala were likely to turn to medicine men for treatment of the disease rather than someone like himself trained in Western medicine. He decided that enlisting the aid of the medicine men rather than an outright suppression of their practices would be a more productive route.

> I then studied their methods of treating the sick, and the results. I found that they have little knowledge of disease, that the most of their medicines are inert, and that their practices consist mostly of mysticism and trickery. But I also learned that the Indians have faith in the power of medicine men to relieve suffering, and that most of the medicine men have a sincere confidence in their power to do so.[71]

Walker went on to explain that the double confidence, on the part of the sick in the medicine men's powers and on the part of the medicine men, did in some minor cases, result in "real and permanent" relief.[72]

The first of the dated interviews conducted by Walker was with Little Wound, a progressive chief. Two days later he interviewed Sword. Sword began in conventional Lakota oral traditional storytelling mode, first substantiating his "authority" for the knowledge he would share.[73]

> I know the old customs of the Lakotas, and all their ceremonies, for I was a *wicasa wakan* (holy man, or shaman), and I have conducted all the ceremonies. I have conducted the Sun Dance, which is the greatest ceremony of the Lakotas. The scars on my body show that I have danced the Sun Dance and no Lakota will dispute my word. I was also a *pejuta wicasa* (medicine man), and belonged with the Bear medicine people. The Bear medicine men have all the medicine ceremonies that other kinds of medicine men have and much more. So I can tell all the medicine ceremonies.

Sword's claims have been accepted and circulated widely. For example, in a biographical entry in the *Encyclopedia of North American Indians*, Harvey Markowitz notes that "Sword achieved great renown as a *wicasa wakan* (holy man, or shaman) and *pejuta wicasa* (medicine man).[74] Jahner remarks that as a result Sword "was remarkably well qualified for his role as Walker's primary teacher and as overseer of the immense task of preserving the holy men's teachings in writing."[75] No one has ever questioned the veracity of Sword's claims made for the first time at the age of fifty.[76] The historical record does not support his claim as it does for some of Walker's other informants such as Little Wound or No-Flesh.[77] In fact, during the era when these men were still actively involved with the Sun Dance, Sword was clearly challenging the practice and conspiring with officials to have it discontinued.

Further, there is a striking omission in Sword's narrative. Jahner and DeMallie rightly locate Sword's biography as following the conventions of Lakota oral tradition. Jahner writes,

> Its primary structure and content clearly follow the traditional Lakota conventions guiding formal, public oral presentations of personal experiences, and it has to be judged first in relation to these conventions. Of all the formalized modes of Sioux narrative, the recounting of one's accomplishments was perhaps the most central—it was the narrative performance for which all other types were prelude and preparation.[78]

Yet, in the case of those claiming to be medicine or holy men, conventions traditionally included some account of the speaker's vision or dream, which substantiated their authority to speak about or conduct the rituals. Little Wound offered this presentation in his interview. "In my boy vision, the Buffalo came to me and when I sought the shaman's vision, the Wind spoke to me."[79] This vital element is missing from Sword's narrative.

By the end of September in 1896 Sword had already agreed to write for Walker and a group of informants including Little Wound, American Horse, and Lone Star agreed to tell Walker "of the ceremonies of the Oglala" if he would "provide a feast."[80] Sword is credited with persuading the others to participate. Just as Sword's claim of being a medicine and holy man requires critical attention, so too, should Walker's claims that he was initiated as a shaman, which has been accepted at face value by scholars. In the introduction to his work on the Sun Dance, Walker writes about himself: "He cultivated the friendship of the shamans, and became a shaman, thus receiving information that it was impossible to get otherwise."[81] Walker claimed that the knowledge of the Shaman was secret and could only be shared with "one who was to become a Shaman."[82] Further, he had agreed not to relate this knowledge until all of his informants were dead.[83] The narrative of Walker's initiation as a shaman is circulated widely. DeMallie and Jahner note, "Through his work and developing knowledge of the sacred, Walker in effect became a holy man himself."[84]

Sword kept, among his letters, several testimonies about his relationship with the Episcopal Church, which relate to Sword's conversion to Christianity. One letter from Bishop W. H. Hare certified that Sword had taken a leadership role in the church by the early 1890s, although his conversion likely came much earlier.[85] In Sword's case, he embraced Christianity in the same way with which he embraced other aspects of dominant culture. "In war with the white people I found their *Wakan Tanka* the Superior, I then took the name of Sword and have served *Wakan Tanka* according the white people's manner with all my power . . . I joined the church and am a deacon in it and shall be until I die. I have done all I was able to do to persuade my people to live according to the teachings of the Christian ministers."[86]

Three decades after Sword's death Dakota ethnographer and linguist Ella Deloria challenged the veracity of his materials. Deloria worked with the Sword material extensively, first translating his written description of the Sun Dance and publishing them in *The Journal of American Folklore* in 1929. Sword's description was originally written in Lakota and Deloria provided a word-for-word translation as well as a version in narrative form—what she referred to as a "free translation."[87] In 1937 Franz Boas asked Deloria to verify the accuracy of the Walker material by conducting interviews with elders on the Pine Ridge and Rosebud Reservations. It is clear that Boas was certain that Deloria *would* be able to confirm the authenticity of the stories and was quite dismayed when she could not. According to historian of religion, Lindsay Jones, "Despite continued checking, however, and despite the fact that many elements . . . did resonate with Indian audiences, Deloria most of all confirmed her initial suspicions that Walker's 'myths' were loaded with features that appeared either twisted or completely unfamiliar to her indigenous contemporaries."[88]

Many contemporary scholars include some reference to this exchange. Some argue that this remained a source of tension between the two throughout the remainder of their association. Others relate the narrative to draw attention to the power differential in the Boas–Deloria relationship.[89] Maria Cotera illuminates one of the most important aspects of the exchange as she observes "Deloria's excitement over her findings . . . Deloria believed that she had uncovered information that would once and for all set the record straight as to the religious practices and mythology of the Sioux."[90] Today scholars continue to obscure Deloria's findings and neglect to ask what it might mean that the Sword materials "have often been presented as constituent elements of pre-colonial ('purely' indigenous and non-Christian) . . . Sioux oral tradition."[91] In spite of Deloria's work, today's leading academics on the Sioux point to the materials as exemplary of Lakota thought and belief.[92]

Returning to the "Two-Worlds" Trope

The two case studies, although very different, offer powerful challenges to the "two-worlds" trope. They illustrate not only that the "two-worlds" trope is not expansive enough to analyze the complex interactions of the contact zone or account for the diverse choices made by Native people, but that the trope is a discourse of power that works to conceal what "*really happened.*" As a result our ability to understand the meaning of Native experience and imagine Native futures is constrained.

In the case of the MMA, the trope is challenged as the medicine men continue to assert that Christianity and Lakota thought are not in opposition. Whereas Giago would lead us to believe that the cultural logics are so incongruent that they are like oil and water, these men, who had continued to practice Lakota ceremony all of their lives in the face of great suppression, were not perplexed by their multiple subject positions and strongly conveyed their understanding that they could be both Christian and Lakota.

The powerful discourse of the "two-worlds" trope obfuscates the profound distinction being made by the medicine men that the root problem facing the Lakota is the inability of individuals to practice the teachings of Christianity. In their reflection the theological underpinnings are not the issue. The problem is not the thought, it is the action.

Sword on the other hand presents a different sort of case study. Throughout his life Sword told about an epiphany he had during a trip to Washington, DC, early in his life. During this visit he became aware that "the white people . . . could not be moved."[93] And, in contrast to the public policy think tank Public Agenda's argument that Native people are caught betwixt and between, unable to assimilate into modernity, it is clear that at that moment he consciously decided to align himself with "the powerful tides of assimilation into modern America."[94] The choices that Sword made are an uncomfortable read for contemporary scholars, because the roles he took on during the turbulent early reservation system locate him as someone who strongly supported the colonizer. He worked for, contributed to, and enforced the programs of colonization, particularly in regards to the suppression of Lakota traditional governance practices and ceremony. Today Sword's contribution to Walker's work is one of the primary sources for understanding Lakota belief and practice. His claims about being a medicine man, which did not emerge until later in his life and remain unsubstantiated, should raise questions. However, this information is obscured, as are the challenges raised by Deloria about the veracity of his contributions. The Sword case study raises questions about the contemporary hesitancy to critically examine Native sources or accept the wide range of Native responses to the colonial project, particularly when the response might entail alliances made with the oppressor. Like the Black Elk case, Sword becomes either a traitor or *the* authority on Lakota belief and culture.

Historian of religions Davíd Carrasco argues that "[y]ou must be in two places at once to have insight!"[95] This is very similar to the argument presented by the MMA who strongly advocated an approach that embraced multiple positionalities in order to come to a better understanding. The development of this capacity is critical to disrupting the dichotomies produced by the "two-worlds" trope.

Notes

1. John Doble and Andrew L. Yarrow, *Walking a Mile: A First Step Toward Mutual Understanding, A Qualitative Study Exploring How Indians and Non-Indians*

Think About Each Other (New York: Public Agenda, 2007), accessed August 29, 2010, <http://www.publicagenda.org/reports/walking-mile-first-step-toward-mutual-understanding>, 19.

2. Ibid., 27.

3. Numerous scholars have offered analyses of *Black Elk Speaks* and its production. See for example: Black Elk, *The Sacred Pipe: Black Elk's Account of the Oglala Sioux,* ed., Joseph Epes Brown (Norman: University of Oklahoma Press, 1953); Clyde Holler, *Black Elk's Religion: The Sun Dance and Lakota Catholicism* (Syracuse, NY: Syracuse University Press, 1995); John G. Neihardt, *The Sixth Grandfather: Black Elk's Teachings Give to John G. Neihardt,* ed., Raymond DeMallie (Lincoln: University of Nebraska Press, 1984); Julian Rice, *Black Elk's Story: Distinguishing its Lakota Purpose* (Albuquerque: University of new Mexico Press, 1991); Michael F. Steltenkamp. *Black Elk: Holy Man of the Oglala* (Norman: University of Oklahoma Press, 1993).

4. Charles H. Long, *Significations: Signs, Symbols, and Images in the Interpretation of Religion* (Philadelphia: Fortress Press, 1986), 141.

5. Ibid.

6. Avery Gordon, *Ghostly Matters: Haunting and the Sociological Imagination (*Minneapolis, MN: University of Minnesota Press, *1997,* 2000), 3–4.

7. Robert Warrior, *Tribal Secrets: Recovering American Indian Intellectual Traditions* (Minneapolis: University of Minnesota Press, 1995).

8. See *Medicine Men and Pastors Meeting, 13 February 1973* (transcripts archived at Marquette University), 2.

9. For a detailed description of the meeting see Paul Chaat Smith and Robert Allen Warrior, *Like a Hurricane: The Indian Movement from Alcatraz to Wounded Knee* (New York: The New Press, 1996), 207.

10. George Eagle Elk, "Transcripts from the Medicine Men and Pastor's Meeting," 13 Feb. 1973, T1, 5, Marquette University Archives, Milwaukee, WI.

11. William Stolzman, "Transcripts," 13 Feb. 1973, T1, 1.

12. Seconding is a rhetorical strategy that affirms the narrator's comments.

13. Emphasis added, Arthur Running Horse, Ben Black Bear, Jr., translator, "Transcripts," 13 Feb. 1973, T1, P2.

14. Warrior, *Tribal Secrets*, 39.

15. Chaat Smith and Warrior, *Like a Hurricane*, 202.

16. Joann Bromberg, "Social Aspects of Story Exchange," *Conversational Narrative,* (Workshop: The Ohio State University, 10/29/2007–11/2/2007), Handout.

17. N. Scott Momaday, "The Man Made of Words." *Native American Literature*, ed. Lawana Trout (Lincolnwood, IL: NTC Publishing Group, 1999), 636.

18. The only text written as a result of the dialogue is William Stolzman, *The Pipe and Christ: A Christian-Sioux Dialogue* (Chamberlain, SD: Tipi Press, *1986*, 2002).

19. Grant's post-Civil War peace policy differed from previous policies of direct colonialism in that the idea was to convince Native of their dependency on the U.S. government. The paternalistic approach was considered a shift in dealing with the Indian problem. The ban on Catholic presence on the reservation reflected

a bias that favored protestant reform. For more on this aspect of the peace policy see, Harvey Markowitz, "The Catholic Mission and the Sioux: A Crisis in the Early Paradigm," *Sioux Indian Religion*, eds. Raymond DeMallie and Douglas Parks. (Norman, OK: University of Oklahoma Press, 1987), 113–137.

20. Marquette University, "St. Francis Mission Records: Catholic Lakota Dakota Indians South Dakota, Scope and Content," 1.

21. Markowitz, "The Catholic Mission and the Sioux," 121.

22. Ibid.

23. Ibid., 122.

24. Robert Hilbert, S.J., "Contemporary Catholic Mission Work Among the Sioux," *Sioux Indian Religion*, eds. Raymond DeMallie and Douglas Parks (Norman, OK: University of Oklahoma Press, 1987), 142.

25. Ibid., 143.

26. Jeffrey Ostler, *The Plains Sioux and U.S. Colonialism from Lewis and Clark to Wounded Knee* (Cambridge, UK: Cambridge University Press, 2004), 174.

27. An account of this event also appears as told by Mary Gertrude Crow Dog. See, Leonard Crow Dog and Richard Erdoes, *Crow Dog: Four Generations of Sioux Medicine Men* (New York: HarperCollins Publishers, 1995), 68.

28. Ibid.

29. Henry Crow Dog, "Old Man Crow Dog, Native American Church," "Transcripts," 24 February, Unnumbered tape, 3.

30. This incident occurred in 1929, see Unknown, "Transcripts," 20 October 1973, T3, 10.

31. Ibid.

32. Stolzman, "Transcripts," 30 April 1974, T8, 1.

33. Charles Kills Enemy, "Transcripts," 20 March 1973, T2, 13.

34. This is similar to the author's findings regarding participants of Aztec dance, who focused on the agentive aspect of cultural syncretism under colonialism rather than the victimization. See, Sandra Garner, "Aztec Dance, Transnational Movements: Conquest of a Different Sort," *Journal of American Folklore*, Vol. 122, No. 486, (October 2009), 414–437.

35. Ben Black Bear, Sr., "Transcripts," 20 March 1973, T2, 9.

36. There is a long history of this sort of Native social commentary. See for example, William Apes. *On Our Own Ground: The Complete Writing of William Apess, a Pequot*, ed., Barry O'Connell (Amherst, MA: The University of Massachusetts Press, 1992); Charles Alexander Eastman (Ohiyesa), *From the Deep Woods to Civilization*, Dover Edition,(Mineola, NY: Dover Publications, Inc., 2003).

37. Lame Deer, "Transcripts," 29 January 1974, T 5, 8.

38. Ibid.

39. Frank Picket Pin, "Transcripts," 29 January 1974, T5, 11.

40. James R. Walker, *Lakota Belief and Ritual*, eds. Raymond J. DeMallie and Elaine A. Jahner (Lincoln: University of Nebraska Press, 1980), xv.

41. James R. Walker, *The Sun Dance and Other Ceremonies of the Oglala Division of the Teton Dakota* (New York: Trustee of the American Museum of Natural History, *1917*, 1979).

42. James R. Walker, *Lakota Belief and Ritual, Lakota Belief and Ritual*, eds. Raymond J. DeMallie and Elaine Jahner (Lincoln: University of Nebraska Press, 1980), xiii.

43. Walker, *The Sun Dance*, 58.

44. Walker, *The Sun Dance*, 59.

45. In an email message to the author on June 24, 2010, DeMallie wrote that the main reason for the delay was technical. He noted that he has freed up time in the spring of 2011 in order to return to and complete the project on the Sword texts.

46. Elaine A. Jahner, "Transitional Narratives and Cultural Continuity" *boundary 2*, Vol. 19, No. 3 (autumn, 1992), 152.

47. Martínez, *Dakota Philosopher*, 4.

48. Jahner, "Transitional Narratives," 149.

49. Ostler, *The Plains Sioux*, 230–231.

50. Edgar Beecher Bronson, *Reminiscences of a Ranchman*, (Lincoln, NE: University of Nebraska Press, 1962), 361.

51. Jahner makes this argument in regards to similar vignettes offered by McGillycuddy's second wife, Julia. I would however, argue that in spite of the troubling language of non-Native accounts from the era, there are enough of them to suggest their reliability. Jahner, "Transitional Narratives," 149 n3.

52. Eli S. Ricker, *Voices of the American West, Vol. 1: The Indian Interviews of Eli S. Ricker, 1903–1919* (Lincoln, NE: University of Nebraska Press, 2005), 330.

53. Walker, *Lakota Belief and Ritual*, 74.

54. Ricker, *Voices of the American West, Vol. 1*, 45.

55. Jahner, "Transitional Narratives," 154.

56. Ibid.

57. Ibid.

58. Robert Utley, *The Last Days of the Sioux Nation* (New Haven, CT: Yale University Press, 1963), 28.

59. There are numerous accounts of this decision. See for example: Julia B. McGillycuddy, *McGillycuddy Agent: A Biography of Dr. Valentine T. McGillycuddy* (Stanford, CA: Stanford University Press, 1941), 113; Agonito, "Young Man Afraid of his Horses," 121; and Bronson, *Reminiscences*, 204.

60. The barbecue represents a traditional feed and because this effort was aborted McGillycuddy issued more beef and told Sword "to assemble his party in a more secluded spot." McGillycuddy, *McGillycuddy*, 113.

61. Agonito, "Young Man Afraid of his Horses," 121.

62. Bronson, *Reminiscences*, 205.

63. Ibid., 212.

64. Ibid., 215.

65. Bronson, *Reminiscences*, 229.

66. Ibid., 230–232.

67. Agonito credits Young Man Afraid of his Horses and Sword with this idea. See Agonito, "Young Man Afraid of his Horses," 122.

68. Ostler, *The Plains Sioux*, 177.

69. Walker's first interview with Sword took place on September 5, 1896, and Bill Means was the interpreter. Walker, *Lakota Belief and Ritual*, 74–80.

70. Ibid., 9.

71. Ibid., 10.

72. Ibid.

73. Walker, *Lakota Belief and Ritual*, 65.

74. Harvey Markowitz, "Sword, George, (c. 1847–1910): Oglala Lakota scholar and leader," *Encyclopedia of North American Indians*, ed. Frederick Hoxie (New York: Houghton Mifflin Company, 1996), 617–618.

75. Sword's claims that he was a medicine man are accepted as fact and they are circulated widely. See for example, James Walker, *Lakota Myth*, ed. Elaine Jahner (Lincoln, NE: University of Nebraska Press, 1983), 43, and Lindsay Jones, "White Myths About American Indian Mythology: Reflections on the Lakota Story of "When the People Laughed at *Hanwi*, the Moon," *Area Studies Tsukuba*, Vol. 17, (1999), 131.

76. In Sword's other activities as a key informant he does not make this claim, but he does repeat his claims regarding his activities as a warrior and magistrate. See for example his interview with Ricker, *Voices of the American West, Vol. 1*, 326–330.

77. For example we read that Little Wound's daughter was the only woman dancer in the Sun Dance held in 1881 and we read about No-Flesh's role as a medicine man at a Sun Dance and how he challenged McGillycuddy's ban on the Sun Dance.

78. Jahner, "Transitional Narratives," 158.

79. Walker, *Lakota Belief and Ritual*, 67.

80. Ibid., 68.

81. Walker, *The Sun Dance*, 55.

82. Ibid., 56.

83. Walker, *Lakota Belief and Ritual*, xx.

84. Walker, *Lakota Belief and Ritual*, xxxii.

85. Ricker, *Voices of the American West, Vol. 1*, 328.

86. Walker, *The Sun Dance*, 159.

87. Ella Deloria, "The Sun Dance of the Oglala Sioux," *The Journal of American Folklore*, Vol. 42, No. 166 (Oct.–Dec., 1929), 388.

88. Jones, "White Myths," 129.

89. Gardner, "Speaking of Ella Deloria," 464.

90. Maria Cotera, *Native Speakers: Ella Deloria, Zora Neale Hurston, Jovita Gonzalez, and the Poetics of Culture* (Austin, TX: University of Texas Press, 2010), 222.

91. Jones, "White Myths," 115.

92. See for example Jones's treatment regarding William Powers work, Jones, "White Myths," 115.

93. Walker, *Lakota Belief and Ritual*, 74.

94. Doble and Yarrow. *Walking a Mile*, 27.

95. Davíd Carrasco, "Proem" in *Significations: Signs, Symbols, and Images in the Interpretation of Religion* (Philadelphia: Fortress Press, 1986), xviii.

Afterword

How Many Worlds?

Place, Power, and Incommensurability

Coll Thrush

Nearly forty years ago, the San Juan Pueblo anthropologist and activist Alfonso Ortiz challenged anthropologists, historians, and others who write about Indigenous issues to take territory seriously. "Historians need to develop a sensitivity to certain tribal traditions that have a bearing on a people's past, present, and aspirations for the future, to wit, on their history, which have no meaning apart from where they occur."[1] Although a number of scholars have risen to Ortiz's challenge, the decline of ethnogeography among anthropologists in favor of other modes of research and writing has largely left the question of place unaddressed. Meanwhile, many historians working on Indigenous peoples and colonialism have tended not to emphasize lived experiences of place, the fine-grained specifics of Indigenous territoriality, or the material processes of local landscape transformation. Regardless of discipline, and especially since the cultural and linguistic turn, scholarly work tends to remain focused primarily on discursive practices and individual and collective identities rather than on the embodied experiences and territorial engagements that are also central to colonialism.[2] Ironically, in all this talk of worlds, we have a tendency to forget the Earth and the specific ways in which human people inhabit it. The great exception to this trend has, not surprisingly, come from Indigenous intellectuals, community-based scholars, and their allies who are closely involved in advocacy and who assert the importance of territory as a strategy for survival and social justice.[3]

In this essay, I want to respond to Ortiz's call, setting aside the usual subjects of the two-world mode—identity and discourse—which have so often been focused on "figuring out the Indian"; even when they do not apply explicit authenticity tests, such studies often rely on binaries of "Indigenous" versus "modern" even as they try to subvert them. This essay, then, is more interested in figuring out *colonialism* and tries to do so by focusing not on people but on places. It uses place-stories of particular locations within the larger Coast Salish world—the homelands of diverse but related peoples in parts of Washington State and British Columbia—to complicate the two-worlds discussion through the specifics of particular landscapes. Each site is also a place in which my own personal history is embedded, both as an American of settler ancestry and as a scholar of Indigenous history, and taken together, their stories are opportunities to think about the ways in which "Indigenous" and "settler" worlds (including the places and practices of academic cultural production) are deeply and profoundly entangled by geography, ecology, the built environment, and vernacular, day-to-day life. Perhaps most importantly, grounding Indigenous and settler histories in place does not lead to clean, positivist assessments of colonialism and "what really happened." Rather, the place-stories below reveal the paradoxical and, pun intended, *unsettling* connections between power and territory, in which there is simultaneously one world, two worlds, and more worlds.

One World: Kitsilano Point

The cedar figure, arms raised in greeting and nearly twenty feet tall, welcomes visitors to the territory. Conical spruce root hat on his head and feathers in his hair, loons on his chest and a fish design on his cedar bark kilt, he is the community's ambassador. Around him lies a vernacular landscape common to the uninhabited corners of any reservation or reserve on the Northwest Coast: a potholed gravel road, long-defunct cars covered in moss and graffiti, evidence of wandering dogs. A glacial erratic, a huge boulder carried by the ice, stands tucked into the wild roses and hardhack, which are in turn being overwhelmed by invasive Scotch broom, Himalayan blackberries, and tansy ragwort. Small flocks of chickadees and bushtits flit through alders and cottonwoods and the last remaining stand of Douglas fir. Down at the shore, crows drop mussels on the rocks at low tide. In the distance, across the inlet, two peaks—ancestral Sisters turned to stone by the Transformers—watch over this place where the people have lived since time immemorial. This is Senákw (a name that means something like "to direct the head there") in the traditional territory of the Sḵwx̱wú7mesh Úxwumixw or Squamish Nation; it is also known as Squamish Reserve No. 6.[4]

The Burrard Street Bridge connects two dense urban neighborhoods. From it come the rushing sounds of car traffic, the metallic pings of bells from the bike lanes, and the too-loud conversations of knots of joggers. Gusts of wind and rain buffet tourists and city workers on their way into or out of downtown, and a billboard blares of cheap flights to San Francisco and Beijing, smart phones and unlimited talk time, the newest Mercedes model, and a women's television network. At the south end of the bridge there is a marina filled with boats, both fishing and pleasure, and a public market where Andean panpipes, piles of heirloom tomatoes, and endless tourist trinkets attract local foodies, families on day trips from the suburbs, and cruise ship passengers. Gulls and sparrows wait at empty tables at the edges of the Sandbar Restaurant's patio. Under the bridge: a kayak rental shop, a Coast Guard office, and dragon boats stored for the summer racing season. Nearby, in a park named for a former Governor General, the Space Centre looks like a landed UFO and huge white tents house the annual Shakespeare festival. To the west, cargo ships swing with the tides in the broad mouth of English Bay. At the north end of the bridge, a skyline of blue-glass high-rises towers above nightclubs, yoga studios, sushi bars, and coffee shops; at night, the constellations of ski areas hang in the darkened mountains behind the city. This is False Creek, Vancouver, Canada.

They are two profoundly different places, Senákw and False Creek, but here is the interesting part: they happen to be in the same location. The calls of birds in the cottonwoods cut through the noise of bridge traffic; the ruined cars are parked behind a condo building. The welcoming figure stands next to the Cultural Harmony Grove Park, where poorly maintained trees—oak, gingko, catalpa, palm, cedar, monkey puzzle—commemorate those who have contributed to the city's diversity: neighborhood houses, knitting clubs, Buddhist Compassion Relief, Vancouver Native Health Society, and individuals with Chinese, Punjabi, Anglo-Celtic, Latino, Jewish, and Muslim names. There is a totem pole just by the Space Centre, and the public market is built on top of an ancient sandbar where the people of Senákw built a maze of vine maple stakes to capture smelt and flounders. The lights of the ski areas are strung along the ridges and bowls near the Sisters, and in between the cooking shows and cheap fares, the billboard advertises a First Nations museum and cultural center in the resort town of Whistler and, occasionally, makes pronouncements on colonialism, sometimes in Indigenous languages: "Under the bridge we remember: the great cedar lodge, the sweet smell of our apple orchard and swish swish of a sea thick with smelt," "Live for aboriginal girls' and women's safety," "RIOT 1492," and "k^{w}em k^{w}em te sq^{w}elewen! 7ey' ey' met Vancouver (Think about it, beautiful Vancouver)."[5] Senákw *and* False Creek, Sḵwx̱wú7mesh homeland *and* City of Vancouver, Squamish Reserve No. 6 *and* Georges Vanier Park, Indigenous territory *and* urban North America. This is also Kitsilano Point, named after Xatsala'nexw, an ancestral Sḵwx̱wú7mesh name carried in the late nineteenth and early twentieth centuries by a leader who had lived there as a child.

Which is to say: there is only one world.

Figure 11. Kitsilano Point.

According to the teleology of empire, a place like Kitsilano Point should not exist. Indeed, around the world, Indigenous peoples and cities occupy opposite ends of a narrative: one represents the past, while the other represents the future. The notion that Indigenous peoples cannot survive—or even be present in—urban places is part of a larger binary that estranges Indigeneity from modernity and helps to undergird the kinds of "two worlds" discourses with which the authors in this volume are concerned.[6] Kits Point, with its hybrid landscape of gravel roads and dragon boats, posh skyline and ancestral mountains, historical sandbar and present-day Sandbar, disrupts these discourses through the interleaving of histories that are supposed to remain distinct, existing as a palimpsest that challenges narratives of conquest. It is also an archive of those narratives, its very physicality an artifact of historical processes of colonialism that took place in a single, deeply contested world. In fact, its history exposes the fatal flaw in the very language of "hybridity" which, in its framing of a blending of two separate things, gives the impression that the urban and Indigenous histories of Kitsilano Point—its two alleged worlds—were ever, in any meaningful way, separate.

As Europeans, Canadians, and others began settling around the shores of what became Vancouver in the 1860s, they did so among the S<u>k</u>w<u>x</u>wú7mesh and other Indigenous peoples. At Senakw, which had been an important seasonal encampment for fishing, S<u>k</u>w<u>x</u>wú7mesh families began to build permanent, year-round homes, attracted by employment in local sawmills or jobs carrying freight from settlement to settlement in their huge dugout canoes, along with the traditional attractions of sandbar, smelt, and flounder. In 1868, the residents of Senákw, more than forty in total and led by Chip-kay-um, formally requested the establishment of a reserve there, and by the 1870s their allotment covered eighty acres at the mouth of False Creek. The families cleared some of the land, set up gardens, raised livestock, planted a cherry orchard, and built a lélem—a cedar "big house" for community gatherings and ceremonies, inspiring one missionary who regularly preached at Senákw to describe the place as a "settlement of consequence" in his memoirs. Other reserves, meanwhile, were established near the mill towns that would become Vancouver and its adjacent suburbs.[7]

But the 1870s also saw the creation of new policies that would have profound consequences for the community of Senákw. In addition to the Indian Act, which set out a plan for "civilizing" Indigenous people, the federal and provincial governments also developed in the 1870s an agreement that any reserve lands "relinquished" by Indigenous people would become provincial property. "To the extent Indians could be persuaded to unsettle reserves," historian Jean Barman has written, "it was British Columbia that benefited." Vancouver would benefit as well. As the city grew, Senákw went from being a source of labor at the edges of colonial settlement to an eyesore in the middle of town, as prim new neighborhoods grew up along the now-fashionable bathing beach facing Senákw from the north shore of False Creek. Meanwhile commercial interests began to develop the south shore for industry and saw the reserve as a key resource; in 1902, for example, one-eighth of the reserve was expropriated by the Canadian Pacific Railroad for a trestle, and soon after, city leaders hatched plans to turn Senákw into a public park for exhibitions and summer festivals. Whether an eyesore to beachgoers or a missed economic opportunity, an Indigenous community in early twentieth-century Vancouver was a problem. This was true of urban reserves in general, according to many civic and national leaders; in 1911, Prime Minister Wilfrid Laurier told Parliament that "where a reserve is in the vicinity of a growing town . . . it becomes a source of nuisance and an impediment to progress." By the time he made that pronouncement, a concerted campaign was well under way to eradicate Senákw. Despite the community's refusal to sell off the reserve, mounting pressure, including threats of police violence, led the residents to sell up in 1913, receiving around one-fifth of the money they had been promised and not receiving the new reserve they had reason to expect. The sale provoked widespread excitement in the city, and the families of Senákw had barely left on a barge when their homes were burned to the ground. Indigenous history on False Creek appeared to have ended.

The experience of Senákw was not unlike that of other Indigenous communities who found themselves in the urbanizing landscapes of the Northwest Coast in the early twentieth century. In the provincial capital of Victoria on Vancouver Island, for example, 1911 saw the liquidation of the Songhees Reserve on the city's Inner Harbour, opposite the site of the current Empress Hotel. While the Songhees did receive a new reserve, the broader narratives of "eyesores" and "impediments," as well as the timeline, mirrored that of Senákw almost exactly.[8] Such events were not limited to Canada; south of the border in Seattle, the 1910s were also a devastating decade for the Indigenous Duwamish people, who still eked out livings in small clusters of shanties and houseboats amid the urban landscape. The straightening of one river and the disappearance of another thanks to the building of a ship canal, as well as new sanitation laws and the privatization of tidelands, meant that Duwamish people either stopped pursuing traditional subsistence practices, left the city for area reservations, or—in at least a few cases—starved to death.[9] Despite the different legal contexts of Canada and the United States and distinct histories of the S<u>k</u>wx<u>x</u>wú7mesh, Songhees, and Duwamish, the stories of urban dispossession in British Columbia and Washington bear striking resemblances to each other.

But as was the case with the Songhees and the Duwamish, the expulsion of the residents of Senákw did not mean that S<u>k</u>wx<u>x</u>wú7mesh memory of—or claims on—the place ended. Two decades after the expulsion, August Jack Khatsalano (after whom Kitsilano Point was named) told historian Major Matthews in great detail about life on the reserve, and similar stories were told among the S<u>k</u>wx<u>x</u>wú7mesh more generally—for example, of the hops that still grew on the site until they were buried under the footings of the new Burrard Bridge.[10] Meanwhile, the specifics of title to the reserve would be disputed for decades to come with various public and private entities laying and abandoning claims to the site, even as squatters occasionally moved in and were run off. Just after the end of World War II, the former reserve was split in half, with the western section being set aside for the creation of Vanier Park and the eastern half opened to commercial and housing development. By that time, the only visible remnant of Senákw was a neglected, dying cherry orchard, and perhaps some lenses of charcoal in the soil where houses had once stood. But in the 1970s and 1980s, the S<u>k</u>wx<u>x</u>wú7mesh (as the Squamish Nation) began a long, slow, and somewhat spectacular return to the site. They initiated a series of lawsuits over the disposition of the reserve, a legal action that would be one of the most protracted in Canadian history. Finally, in 2000, the S<u>k</u>wx<u>x</u>wú7mesh reached a $9.25 million settlement, and in 2002 resumed jurisdiction over the acreage taken for the railway trestle in 1902, now in the shadows of the Burrard Bridge. In addition to the billboard that announces their legal return to the land and the persistence of the memory of Senákw, the S<u>k</u>wx<u>x</u>wú7mesh Úxwumixw has signed a memorandum of understanding with the City of Vancouver over development of the site, which will almost certainly include high-rise towers in keeping with those that already line the shores of False Creek.[11]

The story of Senákw, then, illustrates exactly how deeply entangled urban and Indigenous histories are in this place, in railroad trestles and big houses, bathing beaches and flounder fisheries, cherry orchards and courtrooms. In fact, they are not separate histories at all—they are the same story, embedded in the same place. And yet, as observers, we are often entangled in our own ways in the received narratives of colonialism. Even historian Jean Barman, who has chronicled the story of Senákw and worked closely with local Indigenous families and communities to make visible Vancouver's Indigenous history, falls into the linguistic and teleological trap. Describing the expulsion of 1913, she writes, "the two worlds could not have been further apart."[12] But this is exactly the point of Kits Point: there were never two worlds here. There was only one place. To be sure, it was one that was profoundly contested and engaged by people with widely divergent understandings of land, law, and belonging, no matter how often we might be tempted to talk about "two worlds." By moving away from questions of identity, which so dominate the "two worlds" trope, and turning instead to the material processes by which places are transformed, we have the opportunity to bring both conquest and survival into sharper focus. Where we, like the civic boosters and Indian agents of the past, are tempted to see two discreet worlds—in this case, the Indigenous and the urban—by bringing our attention to place, we are confronted instead, with a single, conflicted, and surprising world.

Two Worlds: The Museum of Anthropology

Vancouver's westernmost promontory juts out into the Strait of Georgia between English Bay and the delta of the great Fraser River. The views from Ulqsun (simply meaning "point" in the local Indigenous language) are spectacular. From the sand below the forested bluffs at Wreck Beach, Canada's largest clothing-optional hangout, and from the offices of the University of British Columbia's Department of History on the twelfth floor of Buchanan Tower, one can see far into Howe Sound and the Tantalus Mountains to the north, across the strait to Vancouver Island in the west, and to the south, the San Juan Islands in Washington State. Whether basking in the afternoon sun of our glorious summers or walloped by winter storms, Point Grey is a quintessentially Northwest Coast place.

It is also a site of transformation and conflict. Its oldest stories, told by the Sḵwx̱wú7mesh Úxwumixw and their southern neighbors the Musqueam (on whose unceded land my university sits), are stories of beings made into landscape. Before their encounters with the Transformer, several large boulders around the long curve of the point's shoreline began their lives in other forms: a widow, someone bending down to drink water, a barking dog, a crying woman. Yet another was a man who dared to threaten the Transformer, and in fact, Point Grey has been influenced by many conflicts. An ancient battle once took place here between the winds, and later a small stockade fort guarded the boundary between the Musqueam and the Sḵwx̱wú7mesh. The threat of violence also echoes throughout the short time since the arrival of the xwenitem ("hungry people") in the territory.

In 1792, it was named Point Grey by British explorer George Vancouver after one of his naval colleagues, and in World War II the point was outfitted with bunkers, magazines, and artillery installed to protect Vancouver, Canada's main Pacific port, from enemy ships and airplanes. Along with all the transformations inherent in the place—widows turned to stone and forests replaced by lecture halls—there is also a history of violence, explicit and implicit, here.[13]

But for most of the world, the most important feature of Point Grey is not the nude beach or the ancient boulder-beings (and it certainly isn't the History Department). Rather, it is the famed Museum of Anthropology, one of the premier institutions of its kind in Canada or even in North America. Originally displayed in the basement of the library, the university's ethnographic collections received widespread attention and acclaim in 1976 with the opening of a new building built literally among the old artillery bunkers. With its seemingly impossible combination of massive bulk and airy openness, Arthur Erickson's award-winning design was created specifically for the collections. The Great Hall is the most obvious example of this: huge blocks of brutalist concrete seem to telescope outward into the weather, while vast expanses of glass render almost invisible the boundary between inside and out. Beyond the glass, a reproduction Haida village stands on the shore of a man-made lake that serves as a backdrop for the most famous treasures of the Great Hall: totem poles from the Tsimshian, Haida, Kwakwa̲ka̲'wakw, and other nations of the British Columbia coast. Along with bentwood boxes, feast dishes, and other objects, the totem poles create a powerful space that is one of Vancouver's top attractions.[14]

Since its opening, the Museum of Anthropology (now known primarily as MOA) has had as a major agenda the elevation of Indigenous material culture to the status of fine art, an agenda that has met with overwhelming success. When anthropologist James Clifford visited the museum in the 1980s, he noted that even though the objects were at times overwhelmed by the architecture that housed them, the "intimate monumentality" of the collections and their presentation was in stark contrast to the practices of other museums. Whether in the darkened smaller galleries with "boutique-style" lighting or in the Great Hall, where visitors could see many objects from all directions under natural light, the Raven masks and mortuary figures of MOA's collection were presented with a degree of aesthetic reverence that was uncommon at the time. With little interpretive context beyond terse labels and with an emphasis on individual artists such as Haida carver Bill Reid, the visitor experience was more akin to that of a high-end art gallery than an ethnographic museum. Clifford proclaimed the fine art approach

Figure 12. University of British Columbia, Museum of Anthropology.

"one of the most effective ways to communicate cross-culturally a sense of quality, meaning, and importance . . . [that] leaves open a possible aesthetic appreciation of the objects on display . . . and evokes both local and global meanings for the interpretive categories (or translation devices) or art, culture, politics, and history."[15]

In the same essay in which he lauded the Museum of Anthropology's curatorial bent, however, Clifford noted the very different approaches taken by Indigenous-run museums in British Columbia. The U'mista Cultural Centre in the 'Na̲mgis Kwakwa̲ka̲'wakw community of Alert Bay and other institutions did not take the decontextualized and depoliticized fine art approach, Clifford observed; rather, they subverted or simply ignored the colonial distinction between "art" and "material culture" while openly challenging unitary, linear constructions of history and the idea of Indigenous as part of Canada's "cultural patrimony." Tribal museums, he wrote, were "oppositional."[16] Such opposition arose directly out of the experiences of colonized peoples in British Columbia, where a lack of recognition for Indigenous title, the cultural genocide of residential schools, and profound economic marginalization meant that in the late twentieth century, the quality of life for Indigenous people and communities in the province contrasted starkly with that of other British Columbians. Of course Indigenous institutions were "oppositional."

While courts, schools, and the media landscape were key venues for the assertion of Indigenous sovereignty, museums like MOA also became a focus of activism. Over the two decades since Clifford wrote about the museum's fine art approach, First Nations communities began to claim authority over their own representation at the Point Grey institution. In 2010, just in time for the Winter Olympics, MOA unveiled its renovated galleries as part of a new way of doing things, titled "A Partnership of Peoples." Based on collaboration with Indigenous communities and nations, the new approach places material objects within deep historical, cultural, and political contexts. Special emphasis is placed on UBC's host nation: Musqueam welcome figures and houseposts outside the museum, Musqueam blankets as the first things encountered once inside, and a recording of the Musqueam language introducing guests to the galleries.

Beyond the acknowledgment of MOA's location on Musqueam land, and in addition to descriptions of the meanings of objects, their proper names in the respective languages, and the presentation of living community practices, the question of territory is now central to the museum's approach. In the case (literally: the museum case) of the Gitxsan Nation, for example, community curators have used MOA to identify both themselves and their territory, articulating "a thriving, active First Nations people who derive their strength from the 33,000 square kilometres of traditional territory in northwest British Columbia, Canada." Their neighbors to the east, the Wet'suwet'en Nation, meanwhile, "assert title, rights, and authority as the original stewards of 22,000 sq. kms of territory encompassing the headwaters of the Wit'zin'kwa (Bulkley-Morice Rivers) and the upper reaches of the Nechako watershed in northwestern British Columbia" in their part of the gallery. The labels there describe the unbroken, autonomous political structures that continue to govern their people, describing the Big Frog, Fireweed, and other clans and houses who own and manage the territory and its resources. A radical departure from MOA's initial practices of fine art curation, the new exhibits create a visitor experience in which it is impossible to avoid Indigenous territoriality and the contested nature of land claims in British Columbia.

In this sense, MOA is not unlike Kitsilano Point: it is an articulation of a single world in which Indigenous and settler peoples engage each other, whereas the old curatorial style was a prime example of the two-world model in which Indigenous objects were unmoored from their context, Indigenous territoriality was largely ignored as being outside the purview of fine art, and most living Indigenous people were rendered invisible. Now, Indigenous territories and the processes of colonialism are projected into the Museum itself: just as the Gitxsan portrait masks and Wet'suwet'en baskets are not only representations of territory but actually the territory itself—yellow cedar and birch bark harvested from traditional places—the claims of Indigenous communities have transformed what was once a locus of ethnographic collection into a space of political and cultural engagement in which the boundaries between places such as MOA and the Wit'zin'kwa begin to break down. There is only one world, whether it is called Ulqsun or Point Grey.

At the same time, however, there is also evidence of two distinct worlds at MOA, and it is a distinction that Indigenous communities have deliberately chosen to make. For the Musqueam and other local Coast Salish communities, for example, there is a critical practice of withholding that takes place in the galleries. While a new engraving on a boulder outside the museum acknowledges Musqueam territory and instructs the people to "REMEMBER YOUR TEACHINGS," and inside a memorial canoe for elder Maggie Point speaks to grief, kinship, and the cultural importance of Elvis Presley, there is also a very clear sense that there are things the community is not willing to share. In a set of cases that includes grave figures, game pieces made from beaver teeth, and spindle whorls, there is a blank space filled only by a white screen and a small label. The label reads:

> Coast Salish spirituality is intensely personal and private. Spiritual knowledge and rights are often passed along family lines. Community members have different feelings regarding public access to spiritual objects and their images.
>
> For some it is acceptable to exhibit their spirituality, while others remain strongly opposed to such displays. With respect to these differences, we have removed spiritual objects from view.
>
> It is important to acknowledge that the Coast Salish still practice their traditional spirituality in the privacy of their own communities.

The screen and label have replaced sacred masks that are only properly seen during ceremonies, yet for years had been openly displayed for all to see.

In the next room, meanwhile, scores of Kwakwa̱ka̱'wakw ceremonial objects—huge raven masks, noisemakers, button blankets, and more—surround an open space with a small stage protected by an alarmed railing.

Beyond the railing a small group of objects lie wrapped in grey fabric, hidden from visitors' view. Mikael Willie of the Dzawada̱'enux̱w Kwakwa̱ka̱'wakw First Nation explains this withholding on a nearby placard:

> In our Kwak'wala language there is a word—k'wik'waladła̱kw—which means "things that are hidden." Traditionally, our wolf headdresses, whistles, and other objects with 'nawalakw, or supernatural power, were put away when not being shown in ceremony.
>
> For some of our people, to have these things on display for the public is very disturbing. That's why we were invited here to the Museum to discuss this issue. Our elders had mixed feelings: some said that we should educate the people of the world by showing the masks; others said that we need to put them away properly and respectfully. I thought that one thing we might be able to do is wrap some of the masks on display. This is so that the public can understand that not everyone is meant to see these things.
>
> Gilakas'la (thank you)!

Sold to the museum and other collectors at a time when the potlatch was outlawed and the future of Kwakwa̱ka̱'wakw cultural traditions was uncertain, such objects are still understood as being owned by particular families. They are also understood as having their own correct places and times, which do not necessarily include a museum.

In both the Musqueam and Kwakwa̱ka̱'wakw examples, the decision to enact ceremonial protocols and cultural privacy at MOA—to explicitly state, *there are some things we will not let you see*—not only flies in the face of hundreds of years of Enlightenment-derived curatorial practice, in which all things are to be revealed and categorized; it also establishes two worlds. Not the two worlds that the liquidation of Senákw was supposed to create, based in colonial policies of dispossession, but rather two worlds in which Indigenous peoples, so long the target of the ethnographic gaze, assert one of the most powerful forms of autonomy: privacy. (This is not to argue that settler society is somehow inherently "public" while Indigenous societies are inherently "private." Indeed, Indigenous communities have their own public spaces: an elders' center at Musqueam, the 'Na̱mg̱is big house in Alert Bay, the Wet'suwet'en band council chambers.)

This assertion of privacy at MOA, however, cannot be disentangled from the political and legal landscapes of British Columbia and the Canadian nation. This is especially true for the Gitxsan and Wet'suwet'en, who, during the decades that MOA was transformed, were involved in a land claims case that also transformed Canadian policy toward Indigenous peoples. Initiated formally in 1984 after much discussion within the two communities, such a claim depended necessarily on the public exposure of traditional knowledge that had long been withheld from outsiders. As Gitxsan scholar and speaker Skanu'u (Ardythe Wilson) noted in 1992,

> there was great reluctance when we saw the history of the courts in our territories—we were always on the losing end. . . . We knew that in order for the courts to understand what it was we were talking about, it was necessary for us to show them our histories, our laws, our practices, our customs, our obligations, our responsibilities. And in order for that to happen, we had to open up our Houses and our families to people who had no understanding or respect for who we are.[17]

For the house chiefs, clan sub-chiefs, and other members of the community, the decision to sing the songs, don the headdresses, and speak the names in a courtroom entailed huge risk. Not only would such knowledge now be available for the scrutiny of outsiders, it did not guarantee success. And in fact, as Skanu'u went on to write, "I think what we dreaded most was exactly what McEachern did."[18] And what McEachern—Alan McEachern, Chief Justice of British Columbia and Chancellor of the University of British Columbia—did was not only to deny the land claims of the Gitxsan and Wet'suwet'en, but to denigrate the knowledge that had been brought forward. Quoting a seventeenth-century European philosopher to say that Indigenous life had been "nasty, brutish, and short," McEachern wrote that he could not accept Indigenous historical narratives such as the Gitxsan adaox as "reliable bases for detailed history," and that he was "able to make the required important findings about these people, sufficient for this case, without this evidence."[19]

It was the worst possible outcome for the Gitxsan and Wet'suwet'en: not only was their claim denied, their societies were openly mocked at the same time their private matters were aired in public. The level of despair and anger within the communities was difficult for outsiders to imagine, and out of these feelings came a renewed commitment to privacy. As Don Ryan, a Gitxsan spokesman under the leadership of the hereditary chiefs, put it in his response to the *Delgamuukw* decision, "This is the last time that the sacred boxes of our people will be opened for the white man to look at."[20]

While the decision would be overturned by the Supreme Court of Canada in 1996, establishing for the first time under Canadian law the notion that Indigenous forms of knowledge constituted legitimate legal evidence, the initial decision reverberated through Indigenous communities not just in British Columbia but throughout Canada and continues to resonate in the choices made by communities as they represent themselves in, for example, the galleries of the Museum of Anthropology.[21]

In a single and profoundly unequal world, then, it is often important for Indigenous peoples to articulate two worlds. Just the boosters and developers of Vancouver sought to create at places like Senákw, a single world in which Indigenous peoples were doomed to irrelevance and extinction, colonial knowledge-making also sought to create a single world in which all things and beings could be catalogued within a unitary taxonomy that ultimately relegated Indigenous and other "primitive" peoples to the past. To most observers, Indigenous resistance to these colonial one-worlds, whether in the form of remaining in territory or maintaining their cultural and political autonomy, was both an impediment to colonial progress and a betrayal of colonial benevolence. In the minds of many Indian agents and Prime Ministers alike, resistance was in fact not in the self-interest of Indigenous peoples. Integration into the one world of, say, Canada, whether through becoming "civilized" and "productive" members of "modern" society or through the willingness to become ethnographic subjects, was of course the ideal outcome. As Cherokee literary scholar Jace Weaver has written, "the concern with getting rid of 'old and isolating world views' and 'unbridgeable chasm[s]' has always been more of a concern for Amer-Europeans than for Natives, who do not view their own cultural responses as 'old and isolating' and who often express scant interest in bridging their worldview with that of the dominant culture."[22] For Indigenous peoples, inclusion in colonial societies has often meant marginalization, while separation has in fact often led to sovereignty—if not legal, then at least cultural.

Here, then, are two worlds, incommensurable not because Indigenous people are incapable of participating in colonial society, but because they shouldn't necessarily have to. Assertions of privacy at the Museum of Anthropology or in a British Columbia law court speak to what is ultimately a deep incommensurability between Indigenous and colonial epistemologies of, for example, the meaning of the territory. For one, place is expressed in collective notions of ownership, sacred obligation, ancestral lineage, and the agency of non-human beings and forces. For the other, place is articulated through notions of liquid property, capitalist modes of production, the idea of an inanimate world, and fantasies of an unpopulated and thus easily exploited wilderness. Such incommensurabilities will continue to be worked out within communities and in courtrooms and classrooms. Meanwhile, Indigenous strategies of resistance, whether in the form of wrapped k'wik'waladłakw in a university museum or the decision to reveal sacred knowledge to a judge, also highlight the incommensurability of the arguments I have been making here. At the same time that there is only one world, symbolized by the place-stories of Senákw, there are also two worlds, symbolized in the place-stories told at the Museum of Anthropology. Both are true. And, it turns out, both statements are insufficient in terms of understanding the full complexities of colonialism.

Many Worlds: Soos Creek

At the rural-suburban boundary about an hour south-southeast of Seattle, there is a third place that suggests, in all this discussion of one world versus two worlds, we may have miscounted. Soos Creek, its name derived from an Indigenous word meaning "face," has its headwaters in marshy forests and wooded ravines of the low foothills just east of my hometown of Auburn, Washington. This is the territory of the Skwupabsh, literally "the people of the rising and falling thing," a reference to the Green River into which Soos Creek empties. Just above the creek's mouth, a massive cedar longhouse with eight fires and some ten acres of cultivated gardens once stood at the center of a densely lived-in landscape. Up-creek to the north, small prairies managed through the use of fire provided important foods for the people. Just to the east, steep, unstable river bluffs were known as the place where evil, child-eating snail women were driven to their death by a bird-hero. The river, meanwhile, provided great wealth through its many runs of salmon and connected the people of Face to their relatives and allies in other towns along its banks, both to the east and the west.[23]

The longhouse at Face was destroyed, almost certainly by settlers, sometime in the late nineteenth century. Most of its inhabitants were forced away to a nearby plateau that is now the Muckleshoot Reservation. Only a handful managed to stay nearby, living in a series of small houses along the river. By the 1920s, the only visible remnant of Face was an old cedar in the woods with a great square scar on its side where a houseplank had once been removed. Meanwhile, across the river from the creek's mouth, a very different kind of house had stood for some time. In 1894, one of the first American families in the area, the Neelys, built a great Victorian homestead back a little from the riverbank, amid newly tilled fields, an orchard, and pasture for Holsteins. Listed on the National Register of Historic Places since 1973, Neely Mansion is one of the area's most important historic landmarks, remembered by many in my generation as the site of annual Halloween haunted houses and slowly being restored to a nostalgic flower-boxes-and-petticoats presentation that would be familiar to any heritage society in the United States or Canada. As such, it is a fairly typical example of pioneer iconography, symbolizing both the resettlement of the Green River Valley and the end of Indigenous inhabitance.

That place-story of endings is true, to some extent—the Skwupabsh history of the valley is largely unknown outside the modern Muckleshoot Tribe—but it is also incomplete. To begin with, the Neely family had close relationships with local Indigenous people. When David Neely and his family arrived in Washington Territory from Tennessee in 1853, they established a farm several miles downriver from Soos Creek. Like many early settlers, they traded with local Indigenous communities and hired Indigenous men and women as laborers, while their children learned the local Indigenous language. When David's son Aaron and his wife moved to Soos Creek, they were relocating among people they knew—a small group of Skwupabsh people and their relatives who, despite the destruction of Face and

Figure 13. Neely Mansion.

the establishment of the reservation, continued to live along the river near Neely's new home. Despite the symbolic work it has done as a pioneer heritage site, Neely Mansion, then, hardly marks the end of one world and the beginning of another.

The house's status as a symbol primarily of Euro-American resettlement rests on shaky ground in another respect, and it is here that the narrative of two worlds becomes complicated in a new way: for much of its life, "Neely Mansion" was not a Euro-American place at all, but an Asian immigrant and Asian-American one. Aaron Neely and his family moved into Auburn in 1908, only fourteen years after the house was built, and went from being pioneers to landlords. From 1912 to 1930—longer than the Neelys were in residence—the house was home to the family of Matasuke and Toku Fukuda and their ten children. The Fukuda home was just one of many Japanese truck farms in the area, producing corn, rhubarb, and milk for markets in Seattle and elsewhere, and often employing Skwupabsh and other Indigenous people. From 1930 to 1942, Shigeichi and Shimanoko Hori, and later Shigeichi's brother leased the property, adding strawberries and other crops to the farmstead's produce. With internment, the Hori, Fukudas, and other families disappeared from the region, but evidence of them remained when the Neelys briefly moved back in during the war: behind the house, there now stood a furoba, a Japanese-style bathhouse.

After World War II, few families of Japanese heritage returned to the Green River Valley, and the Neely house entered a new phase of its history. In 1943, Filipino farmer Pedro "Pete" Acosta and his wife June had begun leasing the property, moving into a second house on the land and turning the 1894 mansion into a boarding house for farm laborers, who in turn transformed its attic into a pigeon coop and source of food. The Acostas remained on the property through the postwar period; theirs was one of the farms on which my mother worked as seasonal stoop labor in the early 1960s, often alongside Indigenous families, some of them descendants specifically of the people of Face. The Acostas are who I remember selling strawberries in June, corn in August, and pumpkins in October during the 1970s, the same decade that the property was officially designated a historic site—and in particular, a site of white settler history.[24]

So what kind of a "world" is this? The simplistic narrative of the land where Soos Creek and the Green River come together describes one world—that of the people of Face—being overwritten by that of white settlers, symbolized by the clapboard and cattle of the Neelys. A more complex story blurs the boundaries between these two worlds, with Skwupabsh cabins and homesteads along the riverbank and postwar Indigenous families picking berries. It would be very easy to imagine Muckleshoot berry-pickers, working in the fields alongside poor white children and teenagers—including my mother and her brothers—as negotiating two worlds. However, if we think of worlds as the spaces of epistemology, cultural practice, and the like—and this is, I think, what we usually mean when we talk of "two worlds"—then two worlds are not enough for Soos Creek. Within the two-worlds framework, what do we "do" with the Fukudas and the Acostas? If historical scholarship is any indicator, then the answer is "not much." The implicit assumptions of the two-world model that has driven much of the literature on Indigenous history all too often erases the non-Indigenous, non-white lives that existed in places like the land around the mouth of Soos Creek, just as the name "Neely Mansion" masked not only Skwupabsh houses along the river but the furo and the Filipino pigeon-coop. There were other worlds, Nikkei and Filipino, at Soos Creek, in which Asian and Asian-American people negotiated their own identities much like Indigenous people did.

Even if we acknowledge that Japanese and Filipino immigration was ultimately a product of American colonialism—these were also newcomers, and in a sense, invaders[25]—not all settlers were the same. Indeed, there were parallel processes of white racial hegemony at work in the valley: the destruction of Soos, the Internment, the deeply entrenched customs of segregation faced by the Filipino community. Such policies were, like those of reservation allotment or residential schools, based on the perceived incommensurability of worlds. Just as policymakers and others believed Indigenous and American identities were ultimately incompatible, policies such as the Alien Land Laws were predicated on the notion that two worlds—say, Japanese and American—were mutually exclusive. Modern or Indian, Japanese or American, brown or white: parallel pairs of "worlds," each with their own assumed "between" in which individuals and communities might theoretically found themselves "caught."

And yet the grounded reality of Soos Creek, like the Kitsilano Reserve, the Museum of Anthropology, or any other place where Indigenous peoples and diverse newcomers have interacted, also attests to the singleness of the world. It shows how a place cannot easily be divided into separate worlds, and certainly cannot be divided into merely two. The bluff of the Snail Women, the Neely family's orchard trees, the furoba, and the attic pigeon-coop together challenge the "two worlds" notion by illustrating just how limited it is. Nearly half a century after the rise of the new social history, only a handful of scholars have begun to investigate encounters between Indigenous people and non-white settlers like those who came to Soos Creek. It is no wonder, then, that we still find ourselves caught in a two-world bind, when the reality was something far more complex. The two-world model simply has no space for the many rich stories that exist, for example, in British Columbia and Washington: shamans of Stó:lo and Chinese ancestry conducting doctoring sessions in the valley of the Fraser River, Suquamish elders with African ancestry teaching anthropologists on the shores of Puget Sound, "Indipino" activists of Indigenous-Filipino ancestry organizing protests in Seattle, or women from the Musqueam Reserve adjacent to Vancouver laboring alongside their Japanese co-workers in a Strait of Georgia salmon cannery. In the end, we need to acknowledge that the two-world model, simply put, is all too often a narrative artifact of white racial hegemony against which we measure Indigeneity while also erasing other communities' histories. Two worlds are not nearly enough.

The Paradox of Place

All of this is to say that Indigenous history (like so many other kinds of history, when done well and honestly) is full of paradoxes. There is only one world, except for the occasions when two worlds are necessary, and two worlds are insufficient. Each of these things is true, just as so many other seeming paradoxes are also true of Indigenous-settler relations. So much has been lost, and so much has been retained. Indigenous people have insisted on their own cultural, economic, and political autonomy, even as they have mobilized for equal inclusion in colonial society. The word "Indian" means nothing, and is one the most important words in North American history. Settlers have been able to carry on as though Indigenous people never existed, and yet settlers have been utterly transformed by the colonial experience. They are the things that make our and our students' heads hurt, and the dynamics with which colonial law and policy struggle, usually unsuccessfully. These are intimate incommensurabilities, the koans of colonialism, and most importantly, they are the complicated shoals that are navigated by Indigenous people.

By grounding these stories in place, however, we can inoculate ourselves against some of the more problematic elements of two-world thinking that continue to influence scholarship, bolster unhelpful notions of authenticity, and focus our gaze primarily on Indigenous people at the expense of attending to the practices and legacies of colonial systems in which we all, Indigenous and settler alike, are entangled. In my case, such places include Kits Point (five blocks from my apartment), the Museum of Anthropology (five minutes from my office), and Soos Creek (a touchstone of my own family history). How might looking at specific sites—not metaphorical sites such as "the Indian mind" or "narrative spaces" but rather actual locations with coordinates and chickadees and concrete—reframe this larger conversation about worlds? In addition to responding to Alfonso Ortiz's call for historians to take place seriously, attending to such questions might also be, to use Kiowa writer N. Scott Momaday's phrase, a "moral act of imagination" that will help all of us learn appropriate relationships to territory.[26]

None of us, Indigenous or settler, can escape the basic fact that we live inside this history. The best we can do is muddle through, with some clarity about our intentions and discernment regarding the ways in which the stories we create all too often replicate the narratives that facilitated conquest in the first place. This is necessarily an inexact process. On the afternoon I spent at Kits Point, collecting the texture of place for this essay, I found a tattered sheet of paper lying in the gravel under the high arches of the Burrard Bridge. On it was a text, perhaps connected to a student project at the nearby art college, that gets at the imperfection of the cultural work we do and the need, perhaps, to make our fumblings more visible:

> Aborted Executions.
>
> The presentation we had originally intended to show proved beyond us. Nearly every element that we had conceived went down in abject failure. Keeping with this theme, we would like to present to you a collection of our failed work. Images, that intended to express certain subject matter, but for one reason or another, did not.
>
> Kept from public consumption, failed works are rarely judged on their merit (or for that matter judged at all). By putting them on display, we feel our stillbirths have just as much to convey as their counterparts. And as there can be no light without darkness, there can be no triumph without utter catastrophe; these are inextricable aspects to our process at large.

Perhaps the parallel is a bit forced; then again, my settler body and this ephemeral, discarded document are also part of the archive that is this place that has carried so many names. As we continue to struggle with ways to speak about what has happened on this continent—a struggle inherent in these discourses of one world, two worlds, and many worlds—such an artifact, and place, is as good a teacher as any.

Notes

1. Alfonso Ortiz, "Some Concerns Central to the Writing of 'Indian' History," *The Indian Historian* (winter 1977), 20, quoted in Peter Nabokov, *A Forest of Time: American Indian Ways of Writing History* (Cambridge, UK: Cambridge University Press, 2002), 131–32.

2. North American examples of this sort of work include Keith H. Basso, *Wisdom Sits in Places: Landscape and Language among the Western Apache* (Albuquerque: University of New Mexico Press, 1996); Julie Cruikshank, *Do Glaciers Listen?: Local Knowledge, Colonial Encounters, and Social Imagination* (Vancouver: UBC Press, 2005); Thomas Thornton, *Being and Place among the Tlingit* (Seattle: University of Washington Press, 2007); and Kirstin C. Erickson, *Yaqui Homeland and Homeplace: The Everyday Production of Ethnic Identity* (Tucson: University of Arizona Press, 2008). Two examples from the territories discussed in this essay include my own *Native Seattle: Histories from the Crossing-Over Place* (Seattle: University of Washington Press, 2007) and Keith Thor Carlson, *The Power of Place, the Problem of Time: Aboriginal Identity and Historical Consciousness in the Cauldron of Colonialism* (Vancouver: UBC Press, 2010).

3. Examples from the American context include Winona LaDuke, *All Our Relations: Native Struggles for Land and Life* (Cambridge, MA: Sound End Press, 1999); *Ecocide of Native America: Environmental Destruction of Indigenous Lands and Peoples*, ed. Donald A. Grinde, Bruce E. Johansen, and Howard Zinn (Santa Fe: Clear Light Books, 1994); Donald L. Fixico, *The Invasion of Indian Country in the Twentieth Century: American Capitalism and Tribal Natural Resources* (Boulder: University Press of Colorado, 1998); and George E. Tinker, *American Indian Liberation: A Theology of Sovereignty* (Maryknoll, NY: Orbis Books, 2008).

4. More commonly known to outsiders as the Squamish Nation, the community has begun to more consistently use its Indigenous name (pronounced "skw-HWOO-mesh OO-hwoo-mee-hw") in its dealings with the public.

5. For these and other billboard texts, as well as related projects, see the Digital Natives website, <digitalnatives.othersights.ca>.

6. For two of the best discussions of the relationship between Indigeneity and modernity, see Paige Raibmon, *Authentic Indians: Episodes of Encounter from the Late-Nineteenth-Century Northwest Coast* (Durham, NC: Duke University Press, 2005) and Philip J. Deloria, *Indians in Unexpected Places* (Lawrence: University Press of Kansas, 2004).

7. Jean M. Barman, "Erasing Indigenous Indigeneity in Vancouver," *BC Studies* 155 (autumn 2007), 7–20.

8. For Indigenous history in Victoria, see Grant Keddie, *Songhees Pictorial: A History of the Songhees People as Seen by Outsiders, 1790–1912* (Victoria: Royal British Columbia Museum, 2004) and Penelope Edmonds, *Urbanizing Frontiers: Indigenous Peoples and Settlers in 19th-Century Pacific Rim Cities* (Vancouver: UBC Press, 2010).

9. Coll Thrush, "City of Changers: Indigenous People and the Transformation of Seattle's Watersheds," *Pacific Historical Review* 75:1 (February 2006), 89–117.

10. The Major Matthews collection at the Vancouver City Archives holds the bulk of Khatsalano's accounts of Vancouver's Indigenous history.

11. Barman, "Erasing Indigenous Indigeneity," 29–30. The full text of the Memorandum of Understanding can be found at <http://vancouver.ca/mediaroom/news/pdf/proclamation_Squamish_Mon.pdf>. For updates on development plans, see the Sḵwx̱wú7mesh Úxwumixw website at <www.squamish.net>.

12. Barman, "Erasing Indigenous Indigeneity," 17.

13. For transformation sites, see Wayne Suttles, "Names of Places and Peoples" in *Musqueam Reference Grammar* (Vancouver: UBC Press, 2004), 570. Sa7plek (Joe Capilano) of the Sḵwx̱wú7mesh Úxwumixw told the story of the West Wind to Mohawk writer and performer E. Pauline Johnson (Tekahionwake), who published her version of it in 1911 as part of *Legends of Vancouver* (Vancouver: Douglas & McIntyre, 1997).

14. For a history of the institution, see *The Museum of Anthropology at the University of British Columbia*, ed. Carol E. Mayer and Anthony Shelton (Vancouver: Douglas & McIntyre, 2010).

15. James Clifford, "Four Northwest Coast Museums: Travel Reflections," in *Routes: Travel and Translation in the Late Twentieth Century* (Cambridge, MA: Harvard University Press), 121.

16. Clifford, "Four Northwest Coast Museums: Travel Reflections."

17. Skanu'u (Ardythe Wilson), "Preface," in *Colonialism on Trial: Indigenous Land Rights and the Gitksan and Wet'suwet'en Sovereignty Case*, ed. Don Monet and Skanu'u (Ardythe Wilson) (Philadelphia: New Society Publishers, 1992), vii.

18. Ibid.

19. *Colonialism on Trial*, 188.

20. Ken MacQueen, "A landmark ruling shocks anthropologists," *Vancouver Sun*, 13 July 1991.

21. For the kind of material made visible to outsiders during the *Delgamuukw* case, see *Hang on to these Words: Johnny David's Delgamuukw Evidence*, ed. Antonia Mills (Toronto: University of Toronto Press, 2005) and Richard Daly, *Our Box was Full: An Ethnography for the Delgamuukw Plaintiffs* (Vancouver: UBC Press, 2004).

22. Jace Weaver, *That the People Might Live: Native American Literatures and Native American Community* (Oxford: Oxford University Press, 1997), 35.

23. The Indigenous history of the Green River has been documented in Coll Thrush, *The Skwupabsh and their River: A Tribal History of the Green River Watershed from Auburn Narrows to the Cascade Crest*, a report held and controlled by the Muckleshoot Indian Tribe, available only by tribal research agreement.

24. For an account of Neely Mansion that does not include its non-white histories (and which represents the dominant public narrative about the place), see Josephine Emmons Vine, *Auburn: A Look Down Main Street* (Auburn, WA: Auburn Centennial Commission and City of Auburn, 1989), 20. For the property's Japanese

and Filipino histories, see Gail Lee Dubrow with Donna Graves, *Sento at Sixth and Main: Preserving Landmarks of Japanese-American Heritage* (Seattle: Seattle Arts Commission, 2002), 24–41.

25. "Colliding Histories: Hawai'i Statehood at the Intersection of Asians 'Ineligible to Citizenship' and Hawaiians 'Unfit for Self-Government,'" in *Journal of Asian American Studies* Vol. 13, No. 3 (October 2010): 283–309.

26. N. Scott Momaday, "Native American Attitudes to the Environment," in *Seeing with a Native Eye: Essays on Native American Religion*, ed. W. Capps (New York: Harper & Row, 1974), 80.

Contributor Biographies

James Joseph Buss, Director of the Thomas E. Bellavance Honors Program and Associate Professor of History at Salisbury University, is the author of *Winning the West with Words: Language and Conquest in the Lower Great Lakes* (Norman: University of Oklahoma Press, 2011). He also has published in *Frontiers: A Journal of Woman's Studies* and is currently completing a manuscript that examines popular constructions of Native and settler histories and memory in nineteenth- and twentieth-century Indiana.

Cathleen D. Cahill, Associate Professor of History at the University of New Mexico, is the author of *Federal Fathers and Mothers: A Social History of the United States Indian Service, 1869–1932* (Chapel Hill: University of North Carolina, 2011). It won the Labriola Center American Indian National Book Award in 2011. She co-edited a special issue on Intermarriage in American Indian History for *Frontiers: A Journal of Woman's Studies* and has published articles addressing the intersections of gender, labor, and race. Her new research focuses on indigenous people's mobility and contributions to the creation of tourist markets throughout the American West.

Ian D. Chambers is an Assistant Professor in the Department of History at the University of Idaho and a faculty member of American Indian Studies, American Studies, and Women Studies programs. He is currently working on a manuscript for UGA Press and has article in *Imago Mundi*, *Native South*, and *History Compass*. He has been a Rockefeller fellow at Colonial Williamsburg, the recipient of a NEH summer fellowship, and is a Fellow of the Royal Geographical Society.

Joseph Cheatle is currently completing his dissertation in English literature at Miami University in Oxford, Ohio. His interests are in twentieth-century British and American literature, particularly on issues of identity. He first became interested in D'Arcy McNickle while working with Dr. Daniel Cobb transcribing McNickle's diaries.

Daniel M. Cobb is Associate Professor of American Studies at the University of North Carolina at Chapel Hill, where he has served as coordinator of American Indian Studies. An award-winning teacher and writer, his publications include *Native Activism in Cold War America* (2008), the co-edited volumes *Beyond Red Power* (2007) and *Memory Matters* (2011), and a revised and updated edition of William T. Hagan's *American Indians* (2012). His current projects include a biography of Ponca activist Clyde Warrior and a collection of primary documents on Native Rights movements from 1887 to the present.

Kyle Fields is a graduate of the Indiana University Maurer School of Law where he obtained his Juris Doctor. After growing up in Fairfield, Ohio, Kyle graduated from Miami University in 2010 with majors in History, Chemistry, and Latin American Studies. He currently lives in Virginia with his wife LiMin and continues to pursue his passion for history.

Sande Garner, Assistant Professor in the American Studies Program at Miami University (Ohio), focuses on Native American and Indigenous ritual and the construction, circulation, and material effects of representations of Native people. She is currently completing her first book, *To Come to a Better Understanding*, which focuses on a five-year-long dialogue between medicine men and priests on the Rosebud Reservation.

C. Joseph Genetin-Pilawa, Assistant Professor of History at George Mason University, is the author of *Crooked Paths to Allotment: The Fight over Federal Indian Policy after the Civil War* (UNC Press, 2012), as well as articles in the *Journal of Women's History* and *Western Historical Quarterly*. His new research, a study of urban Indigenous history in Washington, DC, examines the tensions between the capital's iconographic program and the lived experiences of Native people who visited the city as delegates or spent longer periods there as resident lobbyists and inhabitants.

Susan E. Gray, Associate Professor of History in the School of Historical, Philosophical, and Religious Studies at Arizona State University, is the author or co-editor of several works, including *The Yankee West: Community Life on the Michigan Frontier* (1996), *The Identity of the American Midwest:*

Essays on Regional History (2001), and *Contingent Maps: Re-thinking the North American West and Western Women's History* (2014). At present, she is completing *Lines of Descent: Family Stories from the North Country*, a multigenerational history of a mixed race (Odawa and white) family based on their personal narratives. From 2003 to 2012, Gray was co-editor of *Frontiers: A Journal of Women Studies.*

Brian Hosmer, the H. G. Barnard Chair of Western American History at the University of Tulsa, is author and editor of four books, most recently *Tribal Worlds: Critical Studies in American Indian Nation Building* (co-edited with Larry Nesper, Albany: SUNY Press, 2013). His research typically focuses on intersections between economic change, tribal politics and cultural identity in twentieth-century Indian communities. Hosmer is completing two book manuscripts: a history of Indians in the state of Illinois, and a study of work and attitudes toward working on the Wind River Reservation at midcentury.

Sakina M. Hughes is an Assistant Professor of History at the University of Southern Indiana and held the Du Bois-Mandela-Rodney Postdoctoral Fellow at the University of Michigan in 2012–2013. Her research focuses on the comparative history African-American and American Indian communities in the nineteenth and early twentieth centuries. She is currently working on a project that examines adjacent African-American and Native American communities in nineteenth-century Ohio.

George Ironstrack is Assistant Director and Education Coordinator for the Myaamia Center at Miami University of Ohio. He is a citizen of the Miami Tribe of Oklahoma and has assisted in the organization and administration of the Tribe's Eewansaapita Summer Educational Experience since its inception in 2005. He continues to regularly research and write about Myaamia history. Examples of his work can be found on the Myaamia Community History & Ecology Blog: Aatotamankwi Myaamiaki.

Kathryn Magee Labelle is an Assistant Professor of Aboriginal Canadian History at University of Saskatchewan. Her research and publications focus on the Wendat diaspora with specific emphasis on power, leadership, and women. She is the author of *Dispersed, But Not Destroyed: A History of the Seventeenth Century Wendat People* (Vancouver: University of British Columbia Press, 2013).

Malinda Maynor Lowery is an Associate Professor of History at the University of North Carolina–Chapel Hill and the Director of UNC's Southern Oral History Program. She is a member of the Lumbee Tribe of North Carolina. Her book, *Lumbee Indians in the Jim Crow South: Race, Identity, and the Making of a Nation*, was published by UNC Press in 2010 and won several awards, including "Best 2010 First Book in Native American and Indigenous Studies" from the Native American and Indigenous Studies Association.

Kristalyn Marie Shefveland, Assistant Professor of History at the University of Southern Indiana, is the author of "Cockacoeske and Sarah Harris Stegge Grendon: Bacon's Rebellion and the Roles of Women," contributing essay to *Virginia Women: Their Lives and Times*, edited by Cynthia A. Kierner and Sandy Treadway, Athens: University of Georgia Press, (forthcoming). She is currently completing a manuscript that examines Anglo-Indian interaction in Colonial Virginia and the tributary system.

Nancy Shoemaker, Professor of History at the University of Connecticut, is the author and editor of several books in Native American history, including *A Strange Likeness: Becoming Red and White in Eighteenth-Century North America* (2004) and *Living With Whales: Documents and Oral Histories of Native New England Whaling History* (forthcoming, University of Massachusetts Press). She is finishing up another book that focuses more specifically on Native New England whaling history in the nineteenth century while also starting a new book project on Americans in nineteenth-century Fiji.

Coll Thrush, Associate Professor of History at the University of British Columbia in Vancouver, is the author of *Native Seattle: Histories from the Crossing-Over Place* (Seattle, University of Washington Press, 2007) and the co-editor of *Phantom Past, Indigenous Presence: Native Ghosts in North American Culture & History* (Lincoln: University of Nebraska Press, 2011). He is currently writing a history of London, England, through the experiences of Indigenous people who travelled there, willingly or otherwise, from territories that became Canada, the United States, New Zealand, and Australia.

Index

Acosta, Pedro "Pete," 312–313
Adair, James, 71
Adair, William (Cherokee negotiator), 130
Adam Forepaugh Circus, 142, 144–145, 147
Adam Forepaugh-Sells Brothers Circus, 142, 144–147, 150, 154n3, 157n70
African Methodist Episcopal Church, 139–140
Ahasistari, Eustace (Wendat), 27
Alabama, 88
Albers, Patricia, 244, 247
American Circus Corporation, 150–151, 154n3, 157n70
American Fur Company, 212
American Home Missionary Society, 171
American Indian Movement (AIM), 271–274
American Society for Ethnohistory (ASE), 6, 243, 246, 264n1
Anderson, Gary Clayton, 247
Anglican Church (in Virginia), 41, 57
Anglo-Powhatan War, 40, 42
Antioch Baptist Church, 143–144
Arapaho Training School, 213

Baccas, John, 104
Bah, Che Che (Navajo), 225–226, 234n69
Baldwin, Daryl (Miami), 201
Barker, Joanne (Lenape), 4
Barman, Jean, 300–301
Barnum and Bailey Circus, 146, 148, 157n70
Basso, Keith, 1
Bearskin, Chief Leonard (Wendat), 32, 37n86
Beatty, Clyde (lion tamer), 151
Beaver Wars, 191–192, 197, 206n18, 207n29
Beggs, David, 105
Berkhofer, Robert, 118
Beulah Mission Church, 139–140
Beverley, Robert, 43–44, 52, 62n64
Birkeland, Joran, 256
Bishop, Charles, 245
Bishop of London, 41–59
Black Bear, Ben (Lakota), 278
Black Bear, Jr. Ben (Lakota), 273, 278
Black Elk, Nicholas (Lakota), 270–271, 289
Black Hawk (Sauk), 125
Black Hussar Band, 147
Black River Falls, Wisconsin, 213, 223, 230n21, 234n59
Blackhawk, Ned, 246
Blackmore, William Henry, 127
Blair, Reverend James, 41–42, 57
Boas, Franz, 287–288
Bourdieu, Pierre, 66–67, 81n2
Bourke, Major John, 275–276, 283–284

Bowen, Benjamin (business owner), 143–144
Boxcar Town (African-American community), 139–140, 150
Boyle, Robert, 43–44, 53
Brady, Matthew (photographer), 127
Brebeuf, Father Jean de (Jesuit missionary), 15–16, 19–23, 26, 33
Bronson, Edgar Beecher, 281–284
"Brown Brothers" (Vaudeville act), 137, 152
Brown, Anna (ragtime artist), 149
Brown, Dee, 3
Brown, Harry, 137, 152
Brown, Jennifer S. H., 245
Buffalo Bill's Wild West, 153
Bury My Heart at Wounded Knee, 3
Butler, Hummer (ragtime artist), 149
Byrd II, William, 40, 49, 51, 53–59

Capellano, Antoine (sculptor), 120
Capitalism, 8, 165, 237, 239–240, 242–247
Capitol Building (United States), 117, 119, 121, 123, 128, 133n11
  Rotunda reliefs, 119, 121, 123, 128
Carpenter, Roger, 17
Carrasco, Davíd, 289
Cass, Lewis, 110, 123
Catawba People, xii, 48, 53, 56, 88
Cattelino, Jessica, 205n3, 239, 242
Causici, Enrico (sculptor), 119–122
Champlain, Samuel de, 30
Charles Town, South Carolina, 68, 71, 80–81, 84n19
Cherokee People, 2, 7, 65–81, 87, 90–91, 93, 128–130, 197, 309
  delegation to Washington, DC, 128–130
  town governance, 68–72
  town ceremony, 78–79
  visits to London, 67
Chicago (Illinois), 10, 147, 172, 254
Chickahominy People, 43–44
Chickasaw People, 88
Chicken, George (trader), 68, 72–74, 78, 93
Chilocco Indian School, 209, 216–217
Chin Lee School, 209, 211–212, 214–219, 221–222, 224
Chippewa People, 209, 214–215, 223–224
Choctaw People, 126, 130
Christman, John, 105
Circus, 137–154. *See also* Adam Forepaugh Circus; Adam Forepaugh-Sells Brothers Circus; American Circus Corporation; Barnum and Bailey Circus; Great Wallace Show; Hagenbeck-Wallace Show; Lowery Brothers Circus; Muk-Koons-Kwa Company
Cleveland, Ohio, 150
Clifford, James, 255, 263, 303–305
Clinton Township, Ohio, 141, 143
Coast Salish People, 254, 296, 306
College of William and Mary, 42–43, 45–47, 53, 58
Collier, John, 238, 254
Columbus, Ohio, 141–143, 149
Commissioner of Indian Affairs, 110, 124, 129–130, 145, 212–213, 223
Comparet, Francois (trader), 107
Compton, Henry, 45, 60n16
Congregational Consociation of Connecticut, 171
Cooper, Joseph (trader), 69
Cooper, William, 68
Cottonoir, Leo (Eastern Shoshone), 240–241
Cradic, Richard, 143
Crane, Verner W., 77
Crawford, Thomas Hartley (Commisioner of Indian Affairs), 108, 110
Cosgrove, Denis (geographer), 163, 165

Crow Dog, Henry (Lakota), 276–277
Cumming, Sir Alexander, 68–81

Darwin, Charles, xiii
Dawes Rolls, 3
Dawes, Henry, 3
de Tocqueville, Alexis, 165–166
DeCora, Julla (Ho-Chunk), 214
Delaware People. *See* Lenni-Lenape People
Deloria, Ella, 272, 282
Deloria, Jr., Vine, 1, 4, 153, 161–162, 167, 287–289
Deloria, Philip, 5–6, 153, 210–211, 228, 242, 262–263
Delphi, Indiana, 103
DeMallie, Raymond, 279–280, 285–287
Dinétah (Navajo homelands), 211
Dippie, Brian, 118
Drury, Mary, 143
Duncan, William, 247
Dunn, Jacob Piatt, 186–187
Duquette, John, 102
Dutch East Indies, 163
Duwamish People, 300–301

East India Company, 43, 56
East India School (Charles City, Virginia), 42
Eastern Shoshone People, 240
Eastman, Charles, 3, 4, 280
Edinburgh, Scotland, 67
Edwards, R. A. (banker), 140
Eewansaapita (Miami Youth Education Program), 181
Elliot, Jonathan, 125
Erickson, Arthur, 303
Euler Diagram (Euler, Leonhar), 87–94
Executive Council of Virginia, 45, 49

False Creek, Vancouver, 297–299
Federal Indian Service, 8, 209–228, 229n8, 230n12
Fetterman Fight, 282
Fields, Joshua Ellsworth (United States Postal Service), 144
First Convocation of American Indian Scholars, 274
Flathead People, 253, 256, 264
  Flathead Reservation, 253, 256
Force, William (guidebook author), 121–122, 128
Fort Defiance, Arizona, 211–219, 225–226, 228
Fort Wayne, Indiana, 103, 106, 109–110. Also see *Kiihkayonki*
Foster, Sir Augustus John (travel writer), 126, 128–129
Foucault, Michel, 162, 167
Fontaine, John, 39–40, 47, 49–52, 57, 59
Fowler, Loretta, 243–244
Fryd, Vivian Green, 117–118, 120, 133n11
Fukuda, Matasuke, 312–313
Fukuda, Toku, 312–313

Gallup, New Mexico, 215
Gardner, Alexander (photographer), 127
Gardner, Cheerful (elephant handler), 152
Gertrude, Mary, 276
Gevelot, Nicholas (sculptor), 120, 122
Ghost Dance, 3, 272
Giago, Tim (Lakota), 269–270, 288
Gitxsan People, 305–306, 308
Godfroy, Edward (Miami), 109
Godfroy, Francis/Palaanswa (Miami), 98–99, 102, 104–112, 139
Godfroy, Gabriel/Waapanaakikaapwa (Miami), 139, 141, 150, 185–186
Godfroy, Lewis/Louis (Miami), 107
Godfroy, Washington (Miami), 109
Godfroy, William (Miami), 109
Grand River, 163, 169, 172–173
Grant, Ludovick (trader), 70, 79–80

Grant, Ulysses S., 130, 274, 290n19
Great Depression, 195, 257
Great Tellico (Cherokee town), 75, 76, 80, 81
Great Wallace Show, 138, 145, 146, 148, 154n3

Hagenbeck-Wallace Show, 138, 152
Haida People, 303
Hamilton, Allen (trader), 99, 101, 106–112
Harmon, Alexandra, 242
Harris, LaDonna (Comanche), 256
Harvey, Reverend B. T., 140
Haskell Institute, 216–218
Hayes, Rutherford B., 274
Henderson, Zenas (innkeeper), 103
Henry, Joseph (Secretary of Smithsonian), 127
Hilbert, Father Robert, 275
Hinman, Samuel D. (missionary), 247
Ho-Chunk People, 10, 121, 123, 126, 128, 210–212, 214, 223, 228
Hogan, Ernest (ragtime artist), 149
Hori, Shigeichi, 312
Hori, Shimanoko, 312
House of Burgesses, 45, 47, 56
Hughes, Harley, 143
Hunter, George (Surveyor), 68, 84n18

Illinois People, 183, 185–187, 192–194, 201
Indian Citizenship Act (1924), 196
Indian New Deal, 238, 254
Indian Reorganization Act (1934), 210
Indian School Service, 211
Indian Service. *See* Federal Indian Service
Indian Territory, 194, 198
Indiana State Library, 107, 111
Indianz.com, 269
Innu (Montagnais-Neskapi), 29–32, 33, 88, 91
Ishi, 2

Jackson, Andrew, 97, 169
Jahner, Elaine, 280–282, 285–287
Jamestown (Virginia), 40
Jefferson, Thomas, 165
Jesuit, 15–16, 18–33, 89, 92, 190, 206n23, 275
Jim Crow, 143–144
Jobin, Lucy, 209–210, 214, 216, 218, 221–224
John Robinson Circus, 145, 147
Jones, Reverend Hugh, 43, 48, 58–59
Jones, Reverend Ovie O., 143
Journal of American History, 162

Kalamazoo River, 169, 171
Kaskaskia (*Kaahkaahkia*) People, 194
Kellogg, John R. (lumber businessman), 170
Keowee (Cherokee town), 69–72, 77–78, 81
Kiihkayonki (Fort Wayne, Indiana), 103, 106, 109–110
Kills Enemy, Charles (Lakota), 277
King George II, 68, 69, 79, 80
King William III, 44
King, Charles Bird (artist), 124, 127
King, Thomas (Cherokee), 2, 9
Kinlock, James, 68
Kinnequay (Odawa), 175
Kitsilano Point, 296, 298, 299, 301, 305, 313
Kniffen, Ralph (Fort Hall Shoshone), 240
Knight, Rolf, 242–243
Kroeber, Albert, 2
Kroeber, Theodora, 2
Kwakwa̲ka̲'wakw People, 303, 304, 306–307

Lac du Flambeau Indian School, 213–214, 21
Lake Erie and Western Railroad, 139
Lake Michigan, 169, 171–172
Lakota People, 3, 130, 269–289

Lame Deer, John "Fire" (Lakota), 278
Land Ordinance of 1785, 165
Lassiter, Eric Luke, 255
Laurier, Wilfrid, 300
Le Caron, Father Joseph (Jesuit Missionary), 19
Leelanau Peninsula, 172, 175
Lenni-Lenape People (Delaware), 4, 88, 120, 128
Lightfoot, Thomas (Indian agent), 129
Linworth, Ohio, 141
Little Big Horn, 3
Little, John (Northern Arapaho), 240, 243
Little Turtle. See *Mihšihkinaahkwa*
Logansport, Indiana, 100, 103
London, England, 67, 77, 150
London, Ohio, 143
Long, Charles, 270
Lowery Brothers Circus, 150
Lowery, P. G. (band leader), 147–150
Lumbee People, xi–xiv
Lumber River, xi, xiv

Mackinac Island, 168
Makeabichtichiou (Innu), 31
Maksabe (Odawa), 173, 178n27
Maameewa Siipiiwa (St. Mary's River), 188
Maumee River. See *Taawaawa Siipiiwi*
Markowitz, Harvey, 275, 286
Marks, LaMoine (Miami), 150, 151
Martin, Katie, 143
Marxism, 243
Massey, Doreen (geographer), 163, 167, 168
Mbembe, Achille, 112
McEachern, Alan, 308
McFee, Malcolm, 244
McGillivray, Alexander (Creek), 245–246
McGillycuddy, Dr. Valentine, 275, 281, 282, 283, 284, 292n60, 293n77
McKenney, Thomas (Superintendent of Indian Affairs), 110, 124–126
McNickle, D'Arcy (Flathead), 8, 253, 264
Medicine Men and Pastors Meeting (MMPM), 273–277
Medicine Men's Association (MMA), 271–274, 288–289
Meehcikilita/Le Gros (Miami), 188
Meherrin People, 44, 47, 52, 88
Mellinger, Susie Tucker, 152
Miami County, Indiana, 137–141
Miami Nation of Indiana, 183
Miami/Myaamia People, 8, 97–112, 137–141, 150–154, 181–204
  Archival sources, 110–112
  Circus, 137–141, 150–154
  Miami-Illinois Language, 183, 185–187, 192–193, 201
  Removal Claims, 101–104
  Trade with Americans, 101–108
  Youth education programs, 199–204
Miami Tribe of Oklahoma, 181, 183–185
Miami University of Ohio, 201
Michigan Territory, 123, 166
Mihšihkinaahkwa/Little Turtle (Miami), 185
Miles, Colonel Nelson, 3
Miller, John, 104
Milroy, Samuel (trader), 110
Mississinewa River, 108, 141
Mitchell, William (Army Captain), 129
Mix, Tom (actor), 151
Momaday, N. Scott, 9, 274, 315
Mooney, James, 272
Moss, Jane (teacher), 140, 155n23
Moytoy (Cherokee), 75–80
Muckleshoot Reservation, 310–311, 313
Mugivan, Jerry, 150, 157n70
Muk-Koons-Kwa Company, 152, 159n116

Murphy, Lucy, xv, 245
Museum of Anthropology (British Columbia), 303–304, 309–310, 313–314
Musqueam People, 302, 305–307, 314
Myaamiaki (Miami People), 183. *See also* Miami People
Myaamionki (the place of the Miami), 182, 194, 202

Nahyssan People, 47
Nansemond People, 44
National Congress of American Indians, 254
National Industrial Recovery Act (1933), 257
National Museum of the American Indian (NMAI), 4
Navajo People, 209–216, 223–228
Navajo Reservation, 209, 211, 213, 223
Nea, Huskay Yee Chee (Navajo), 225–226
Neely Mansion, 311–313, 317n24
Neosho River, 198
New Deal, 237–238, 240–241, 254, 257–258
New France, 19–31
Newberry Library, 254
Northern Arapaho People, 237, 240, 241
Nottoway People, 44, 47, 57, 88

O'Connell, Dometilla "Tillie," 214, 228
O'Neill, Colleen, 242
Occaneechee People, 47
Odawa People, 163, 167–175
Office of Indian Affairs, 127, 210
Ogemainne (Odawa), 168–175, 178n27
Oglala People, 130, 275, 279–282, 285, 287
Oglala Sioux Civil Rights Organization, 272
Ojibwe People, 129–130, 163, 167–168, 170
Oklahoma, 32, 181–185, 194–195, 197, 198, 200, 213
Old Coyote, Henry (Crow), 117, 119, 131
Old Wing Mission, 163–164, 168–170, 173, 177n19
Olentangy River, 141
Ookunny (Cherokee Town), 80–81
Ortiz, Alfonso (San Juan Pueblo), 295, 315
Osage People, 126, 128, 197
Oshkenaniew, Mitchell, 244–246
Oshkosh, Reginald, 244–246
Oscotarach (Wendat), 18–19
Owens, Louis, 254
Owl (Miami), 103
Oxford University, 256

P. J. Lowery Band, 148
Pamunkey People, 41, 43–44
Paquette, Dora (Ho-Chunk), 212–215
Paquette, Mary (Ho-Chunk), 212–216, 223
Paquette, Peter (Ho-Chunk), 212–216, 218–219, 222–228
Parker, Ely (Tonawanda Seneca), 2, 128, 130
Peace with Necotowance, 40
Peewaalia/Peoria People, 194, 198
Peeyankihšia/Piankashaw People, 192, 194
Pendunwan (Odawa), 173, 175
Pepper, Able C. (American Agent), 110
Perry, Ruben, 213
Portage, Wisconsin, 212
Peru, Indiana, 8, 138–139, 140, 148–151
Peterson, Jacqueline, 245
Piankashaw People. See *Peeyankihšia* People
Pine Ridge Agency, 272, 275, 280, 282

Pine Ridge Reservation, 272, 274, 279–280, 285
Pinšiwa. See *Richardville, Jean Baptiste*
Pitchlynn, Peter (Choctaw), 130
Pocahontas, 119, 120, 128, 130
Podruchny, Carolyn, 245
Point Grey, Vancouver, 302–303, 305–306
Point, Maggie (Coast Salish), 306
Polkadot School, 143–144
Poore, Benjamin Perley (author), 128
Porter, Peter (Secretary of War), 123
Portwood, Alfred "Sunny" (Northern Arapaho), 241
Povinelli, Elizabeth, 242
Powhatan, 40–42, 44
Presbyterian General Assembly, 171
Preuss, Henry Clay (playwright), 123
Public Broadcasting Service (PBS), 2

Quapaw People, 197
Quebec, 19, 28, 30
Quebec City, 28, 30
Quinney, John W. (Stockbridge-Munsee delegate), 130

Raibmon, Paige, 242, 253
Rappahannock County, Virginia, 41
Red Cloud (Oglala), 3, 124, 130, 280, 282, 285
Red Dog (Oglala), 275
Reid, Bill (Haida), 303
Reynolds, James (escaped slave), 144
Richardville, Jean Baptiste/*Pinšiwa* (Miami), 98–99, 102–112, 139, 188
Ringling Brothers Circus, 149–150, 157n70
Roberts, Reverend Zachariah, 140
Roosevelt, Franklin Delano, 257–259
Rosebud Reservation, 271, 274–275, 288
Ross, John (Cherokee), 125, 130
Running Horse, Arthur (Lakota), 273
Ryan, Don (Gitxsan spokesperson), 308

Saakiiweeyonki, 185–186, 188
Sackett, Minnie, 130
Sagard, Brother Gabriel (Jesuit missionary), 19, 34n13
San Juan Pueblo, 295
Sandys, Sir William, 42
Saponi People, 47–48, 50–52, 55–56
Sarris, Greg, 131
Schoolcraft, Henry Rowe (Superintendent of Indian Affairs), 167–170
Scurry, James (United States Postal Service), 144
Sellsville, Ohio, 137, 141–144
Seminole People, 239
Senákw, 296–301, 307, 309–310
Seneca-Cayuga People, 198
Shakespeare, Tom (Northern Arapaho), 237–240
Shawnee People, 88, 198
Sitting Bull/Tatanka Iyotanka (Lakota), 3, 153, 269
Skanu'u/Ardythe Wilson (Gitxsan), 308
Skwupabsh People, 310–313
Sleeper-Smith, Susan, 214–215, 245
Smith, Arvilla, 171–172, 174–175
Smith, John, 119, 128
Smith, Margaret Bayard, 123, 126
Smith, Mary Jane, 175
Smith, Paul Chaat, 4, 10, 263, 272, 274
Smith, Reverend George Nelson, 171–175
Smithsonian Institution, 4, 125, 127
Social Darwinism, 275
Society for the Propagation of the Gospel (SPG), 44–45
Sondaarouhane, Joseph (Wendat), 22
Songhees Reserve, 300–301
Soos Creek (Washington State), 310–315

Spivak, Gayatri, 9, 263
Spotswood, Alexander, 39, 42, 44–59
Spotted Tail (Lakota), 124, 130, 274
Squamish Nation, 296, 298, 301
St. Mary's River (*Maameewa Siipiiwa*), 188
Stockbridge-Munsee People, 129–130
Stoler, Ann, 110, 162–164, 167, 175
Stolzman, Father William, 273, 277
Stony Point School, 139, 155n15
Strack, Andrew (Miami), 201
Straits of Mackinac, 168
Sun Dance, 272, 275, 278, 279–280, 283–287, 293n77
Supreme Court of Canada, 309
Swift Bear (Lakota), 124
Sword, George (Lakota), 272, 279–289

Taawaawa Siipiiwi (Maumee River), 188
Tannassy (Cherokee Town), 76, 78–79
Taondechoren, Joseph (Wendat), 28–29
Tassetchee (Cherokee Town), 74–75
Tatanka Iyotanka. *See* Sitting Bull
The Carlisle Arrow, 217
The Indian Leader, 217, 218
The Indian School Journal, 217
The Sells Brothers Circus, 137, 141–142, 144–148, 154n3
Thompson, Eph (elephant trainer), 147, 150
Thornton, Reverend I. A., 143
Trigger, Bruce, 25
Toxsoah (Cherokee Town), 73–74
Traverse City, Michigan, 172
Treaty of Washington (1836), 163, 167–168, 170, 173
Trollope, Francis, 125
Tsicok, Martin (Wendat), 20
Tsimshian People, 245–246, 303
Tucker, Gabe, 152
Tucker, Mary, 152
Turner, Frederick Jackson, 1
Tuscarora People, 3, 44, 46–47, 51, 53, 57, 88
Tuscarora War, 46–47, 51
Tuskegee College, 140
Tutelo People, 47, 56

U'mista Cultural Centre (Alert Bay), 304
United States Postal Service, 144
University of British Columbia, 302, 304–305, 308
Usner, Daniel, 241–242

Van Buren, Martin, 97
Vancouver, Canada, 297–303, 309, 314
Vancouver, George, 303
Venn Diagram/John Venn, 87, 94n1
Viel, Father Nicholas (Jesuit missionary), 19
Viola, Herman, 118, 126–127, 129–130
Virginia Company, 42

Wa Pawni Ha (Sauk), 129
Waapanaakikaapwa (Miami). *See* Gabriel Godfroy
Waayaahtanwa (Wea People), 192, 194
Wabash River/*Waapaahšiki Siipiiwi*, 106–108, 155n18, 183, 186, 188, 192
Walker, James R., 272, 279–282, 285–289
Walker, Reverend George, 144
Wallace, Benjamin, 140, 141, 145–148, 150–151, 157n70
Warm Springs Indian Agency, Oregon, 129
Warren, Jr., Ben (Northern Arapaho), 240
Warrior, Robert, 271–274

Washington, DC, 7, 117–132, 164, 169, 258, 266n9, 280, 282, 289
- Artwork, 119–123
- Native people traveling to, 118, 121, 123–128, 130–131, 280, 282, 289
- Travel guides, 119, 121, 125, 128, 131

Wawgawnawkezee (Odawa village), 173–174
Weaver, Jace, 309
Weber, Father Anselm, 213, 215, 222, 224–225
Webster, Jodi (Potowatomi-Ho-Chunk), 10
Weekwitonsing (Odawa village), 168
Weisenberger, Sarah Tucker, 152
Wells, Al (performer), 153
Wendat/Wyandot People, 7, 15–33, 88, 90–92, 187, 198
West, Nathaniel, 101–105
Western Michigan Society to Benefit the Indians, 169
Wet'suwet'en Nation, 305–308
White, Sol (band leader), 147
Wilkins, Bill (ragtime artist), 149
Willard, Mary Ann (métis), 175
Williams, Ephraim (equestrian trainer), 141, 147, 150
Willie, Mikael (Kwakwa̱ka̱'wakw), 307
Winter, George (painter), 107
Wolfe, Payson (Odawa), 175
World Systems Theory, 24
Wounded Knee, 3, 272, 274